2004 UPDATE

Third Edition

TEXAS REAL ESTATE CONTRACTS

Ralph Tamper, ABR, CREI, DREI, GRI, LTG

Dearborn™
Real Estate Education

President: Roy Lipner
Publisher: Evan Butterfield
Managing Editor, Print Products: Louise Benzer
Development Editor: Tony Peregrin
Production Coordinator: Daniel Frey
Quality Assurance Editor: David Shaw
Typesetter: Janet Schroeder
Creative Director: Lucy Jenkins

Published by Dearborn™ Real Estate Education
a division of Dearborn Financial Publishing, Inc.®
30 South Wacker Drive
Chicago, IL 60606-7481
(313) 836-4400
http://www.REcampus.com

Printed in the United States of America.
04 05 06 10 9 8 7 6 5 4 3 2 1

Library of Congress Cataloging-in-Publication Data

Tamper, Ralph.
Texas real estate contracts / Ralph Tamper.—3rd. ed., Revised
Includes index.
p. cm.
ISBN 0-7931-9436-9
1. Vendors and purchasers—Texas. 2. Real property—Texas—Forms. I. Title.

KFT1326.T36 2002
346.76404'3—dc21 2002025951

Table of Contents

Preface

This book was created to provide a clear, practical approach to one of the most important things a Texas real estate broker or salesperson will do for a buyer or seller: filling in the blanks on the purchase agreement. The book is not designed as a definitive legal text, nor does it provide legal advice to license holders or their customers and clients. Readers are advised that it is always desirable to read every word of a legal document carefully and understand it before signing. When unusual matters arise or a party does not understand what he or she is being asked to sign, legal counsel should be sought before proceeding. Real estate license holders may not give legal advice or write documents defining legal rights and remedies of the parties. License holders may only add business details desired by the parties.

At the conclusion of your study of the material in this volume, you will

- be able to professionally fulfill the role of the license holder by accurately setting down the wishes and intent of the parties and refrain from making decisions for them or imposing the broker's or salesperson's will upon them;
- be able to clearly state the elements of a contract;
- be able to explain and comply with the provisions of the Statute of Frauds, the Texas Real Estate License Act, and the Rules of the Texas Real Estate Commission as they relate to the creation of executory purchase contracts between sellers and buyers;
- be able to write down a business detail and know the difference between a word or phrase that establishes a business detail and one that defines legal rights and remedies of the parties;
- be able to select the correct form or forms that are appropriate to define the agreement of the parties;

- be able to recognize potential legal problems and know when to encourage the parties to seek competent legal advice from a competent real estate attorney;
- be able to explain to a seller what is required by statute with regard to property disclosure requirements;
- be able to assist buyers and sellers in gaining understanding of the options available to them when a breach of contract occurs; and
- be able to estimate the bottom line accurately for the seller and the buyer.

The book is intended for use by both new license holders and seasoned practitioners. As you begin your study, remember that what others do and what is popular are not always correct, and what is correct is not always popular. Real professionals accept the responsibility of verifying and making certain that the approach being used is accurate and appropriate.

Learn what is correct and do not let others intimidate you or put you at risk just because they have been in the business longer than you have. Many practicing license holders have never carefully read the forms. A truly competent real estate broker or salesperson should be able to discuss in detail every one of the promulgated contracts and addenda. A competent license holder should know exactly when to use and when not to use each of the forms.

Great care has been taken to ensure that every detail about contracts that is covered on the state licensing exams has been thoroughly explored in these pages.

The Texas Real Estate Broker-Lawyer Committee and the Texas Real Estate Commission meet on a regular basis to review and modify the forms. The commission makes license holders aware of any changes and any newly adopted forms through *The Advisor* the official publication of the Texas Real Estate Commission (TREC) for the distribution of important information to license holders. Carefully read every word of a new form before you use it. Additionally, you can always obtain current, accurate information at the TREC Web site where back issues of *The Advisor* are available.

If necessary, a supplement will be added to this book that will give you current information about revisions and new forms that have been promulgated since the publication of this third edition. A visit to the TREC Web site at *www.trec.state.tx.us* offers the opportunity for you to download the latest version of the forms.

This book explores TREC published forms. Forms made available for use by members of trade organizations such as local REALTOR® associations and the Texas Association of REALTORS® are referenced sparingly because they are available only to association members.

New features of the third edition include an extensive glossary and additional opportunities to apply what you are learning. Answer keys for chapter review questions, Chapter 10 Settlement Statement, and Appendix A Contract Review and Practice Exam are found in Appendix B. Answers for case studies for Chapters 5 and 9 will be provided by your instructor after the exercises have been completed in class. Appendix C provides a complete inventory of TREC forms approved and promulgated as of the publication date.

Acknowledgments

The author would like to thank Lloyd Hampton, Chuck Hutchinson, and Carolyn Rogers, instructors at The Real Estate School, Houston, Texas, for their invaluable input. In addition to offering valuable suggestions for the content, they field-tested the case studies. Appreciation is also expressed to Don Shrum for his assistance in preparing the manuscript.

The author also thanks the following reviewers for their valuable contributions to this edition: Rick Knowles, Capital Real Estate Training and Philip G. Schoewe, DREI, HomeIndex Real Estate Company.

In addition, the author wishes to thank those who have helped with the previous editions, including Harold Grimes, Tyler Real Estate College; Nanci Hawes, DREI, Leonard-Hawes Real Estate School; Frankie Jefferson, Houston Community College; Randy McKechnie, University of Texas at Arlington; Kevin S. Morris, San Jacinto College; Marga Shefman, formerly with the Austin Association of REALTORS®, and Ken Trussell, Continuing Education for Licensing, Inc. (C.E.L.I.) and Texas A&M University—Commerce.

About the Author

Ralph Tamper, owner and director of The Real Estate School of Houston, Texas, received his real estate training at the University of Houston. He is author of *Mastering Real Estate Math,* Seventh Edition, 2002, published by Dearborn Real Estate Education of Chicago and *MCE for Texas Real Estate Professionals,* 1999, also published by Dearborn Real Estate Education of Chicago. He is in demand as a reviewer of real estate related texts and computer software for real estate study.

Mr. Tamper is active as a presenter of continuing education classes for real estate brokers and salespersons, attorneys, appraisers, and accountants. He is a popular senior instructor for the Graduate REALTOR® Institute program in which he teaches legal issues, pricing property, contracts, technology applications for REALTORS®, taxation, and investments.

He has been awarded the prestigious Distinguished Real Estate Instructor (DREI) designation by the Real Estate Educators Association. He serves on the Board of Directors, was program chairman of the 1998 Annual Conference, and was president of the Real Estate Educators Association for 2000–2001. Additionally, he is a senior instructor for the Real Estate Educators Association's Instructor Development Workshops.

He is a life member of the Texas Real Estate Teachers Association and has been awarded its Certified Real Estate Instructor (CREI) designation. He also holds memberships in the national, Texas, and Houston Associations of REALTORS®. In 2000, the Texas Association of REALTORS® named him Real Estate Educator of the Year.

Chapter 1

The Texas Real Estate License Act (TRELA) and the Rules of the Texas Real Estate Commission (TREC)

Key Terms

addenda
addendum
Broker-Lawyer Committee
business detail
lease
legal right
promulgate
remedy
temporary lease

Under its police power, the state of Texas has the legal right to enact and enforce laws to protect the health, safety, and general welfare of the public. Since 1949, Texas has had the TRELA (Chapter 1101 of the Texas Occupations Code) to regulate those who, for a fee or other valuable consideration, sell, exchange, procure, prospect, or inspect real property. The law holds brokers responsible for all professional and vocational acts performed by any real estate salesperson associated with or acting for the broker. Brokers must pay close attention to the activities of their licensed staff.

TRELA Sections 1101.155; 1101.251; 1101.252; 1101.654

The TRELA specifically prohibits license holders from practicing law by giving opinions or counsel regarding the validity or legal sufficiency of an instrument that addresses real property rights or as to the status of title to real estate. Throughout the act, it is clearly established that, prior to signing a purchase contract, the license holder must give a buyer written advice to have the abstract covering the property examined by an attorney of the buyer's selection or to obtain an owner's title insurance policy prior to closing. Failure to do so may result in disciplinary action by TREC.

Those who choose to become REALTORS® will subscribe to a Code of Ethics that demands a very high level of professional conduct. Article 13 of that Code addresses the unauthorized practice of law.

National Association of REALTORS® Code of Ethics, Article 13

> REALTORS® shall not engage in activities that constitute the unauthorized practice of law and shall recommend that legal counsel be obtained when the interest of any party to the transactions requires it.

The TRELA clearly establishes that it is illegal for the license holder to draw a deed, note, deed of trust, will, or other written instrument that transfers or may transfer an interest in or title to real property. However, the act goes on to give permission for a license holder to complete a contract form that may bind the sale, exchange, option, lease, or rental of any interest in real property as long as forms are used that have been prepared by or are required by the property owner or have been provided by the real estate commission, prepared by an attorney licensed by Texas, and approved by that attorney for a particular type of transaction.

> Sec. 1101.654. SUSPENSION OR REVOCATION OF LICENSE OR CERTIFICATE FOR UNAUTHORIZED PRACTICE OF LAW. (a) The commission shall suspend or revoke the license or certificate of registration of a license or certificate holder who is not a licensed attorney in this state and who, for consideration, a reward, or in a pecuniary benefit, present or anticipated, direct or indirect, or in connection with the person's employment, agency, or fiduciary relationship as a license or certificate holder:
>
> (1) drafts an instrument, other than a form described by Section 1101.155, that transfers or otherwise affects an interest in real property; or
>
> (2) advises a person regarding the validity or legal sufficiency of an instrument or the validity of title to real property.
>
> (b) Notwithstanding any other law, a license or certificate holder who completes a contract form for the sale, exchange, option, or lease of an interest in real property incidental to acting as a broker is not engaged in the unauthorized or illegal practice of law in this state if the form was:
>
> (1) adopted by the commission for the type of transaction for which the form is used;
>
> (2) prepared by an attorney licensed in this state and approved by the attorney for the type of transaction for which the form is used; or
>
> (3) prepared by the property owner or by an attorney and required by the property owner.

The legislature created an advisory body to develop and recommend various contract forms to the Texas Real Estate Commission (TREC) for use by license holders when performing the tasks for which they have been licensed. This body, the Texas Real Estate **Broker-Lawyer Committee,** does not **promulgate,** or publish, forms for mandatory use by license holders. Only the TREC has been given rule-making authority. The Broker-Lawyer Committee develops forms and recommends their adoption, but it is the TREC that *promulgates* the forms for mandatory use. The act clearly establishes the responsibilities of the committee, composed of six brokers appointed by TREC and six attorneys appointed by the president of the State Bar of Texas and one public member appointed by the governor.

SUBCHAPTER F
TEXAS REAL ESTATE BROKER-LAWYER COMMITTEE

Sec. 1101.251. DEFINITION OF COMMITTEE. In this subchapter, "committee" means the Texas Real Estate Broker-Lawyer Committee. (New.)

Sec. 1101.252. COMMITTEE MEMBERSHIP. (a) The Texas Real Estate Broker-Lawyer Committee consists of 13 members appointed as follows:

(1) six members appointed by the commission; and

(2) six members of the State Bar of Texas appointed by the president of the state bar; and

(3) one public member appointed by the governor.

(b) Appointments to the committee shall be made without regard to the race, creed, sex, religion, or national origin of the appointee.

The license holder also needs to be aware that the legislature has given the commission rule-making authority and that the rules of the commission are just as binding on license holders as are the provisions of the act. With regard to contracts, specific authority is given in the act.

Sec. 1101.155. RULES RELATING TO CONTRACT FORMS. (a) The commission may adopt rules in the public's best interest that require license holders to use contract forms prepared by the Texas Real Estate Broker-Lawyer Committee and adopted by the commission.

(b) The commission may not prohibit a license holder from using for sale, exchange, option, or lease of an interest in real property a contract form that is:

(1) prepared by the property owner; or

(2) prepared by an attorney and required by the property owner.

(c) A listing contract form adopted by the commission that relates to the contractual obligations between a seller of real estate and a license holder acting as an agent for the seller must include:

(1) a provision informing the parties to the contract that real estate commissions are negotiable; and

(2) a provision explaining the availability of Texas coastal natural hazards information important to coastal residents, if that information is appropriate.

Before engaging in the business of completing any contract forms that bind the sale, **lease, temporary lease,** or rental of any real property, the license holder should become thoroughly familiar with what the rules do and do not permit.

TREC Rule 537.11

The first part of Rule 537.11 lists the forms that are currently promulgated, that is, published, for mandatory use by a license holder when the form fits a particular transaction. The following list gives the date on which the form was promulgated, as well as the name of the form and the TREC form reference number. Earlier versions of forms may not be used; to do so could be considered the unauthorized practice of law, an illegal act.

Texas Real Estate Commission Forms

Promulgated Contracts:

Number	Name	Adoption Date
9-5	Unimproved Property Contract	01/03
20-6	One to Four Family Residential Contract (Resale)	01/03
23-5	New Home Contract (Incomplete Construction)	01/03
24-5	New Home Contract (Completed Construction)	01/03
25-4	Farm and Ranch Contract	01/03
30-4	Residential Condominium Contract (Resale)	01/03

Promulgated Addenda:

Number	Name	Adoption Date
10-4	Addendum for Sale of Other Property by Buyer	10/01
11-5	Addendum for "Back-Up" Contract	02/04
12-1	Addendum for Release of Liability on Assumption of FHA, VA or Conventional Loan/Restoration of Seller's Entitlement for VA Guaranteed Loan	03/92

15-3	Seller's Temporary Residential Lease	12/98
16-3	Buyer's Temporary Residential Lease	12/98
26-4	Seller Financing Addendum	10/01
28-0	Environmental Assessment, Threatened or Endangered Species, and Wetlands Addendum	10/93
33-0	Addendum for Coastal Area Property	12/94
34-1	Addendum for Property Located Seaward of the Gulf Intracoastal Waterway	10/01
36-3	Addendum for Property Subject to Mandatory Membership in an Owners' Association	02/04
40-1	Third Party Financing Condition Addendum	02/04
41-0	Loan Assumption Addendum	10/01

Promulgated Amendment:

39-4	Amendment	01/03

Promulgated Resale Certificates:

32-0	Condominium Resale Certificate	04/94
37-1	Subdivision Information, Including Resale Certificate for Property Subject to Mandatory Membership in an Owners' Association	09/99

Promulgated Notice:

38-1	Notice of Termination of Contract	10/01
42-0	Notice Pursuant to Third Party Financing Addendum	02/04

Promulgated Consumer Disclosure:

	* Consumer Information Form 1-1	08/91

Optional/Voluntary Use Forms:

OP-C	Notice to Prospective Buyer	12/90
OP-H	Seller's Disclosure of Property Condition	10/93
OP-I	Texas Real Estate Consumer Notice Concerning Hazards or Repairs	04/02
OP-K	Information About Brokerage Services	01/96
OP-L	Lead-based Paint Addendum	02/04
OP-M	Addendum for Unimproved Property Located in a Certificated Service Area of a Utility Service Provider	07/01

After itemizing the current inventory of available forms, the commission set down the do's and don'ts for the completion of those forms. A careful reading of the rules tells you all you need to know. The underlining has been added for emphasis.

(b) When negotiating contracts binding the sale, exchange, option, lease or rental of any interest in real property, a real estate licensee shall use only those contract forms promulgated by the Texas Real Estate Commission for that kind of transaction with the following exceptions:

(1) transactions in which the licensee is functioning solely as a principal, not an agent;

(2) transactions in which an agency of the United States government requires a different form to be used;

(3) transactions for which a contract form has been prepared by the property owner or prepared by an attorney and required by the property owner;

(4) transactions for which no standard contract form has been promulgated by the Texas Real Estate Commission, and the licensee uses a form prepared by an *attorney at law* licensed by this state and approved by the attorney for the particular kind of transactions involved or prepared by the Texas Real Estate Broker-Lawyer Committee and made available for trial use by licensees with the consent of the Texas Real Estate Commission.

(c) A licensee may not practice law, offer, give nor attempt to give advice, directly or indirectly; the licensee may not act as a public conveyancer nor give advice or opinions as to the legal effect of any contracts or other such instruments which may affect the title to real estate; the licensee may not give opinions concerning the status or validity of title to real estate; and the licensee may not attempt to prevent nor in any manner whatsoever discourage any principal to a real estate transaction from employing a lawyer. However, nothing herein shall be deemed to limit the licensee's fiduciary obligation to disclose to his principals all pertinent facts which are within the knowledge of the licensee, including such facts which might affect the status of or title to real estate.

(d) A licensee may not undertake to draw or prepare documents fixing and defining the *legal rights* of the principals to a transaction. In negotiating real estate transactions, the licensee may fill in forms for such transactions, using exclusively forms which have been approved and promulgated by the Texas Real Estate Commission or such forms as are otherwise permitted by these rules. When filling in such a form, the licensee may only fill in the blanks provided and may not add to or strike matter from such form, except that licensees shall add factual statements and business details desired by the principals and shall strike only such matter as is desired by the principals and as is necessary to conform the instrument to the intent of the parties. A licensee may not add to a promulgated earnest money contract form factual statements or business details for which a contract

addendum, lease or other form has been promulgated by the commission for mandatory use. Nothing herein shall be deemed to prevent the licensee from explaining to the principals the meaning of the factual statements and business details contained in the said instrument so long as the licensee does not offer or give legal advice. It is not the practice of law as defined in this Act for a real estate licensee to complete a contract form which is either promulgated by the Texas Real Estate Commission or prepared by the Texas Real Estate Broker-Lawyer Committee and made available for trial use by licensees with the consent of the Texas Real Estate Commission. Contract forms prepared by the Texas Real Estate Broker-Lawyer Committee for trial use may be used on a voluntary basis after being approved by the commission. Contract forms prepared by the Texas Real Estate Broker-Lawyer Committee and approved by the commission to replace previously promulgated forms may be used by licensees on a voluntary basis prior to the effective date of rules requiring use of the replacement form.

(e) Where it appears that, prior to the execution of any such instrument, there are unusual matters involved in the transaction which should be resolved by legal counsel before the instrument is executed or that the instrument is to be acknowledged and filed for record, the licensee shall advise the principals that each should consult a lawyer of the principal's choice before executing same.

(f) A licensee may not employ, directly or indirectly, a lawyer nor pay for the services of a lawyer to represent any principal to a real estate transaction in which the licensee is acting as an agent. The licensee may employ and pay for the services of a lawyer to represent only the licensee in a real estate transaction, including preparation of the contract, agreement, or other legal instruments to be executed by the principals to the transactions.

(g) A licensee shall advise the principals that the instrument they are about to execute is binding on them.

(h) Forms approved or promulgated by the commission may be reproduced only from the following sources:

(1) numbered copies obtained from the commission, whether in a printed format or electronically reproduced from the files available on the commission's Internet site;

(2) printed copies made from copies obtained from the commission;

(3) legible photocopies made from such copies; or

(4) computer-driven printers following these guidelines:

(A) The computer file or program containing the form text must not allow the end-user direct access to the text of the form and may only permit the user to insert language in blanks in the forms or to strike through language at the direction of the parties to the contract.

(B) Typefaces or fonts must appear to be identical to those used by the commission in printed copies of the particular form.

(C) The text and number of pages must be identical to that used by the commission in printed proofs of the particular form.

(D) The spacing, length of blanks, borders and placement of text on the page must appear to be identical to that used by the commission in printed copies of the form.

(E) The name and address of the person or firm responsible for developing the software program must be legibly printed below the border at the bottom of each page in no less than 6 point type and in no larger than 10 point type.

(F) The text of the form must be obtained from a copy of the form bearing a control number assigned by the commission.

(i) The control number of each copy must appear on all forms reproduced from the copy, including forms reproduced by computer-driven printers.

(j) Forms approved or promulgated by the commission must be reproduced on the same size of paper used by the commission with the following changes or additions only.

(1) The business name or logo of a broker, organization or printer may appear at the top of a form outside the border.

(2) The broker's name may be inserted in any blank provided for that purpose.

The commission and the Broker-Lawyer Committee are charged with serving the best interest of the public and have adopted the foregoing to accomplish that purpose. They are always willing to hear comments from the license holders whom they regulate. Address your suggestions for contract and addenda revisions to:

General Counsel
Texas Real Estate Commission
P.O. Box 12188
Austin, TX 78711-2188

From time to time *The Advisor* will carry a message from TREC's enforcement division relating to the proper approach to structuring, presenting, and negotiating purchase agreements. Volume 9, No. 4 addresses the proper handling of multiple offers, a common challenge in a seller's market. In response to the commonly asked questions about the listing agent's duty to notify the seller of multiple offers, TREC responded:

> TREC rule 535.156(a) specifically requires a licensee to "convey to the principal all known information which would affect the principal's decision on whether or not to accept or reject offers." Subsection 535.156(c) further provides that "a licensee has an affirmative duty to keep the principal informed at all times of significant information applicable to the transaction or transactions in which the licensee is acting as agent for the principal." Thus the rules require the listing agent to submit all written purchase offers to the seller until a buyer and the seller have a fully executed contract.

Although the general rule is that all offers must be communicated to the seller by the listing agent, there are a few exceptions. These include instances where the seller has specifically instructed the listing broker not to bring the seller any offers below a certain price, or situations in which a binding contract has been executed between a seller and buyer. In the latter situation, Rule 535.156(a) provides that "the license holder shall have no duty to submit offers to the principal after the principal has accepted an offer." Furthermore, the listing agent is prohibited from sharing any information about one buyer's offer with another buyer. Note, however, that in the end, it is always the sellers' decision whether to accept or reject offers they receive. The listing should address the broker's duty regarding back-up offers to avoid confusion on the issue. Also, trade association rules may affect the broker's duty.

Remember that the latest forms are available and can be downloaded and printed from *www.trec.state.tx.us.*

Summary

The purpose of the license act and the rules of the commission are to protect the public. The provisions prohibit the unauthorized practice of law by real estate license holders both in the area of structuring instruments and in the area of giving legal advice and opinions as to the legal sufficiency of instruments or the status of title.

To assist license holders, the commission has promulgated various forms for use by license holders. These forms must be used for all transactions assisted by license holders unless the transaction meets one of the defined exceptions itemized in the TREC rule. Remember that you must use promulgated contracts and addenda. Do not write a **business detail** addressing the business detail into the "Special Provisions" paragraph when there is a promulgated addendum. A business detail states what someone will or will not do. The license holder may only fill in the blanks provided and may not add material to or strike wording from the forms except to add business details to conform the instrument to the intent of the parties. When the license holder describes what will happen if someone does or does not do a certain act (e.g., terminate the contract, refund earnest money), the license holder steps over the line and begins defining **legal rights** and **remedies.** A thorough discussion and example of what is and is not acceptable wording for paragraph 11 is provided in a later chapter.

The license holder may help a customer or client read the document, but shall not give legal advice or opinions. Never discourage a customer or client from employing a competent real estate attorney. It is good practice to encourage buyers and sellers to carefully read any document before they sign it and seek legal counsel to clarify anything they do not understand. Encourage buyers and sellers to provide the information to complete paragraph 24 of the contract.

CHAPTER 1

REVIEW QUESTIONS

1. Which of the following defines a legal right as opposed to simply stating a business detail?

    A. The buyer will inspect the property again during the four hours immediately preceding closing.
    B. The buyer will pay for the owner's title policy.
    C. The seller will pay for all of the buyer's normal closing costs.
    D. The buyer may terminate the contract if the foundation needs to be repaired.

2. Identify which of the following addenda is not a promulgated form.

    A. Lead-Based Paint Addendum
    B. Seller's Temporary Residential Lease
    C. Seller Financing Addendum
    D. Addendum for Coastal Area Property

3. Who must notify the buyer to have the abstract examined by an attorney or obtain a policy of title insurance?

    A. The seller
    B. The license holder
    C. The lender
    D. The buyer's attorney

4. A license holder may use a contract form that has been prepared by the property owner when instructed by the property owner to do so.

    A. True
    B. False

5. What should a license holder do when there are unusual matters involved in a transaction?

    A. Explain it to the best of his/her ability before letting the prospect sign the contract.
    B. Ignore it and hope that the client understands it.
    C. Have the client sign the form and then advise him/her to talk to an attorney.
    D. Advise the client to seek legal advice before signing anything.

6. For which of the following is there no promulgated form?

    A. Sale of an unimproved residential lot
    B. Contract for deed
    C. Lease for temporary occupancy by a seller after the closing
    D. Request for information about an owner's association

7. As an added value to the service provided by a broker, may a broker retain and pay for the services of an attorney to provide legal counsel to a client?

   A. Yes
   B. No

8. Which of the following actions might leave a license holder open to a charge of practicing law without a license?

   A. License holder advises the seller that the property probably won't sell because it is overpriced.
   B. License holder advises the buyer in writing that a title policy should be obtained as well as a survey.
   C. License holder advises both the seller and the buyer that, in his opinion, title to the subject property is encumbered.
   D. License holder adds factual statements and business details to a promulgated form as requested by the client.

9. Which of the following is true about TREC promulgated contract forms?

   A. They must be used by all real estate license holders and Texas attorneys handling real estate transactions.
   B. They must be used by real estate license holders in all transactions to which the forms are applicable unless one of the four exceptions apply.
   C. They contain suggested language that a license holder may include when writing an agreement of purchase between a seller and a buyer.
   D. They are written and published by the Broker-Lawyer Committee and must be used for those transactions identified by the commission.

10. When no promulgated form meets the needs of a particular transaction, the license holder may use which of the following?

   A. Any standard form sold at the office supply store
   B. Any of the State Bar standard forms
   C. A form structured and approved by a licensed attorney at law
   D. A form created by a Texas licensed attorney for that type of transaction

Chapter 2

An Agreement or a Contract?

Key Terms

assignment
attorney-in-fact
bilateral contract
breach of contract
competent party
contract
default
earnest money
executed
executory contract
forbearance
fraud
incompetent party
liquidated damages
minor
money damages
novation
performance
statute of frauds
unenforcable
unilateral contract
valid
void
voidable

Elements of a Valid Contract

Every day individuals enter into agreements to do or to refrain from doing specific acts. Some of these agreements can be classified as contracts; others are simply agreements. A **contract** is a legally enforceable agreement to do **(performance)** or not to do **(forbearance)** a specific thing. Our Texas statutes protect contractual rights. Those who enter a contract and fail to perform **(default)** may be sued by the other party or parties to the agreement. To be considered an enforceable contract, the agreement must meet certain requirements. The six elements of a valid real estate contract include the following:

1. ***Competent Parties***–A party who does not have legal capacity **(incompetent party)** cannot be held to the terms of an agreement. To be legally competent, a party must have attained the age of majority, which in Texas is 18 years old. An individual under the age of 18 can be emancipated by a court of competent jurisdiction and declared an adult with contractual capacity. A contract

signed by a **minor** (younger than 18) is classified as voidable; that is, it can be set aside at the sole option of the minor party. If the minor chooses to uphold and fulfill the terms of the agreement, the contract is binding. The parties must be in control of their mental faculties. Individuals are considered sane or mentally competent until declared otherwise by a court. The parties must also be sober and demonstrate contractual intent. Any person who meets the **competent party** test may, through a duly executed specific *power of attorney,* name and appoint another to act as an **attorney-in-fact.** The attorney-in-fact serves in a fiduciary capacity to the one who makes the appointment. The signature of the attorney-in-fact binds a party just as effectively as the party's own signature. License holders dealing with corporate-owned real estate should remember that only an officer named in a *corporate resolution* passed at a meeting of the board of directors can sign a contract for and on behalf of the corporation.

2. ***Consideration***–To be valid, a contract must specifically identify that something, usually money, is being given in exchange for something else. Texas courts have clearly provided that a promise given in exchange for a promise is adequate consideration to bind a purchase agreement. The promise to sell and the promise to purchase in paragraph 1 of the promulgated forms serve as adequate consideration to bind the contract.

Figure 2.1 TREC 20-6 Paragraph 1

1. PARTIES: ______________________________ (Seller) agrees
sell and convey to ______________________________(Buyer) ar
Buyer agrees to buy from Seller the Property described below.

With regard to a purchase contract, the listing broker best fulfills the fiduciary duty to the seller by encouraging a substantial amount of **earnest money.** The earnest money can demonstrate the buyer's serious intent to purchase and may serve as liquidated damages in the event of a breach of contract as defined in paragraph 15 of the TREC promulgated contracts.

3. ***Mutual Agreement*** *(mutual assent)*–The parties must enter the contract freely and voluntarily. Their decisions must be based on truthful, accurate information. The presence of false information or fraud, by either acts of commission or acts of omission, precludes an enforceable agreement. License holders should take decisive action to ensure that full disclosure is made and that the parties to a purchase agreement are making their decisions based on truthful, accurate information.
4. ***Lawful Objective***–The provisions of an agreement must call for lawful activity. A provision that does not comply with federal, state, or local law cannot be upheld by a court. Suppose a tenant signs a lease stating that if the tenant fails to pay the rent, the landlord may enter the premises, seize all of the tenant's personal possessions, and immediately sell them to satisfy the rent obli-

gation. This provision is in violation of the homestead law and therefore unenforceable.

5. ***In Writing and Signed by the Parties***–The **Statute of Frauds** requires that, to be enforceable, all agreements affecting title to or interest in real estate in Texas be reduced to writing and signed by the parties. An oral agreement of sale is unenforceable in Texas and it is inadvisable for license holders to conduct real estate negotiations orally. Offers and counteroffers should be in writing. One does not have a binding executory contract until an offer has been made and accepted in writing and the offeror has been notified of the acceptance. The only exception to the "in writing" rule is a lease for one year or less. All other agreements must be in writing to be enforceable.
6. ***Contain a Legal Description***–A street address does not constitute an adequate description of the property for contract and conveyance purposes. The Statute of Frauds calls for the agreement to have a description that is of such certainty and accuracy that one can go to and identify it. The two commonly used are (1) reference to a recorded plat (lot, block, section number, subdivision name) and (2) metes and bounds.

Valid/Void/Unenforceable/Voidable

If an agreement meets all the above requirements, it is considered **valid** and will be upheld by Texas courts. If it does not meet the requirements, it is identified as a **void** (the absence of) contract. Due to a change in the law or the passage of time, a contract or certain provisions of a contract may become **unenforceable.**

As mentioned earlier, contracts can also be **voidable** (set aside at the option of one of the contracting parties). Voidable contracts typically exist in the following instances.

1. When entered into with a minor, the agreement is voidable at the option of the minor party.
2. When **fraud** by acts of commission or acts of omission can be proven, the agreement is voidable at the option of the nonfraudulent party.
3. When the seller fails to provide and the buyer of a previously occupied single-family residence fails to receive the Texas legislature-mandated "Seller's Disclosure of Property Condition," as required by section 5.008 of the Texas Property Code, the contract can be terminated at the sole option of the buyer and is therefore voidable at the option of the buyer. If it is presented after the agreement is signed, the buyer may terminate the contract within seven days after receipt of the disclosure.
4. When homeowner's association information and "Resale Certificate" have not been provided to the buyer prior to creating an executory contract to purchase, the buyer has the unrestricted right to terminate the agreement per section 5.012 of the Texas Property Code.

5. When the property is situated in a utility district or other statutorily created district providing water, sewer, drainage, or flood control, chapter 49 of the Texas Water Code establishes the contract voidable by the buyer if the seller has not forwarded the appropriate notice prior to creating an executory contract to purchase.

Presenting Offers

All offers should be in writing and presented to the property owner as quickly as reasonably practical. TREC rules call for "immediate" presentation. No real estate broker or salesperson has the right to withhold an offer from a property owner. To do so may result in suspension or revocation of one's license under the provisions of the TRELA or, worse, result in an unpleasant lawsuit for tortious interference. A tort is an act that damages another individual and gives rise to legal action. A property owner may consider the license holder's failure to present an offer in a timely manner a tortious interference with his or her ability to sell the property. The reader would do well to explore the possible consequences of this further before failing to present an offer in a timely manner.

Every license holder in Texas must successfully complete a 30-hour course in the law of agency to obtain a license. As you are taught in the law of agency, never lose sight of your fiduciary duties to your clients when helping them negotiate contracts. In addition to obedience (finding a buyer for the property), loyalty (putting the client's interest above all others, including your own), confidentiality (not revealing the client's personal information, although you have the duty to disclose all material facts about the property not specifically excluded by statute), reasonable care and due diligence, you owe your client disclosure and accounting. *Failure to present an offer* is certainly a breach of one's fiduciary duties, as well as the possible basis for a tortious interference lawsuit. Unless instructed otherwise by the owner, all offers must be presented! A seller's instruction not to present back-up offers must be to the agent in writing.

When an offer is unacceptable to the property owner, the owner's interest is best served when the owner gives written notice that the offer is unacceptable, thanks the offeror for the prospect's interest in the property and invites the offeror to submit another offer. The owner should give the offeror information that will shed some light upon what terms would be more acceptable to the offeree. A REALTOR® and his or her client might use the TAR "Rejection of Offer with Invitation to Submit a New Offer" form designed for this purpose or might simply create a letter to convey the message to the offeror. An example of such a letter follows.

Dear Mr. and Mrs. Prospect:

Thank you for your offer to purchase our home at 4321 Pine Hollow Drive. We cannot accept your offer as presented. We appreciate your interest and encourage you to submit another offer which will be more favorably considered if you will:

- offer a purchase price more in line with current market value,
- close within 20 to 30 days,
- purchase the property in its present condition, and
- pay your own loan origination costs including the fee for the survey required by your lender.

Although this is not a counteroffer, we look forward to hearing from you soon and wish you a very pleasant day.

Sincerely,

Although the majority of lawsuits against license holders are still brought by buyers dissatisfied with the condition of the property after the sale closes, each year more and more suits are being brought by clients or customers who feel that the selling agent breached one or more fiduciary duties or treated them unfairly.

Failure to present an offer can also result in disciplinary action against the license holder by TREC.

The seller presented with a written offer may

- accept it,
- reject it,
- counter it, or
- do nothing, ignore it.

The offeror may withdraw an offer any time before the offeree's acceptance or the offeror's receiving notification of the offeree's acceptance. Other things that may terminate an offer include

- lapse of reasonable time,
- destruction of the subject matter, and
- death or insanity of the offeror.

Performance

When an offeror has presented an offer to a seller, the offeree has accepted it, and the offeror has been notified of the acceptance, an **executory contract** exists. If and when everyone does what was promised in the agreement, closing will generally occur in 15 to 25 days. Of course, the time frame can be shorter or considerably longer.

When closing and funding occur, the contract is considered fully **executed.** An executory contract is one that is fully negotiated and signed by the parties. The parties still have obligations to fulfill before all things called for in the agreement have been performed. A *fully executed contract* is one in which all parties have fulfilled all promises made in the agreement. When the seller has delivered the deed, received the proceeds, and granted possession to the purchaser, a fully executed contract exists.

If one of the parties defaults or violates the agreement **(breach of contract),** the nondefaulting party may

- sue the defaulting party for specific performance,
- sue the defaulting party for **money damages,** or
- accept the earnest money as liquidated damages.

The TREC-promulgated contracts specify that the acceptance of the earnest money as liquidated damages releases the parties from further obligations to each other.

Figure 2.2 TREC 20-6 Paragraph 15

15. DEFAULT: If Buyer fails to comply with this contract, Buyer will be in default, and Seller may (a enforce specific performance, seek such other relief as may be provided by law, or both, or (b terminate this contract and receive the earnest money as liquidated damages, thereby releasin both parties from this contract. If, due to factors beyond Seller's control, Seller fails within th time allowed to make any non-casualty repairs or deliver the Commitment, or survey, if require of Seller, Buyer may (a) extend the time for performance up to 15 days and the Closing Date w be extended as necessary or (b) terminate this contract as the sole remedy and receive th earnest money. If Seller fails to comply with this contract for any other reason, Seller will be default and Buyer may (a) enforce specific performance, seek such other relief as may b provided by law, or both, or (b) terminate this contract and receive the earnest money, thereb releasing both parties from this contract.

Bilateral versus Unilateral

Purchase contracts are **bilateral contracts** that involve a promise in exchange for a promise. The seller in a purchase agreement agrees to deliver clear title and the buyer agrees to deliver money. A **unilateral contract** involves a promise in exchange for an act. The seller agrees to pay the listing broker when and if the broker produces a ready, willing, and able buyer.

Interpreting Contracts

When a court is called upon to settle a dispute between the parties to a contract, the court examines the entire agreement in an attempt to discover the intent of the parties. The court reads the preprinted form and presumes that anything added to the preprinted agreement more clearly shows the intent of the parties. Something handwritten overrides anything typewritten or preprinted, and an addendum takes precedence over the preprinted form. Once an *executory contract* has been created, the court favors upholding the agreement and applies the *parol evidence rule* when called upon to make a decision. The parol evidence rule prohibits the consideration of later written or oral agreements unless those agreements clear up any ambiguity in the original agreement. For example, if the original agreement called for closing in "late July" and a separate written agreement called for closing on "July 28," the court would accept the additional "evidence" as a more specific time to close. When parties wish to alter the provisions of an executory contract, they may execute a new contract in place of the existing agreement or amend the existing contract by using the TREC-promulgated amendment. In legal terms, a replacement contract is known as a **novation.** A novation or new contract should clearly reference the original agreement and state that the old agreement is replaced by the novation.

Reasonable Time versus "Time Is of the Essence"

With regard to time frames established in contracts, Texas courts always favor upholding the provisions of the contract when the parties have acted in good faith and have performed within a *reasonable time.* The court must hold the parties to exact performance within the time specified only when the agreement has incorporated the words, "*time is of the essence.*" Only the Option to Terminate clause in the contract and three addenda include those words: Addendum for Sale of Other Property by Buyer (TREC form 10-4), Addendum for "Back-Up" Contract (TREC form 11-5), and "Third Party Financing Condition Addendum" (TREC Form 40-1).

A real estate broker or salesperson should *never* add "time is of the essence" to a contract or advise a customer or client to do so. If a party wants to add the words, that party and the other party should be advised to seek the counsel of a real estate attorney before proceeding.

The TREC-promulgated contracts call for things to occur within a certain number of days AFTER the effective date of the contract. The effective date is filled in above the signature lines by the broker after the last party, usually the seller, has signed, and the other party, usually the buyer, has been notified of the acceptance. It is very difficult to establish performance and nonperformance when a careless license holder fails to fill in the appropriate date before opening title.

It is important to note that all 365 days (366 days in leap year) of the year have equal status. It is also important to learn that the word *after* does not include the effective day of the contract. Therefore, if the effective date of the contract is June 14, and the time frame calls for seven days, the time period will end at midnight on June 21.

Assignment versus Novation

Once an executory contract has been created, a party may transfer his or her interest to another legal entity **(assignment)** unless prohibited by statute or written agreement of the parties. Purchase contracts are typically assignable. Leases, by statute, may not be assigned without the express written permission of the property owner. The assignor is the party who transfers a right and the assignee is the party to whom the right is assigned. The assignee takes on all of the rights and obligations of the contract being assigned. However, the assignor is not released from the obligations.

The replacement of an existing contract with a new contract is known as a **novation.** The new contract must reference the contract that is being replaced. There can also be a novation of the parties. A novation releases the assignor from the obligations.

Summary

For a contract to be valid, the parties involved must be competent and must have reached mutual agreement and have tendered consideration. The acts agreed to must be lawful, and the agreement must be in writing if it involves rights and interest in real estate. Once the agreement is signed, it can be valid, void, unenforceable, or voidable.

The license holder should present all offers as quickly as possible to avoid disciplinary action by the Texas Real Estate Commission or a possible suit for tortious interference brought by the property owner.

Texas courts favor upholding the provisions of contracts and apply the reasonable-time rule when interpreting contracts unless the parties have specifically stated that "time is of the essence."

CHAPTER 2

REVIEW QUESTIONS

1. What kind of contract exists when a promise is exchanged for a promise?

   A. Unilateral
   B. Executed
   C. Bilateral
   D. Defaulted

2. When all parties have signed a contract and the offeror has been notified of the offeree's acceptance, what exists?

   A. Executed contract
   B. Expired contract
   C. Unenforceable contract
   D. Executory contract

3. When there is a default on the part of one party and the other party wants the defaulting party to do what was agreed in the contract, for what would the non-defaulting party sue?

   A. Money damages
   B. Specific performance
   C. Liquidated damages
   D. Injunctive relief

4. What word best describes a contract entered into with a minor?

   A. Void
   B. Voidable
   C. Valid
   D. Venued

5. Which of the following is an example of a unilateral contract?

   A. Contract for sale
   B. Lease
   C. Contract for deed
   D. Listing agreement

6. When an agreement is unenforceable because it does not fulfill the statutory requirements of a contract, it is identified as

   A. valid.
   B. void.
   C. voidable.
   D. invalid.

7. An offer made in response to an offer is known as what?

   A. Contract
   B. Assignment
   C. Counteroffer
   D. Novation

8. The substitution of a new contract for an existing contract is known as what?

   A. Amendment
   B. Novation
   C. Cancellation
   D. Rescission

9. What do you call a deliberate act of deception for the purpose of inducing another to part with something of value or to enter into a contract?

   A. Innocent misrepresentation
   B. Duress
   C. Mistake
   D. Fraud

10. The transfer of a party's rights and obligations created by the contract to a third party is

    A. cancellation.
    B. assignment.
    C. amendment.
    D. specific performance.

Chapter 3

The Three Ps (Parties, Property, Price)

Key Terms

accessories
baron sole
consideration
et ux
et vir
femme sole
fixture
land
legal description
metes and bounds
recorded plat
Statute of Frauds

Now that we have been introduced to the basic terminology of contracts and the requirements for creating a legally enforceable agreement between parties, we can begin to make an in-depth examination of the TREC-promulgated forms. Unfortunately, many license holders fail to take the time to carefully read and understand the content of the forms before attempting to use them to capture the wishes of the party or parties whom they represent.

Common Contract Errors

Through extensive interviews with over 40 escrow officers over an 18 month period, we identified and ranked the most commonly recurring errors made in the completion of the contract and addenda forms. Unfortunately, many of them can lead to serious legal complications, confusion, and unhappy clients. You might want to reproduce the following list of the ten most common contract errors and use it as a checklist to keep you on track when completing forms for customers and your clients.

1. Missing signatures or initials of the parties
2. No effective date
3. Addenda attached that are not listed in the contract

4. Incomplete or incorrect legal descriptions
5. Documents, such as the Seller's Disclosure Form, listed as addenda that should not be listed as such
6. Failure to use the appropriate TREC temporary leases when possession is to be granted before or after the funding of the transation
7. Cash down payments and loan amounts in the Sales Price paragraph that do not total the sales price (3A plus 3B must equal 3C)
8. Lack of coordination of the time frames established in the contract such as giving the buyer 30 days to obtain financing and calling for closing of the transaction in 20 days
9. Failure to define where notices can be effectively delivered to the buyer and the seller
10. Legal remedies written into paragraph 11, Special Provisions, by the license holders

Information Needed to Complete Contract Forms

The various paragraphs of the contract forms might be thought of as the building blocks of a solid transaction. The parties can choose the size and shape of the blocks to be used to build their transaction. Some of the blocks will need to be modified to create the transaction desired by the principals. The wise agent will help the parties identify the alternatives available to them and then let the parties choose the details of their transaction. The answers to the following 37 questions will enable the agent to guide the parties in the selection of the appropriate contract form for their situation and the needed addenda to clearly define the details of a particular transaction.

1. Name(s) of Seller(s) as on deed or owner's title policy including marital status.

   ____

2. Name(s) of Buyer(s) as buyers wish to take title; include marital status.

   ____

3. Legal description including:

   Lot number _______; Block number _______;

   Section number _______; Subdivision name ____________________;

   County ____________________; City ____________________;

   Address ______________________________; Zip code __________

4. Excluded fixtures and accessories ______________________________

____

5. Cash down payment $ ______________________________

6. Amount of 1st loan $______________; 2nd loan $ ______________

7. Sales price $ ______________________________

8. Type of financing ____________ Addenda needed ______________

9. Term of loan 1st ______________; 2nd ______________

10. Interest Rate 1st ______________; 2nd ______________

11. Assumption of loan balance $______________________________

12. Earnest money amount $ ______________________________

13. Escrow officer ______________________________

Address ______________________________

14. Additional earnest money $ ______________________________

15. Who will pay for title policy? ______________________________

16. Who will issue the title policy? ______________________________

17. Survey: Who will furnish? ______________________________

18. Number of days to furnish? ______________________________

19. How may days for buyer to raise title objections? ______________

20. Concern about what prohibited activities? ______________________

21. Is property subject to mandatory membership in HOA? ____________

22. Has buyer received seller's disclosure notice? ________________

23. If not, how many days for seller to furnish? ________________

24. Was house built prior to 1978? ______________________________

25. Are there specific repairs required by the buyer? ________________

____

____

____

26. How much does the buyer want the seller to contribute to the price of a residential service contract?
$ ____

27. By what date will closing hopefully take place? __________________

28. When will possession occur? ______________________________

29. Any special provisions?

____

____

30. How much will seller contribute toward buyer's expenses? $ _______

31. Do the parties agree to submit disputes to mediation? ____________

32. At what address will buyers receive notices?

____

phone number:________________; fax number:___________________

33. At what address will sellers receive notices?

____

phone number:________________; fax number:___________________

34. What addenda will need to be added to the agreement?

- ❑ Third Party Financing Condition Addendum
- ❑ Seller Financing Addendum
- ❑ Buyer's Temporary Residential Lease
- ❑ Seller's Temporary Residential Lease
- ❑ Addendum for Sale of Other Property by Buyer
- ❑ Addendum for "Back-Up" Contract
- ❑ Addendum for Seller's Disclosure of Information on Lead-based Paint and Lead-based Paint Hazards as Required by Federal Law
- ❑ Loan Assumption Addendum
- ❑ Addendum for Property Subject to Mandatory Membership in an Owners' Association
- ❑ Environmental Assessment, Threatened or Endangered Species and Wetlands Addendum
- ❑ Addendum for Coastal Area Property
- ❑ Addendum for Property Located Seaward of the Gulf Intracoastal Waterway
- ❑ Addendum for Release of Liability on Assumption of FHA, VA, or Conventional Loan/Restoration of Seller's Entitlement for VA Guaranteed Loan
- ❑ Other (list): ____________________

____

35. Does the buyer wish to purchase an option period? __________

How many days? __________ At what fee? __________

Credited or not credited to the sales price at closing? __________

36. Who is the buyer's attorney? __________

The address of the buyer's attorney __________

____

Telephone __________; Facsimile __________

37. Who is the seller's attorney? __________

The address of the seller's attorney __________

Telephone __________; Facsimile __________

A thorough understanding of the content of each of the paragraphs of any form to be used is essential. As we embark upon a detailed examination of the 24 paragraphs of the most commonly used of the TREC-promulgated contract forms, TREC 20-6, One To Four Family Residential Contract (Resale), we will give you the opportunity to read the text of each paragraph and make suggestions for proper completion of the blanks. We will also introduce various addenda that may be needed to add business details or create contingencies.

The remainder of this chapter is devoted to the three paragraphs that will be found in every real estate purchase agreement.

- Identification of the **P**arties
- Identification of the **P**roperty
- Establishment of the **P**rice

Before we look at the three Ps, take just a moment to examine the beginning of each form, its title, and statement of intended use. The forms may also carry a notice of purposes for which the form was not designed. Heed these notices and warnings.

Figure 3.1 TREC 20-6 Heading

EQUAL HOUSING OPPORTUNITY

PROMULGATED BY THE TEXAS REAL ESTATE COMMISSION (TREC) 01-06-03

ONE TO FOUR FAMILY RESIDENTIAL CONTRACT (RESALE)

NOTICE: Not For Use For Condominium Transactions

You will notice that the intended use of the form is identified in its title.

- Resale–not for use with new construction
- One to four family–not for larger residential or commercial
- Not for use with condominiums

In the upper right-hand corner of each form is the date of the Commission meeting at which the form was promulgated. To make certain that you are using correct forms, verify the date on any form against the date on the list in Chapter 1 of this book or verify current forms at the TREC Web site: *www.trec.state.tx.us.* If you have forms with an earlier date than those found on the list, do not use them. Once an earlier version of a form has been retired, it is illegal for a license holder to use it in structuring a transaction. To do so would constitute the illegal practice of law as defined by the TRELA.

The various addenda designed to add specific business details, contingencies, and temporary leasehold arrangements to the transaction are introduced throughout the discussion of the provisions of the basic contract form.

Unfortunately, many license holders attempt to complete the forms without ever having read them. The best approach is to read the form carefully and simply add the appropriate business detail called for by a blank line. We shall discuss what needs to be added where blanks appear. The information should have been gathered when answering the 37 questions printed in this chapter.

The executory contract provides the escrow officer and all affected parties with definitive instructions for closing the real estate transaction. The executory contract serves as a blueprint for the closing. It should address every detail relating to what must be done to close the sale of the property and have a fully executed contract.

There should be no reason for anyone to contact the license holder to interpret the phraseology of the special provisions or any filled in blanks if the license holder has performed competently.

As you proceed through the various provisions of the contract, remember that reasonable, realistic time frames need to be defined. One cannot close in 15 days if it is going to take 25 days to get loan approval and 20 days to get the results of an environmental inspection. It makes no sense to structure an executory contract that is contingent upon obtaining a 97 percent LTV loan at 5 percent annual interest for 40 years if only 90 percent LTV loans at 6.5 percent annual interest for 30 years are currently available from lenders.

Parties

Figure 3.2 TREC 20-6 Paragraph 1

1. PARTIES: ______________________________ (Seller) agrees to sell and convey to ______________________________(Buyer) and Buyer agrees to buy from Seller the Property described below.

The seller(s) and buyer(s) must be identified in the first paragraph. Because Texas is a community property state, it is important to include marital status. The following are acceptable ways to identify the marital status of parties.

Unmarried	NAME, **baron sole** (An unmarried male) NAME, **femme sole** (An unmarried female) NAME, **an unmarried person** NAME, **a widow or** NAME, **a widower**
Married	(When spouse is not joining in the conveyance) NAME, **as separate property**
Married	(Community property) NAME, **et ux** NAME (and wife) NAME, **et vir** NAME (and husband) NAME, **and spouse** NAME Husband's NAME **and wife** wife's NAME Wife's NAME **and husband** husband's NAME
Unmarried Persons Buying Together	NAME and NAME, **as tenants in common** **NOTE:** When parties wish to create rights of survivorship or fractional interests are involved, the parties should be advised to seek the advice of a competent real estate attorney before proceeding.

Executor or Administrator of an Estate	Executor's or administrator's NAME, **executor (administrator) of the estate of (decedent's name), deceased**
General Partnership	Business NAME, **a Texas partnership** or Business NAME, **a Texas partnership composed of name, name, and name**
Limited Partnership	Business NAME, **a Texas limited partnership, name, as general partner acting for and on behalf of the partnership**
Corporation	Company NAME, **a Texas* corporation** * or the name of the state in which the corporation is chartered **NOTE:** A corporate resolution issued by the board of directors names the officers appointed to execute the instruments for and on behalf of the corporation. A license holder should request a copy of the corporate resolution prior to the execution of any written agreements. It is to be retained in the transaction file.
Texas Limited Liability Company	Company NAME, **a Texas limited liability company** or Company NAME, **LLC**
Nonprofit	NAME, NAME, and NAME, **trustees for and on behalf of (corporate name)** Make certain that all names are complete and spelled correctly. To verify sellers' names, check the owner's title policy issued when title was taken or examine the name(s) appearing on the deed used to convey title and recorded at the county courthouse of the county in which the property is located. Remember that the tax records often contain significant errors and should not be relied upon as the final authority in these matters.

It is in this paragraph that the first **consideration** to bind the contract is expressed. The promise to sell by the seller and the promise to buy by the buyer is adequate consideration to bind the contract.

Property

Figure 3.3 TREC 20-6 Paragraph 2

2. PROPERTY:

A. LAND: Lot ______________________________,Block_____, ______________________________ ______________________________Addition, City of ________________ , ______________ County, Texas, known as ______________________________ ______________________________(address/zip code), or as described on attached exhibit.

B. IMPROVEMENTS: The house, garage and all other fixtures and improvements attached to the above-described real property, including without limitation, the following permanently installed and built-in items, if any: all equipment and appliances, valances, screens, shutters, awnings, wall-to-wall carpeting, mirrors, ceiling fans, attic fans, mail boxes, television antennas and satellite dish system and equipment, heating and air-conditioning units, security and fire detection equipment, wiring, plumbing and lighting fixtures, chandeliers, water softener system, kitchen equipment, garage door openers, cleaning equipment, shrubbery, landscaping, outdoor cooking equipment, and all other property owned by Seller and attached to the above described real property.

C. ACCESSORIES: The following described related accessories, if any: window air conditioning units, stove, fireplace screens, curtains and rods, blinds, window shades, draperies and rods, controls for satellite dish system, controls for garage door openers, entry gate controls, door keys, mailbox keys, above ground pool, swimming pool equipment and maintenance accessories, and artificial fireplace logs.

D. EXCLUSIONS: The following improvements and accessories will be retained by Seller and excluded: ______________________________ ______________________________.

The land, improvements and accessories are collectively referred to as the "Property".

The **Statute of Frauds** requires that agreements affecting title to real property have a **legal description,** a description of such certainty and accuracy that one can go to the property and identify it. Most urban residential properties are described by reference to a **plat recorded** at the courthouse of the county where the property is located.

The form provides a blank for the lot number, the block number, the name of the subdivision, the name of the city, and the informal street or post office address. When the subdivision has multiple sections, it is important to include the section number either before or after the name of the addition.

Example: Lot 3, Block 5, Section 2 of Shady Hollow Addition . . .

When the property is located in a city, include the name of the city. If the property is located in an unincorporated area, put "unincorporated" or "none" in the blank for city. Be sure to provide the zip code as called for in the contract form.

If the property is described by a **metes-and-bounds** description, put "N/A" in the blanks for lot and block. You may or may not have a subdivision name. Add the description as an attached exhibit to the contract.

Often townhouses are located in a platted subdivision but are described by a metes-and-bounds description. Fill in any blanks that apply, put N/A in those that do not apply and be sure to attach the metes-and-bounds descriptions as Exhibit A. If the legal description uses a building letter and unit number, use the TREC 30-3 Condominium contract form.

After describing the **land** in 2A, you move on to 2B and 2C. Part B lists the **fixtures**. Part C lists the **accessories** such as the curtains, draperies, and stove that usually remain with the property upon the transfer of ownership. **Do not strike any words in this paragraph.** When any of these items are to be removed by the seller, carefully list in 2D the items that do not remain. If there are no exclusions, be sure that you enter "N/A" or "none" in the space provided for the purpose of listing any exclusions.

Make certain that both buyers and sellers carefully read and understand what does and does not stay with the property at closing. This is no place for assumptions and guesswork. A clear understanding and realistic expectations create the atmosphere for happy buyers and sellers after closing.

Do not attempt in this paragraph to deal with personal property that might remain with the property. It is best to keep personal property completely out of the contract. The contract addresses the proposed transfer of real property. Personal property should be handled by a bill of sale as an entirely separate transaction between the parties. However, if the parties insist on putting personal property in the contract, it may be addressed in paragraph 11 or by using the appropriate TAR addendum for Non-Realty items. Use the TAR form only if you are a REALTOR®.

Figure 3.4 TAR Addendum for Non-Realty Items

TEXAS ASSOCIATION OF REALTORS®

NON-REALTY ITEMS ADDENDUM TO CONTRACT

ADDENDUM TO CONTRACT BETWEEN THE UNDERSIGNED PARTIES CONCERNING THE PROPERTY AT

____

(Street Address and City)

A. Seller shall convey to Buyer at closing the following personal property *(specify each item carefully, include description, model numbers, serial numbers, location, and other information)*:

____
____
____
____
____

B. Seller represents and warrants that Seller owns the personal property described in Paragraph A free and clear of all encumbrances. Seller shall convey the personal property:

☐ (1) at no cost to Buyer at closing.

☐ (2) for an additional sum of $ ____________________ as separate consideration for the personal property.

C. Seller does not warrant or guarantee the condition or future performance of the personal property conveyed by this document.

______________________	______________________
Buyer	Seller
______________________	______________________
Buyer	Seller

(TAR-1924) 01-27-98

Page 1 of 1

TAR, P.O. Box 2246, Austin, TX 78768-2246

Paragraph 3 is one of the easiest to complete correctly. Enter the sales price on line C. Add all loans that will be used to finance the purchase and enter the amount on line B. Most of the time you will deal with only one loan. Sometimes you may have a buyer assuming an existing loan and asking a seller to carry back a second.

Price

Figure 3.5 TREC 20-6 Paragraph 3

3. SALES PRICE:
A. Cash portion of Sales Price payable by Buyer at closing................. $_______________
B. Sum of all financing described below (excluding any loan funding fee or mortgage insurance premium) .... $_______________
C. Sales Price (Sum of A and B) .... $_______________

Example: The buyer is assuming a first lien note with an outstanding balance of $83,400 and a home improvement loan with a balance of $21,680 and asking the seller to carry back a note for $30,000. To get the correct number to enter in 3B, add $83,400 + $21,680 + $30,000 for a total of $135,080. To get the correct number to put in 3A, simply subtract 3B from 3C.

If the sales price in the above example is $160,000, line 3A would be $24,920 ($160,000 minus $135,080). Make certain that the buyer realizes that 3A represents only the cash portion of the sales price to be paid at closing by the buyer. Prepaids, reserve impounds, and closing costs are not included in this number.

For an all-cash transaction, the same number will be entered on line 3A and 3C with N/A, none, or -0- being entered on line 3B.

When financing is involved and the transaction is subject to or contingent upon receiving financing approval, one of two TREC addenda will be used to establish these details.

1. TREC 40-1; Third Party Financing Condition Addendum
2. TREC 41-0; Loan Assumption Addendum

If the seller is financing the purchase and receiving part of the consideration in the form of a promissory note secured by a Deed of Trust, the Seller Financing Addendum (TREC 26-4) will be used to define the details of the financing transaction.

Financing details will be discussed in the next chapter.

CHAPTER 3

REVIEW QUESTIONS

1. An unmarried female might appropriately be identified by all of the following except
   A. femme sole.
   B. an unmarried person.
   C. as separate property.
   D. a single woman.

2. The One To Four Family Residential Contract (Resale) can be used for all but which one of the following properties?
   A. A patio home
   B. A townhome identified as Unit 16, Building H of Phase One, Easy Living Estates
   C. A townhome identified as Lot 6, Block 2 of Section 1 of Carefree Living Estates
   D. A duplex with 2 garage apartments

3. A TREC contract form has the date on which it was promulgated printed on the form.
   A. True
   B. False

4. When property owned by a married couple is being sold, what is the best way to identify the sellers?
   A. Mr. and Mrs. Thomas Bud Smith
   B. Thomas Bud Smith and spouse Mary Ann Smith
   C. Thomas Bud Smith and his wife
   D. Thomas Bud Smith et vir Mary Ann Smith

5. The loan amount listed as the "sum of all financing listed below" (3B) includes PMI, MIP, or a VA funding fee.
   A. True
   B. False

Chapter 4

If I Can Get A Loan ...

Key Terms

assumption
escrow account
FHA insured
financing approval
first mortgage loan
loan approval
loan fees
MIP
PMI
promissory note
release of lien
second mortgage loan
seller financing
VA guaranteed
vendor's lien

One of the significant roadblocks to the consummation of many real estate transactions is the buyer's ability to obtain a loan. Sellers are well advised to require evidence of the buyer's ability to obtain financing before entering into purchase agreements with them. Competent buyer agents will encourage their clients to become preapproved by a lender before preceding with searching for the ideal property and attempting to convince the owner to enter into a purchase agreement subject to their ability to obtain financing approval.

Paragraph 4 of the promulgated contracts describes the manner in which the transaction will be financed. You will check no boxes or fill in any blanks if line 3B is zero. (Refer to page 34.)

Figure 4.1 TREC 20-6 Paragraph 4

4. FINANCING: The portion of Sales Price not payable in cash will be paid as follows: (Check applicable boxes below)

❑ A. THIRD PARTY FINANCING: One or more third party mortgage loans in the total amount of $____________________. If the Property does not satisfy the lenders' underwriting requirements for the loan(s), this contract will terminate and the earnest money will be refunded to Buyer. (Check one box only)

❑(1) This contract is subject to Buyer being approved for the financing described in the attached Third Party Financing Condition Addendum.

❑(2) This contract is not subject to Buyer being approved for financing and does not involve FHA or VA financing.

❑ B. ASSUMPTION: The assumption of the unpaid principal balance of one or more promissory notes described in the attached TREC Loan Assumption Addendum.

❑ C. SELLER FINANCING: A promissory note from Buyer to Seller of $________________, bearing _______ % interest per annum, secured by vendor's and deed of trust liens, and containing the terms and conditions described in the attached TREC Seller Financing Addendum. If an owner policy of title insurance is furnished, Buyer shall furnish Seller with a mortgagee policy of title insurance.

Three choices are available and can be used solo or in combination. You will notice that the forms instruct us to check the applicable boxes; in other places, the form instructs us to check one box only. Each of the three choices requires the use of an addendum to define the conditions.

A. Third party financing requires the use of TREC 40-1 unless 4A2 is selected. The Third Party Financing Conditions Addendum will be used when the borrower seeks conventional financing, FHA insured, or VA guaranteed financing.
B. Assumption of existing financing requires the use of TREC 41-0, Loan Assumption Addendum. If, as a condition of permitting assumption of existing financing, the seller wants to make the assumption subject to the seller being released from future liability for the loan, the parties will need to use TREC 12-1, Release of Liability on Assumption of FHA, VA or Conventional Loan/Restoration of Seller's Entitlement for VA Guaranteed Loan.
C. Seller financing requires the use of TREC 26-4, Seller Financing Addendum.

The real estate professional needs to carefully read paragraph 4 and each of the addenda and encourage the buyer and seller to carefully read and understand the portions that are applicable to their transaction. As you read, be sure to make note of the details itemized and discussed in the following paragraphs.

Paragraph 4A provides for one or more third party loans and provides a blank for entering the total of multiple third party loans. Point out to the buyer that the loan amount entered does not include **PMI, MIP,** or **VA funding fee.**

The next two check boxes in paragraph 4A are very significant. Checking the wrong box could have far-reaching financial implications for both you and the parties.

Box one (1) establishes that the parties agree that the contract **is** subject to the buyer being approved for the financing described in the attached addendum. Box two (2) states that the contract **is not** subject to the buyer being approved. These boxes do not establish that the property has been approved by the lender and is acceptable collateral to approve the loan.

Please note that **financing approval** and **loan approval** are two different things. Financing approval comes when the borrower is acceptable to and approved by the lender; when the buyer's assets, income and credit history are adequate to meet the lender's underwriting requirements. Loan approval comes when both the borrower and the property being offered as collateral meet the lender's underwriting guidelines.

NEVER check box two when FHA or VA financing is being sought.

Third Party Financing

TREC 40-1, Third Party Financing Condition Addendum is on the next two pages.

TREC 40-1, Third Party Financing Condition Addendum, is the most used of the promulgated addenda. Its use creates a very significant contingency in the contract. It places a responsibility on the buyer to apply promptly for the described financing, to furnish information and documents required by the lender, and to notify the seller timely if the buyer is unable to obtain the described loan. Time is of the essence for the purposes of performance and the giving of notice in this addendum. Failure to give the seller notice that the buyer is unable to obtain the loan removes the contingency and obligates the buyer to complete the transaction without the loan.

Failure to close becomes an act of default under the terms of the contract. Upon said default, the seller may invoke the remedies established in paragraph 15 of the contract. The parties must be encouraged to carefully read and understand the first paragraph in the text of the addendum. Give particular attention to the bold print.

When the buyer is unable to obtain the loan, most sellers will undoubtedly require documentation from the lender that the buyer did indeed exercise good faith in the attempt to obtain the desired loan. Buyer agents must make certain that the buyer client gives the required notice timely. Failure to do so will create great problems for most buyers.

A discussion of the types of third party financing follows the addendum and notice forms.

Figure 4.2 TREC 40-1

02-09-2004

EQUAL HOUSING OPPORTUNITY

PROMULGATED BY THE TEXAS REAL ESTATE COMMISSION (TREC)

THIRD PARTY FINANCING CONDITION ADDENDUM

TO CONTRACT CONCERNING THE PROPERTY AT

____

(Street Address and City)

Buyer shall apply promptly for all financing described below and make every reasonable effort to obtain financing approval including but not limited to furnishing all information and documents required by lender for approval. Financing approval will be deemed to have been obtained when the lender determines that Buyer has satisfied all of lender's financial requirements (those items relating to Buyer's assets, income and credit history). If Buyer cannot obtain financing approval, Buyer must give written notice to Seller within ____ days after the effective date of this contract and this contract will terminate and the earnest money will be refunded to Buyer. **If Buyer does not give such notice within the time allowed, this contract will no longer be subject to Buyer being approved for the financing described below. For purposes of this paragraph, time is of the essence; strict compliance with the times for performance herein stated is required.**

Each note must be secured by vendor's and deed of trust liens.

❑ A. CONVENTIONAL FINANCING:

❑ (1) A first mortgage loan in the principal amount of $ __________________ (excluding any financed PMI premium), due in full in _________ year(s), with interest not to exceed ______% per annum for the first _______year(s) of the loan with Loan Fees (loan origination, discount, buy-down, and commitment fees) not to exceed _______% of the loan.

❑ (2) A second mortgage loan in the principal amount of $_________________(excluding any financed PMI premium), due in full in __________year(s), with interest not to exceed ______% per annum for the first ___________year(s) of the loan with Loan Fees (loan origination, discount, buy-down, and commitment fees) not to exceed _________ % of the loan.

❑ B. TEXAS VETERANS' HOUSING ASSISTANCE PROGRAM LOAN: A Texas Veteran's Housing Assistance Program Loan of $_______________ for a period of at least ______years at the interest rate established by the Texas Veteran's Land Board at the time of closing.

❑ C. FHA INSURED FINANCING: A Section ________________ FHA insured loan of not less than $_________________ (excluding any financed MIP), amortizable monthly for not less than _______years, with interest not to exceed _______% per annum for the first ______year(s) of the loan with Loan Fees (loan origination, discount, buy-down, and commitment fees) not to exceed _________ % of the loan. As required by HUD-FHA, if FHA valuation is unknown, "*It is expressly agreed that, notwithstanding any other provision of this contract, the purchaser (Buyer) shall not be obligated to complete the purchase of the Property described herein or to incur any penalty by forfeiture of earnest money deposits or otherwise unless the purchaser (Buyer) has been given in accordance with HUD/FHA or VA requirements a written statement issued by the Federal Housing Commissioner, Department of Veterans Affairs, or a Direct Endorsement Lender setting forth the appraised value of the Property of not less than $__________________. The purchaser (Buyer) shall have the privilege and option of proceeding with consummation of the contract without regard to the amount of the appraised valuation. The appraised valuation is arrived at to determine the maximum mortgage the Department of Housing and Urban Development will insure. HUD does not warrant the value or the condition of the Property. The purchaser (Buyer) should satisfy himself/herself that the price and the condition of the Property are acceptable.*"

Initialed for identification by Buyer_______ _______ and Seller________ ________ 01A

Figure 4.2 TREC 40-1 (continued)

Third Party Financing Condition Addendum Concerning Page Two 02-09-2004

____
(Address of Property)

☐ D. VA GUARANTEED FINANCING: A VA guaranteed loan of not less than $__________________ (excluding any financed Funding Fee), amortizable monthly for not less than________years, with interest not to exceed________% per annum for the first ________year(s) of the loan with Loan Fees (loan origination, discount, buy-down, and commitment fees) not to exceed ________% of the loan.

VA NOTICE TO BUYER: "*It is expressly agreed that, notwithstanding any other provisions of this contract, the Buyer shall not incur any penalty by forfeiture of earnest money or otherwise or be obligated to complete the purchase of the Property described herein, if the contract purchase price or cost exceeds the reasonable value of the Property established by the Department of Veterans Affairs. The Buyer shall, however, have the privilege and option of proceeding with the consummation of this contract without regard to the amount of the reasonable value established by the Department of Veterans Affairs.*"

If Buyer elects to complete the purchase at an amount in excess of the reasonable value established by VA, Buyer shall pay such excess amount in cash from a source which Buyer agrees to disclose to the VA and which Buyer represents will not be from borrowed funds except as approved by VA. If VA reasonable value of the Property is less than the Sales Price, Seller may reduce the Sales Price to an amount equal to the VA reasonable value and the sale will be closed at the lower Sales Price with proportionate adjustments to the down payment and the loan amount.

Buyer hereby authorizes any lender to furnish to the Seller or Buyer or their representatives information relating only to the status of financing approval of Buyer.

______________________	______________________
Buyer	Seller
______________________	______________________
Buyer	Seller

This form has been approved by the Texas Real Estate Commission for use with similarly approved or promulgated contract forms. Such approval relates to this form only. TREC forms are intended for use only by trained real estate licensees. No representation is made as to the legal validity or adequacy of any provision in any specific transactions. It is not suitable for complex transactions. Texas Real Estate Commission, P.O. Box 12188, Austin, TX 78711-2188, 1-800-250-8732 or (512) 459-6544 (http://www.trec.state.tx.us) TREC No. 40-1. This form replaces TREC No. 40-0.

Figure 4.3 TREC 42-0

02-09-2004

PROMULGATED BY THE TEXAS REAL ESTATE COMMISSION (TREC)

NOTICE PURSUANT TO THIRD PARTY FINANCING CONDITION ADDENDUM

To: Seller(s)

In accordance with the Third Party Financing Condition Addendum attached to the Contract between ______________________________ as Seller and ______________________________ as Buyer dated ______________________, _____ for the Property located at __________ ______________________________ Buyer notifies Seller that Buyer cannot obtain financing approval.

Buyer Date	Buyer Date

To complete the blanks in the addendum, one needs to know what loan products are available. It makes no sense to structure an agreement that calls for a 10-day approval when it is taking 20 days to obtain approvals. It also makes no sense to cap the interest rate at 6 percent when nothing is available at less than 6.5 percent. Checking box A establishes a contingency of obtaining a conventional loan for a defined term at a maximum interest rate of not less than a certain amount. You must enter specific numbers in the blanks. "Market Rate" or "TBD" (to be determined) is never acceptable.

Often a borrower will obtain two loans to avoid PMI. A very popular approach is to obtain a first lien loan for 80 percent or less of the purchase price and a second for 10 percent or so.

> ***Example:*** The buyers are purchasing a new home for $450,000. They want to finance $405,000 after paying $45,000 cash. For year 2004, the Fannie Mae conforming loan limit is $333,700. A loan for more than this amount will be a nonconforming loan that will be made at a higher interest rate. The buyer has some alternatives to consider.
>
> 1. Pay $116,300 cash down payment and finance $333,700 at a favorable rate.
> 2. Pay $45,000 cash down payment and obtain a first lien at $333,700 at a favorable rate and a second lien for $71,300 at a rate about 2 points higher than the first.
> 3. Pay $45,000 cash down payment and obtain a first lien of $333,700 and ask the seller to carry back a second lien for $71,300.
> 4. An eligible Texas Veteran could use the Texas Housing Assistance Program Loan in concert with a first lien that conforms to Fannie Mae guidelines.

A challenge is faced when the buyer wants to pay a large amount of cash down payment and obtain a loan of significantly less than 80 percent. Most buyers do not want to pay more than the amount the lender's appraiser indicates the property is worth. If the LTV is 80 percent or greater and an appraisal is for less than the sales price listed in line 3B of the contract, the buyer can walk or attempt to renegotiate the sales price. This is not the case when dealing with a lower than 80 percent LTV.

One possible solution is for the buyer to add as a business detail to paragraph 11, the Special Provisions paragraph, a statement to the effect that the loan in 4B and the Third Party Financing Conditions Addendum is to be for an LTV as established by the lender's appraisal not to exceed _____%. To calculate the LTV, simply divide the amount entered on line 3B by the amount entered on 3C of the contract to get the LTV. If the lender's appraisal is less than 3B, the LTV will be higher.

Example: 3 A $300,000
B $175,000
C $475,000

$175,000 ÷ $475,000 = .37, or 37% LTV

After the lender's appraiser does the appraisal, the indicated value is $456,000.

$175,000 ÷ $456,000 = .38, or 38% LTV

The parties may agree to renegotiate the sales price or to release the buyer from the contract. Buyers in this type of situation will do well to consult competent legal counsel to write language that accurately defines their wishes.

License holders, especially buyer's agents, would do well to become thoroughly familiar with all of the financing options open to their clients. An especially good program is available to eligible Texas Veterans known as the Texas Veteran's Housing Assistance Program Loan. It is box B on the Third Party Financing Addendum. Buyers and their agents can learn more about the program by calling 1-800-252-VETS or going to *www.TexasVeterans.com.* The interest rate can be as much as 2 percent below the going rate on other available loans. The current maximum loan amount is $240,000. The program can be alone or in combination with conventional, FHA insured, or VA guaranteed loans.

Frequently, buyers with limited up-front cash use the FHA insurance program. Remember that FHA does not loan money; it insures high LTV-ratio loans and reduces the risk to the lenders loaning the money.

Early in 1999 the FHA greatly simplified the rules for **FHA insured** loan amounts and down payment requirements. The maximum loan amounts are a percentage of Fannie Mae's maximum conforming loan amount in the highest cost areas. Check FHA's Web site for the maximum insured loan for your county.

For current limits on high cost counties, go to the HUD Web site (*https://entp.hud.gov/idapp/html/hicostlook.cfm*), which always has the most recent numbers available when changes are made.

Under current regulations, a buyer obtaining an FHA insured loan must invest at least 3 percent in down payment and/or closing costs. If the sales price is $50,000 or less, the maximum LTV is 98.75 percent. The borrower must pay 1.25 percent down and costs equal to a minimum of 1.75 percent. When the sales price is more than $50,000, the maximum LTV is 97.75 percent. The borrower must pay 2.25 percent down and costs equal to a minimum of .75 percent. Any closing costs in excess of these amounts may be paid by the seller who is willing to pay them.

For current information, go to a finance book or check with the buyer's loan officer.

HUD Form: HUD-92564-CN (12/03) must be used when a buyer is getting an FHA insured loan.

Figure 4.4 HUD 92564

US Department of Housing and Urban Development (HUD)
Federal Housing Administration

OMB Approval No: 2502
(exp. 06/30

For Your Protection: Get a Home Inspectio

Name of Buyer (s) ______________________

Property Address ______________________

____

Why a Buyer Needs a Home Inspection

A home inspection gives the buyer more detailed information about the overall condition of the home prior to purchase. In a home inspection, a qualified inspector takes an in-depth, unbiased look at your potential new home to:

- evaluate the physical condition: structure, construction, and mechanical systems
- identify items that need to be repaired or replaced
- estimate the remaining useful life of the major systems, equipment, structure, and finishes

Appraisals are Different from Home Inspections

An appraisal is different from a home inspection. Appraisals are for lenders; home inspections are for buyers. An appraisal is required for three reasons:

- to estimate the market value of a house
- to make sure that the house meets FHA minimum property standards/requirements
- to make sure that the house is marketable

FHA Does Not Guarantee the Value or Condition of your Potential New Home

If you find problems with your new home after closing, FHA can not give or lend you money for repairs, and FHA can not buy the home back from you.

Radon Gas Testing

The United States Environmental Protection Agenc the Surgeon General of the United States have recommended that all houses should be tested for ra For more information on radon testing, call the Nati Radon Information Line at 1-800-SOS-Radon (1-80 644-6999). As with a home inspection, if you decid test for radon, you may do so before signing your contract, or you may do so after signing the contract long as your contract states the sale of the home dep on your satisfaction with the results of the radon tes

Be an Informed Buyer

It is your responsibility to be an informed buyer. Be that what you buy is satisfactory in every respect. Y have the right to carefully examine your potential ne home with a qualified home inspector. You may ar to do so before signing your contract, or may do so signing the contract as long as your contract states t the sale of the home depends on the inspection.

I/we understand the importance of getting an independent home inspection. I/we have considered this before si contract with the seller for a home. Furthermore, I/we have carefully read this notice and fully understand that will not perform a home inspection nor guarantee the price or condition of the property.

______ **I/We choose to have a home inspection performed.**

______ **I/We choose not to have a home inspection performed.**

X ______________________ X ______________________

Signature & Date Signature & Date

The final choice on the Third Party Financing Condition Addendum is for **VA guaranteed** financing. Before structuring a contract that calls for a VA loan, the borrower must contact the Department of Veterans Affairs to determine eligibility and the amount of available entitlement. VA guaranteed loans are often used when the eligible veteran has limited cash available. These loans can also be a good choice for a buyer who is putting a large amount of cash into the property. The loans are assumable with VA approval. When assumed, the interest rate does not increase. One buying when loan interest rates are low might have a very significant advantage by being able to offer an **assumption** if interest rates are high at a point in the future when the buyer is ready to sell.

Assumption

The second choice offered in paragraph 4 is for the financing to be the assumption of an existing loan or loans. Two addenda may need to be used.

- TREC 12-1, Release of Liability on Assumption of FHA, VA or Conventional Loan/Restoration of Seller's Entitlement for VA Guaranteed Loan
- TREC 41-0, Loan Assumption Addendum

Unfortunately, the TREC 41-0 does not address when a buyer must apply for assumption approval when assuming a conventional, FHA insured or VA guaranteed loan. It would be prudent to address this important business detail in paragraph 11 of the contract. Simply state that the buyer will apply to the lender for assumption approval within a specific number of days after the effective date of the contract.

Figure 4.5 TREC 12-1

EQUAL HOUSING OPPORTUNITY

03-17-92

ADDENDUM FOR
RELEASE OF LIABILITY ON ASSUMPTION OF FHA, VA OR CONVENTIONAL LOAN
RESTORATION OF SELLER'S ENTITLEMENT FOR VA GUARANTEED LOAN

PROMULGATED BY THE TEXAS REAL ESTATE COMMISSION (TREC)

ADDENDUM TO EARNEST MONEY CONTRACT BETWEEN THE UNDERSIGNED PARTIES CONCERNING THE PROPERTY AT______________________________________
(Street Address and City)

☐ **A. RELEASE OF SELLER'S LIABILITY ON LOAN TO BE ASSUMED:**

Within ___________ days from the effective date of this contract Seller and Buyer shall apply for release of Seller's liability from (a) any conventional lender, (b) VA and any lender whose loan has been guaranteed by VA, or (c) FHA and any lender whose loan has been insured by FHA. Seller and Buyer shall furnish all required information and documents. If any release of liability has not been approved by the Closing Date: (check 1 or 2 below)

☐ 1. This contract shall terminate and the Earnest Money shall be refunded to Buyer.

☐ 2. Failure to obtain release approval shall not delay closing and Seller and Buyer shall continue to seek release of Sellers' liability.

☐ **B. RESTORATION OF SELLERS ENTITLEMENT FOR VA LOAN:**

Within __________ days from the effective date of this contract Seller and Buyer shall apply for restoration of Seller's VA entitlement and shall furnish all information and documents required by VA. If restoration has not been approved by the Closing Date: (check 1 or 2 below)

☐ 1. This contract shall terminate and the Earnest Money shall be refunded to Buyer.

☐ 2. Failure to obtain restoration approval shall not delay closing and Seller and Buyer shall continue to seek restoration of Seller's VA entitlement.

NOTICE: VA will not restore Seller's VA entitlement unless Buyer: (a) is a veteran, (b) has sufficient unused VA entitlement and (c) is otherwise qualified. If Seller desires release of liability from VA and the lender together with restoration of VA entitlement, paragraphs A and B should be used.

Seller shall pay the cost of securing the release and restoration. If Seller's cost will exceed $______________________, and Buyer declines to pay the excess, Seller may (a) waive release or restoration, (b) pay the excess, or (c) terminate this contract and the Earnest Money shall be refunded to Buyer.

Seller's deed shall contain any loan assumption clause required by FHA, VA or any lender. The provisions of this addendum are enforceable after closing.

____________________	____________________
Buyer	Seller
____________________	____________________
Buyer	Seller

The form of this Addendum has been approved by the Texas Real Estate Commission for use with similarly approved or promulgated contract forms. Such approval relates to this form only. No representation is made as to the legal validity or adequacy of any provision in any specific transactions. It is not suitable for complex transactions. (03-92) TREC No. 12-1. This form replaces TREC No. 12-0.

01A TREC No. 12-1

Figure 4.6 TREC 41-0

PROMULGATED BY THE TEXAS REAL ESTATE COMMISSION (TREC) 10-29-01

EQUAL HOUSING OPPORTUNITY

LOAN ASSUMPTION ADDENDUM

TO CONTRACT CONCERNING THE PROPERTY AT

____

(Street Address and City)

A. CREDIT DOCUMENTATION. Within______days after the effective date of this contract, Buyer shall deliver to Seller ❑ credit report ❑ verification of employment, including salary ❑ verification of funds on deposit in financial institutions ❑ current financial statement to establish Buyer's creditworthiness and ❑ ________ ____.
Buyer hereby authorizes any credit reporting agency to furnish to Seller at Buyer's sole expense copies of Buyer's credit reports.

B.CREDIT APPROVAL. If Buyer's documentation is not delivered within the specified time, Seller may terminate this contract by notice to Buyer within 7 days after expiration of the time for delivery, and the earnest money will be paid to Seller. If the documentation is timely delivered, and Seller determines in Seller's sole discretion that Buyer's credit is unacceptable, Seller may terminate this contract by notice to Buyer within 7 days after expiration of the time for delivery and the earnest money will be refunded to Buyer. If Seller does not terminate this contract, Seller will be deemed to have accepted Buyer's credit.

C. ASSUMPTION.

❑ (1) The unpaid principal balance of a first lien promissory note payable to ______________________ ______________________ which unpaid balance at closing will be $ ______________. The total current monthly payment including principal, interest and any reserve deposits is $ ______________. Buyer's initial payment will be the first payment due after closing.

❑ (2) The unpaid principal balance of a second lien promissory note payable to ______________________ ______________________ which unpaid balance at closing will be $ ______________. The total current monthly payment including principal, interest and any reserve deposits is $ ______________. Buyer's initial payment will be the first payment due after closing.

Buyer's assumption of an existing note includes all obligations imposed by the deed of trust securing the note. If the unpaid principal balance(s) of any assumed loan(s) as of the Closing Date varies from the loan balance(s) stated above, the ❑ cash payable at closing ❑ Sales Price will be adjusted by the amount of any variance; provided, if the total principal balance of all assumed loans varies in an amount greater than $350.00 at closing, either party may terminate this contract and the earnest money will be refunded to Buyer unless the other party elects to eliminate the excess in the variance by an appropriate adjustment at closing. Buyer may terminate this contract and the earnest money will be refunded to Buyer if the noteholder requires (a) payment of an assumption fee in excess of $ ______________in (1) above or $ ______________in (2) above and Seller declines to pay such excess, (b) an increase in the interest rate to more than _______% in (1) above, or ______% in (2) above, (c) any other modification of the loan documents, or (d) consent to the assumption of the loan and fails to consent. A vendor's lien and deed of trust to secure assumption will be required which will automatically be released on execution and delivery of a release by noteholder. If Seller is released from liability on any assumed note, the vendor's lien and deed of trust to secure assumption will not be required.
If noteholder maintains an escrow account, the escrow account must be transferred to Buyer without any deficiency. Buyer shall reimburse Seller for the amount in the transferred accounts.

NOTICE TO BUYER: The monthly payments, interest rates or other terms of some loans may be adjusted by the noteholder at or after closing. If you are concerned about the possibility of future adjustments, do not sign the contract without examining the notes and deeds of trust.

NOTICE TO SELLER: Your liability to pay the note assumed by Buyer will continue unless you obtain a release of liability from the noteholder. If you are concerned about future liability, you should use the TREC Release of Liability Addendum.

______________________	______________________
Buyer	Seller
______________________	______________________
Buyer	Seller

This form has been approved by the Texas Real Estate Commission for use with similarly approved or promulgated contract forms. Such approval relates to this form only. TREC forms are intended for use only by trained real estate licensees. No representation is made as to the legal validity or adequacy of any provision in any specific transactions. It is not suitable for complex transactions. Texas Real Estate Commission, P.O. Box 12188, Austin, TX 78711-2188, 1-800-250-8732 or (512) 459-6544 (http://www.trec.state.tx.us) TREC No. 41-0.

01A

Before completing the blanks on the Loan Assumption Addendum, check with the seller for what documentation the seller will want to review and then make certain that both parties understand the time frames to which they are agreeing in the Credit Documentation and Credit Approval sections.

Be sure to obtain accurate information for the Assumption section and have the parties decide about adjusting the sales price or the buyer's cash payable at closing. Give careful attention to the discussion of liens, securing of assumptions, and transfer of **escrow accounts,** if any. Buyers and sellers should carefully read the notices on the addendum with buyers taking seriously the advice to carefully examine any notes and deeds of trust to be assumed.

Seller Financing

The final choice offered in paragraph 4 of the contract is for the seller to accept part of the consideration in the form of a note secured by a deed of trust.

The Seller Financing Addendum is added to the contract to address how the loan will be repaid, whether the note is assumable, and how payment of ad valorem taxes and insurance will be handled. A prudent seller should have an attorney any time **seller financing** is a part of the transaction. The attorney should be experienced in real estate law and understand the potential risks to the seller's financial well-being when the buyer defaults on the payments and decisive legal action against the borrower becomes necessary.

Figure 4.7 TREC 26-4

PROMULGATED BY THE TEXAS REAL ESTATE COMMISSION (TREC) 10-29-01

EQUAL HOUSING OPPORTUNITY

SELLER FINANCING ADDENDUM

TO CONTRACT CONCERNING THE PROPERTY AT

____
(Street Address and City)

A. CREDIT DOCUMENTATION. Within__________days after the effective date of this contract, Buyer shall deliver to Seller ❑ credit report ❑ verification of employment, including salary ❑ verification of funds on deposit in financial institutions ❑ current financial statement to establish Buyer's creditworthiness and ❑ ____
____.
Buyer hereby authorizes any credit reporting agency to furnish to Seller at Buyer's sole expense copies of Buyer's credit reports.

B. CREDIT APPROVAL. If Buyer's documentation is not delivered within the specified time, Seller may terminate this contract by notice to Buyer within 7 days after expiration of the time for delivery, and the earnest money will be paid to Seller. If the documentation is timely delivered, and Seller determines in Seller's sole discretion that Buyer's credit is unacceptable, Seller may terminate this contract by notice to Buyer within 7 days after expiration of the time for delivery and the earnest money will be refunded to Buyer. If Seller does not terminate this contract, Seller will be deemed to have accepted Buyer's credit.

C. PROMISSORY NOTE. The promissory note (Note) described in Paragraph 4 of this contract payable by Buyer to the order of Seller will be payable at the place designated by Seller. Buyer may prepay the Note in whole or in part at any time without penalty. Any prepayments are to be applied to the payment of the installments of principal last maturing and interest will immediately cease on the prepaid principal. The Note will contain a provision for payment of a late fee of 5% of any installment not paid within 10 days of the due date. The Note will be payable as follows:

❑ (1) In one payment due ______________________________ after the date of the Note with interest payable ____.

❑ (2) In ________________ installments of $ ___________________ ❑ including interest ❑ plus interest beginning ______________________________ after the date of the Note and continuing at _____________ intervals thereafter for ________________when the balance of the Note will be due and payable.

❑ (3) Interest only in ______ installments for the first ________________________ month(s) and thereafter in installments of $________________ ❑ including interest ❑ plus interest beginning ______________________________ after the date of the Note and continuing at ______________ intervals thereafter for __________________ when the balance of the Note will be due and payable.

D. DEED OF TRUST. The deed of trust securing the Note will provide for the following:

(1) PROPERTY TRANSFERS: (check only one)

❑ (a) Consent Not Required: The Property may be sold, conveyed or leased without the consent of Seller, provided any subsequent buyer assumes the Note.

❑ (b) Consent Required: If all or any part of the Property is sold, conveyed, leased for a period longer than 3 years, leased with an option to purchase, or otherwise sold (including any contract for deed), without the prior written consent of Seller, Seller may declare the

01A

Initialed for identification by Buyer_______ _______ and Seller_______ _______

Figure 4.7 TREC 26-4 (continued)

Seller Financing Addendum Concerning Page Two 10-29-01

____
(Address of Property)

balance of the Note, to be immediately due and payable. The creation of a subordinate lien, any conveyance under threat or order of condemnation, any deed solely between buyers, the passage of title by reason of the death of a buyer or by operation of law will not entitle Seller to exercise the remedies provided in this paragraph.

(2) TAX AND INSURANCE ESCROW: (check only one)

❑ (a) Escrow Not Required: Buyer shall furnish Seller annually, before the taxes become delinquent, evidence that all taxes on the Property have been paid. Buyer shall furnish Seller annually evidence of paid-up casualty insurance naming Seller as an additional loss payee.

❑ (b) Escrow Required: With each installment Buyer shall deposit with Seller in escrow a pro rata part of the estimated annual ad valorem taxes and casualty insurance premiums for the Property. Buyer shall pay any deficiency within 30 days after notice from Seller. Buyer's failure to pay the deficiency constitutes a default under the deed of trust. Buyer is not required to deposit any escrow payments for taxes and insurance that are deposited with a superior lienholder. The casualty insurance must name Seller as an additional loss payee.

(3) PRIOR LIENS: Any default under any lien superior to the lien securing the Note constitutes default under the deed of trust securing the Note.

______________________	______________________
Buyer	Seller
______________________	______________________
Buyer	Seller

This form has been approved by the Texas Real Estate Commission for use with similarly approved or promulgated contract forms. Such approval relates to this form only. TREC forms are intended for use only by trained real estate licensees. No representation is made as to the legal validity or adequacy of any provision in any specific transactions. It is not suitable for complex transactions. Texas Real Estate Commission, P.O. Box 12188, Austin, TX 78711-2188, 1-800-250-8732 or (512) 459-6544 (http://www.trec.state.tx.us) TREC No. 26-4. This form replaces TREC No. 26-3.

01A

Once the financing is in place, the transaction will be a giant step closer to closing. An important part of the agreement between the parties addresses who will pay for what at or prior to the closing. Many of the expenses to be paid are loan related. Paragraph 12 reflects the most current practice and custom in Texas of who pays for what. Any of the items listed for the seller can be paid for by the buyer and many of the expenses listed for the buyer can be paid by the seller with the lender's knowledge and approval. Generally, who pays for what is negotiable between the parties; however, with certain loan programs the buyers may be prohibited from paying certain expenses and may be required to pay certain things on their own behalf. It is best to check with a loan officer for current requirements.

To replace any definition of who pays for what in paragraph 12, the parties can define their agreement in the Special Provisions paragraph. Who pays for something is a business detail that is appropriately addressed in the Special Provisions paragraph.

It Takes More than a Down Payment to Close a Transaction

Figure 4.8 TREC 20-6 Paragraph 12

12. SETTLEMENT AND OTHER EXPENSES:

A. The following expenses must be paid at or prior to closing:

(1) Expenses payable by Seller (Seller's Expenses):

(a) Releases of existing liens, including prepayment penalties and recording fees; release of Seller's loan liability; tax statements or certificates; preparation of deed; one-half of escrow fee; and other expenses payable by Seller under this contract.

(b) Seller shall also pay an amount not to exceed $ ______________ to be applied in the following order: Buyer's Expenses which Buyer is prohibited from paying by FHA, VA, Texas Veteran's Housing Assistance Program or other governmental loan programs; Buyer's prepaid items; other Buyer's expenses.

(2) Expenses payable by Buyer (Buyer's Expenses):

(a) Loan origination, discount, buy-down, and commitment fees (Loan Fees).

(b) Appraisal fees; loan application fees; credit reports; preparation of loan documents; interest on the notes from date of disbursement to one month prior to dates of first monthly payments; recording fees; copies of easements and restrictions; mortgagee title policy with endorsements required by lender; loan-related inspection fees; photos, amortization schedules, one-half of escrow fee; all prepaid items, including required premiums for flood and hazard insurance, reserve deposits for insurance, ad valorem taxes and special governmental assessments; final compliance inspection; courier fee, repair inspection, underwriting fee and wire transfer, expenses incident to any loan, and other expenses payable by Buyer under this contract.

B. Buyer shall pay Private Mortgage Insurance Premium (PMI), VA Loan Funding Fee, or FHA Mortgage Insurance Premium (MIP) as required by the lender.

C. If any expense exceeds an amount expressly stated in this contract for such expense to be paid by a party, that party may terminate this contract unless the other party agrees to pay such excess. Buyer may not pay charges and fees expressly prohibited by FHA, VA, Texas Veteran's Housing Assistance Program or other governmental loan program regulations.

Two points need to be considered in paragraph 12.

1. **Loan Fees** are defined in paragraph 12A(2)(a). These are the same Loan Fees referenced in the Third Party Financing Condition Addendum. They include:
   - loan origination fees,
   - discount points,
   - buy-down, and
   - commitment fees.

   These Loan Fees are usually expressed as points. Remember that 1 point is equal to 1 percent of the loan amount. Interestingly, Loan Fees are not defined for VA financing.

2. The order of the application of what the seller might agree to pay as additional expenses on the buyer's behalf is clearly established in 12A(1)(b).
   - Buyer's expense which buyer is prohibited by FHA or VA from paying
   - Buyer's prepaid items
   - Other buyer's expenses

The buyer is required by the contract to pay private mortgage insurance. It can be paid in cash at closing or added to the amount of the loan. This is a point to be negotiated between a buyer and the lender and does not involve the sellers or license holders.

Finally, note that if any expense exceeds an amount set as an upper limit in the contract, a party may terminate the contract unless the other party agrees to pay the excess.

Summary

A very large percentage of the blanks that must be completed in the purchase agreement address the financing. Most buyers will use some borrowed funds to complete the purchase; therefore, it is important for the professional real estate practitioner to be well informed about the available options and be able to guide the parties to a financing arrangement that best suits the needs of both parties. Be thoroughly familiar with the contract provisions and the content of each of the three addenda that are available to help the parties define their wishes.

Remember that there is a difference between financing approval and loan approval. Also, Loan Fees are a clearly defined term in the contract and the order for the application of any money paid by the seller to assist the buyer with loan expenses is clearly defined in the contract.

Encourage parties to read and understand before signing and always advise one who does not understand to seek legal counsel before signing. Loans should never be assumed until the buyer has carefully reviewed the note and deed of trust that is being assumed.

Carefully read and study the content of the promulgated forms before you attempt to act on behalf of a client or customer. Inexperienced salespersons should consult more experienced persons such as the broker or the loan officer for guidance.

CHAPTER 4

REVIEW QUESTIONS

1. Which of the following options would never require the use of a TREC promulgated addendum to define the transaction's financial details?

   A. Seller financing
   B. Third party financing
   C. Cash
   D. Assumption of existing lien

2. If the property does not satisfy the lender's underwriting requirements, the contract will terminate and the earnest money will be returned to the buyer.

   A. True
   B. False

3. Which of the following loan combinations is least likely to occur?

   A. Third party conventional first lien with Texas Veterans Housing assistance loan
   B. Third party conventional first lien with a third party conventional second lien
   C. Third party conventional second lien with assumption of a FHA insured loan
   D. FHA insured loan with a third party conventional second lien

4. When a loan is assumed with lender approval and modification of the interest rate has occurred, the original borrower, seller, is automatically released from liability.

   A. True
   B. False

5. How many days does the contract give the seller to terminate the contract after expiration of the time for the buyer to deliver documentation for credit approval purposes?

   A. 5 days
   B. 7 days
   C. 10 days
   D. 15 days

6. What two documents are required to be executed when an assumption takes place without the release of liability being granted by the lender to the seller?

   A. Vendor's lien and deed of trust to secure assumption
   B. A reaffirmation promissory note and deed of trust
   C. A release of original lien and deed of trust to secure assumption
   D. A special warranty deed and deed of trust to secure assumption

7. In paragraph 3 of the contract and the Third Party Financing Condition Addendum, each time the loan amount is recited it is with PMI, MIP or VA funding fee included in the amount.

   A. True
   B. False

8. Who establishes the interest rate for Texas Veterans' Housing Assistance Program Loans?

   A. The Department of Veterans Affairs
   B. The local VA field office
   C. The individual lender
   D. The Texas Veterans Land Board

9. Conventional loan amounts in excess of what LTV will require the purchaser to obtain PMI?

   A. 95%
   B. 90%
   C. 80%
   D. 75%

10. Financing approval and loan approval are the same thing.

    A. True
    B. False

Chapter

5

Practice with the Money

Now that you have become familiar with the paragraphs of the contract and the addenda relating to financing, it is time to practice filling in the applicable blanks for a variety of financing scenarios.

We will give the relevant data needed to structure the following types of financing. You are to fill in the appropriate contract paragraphs and addenda that are furnished following each scenario.

The scenarios will cover several of the more commonly encountered financing choices made by buyers of Texas properties. These include the following:

Scenario 1	All Cash—No Financing
Scenario 2	Third Party 80% Conventional
Scenario 3	Third Party 90% Conventional
Scenario 4	Third Party 80/10/10 Conventional
Scenario 5	FHA Insured
Scenario 6	VA Guaranteed
Scenario 7	Assumption with Seller 2nd

The solutions for these scenarios will be provided by your instructor and serve as a basis for class discussion of situations that a license holder may experience in the brokerage business.

Scenario 1 All Cash–No Financing

The Thompsons want to purchase the Johnsons' home and offer a purchase price of \$340,000. Mr. Thompson has recently inherited \$400,000. They decide to save money and to enjoy the benefits of having a home with no mortgage. They have studied the market carefully and know that they are paying a fair price.

Since there is no loan involved, they will not need to use any of the financing addenda.

Complete paragraphs 3, 4, and 12 of their purchase agreement.

May you enjoy a career with many transactions of this type.

Scenario 1

Figure 5.1 TREC 20-6 Paragraph 3

3. SALES PRICE:
A. Cash portion of Sales Price payable by Buyer at closing.................. \$____________________
B. Sum of all financing described below (excluding any loan funding fee or mortgage insurance premium) .... \$____________________
C. Sales Price (Sum of A and B) .... \$____________________

Figure 5.2 TREC 20-6 Paragraph 4

4. FINANCING: The portion of Sales Price not payable in cash will be paid as follows: (Check applicable boxes below)

❑ A. THIRD PARTY FINANCING: One or more third party mortgage loans in the total amount of $__________________. If the Property does not satisfy the lenders' underwriting requirements for the loan(s), this contract will terminate and the earnest money will be refunded to Buyer. (Check one box only)

❑(1) This contract is subject to Buyer being approved for the financing described in the attached Third Party Financing Condition Addendum.

❑(2) This contract is not subject to Buyer being approved for financing and does not involve FHA or VA financing.

❑ B. ASSUMPTION: The assumption of the unpaid principal balance of one or more promissory notes described in the attached TREC Loan Assumption Addendum.

❑ C. SELLER FINANCING: A promissory note from Buyer to Seller of $______________ bearing ______ % interest per annum, secured by vendor's and deed of trust liens, and containing the terms and conditions described in the attached TREC Seller Financing Addendum. If an owner policy of title insurance is furnished, Buyer shall furnish Seller with a mortgagee policy of title insurance.

Figure 5.3 TREC 20-6 Paragraph 12

12. SETTLEMENT AND OTHER EXPENSES:

A. The following expenses must be paid at or prior to closing:

(1) Expenses payable by Seller (Seller's Expenses):

(a) Releases of existing liens, including prepayment penalties and recording fees; release Seller's loan liability; tax statements or certificates; preparation of deed; one-half o escrow fee; and other expenses payable by Seller under this contract.

(b) Seller shall also pay an amount not to exceed $ ____________ to be applied in the following order: Buyer's Expenses which Buyer is prohibited from paying by FHA, V Texas Veteran's Housing Assistance Program or other governmental loan programs; Buyer's prepaid items; other Buyer's expenses.

(2) Expenses payable by Buyer (Buyer's Expenses):

(a) Loan origination, discount, buy-down, and commitment fees (Loan Fees).

(b) Appraisal fees; loan application fees; credit reports; preparation of loan documents; interest on the notes from date of disbursement to one month prior to dat of first monthly payments; recording fees; copies of easements and restrictions mortgagee title policy with endorsements required by lender; loan-related inspecti fees; photos, amortization schedules, one-half of escrow fee; all prepaid items, including required premiums for flood and hazard insurance, reserve deposits fo insurance, ad valorem taxes and special governmental assessments; final complian inspection; courier fee, repair inspection, underwriting fee and wire transfer, expens incident to any loan, and other expenses payable by Buyer under this contract.

B. Buyer shall pay Private Mortgage Insurance Premium (PMI), VA Loan Funding Fee, or FH Mortgage Insurance Premium (MIP) as required by the lender.

C. If any expense exceeds an amount expressly stated in this contract for such expense to be paid by a party, that party may terminate this contract unless the other party agrees to p such excess. Buyer may not pay charges and fees expressly prohibited by FHA, VA, Tex Veteran's Housing Assistance Program or other governmental loan program regulations.

Scenario 2 Third Party 80% Conventional

Philip Schoewe and his wife, Karen Nichols, have been saving their money and investing it wisely to accumulate a significant down payment to purchase their dream home. They have about $110,000 to use as a down payment, pay closing costs and prepaids, and hope to have $15,000 to $20,000 remaining to spend on decorating.

They find a 4/2/2 in a wonderful neighborhood for $250,300. They offer $249,000, which the owners readily accept.

The contract is contingent upon the buyers being approved for an 80 percent conventional loan and invest their extra savings to let the income help pay the note. They will not need to purchase PMI, pay discount, buydown, or commitment fees or ask the seller to help them with any loan costs. They can obtain a 15-year fixed rate loan at 6.25 percent annual interest and anticipate that they can have financing approval within 20 days after the effective date of the contract. To provide a cushion for a possible upward adjustment in the market rate, they write the offer with a 6.5% maximum acceptable rate. They have not yet applied for financing approval. They do know that they will be charged a 1 percent loan origination fee.

Scenario 2

Figure 5.4 TREC 20-6 Paragraph 3

3. SALES PRICE:

A. Cash portion of Sales Price payable by Buyer at closing.................. $________________

B. Sum of all financing described below (excluding any loan funding fee or mortgage insurance premium) .... $________________

C. Sales Price (Sum of A and B) .... $________________

Figure 5.5 TREC 20-6 Paragraph 4

4. FINANCING: The portion of Sales Price not payable in cash will be paid as follows: (Check applicable boxes below)

❑ A. THIRD PARTY FINANCING: One or more third party mortgage loans in the total amount of $__________________. If the Property does not satisfy the lenders' underwriting requirements for the loan(s), this contract will terminate and the earnest money will be refunded to Buyer. (Check one box only)

❑(1) This contract is subject to Buyer being approved for the financing described in the attached Third Party Financing Condition Addendum.

❑(2) This contract is not subject to Buyer being approved for financing and does not involve FHA or VA financing.

❑ B. ASSUMPTION: The assumption of the unpaid principal balance of one or more promissory notes described in the attached TREC Loan Assumption Addendum.

❑ C. SELLER FINANCING: A promissory note from Buyer to Seller of $_______________ bearing ______ % interest per annum, secured by vendor's and deed of trust liens, and containing the terms and conditions described in the attached TREC Seller Financing Addendum. If an owner policy of title insurance is furnished, Buyer shall furnish Seller with a mortgagee policy of title insurance.

Figure 5.6 TREC 20-6 Paragraph 12

12. SETTLEMENT AND OTHER EXPENSES:

A. The following expenses must be paid at or prior to closing:

(1) Expenses payable by Seller (Seller's Expenses):

(a) Releases of existing liens, including prepayment penalties and recording fees; release of Seller's loan liability; tax statements or certificates; preparation of deed; one-half of escrow fee; and other expenses payable by Seller under this contract.

(b) Seller shall also pay an amount not to exceed $ ____________ to be applied in the following order: Buyer's Expenses which Buyer is prohibited from paying by FHA, VA, Texas Veteran's Housing Assistance Program or other governmental loan programs; Buyer's prepaid items; other Buyer's expenses.

(2) Expenses payable by Buyer (Buyer's Expenses):

(a) Loan origination, discount, buy-down, and commitment fees (Loan Fees).

(b) Appraisal fees; loan application fees; credit reports; preparation of loan documents; interest on the notes from date of disbursement to one month prior to dates of first monthly payments; recording fees; copies of easements and restrictions; mortgagee title policy with endorsements required by lender; loan-related inspection fees; photos, amortization schedules, one-half of escrow fee; all prepaid items, including required premiums for flood and hazard insurance, reserve deposits for insurance, ad valorem taxes and special governmental assessments; final compliance inspection; courier fee, repair inspection, underwriting fee and wire transfer, expenses incident to any loan, and other expenses payable by Buyer under this contract.

B. Buyer shall pay Private Mortgage Insurance Premium (PMI), VA Loan Funding Fee, or FHA Mortgage Insurance Premium (MIP) as required by the lender.

C. If any expense exceeds an amount expressly stated in this contract for such expense to be paid by a party, that party may terminate this contract unless the other party agrees to pay such excess. Buyer may not pay charges and fees expressly prohibited by FHA, VA, Texas Veteran's Housing Assistance Program or other governmental loan program regulations.

Figure 5.7 TREC 40-1

02-09-2004

EQUAL HOUSING OPPORTUNITY

PROMULGATED BY THE TEXAS REAL ESTATE COMMISSION (TREC)

THIRD PARTY FINANCING CONDITION ADDENDUM

TO CONTRACT CONCERNING THE PROPERTY AT

____

(Street Address and City)

Buyer shall apply promptly for all financing described below and make every reasonable effort to obtain financing approval including but not limited to furnishing all information and documents required by lender for approval. Financing approval will be deemed to have been obtained when the lender determines that Buyer has satisfied all of lender's financial requirements (those items relating to Buyer's assets, income and credit history). If Buyer cannot obtain financing approval, Buyer must give written notice to Seller within _____ days after the effective date of this contract and this contract will terminate and the earnest money will be refunded to Buyer. **If Buyer does not give such notice within the time allowed, this contract will no longer be subject to Buyer being approved for the financing described below. For purposes of this paragraph, time is of the essence; strict compliance with the times for performance herein stated is required.**

Each note must be secured by vendor's and deed of trust liens.

❑ A. CONVENTIONAL FINANCING:

❑ (1) A first mortgage loan in the principal amount of $ ____________________ (excluding any financed PMI premium), due in full in __________ year(s), with interest not to exceed ______% per annum for the first ________year(s) of the loan with Loan Fees (loan origination, discount, buy-down, and commitment fees) not to exceed ________% of the loan.

❑ (2) A second mortgage loan in the principal amount of $___________________(excluding any financed PMI premium), due in full in ___________year(s), with interest not to exceed ______% per annum for the first ____________year(s) of the loan with Loan Fees (loan origination, discount, buy-down, and commitment fees) not to exceed _________ % of the loan.

❑ B. TEXAS VETERANS' HOUSING ASSISTANCE PROGRAM LOAN: A Texas Veteran's Housing Assistance Program Loan of $________________ for a period of at least ______years at the interest rate established by the Texas Veteran's Land Board at the time of closing.

❑ C. FHA INSURED FINANCING: A Section _________________ FHA insured loan of not less than $___________________ (excluding any financed MIP), amortizable monthly for not less than ________years, with interest not to exceed _______% per annum for the first ______year(s) of the loan with Loan Fees (loan origination, discount, buy-down, and commitment fees) not to exceed __________ % of the loan. As required by HUD-FHA, if FHA valuation is unknown, *"It is expressly agreed that, notwithstanding any other provision of this contract, the purchaser (Buyer) shall not be obligated to complete the purchase of the Property described herein or to incur any penalty by forfeiture of earnest money deposits or otherwise unless the purchaser (Buyer) has been given in accordance with HUD/FHA or VA requirements a written statement issued by the Federal Housing Commissioner, Department of Veterans Affairs, or a Direct Endorsement Lender setting forth the appraised value of the Property of not less than $___________________. The purchaser (Buyer) shall have the privilege and option of proceeding with consummation of the contract without regard to the amount of the appraised valuation. The appraised valuation is arrived at to determine the maximum mortgage the Department of Housing and Urban Development will insure. HUD does not warrant the value or the condition of the Property. The purchaser (Buyer) should satisfy himself/herself that the price and the condition of the Property are acceptable."*

Initialed for identification by Buyer_______ _______ and Seller_________ _______

Figure 5.7 TREC 40-1 (continued)

Third Party Financing Condition Addendum Concerning Page Two 02-09-2004

____
(Address of Property)

❑ D. VA GUARANTEED FINANCING: A VA guaranteed loan of not less than $________________ (excluding any financed Funding Fee), amortizable monthly for not less than________years, with interest not to exceed________% per annum for the first ________year(s) of the loan with Loan Fees (loan origination, discount, buy-down, and commitment fees) not to exceed ________% of the loan.

VA NOTICE TO BUYER: "*It is expressly agreed that, notwithstanding any other provisions of this contract, the Buyer shall not incur any penalty by forfeiture of earnest money or otherwise or be obligated to complete the purchase of the Property described herein, if the contract purchase price or cost exceeds the reasonable value of the Property established by the Department of Veterans Affairs. The Buyer shall, however, have the privilege and option of proceeding with the consummation of this contract without regard to the amount of the reasonable value established by the Department of Veterans Affairs.*"

If Buyer elects to complete the purchase at an amount in excess of the reasonable value established by VA, Buyer shall pay such excess amount in cash from a source which Buyer agrees to disclose to the VA and which Buyer represents will not be from borrowed funds except as approved by VA. If VA reasonable value of the Property is less than the Sales Price, Seller may reduce the Sales Price to an amount equal to the VA reasonable value and the sale will be closed at the lower Sales Price with proportionate adjustments to the down payment and the loan amount.

Buyer hereby authorizes any lender to furnish to the Seller or Buyer or their representatives information relating only to the status of financing approval of Buyer.

Buyer	Seller
Buyer	Seller

This form has been approved by the Texas Real Estate Commission for use with similarly approved or promulgated contract forms. Such approval relates to this form only. TREC forms are intended for use only by trained real estate licensees. No representation is made as to the legal validity or adequacy of any provision in any specific transactions. It is not suitable for complex transactions. Texas Real Estate Commission, P.O. Box 12188, Austin, TX 78711-2188, 1-800-250-8732 or (512) 459-6544 (http://www.trec.state.tx.us) TREC No. 40-1. This form replaces TREC No. 40-0.

01A

Scenario 3 Third Party 90% Conventional

John Paul Gordon and his wife, Mary Ann Gordon, are offering Isabelle Gerhard $176,400 for her home. They have been preapproved for a loan not to exceed $160,400. The loan will be for 30 years and will have an interest rate of 6.75 percent for the first 3 years. After that it will be adjusted annually with adjustments being tied to the 11th Federal Reserve District Cost of Funds.

They will pay 10 percent down payment. They will be charged a 1 percent origination fee. The Gordons are asking Ms. Gerhard to assist the buyers with their closing costs and related expenses in an amount of $1,500. The contract is not subject to borrower approval for financing.

Scenario 3

Figure 5.8 TREC 20-6 Paragraph 3

3. SALES PRICE:

A. Cash portion of Sales Price payable by Buyer at closing.................. $________________

B. Sum of all financing described below (excluding any loan funding fee or mortgage insurance premium) .... $________________

C. Sales Price (Sum of A and B) .... $________________

Figure 5.9 TREC 20-6 Paragraph 4

4. FINANCING: The portion of Sales Price not payable in cash will be paid as follows: (Check applicable boxes below)

❑ A. THIRD PARTY FINANCING: One or more third party mortgage loans in the total amount of $__________________. If the Property does not satisfy the lenders' underwriting requirements for the loan(s), this contract will terminate and the earnest money will be refunded to Buyer. (Check one box only)

❑(1) This contract is subject to Buyer being approved for the financing described in the attached Third Party Financing Condition Addendum.

❑(2) This contract is not subject to Buyer being approved for financing and does not involve FHA or VA financing.

❑ B. ASSUMPTION: The assumption of the unpaid principal balance of one or more promissory notes described in the attached TREC Loan Assumption Addendum.

❑ C. SELLER FINANCING: A promissory note from Buyer to Seller of $______________ bearing ______ % interest per annum, secured by vendor's and deed of trust liens, and containing the terms and conditions described in the attached TREC Seller Financing Addendum. If an owner policy of title insurance is furnished, Buyer shall furnish Seller with a mortgagee policy of title insurance.

Figure 5.10 TREC 20-6 Paragraph 12

12. SETTLEMENT AND OTHER EXPENSES:

A. The following expenses must be paid at or prior to closing:

(1) Expenses payable by Seller (Seller's Expenses):

(a) Releases of existing liens, including prepayment penalties and recording fees; release of Seller's loan liability; tax statements or certificates; preparation of deed; one-half of escrow fee; and other expenses payable by Seller under this contract.

(b) Seller shall also pay an amount not to exceed $ ____________ to be applied in the following order: Buyer's Expenses which Buyer is prohibited from paying by FHA, VA, Texas Veteran's Housing Assistance Program or other governmental loan programs; Buyer's prepaid items; other Buyer's expenses.

(2) Expenses payable by Buyer (Buyer's Expenses):

(a) Loan origination, discount, buy-down, and commitment fees (Loan Fees).

(b) Appraisal fees; loan application fees; credit reports; preparation of loan documents; interest on the notes from date of disbursement to one month prior to dates of first monthly payments; recording fees; copies of easements and restrictions; mortgagee title policy with endorsements required by lender; loan-related inspection fees; photos, amortization schedules, one-half of escrow fee; all prepaid items, including required premiums for flood and hazard insurance, reserve deposits for insurance, ad valorem taxes and special governmental assessments; final compliance inspection; courier fee, repair inspection, underwriting fee and wire transfer, expenses incident to any loan, and other expenses payable by Buyer under this contract.

B. Buyer shall pay Private Mortgage Insurance Premium (PMI), VA Loan Funding Fee, or FHA Mortgage Insurance Premium (MIP) as required by the lender.

C. If any expense exceeds an amount expressly stated in this contract for such expense to be paid by a party, that party may terminate this contract unless the other party agrees to pay such excess. Buyer may not pay charges and fees expressly prohibited by FHA, VA, Texas Veteran's Housing Assistance Program or other governmental loan program regulations.

Scenario 4 Third Party 80/10/10 Conventional

The buyers are under contract to buy their dream home for $435,000. They have been planning to make a 10 percent down payment and to finance the balance for 30 years, which would result in a loan of $391,500, a jumbo loan that would require PMI and would be available at 7.875 percent for 30 years. They can comfortably afford the resulting monthly payment.

Their buyer agent and the loan officer recommend that they get a conforming loan of $300,700, currently available at 6.75 percent annual interest AND simultaneously get a second mortgage loan of $90,800 at 8.25 percent for 15 years. After being shown the numbers, they decide that going for two loans is a wonderful idea. The second will not require any origination fee and will eliminate the need for them to carry PMI. As long as the conforming loan does not exceed an 80 percent loan-to-value ratio, Fannie Mae will not require PMI.

The buyers do not ask the sellers to contribute anything to the payment of their loan costs. The buyers will pay the 1 point origination fee required on the first lien note.

They will apply immediately for the financing and have been assured by the loan officer that they will be able to obtain financing approval within 15 days after the effective date of the contract and the submission of their loan application. They decide to write the purchase agreement with 20 days for financing approval just to be on the safe side. The transaction is subject to financing approval.

Scenario 4

Figure 5.11 TREC 20-6 Paragraph 3

3. SALES PRICE:

A. Cash portion of Sales Price payable by Buyer at closing................. $____________________

B. Sum of all financing described below (excluding any loan funding fee or mortgage insurance premium) .... $____________________

C. Sales Price (Sum of A and B) .... $____________________

Figure 5.12 TREC 20-6 Paragraph 4

4. FINANCING: The portion of Sales Price not payable in cash will be paid as follows: (Check applicable boxes below)

❑ A. THIRD PARTY FINANCING: One or more third party mortgage loans in the total amount of $__________________. If the Property does not satisfy the lenders' underwriting requirements for the loan(s), this contract will terminate and the earnest money will be refunded to Buyer. (Check one box only)

❑(1) This contract is subject to Buyer being approved for the financing described in the attached Third Party Financing Condition Addendum.

❑(2) This contract is not subject to Buyer being approved for financing and does not involve FHA or VA financing.

❑ B. ASSUMPTION: The assumption of the unpaid principal balance of one or more promissory notes described in the attached TREC Loan Assumption Addendum.

❑ C. SELLER FINANCING: A promissory note from Buyer to Seller of $_______________ bearing ______ % interest per annum, secured by vendor's and deed of trust liens, and containing the terms and conditions described in the attached TREC Seller Financing Addendum. If an owner policy of title insurance is furnished, Buyer shall furnish Seller with a mortgagee policy of title insurance.

Figure 5.13 TREC 20-6 Paragraph 12

12. SETTLEMENT AND OTHER EXPENSES:

A. The following expenses must be paid at or prior to closing:

(1) Expenses payable by Seller (Seller's Expenses):

(a) Releases of existing liens, including prepayment penalties and recording fees; release of Seller's loan liability; tax statements or certificates; preparation of deed; one-half of escrow fee; and other expenses payable by Seller under this contract.

(b) Seller shall also pay an amount not to exceed $ ____________ to be applied in the following order: Buyer's Expenses which Buyer is prohibited from paying by FHA, VA, Texas Veteran's Housing Assistance Program or other governmental loan programs; Buyer's prepaid items; other Buyer's expenses.

(2) Expenses payable by Buyer (Buyer's Expenses):

(a) Loan origination, discount, buy-down, and commitment fees (Loan Fees).

(b) Appraisal fees; loan application fees; credit reports; preparation of loan documents; interest on the notes from date of disbursement to one month prior to dates of first monthly payments; recording fees; copies of easements and restrictions; mortgagee title policy with endorsements required by lender; loan-related inspection fees; photos, amortization schedules, one-half of escrow fee; all prepaid items, including required premiums for flood and hazard insurance, reserve deposits for insurance, ad valorem taxes and special governmental assessments; final compliance inspection; courier fee, repair inspection, underwriting fee and wire transfer, expenses incident to any loan, and other expenses payable by Buyer under this contract.

B. Buyer shall pay Private Mortgage Insurance Premium (PMI), VA Loan Funding Fee, or FHA Mortgage Insurance Premium (MIP) as required by the lender.

C. If any expense exceeds an amount expressly stated in this contract for such expense to be paid by a party, that party may terminate this contract unless the other party agrees to pay such excess. Buyer may not pay charges and fees expressly prohibited by FHA, VA, Texas Veteran's Housing Assistance Program or other governmental loan program regulations.

Figure 5.14 TREC 40-1

02-09-2004

EQUAL HOUSING OPPORTUNITY

PROMULGATED BY THE TEXAS REAL ESTATE COMMISSION (TREC)

THIRD PARTY FINANCING CONDITION ADDENDUM

TO CONTRACT CONCERNING THE PROPERTY AT

____

(Street Address and City)

Buyer shall apply promptly for all financing described below and make every reasonable effort to obtain financing approval including but not limited to furnishing all information and documents required by lender for approval. Financing approval will be deemed to have been obtained when the lender determines that Buyer has satisfied all of lender's financial requirements (those items relating to Buyer's assets, income and credit history). If Buyer cannot obtain financing approval, Buyer must give written notice to Seller within _____ days after the effective date of this contract and this contract will terminate and the earnest money will be refunded to Buyer. **If Buyer does not give such notice within the time allowed, this contract will no longer be subject to Buyer being approved for the financing described below. For purposes of this paragraph, time is of the essence; strict compliance with the times for performance herein stated is required.**

Each note must be secured by vendor's and deed of trust liens.

❑ A. CONVENTIONAL FINANCING:

❑ (1) A first mortgage loan in the principal amount of $ ____________________ (excluding any financed PMI premium), due in full in _________ year(s), with interest not to exceed ______% per annum for the first ________year(s) of the loan with Loan Fees (loan origination, discount, buy-down, and commitment fees) not to exceed ________% of the loan.

❑ (2) A second mortgage loan in the principal amount of $__________________(excluding any financed PMI premium), due in full in ___________year(s), with interest not to exceed ______% per annum for the first ____________year(s) of the loan with Loan Fees (loan origination, discount, buy-down, and commitment fees) not to exceed _________ % of the loan.

❑ B. TEXAS VETERANS' HOUSING ASSISTANCE PROGRAM LOAN: A Texas Veteran's Housing Assistance Program Loan of $________________ for a period of at least ______years at the interest rate established by the Texas Veteran's Land Board at the time of closing.

❑ C. FHA INSURED FINANCING: A Section _________________ FHA insured loan of not less than $__________________ (excluding any financed MIP), amortizable monthly for not less than _______years, with interest not to exceed _______% per annum for the first ______year(s) of the loan with Loan Fees (loan origination, discount, buy-down, and commitment fees) not to exceed _________ % of the loan. As required by HUD-FHA, if FHA valuation is unknown, *"It is expressly agreed that, notwithstanding any other provision of this contract, the purchaser (Buyer) shall not be obligated to complete the purchase of the Property described herein or to incur any penalty by forfeiture of earnest money deposits or otherwise unless the purchaser (Buyer) has been given in accordance with HUD/FHA or VA requirements a written statement issued by the Federal Housing Commissioner, Department of Veterans Affairs, or a Direct Endorsement Lender setting forth the appraised value of the Property of not less than $___________________. The purchaser (Buyer) shall have the privilege and option of proceeding with consummation of the contract without regard to the amount of the appraised valuation. The appraised valuation is arrived at to determine the maximum mortgage the Department of Housing and Urban Development will insure. HUD does not warrant the value or the condition of the Property. The purchaser (Buyer) should satisfy himself/herself that the price and the condition of the Property are acceptable."*

Initialed for identification by Buyer_______ _______ and Seller________ ________

Figure 5.14 TREC 40-1 (continued)

Third Party Financing Condition Addendum Concerning Page Two 02-09-2004

____

(Address of Property)

❑ D. VA GUARANTEED FINANCING: A VA guaranteed loan of not less than $________________ (excluding any financed Funding Fee), amortizable monthly for not less than________years, with interest not to exceed________% per annum for the first ________year(s) of the loan with Loan Fees (loan origination, discount, buy-down, and commitment fees) not to exceed ________% of the loan.

VA NOTICE TO BUYER: "*It is expressly agreed that, notwithstanding any other provisions of this contract, the Buyer shall not incur any penalty by forfeiture of earnest money or otherwise or be obligated to complete the purchase of the Property described herein, if the contract purchase price or cost exceeds the reasonable value of the Property established by the Department of Veterans Affairs. The Buyer shall, however, have the privilege and option of proceeding with the consummation of this contract without regard to the amount of the reasonable value established by the Department of Veterans Affairs.*"

If Buyer elects to complete the purchase at an amount in excess of the reasonable value established by VA, Buyer shall pay such excess amount in cash from a source which Buyer agrees to disclose to the VA and which Buyer represents will not be from borrowed funds except as approved by VA. If VA reasonable value of the Property is less than the Sales Price, Seller may reduce the Sales Price to an amount equal to the VA reasonable value and the sale will be closed at the lower Sales Price with proportionate adjustments to the down payment and the loan amount.

Buyer hereby authorizes any lender to furnish to the Seller or Buyer or their representatives information relating only to the status of financing approval of Buyer.

____________________ Buyer	____________________ Seller
____________________ Buyer	____________________ Seller

This form has been approved by the Texas Real Estate Commission for use with similarly approved or promulgated contract forms. Such approval relates to this form only. TREC forms are intended for use only by trained real estate licensees. No representation is made as to the legal validity or adequacy of any provision in any specific transactions. It is not suitable for complex transactions. Texas Real Estate Commission, P.O. Box 12188, Austin, TX 78711-2188, 1-800-250-8732 or (512) 459-6544 (http://www.trec.state.tx.us) TREC No. 40-1. This form replaces TREC No. 40-0.

Scenario 5 FHA 203(b) Insured Loan

Manuel Moritz and his wife, Estella Moritz, are first-time buyers with limited funds who want to obtain an FHA 203(b) loan. They want to buy the property owned by Barbara Johnson, who owns it as her separate property.

Ms. Johnson is asking $118,500, but the Moritzes offer $115,000, which is accepted. They will apply for the FHA insured loan within 5 days after the date of the contract and anticipate that they can get financing approval within 40 days after the effective date of the contract. Knowing that it will table fund, the Moritzes request possession at funding. They will pay the minimum down and ask the seller to contribute $1,200 toward their closing expenses in addition to the $750 that FHA prohibits the borrower from paying.

The Moritzes will use an FHA 203(b) insured loan, which will enable them to move in with minimal cash up front. They can obtain a 30-year fixed rate loan at 5.75 percent annual interest.

The buyers will pay the 1 point origination fee and 1 discount point.

Scenario 5

Figure 5.15 TREC 20-6 Paragraph 3

3. SALES PRICE:
A. Cash portion of Sales Price payable by Buyer at closing................. $______________
B. Sum of all financing described below (excluding any loan funding fee or mortgage insurance premium) .... $______________
C. Sales Price (Sum of A and B) .... $______________

Figure 5.16 TREC 20-6 Paragraph 4

4. FINANCING: The portion of Sales Price not payable in cash will be paid as follows: (Check applicable boxes below)

❑ A. THIRD PARTY FINANCING: One or more third party mortgage loans in the total amount of $____________________. If the Property does not satisfy the lenders' underwriting requirements for the loan(s), this contract will terminate and the earnest money will be refunded to Buyer. (Check one box only)

❑(1) This contract is subject to Buyer being approved for the financing described in the attached Third Party Financing Condition Addendum.

❑(2) This contract is not subject to Buyer being approved for financing and does not involve FHA or VA financing.

❑ B. ASSUMPTION: The assumption of the unpaid principal balance of one or more promissory notes described in the attached TREC Loan Assumption Addendum.

❑ C. SELLER FINANCING: A promissory note from Buyer to Seller of $________________ bearing _______ % interest per annum, secured by vendor's and deed of trust liens, and containing the terms and conditions described in the attached TREC Seller Financing Addendum. If an owner policy of title insurance is furnished, Buyer shall furnish Seller with a mortgagee policy of title insurance.

Figure 5.17 TREC 20-6 Paragraph 12

12. SETTLEMENT AND OTHER EXPENSES:

A. The following expenses must be paid at or prior to closing:

(1) Expenses payable by Seller (Seller's Expenses):

(a) Releases of existing liens, including prepayment penalties and recording fees; release of Seller's loan liability; tax statements or certificates; preparation of deed; one-half of escrow fee; and other expenses payable by Seller under this contract.

(b) Seller shall also pay an amount not to exceed $ ____________ to be applied in the following order: Buyer's Expenses which Buyer is prohibited from paying by FHA, VA, Texas Veteran's Housing Assistance Program or other governmental loan programs; Buyer's prepaid items; other Buyer's expenses.

(2) Expenses payable by Buyer (Buyer's Expenses):

(a) Loan origination, discount, buy-down, and commitment fees (Loan Fees).

(b) Appraisal fees; loan application fees; credit reports; preparation of loan documents; interest on the notes from date of disbursement to one month prior to dates of first monthly payments; recording fees; copies of easements and restrictions; mortgagee title policy with endorsements required by lender; loan-related inspection fees; photos, amortization schedules, one-half of escrow fee; all prepaid items, including required premiums for flood and hazard insurance, reserve deposits for insurance, ad valorem taxes and special governmental assessments; final compliance inspection; courier fee, repair inspection, underwriting fee and wire transfer, expenses incident to any loan, and other expenses payable by Buyer under this contract.

B. Buyer shall pay Private Mortgage Insurance Premium (PMI), VA Loan Funding Fee, or FHA Mortgage Insurance Premium (MIP) as required by the lender.

C. If any expense exceeds an amount expressly stated in this contract for such expense to be paid by a party, that party may terminate this contract unless the other party agrees to pay such excess. Buyer may not pay charges and fees expressly prohibited by FHA, VA, Texas Veteran's Housing Assistance Program or other governmental loan program regulations.

Figure 5.18 TREC 40-1

02-09-2004

EQUAL HOUSING OPPORTUNITY

PROMULGATED BY THE TEXAS REAL ESTATE COMMISSION (TREC)

THIRD PARTY FINANCING CONDITION ADDENDUM

TO CONTRACT CONCERNING THE PROPERTY AT

____
(Street Address and City)

Buyer shall apply promptly for all financing described below and make every reasonable effort to obtain financing approval including but not limited to furnishing all information and documents required by lender for approval. Financing approval will be deemed to have been obtained when the lender determines that Buyer has satisfied all of lender's financial requirements (those items relating to Buyer's assets, income and credit history). If Buyer cannot obtain financing approval, Buyer must give written notice to Seller within _____ days after the effective date of this contract and this contract will terminate and the earnest money will be refunded to Buyer. **If Buyer does not give such notice within the time allowed, this contract will no longer be subject to Buyer being approved for the financing described below. For purposes of this paragraph, time is of the essence; strict compliance with the times for performance herein stated is required.**

Each note must be secured by vendor's and deed of trust liens.

❑ A. CONVENTIONAL FINANCING:

❑ (1) A first mortgage loan in the principal amount of $ ____________________ (excluding any financed PMI premium), due in full in _________ year(s), with interest not to exceed ______% per annum for the first ________year(s) of the loan with Loan Fees (loan origination, discount, buy-down, and commitment fees) not to exceed ________% of the loan.

❑ (2) A second mortgage loan in the principal amount of $__________________(excluding any financed PMI premium), due in full in ___________year(s), with interest not to exceed ______% per annum for the first ____________year(s) of the loan with Loan Fees (loan origination, discount, buy-down, and commitment fees) not to exceed _________ % of the loan.

❑ B. TEXAS VETERANS' HOUSING ASSISTANCE PROGRAM LOAN: A Texas Veteran's Housing Assistance Program Loan of $________________ for a period of at least ______years at the interest rate established by the Texas Veteran's Land Board at the time of closing.

❑ C. FHA INSURED FINANCING: A Section _________________ FHA insured loan of not less than $__________________ (excluding any financed MIP), amortizable monthly for not less than ________years, with interest not to exceed _______% per annum for the first ______year(s) of the loan with Loan Fees (loan origination, discount, buy-down, and commitment fees) not to exceed _________ % of the loan. As required by HUD-FHA, if FHA valuation is unknown, *"It is expressly agreed that, notwithstanding any other provision of this contract, the purchaser (Buyer) shall not be obligated to complete the purchase of the Property described herein or to incur any penalty by forfeiture of earnest money deposits or otherwise unless the purchaser (Buyer) has been given in accordance with HUD/FHA or VA requirements a written statement issued by the Federal Housing Commissioner, Department of Veterans Affairs, or a Direct Endorsement Lender setting forth the appraised value of the Property of not less than $__________________. The purchaser (Buyer) shall have the privilege and option of proceeding with consummation of the contract without regard to the amount of the appraised valuation. The appraised valuation is arrived at to determine the maximum mortgage the Department of Housing and Urban Development will insure. HUD does not warrant the value or the condition of the Property. The purchaser (Buyer) should satisfy himself/herself that the price and the condition of the Property are acceptable."*

Initialed for identification by Buyer_______ _______ and Seller________ ________

Figure 5.18 TREC 40-1 (continued)

Third Party Financing Condition Addendum Concerning Page Two 02-09-2004

____
(Address of Property)

❑ D. VA GUARANTEED FINANCING: A VA guaranteed loan of not less than $________________ (excluding any financed Funding Fee), amortizable monthly for not less than________years, with interest not to exceed________% per annum for the first ________year(s) of the loan with Loan Fees (loan origination, discount, buy-down, and commitment fees) not to exceed ________% of the loan.

VA NOTICE TO BUYER: "*It is expressly agreed that, notwithstanding any other provisions of this contract, the Buyer shall not incur any penalty by forfeiture of earnest money or otherwise or be obligated to complete the purchase of the Property described herein, if the contract purchase price or cost exceeds the reasonable value of the Property established by the Department of Veterans Affairs. The Buyer shall, however, have the privilege and option of proceeding with the consummation of this contract without regard to the amount of the reasonable value established by the Department of Veterans Affairs.*"

If Buyer elects to complete the purchase at an amount in excess of the reasonable value established by VA, Buyer shall pay such excess amount in cash from a source which Buyer agrees to disclose to the VA and which Buyer represents will not be from borrowed funds except as approved by VA. If VA reasonable value of the Property is less than the Sales Price, Seller may reduce the Sales Price to an amount equal to the VA reasonable value and the sale will be closed at the lower Sales Price with proportionate adjustments to the down payment and the loan amount.

Buyer hereby authorizes any lender to furnish to the Seller or Buyer or their representatives information relating only to the status of financing approval of Buyer.

______________________	______________________
Buyer	Seller
______________________	______________________
Buyer	Seller

This form has been approved by the Texas Real Estate Commission for use with similarly approved or promulgated contract forms. Such approval relates to this form only. TREC forms are intended for use only by trained real estate licensees. No representation is made as to the legal validity or adequacy of any provision in any specific transactions. It is not suitable for complex transactions. Texas Real Estate Commission, P.O. Box 12188, Austin, TX 78711-2188, 1-800-250-8732 or (512) 459-6544 (http://www.trec.state.tx.us) TREC No. 40-1. This form replaces TREC No. 40-0.

Scenario 6 VA Guaranteed Loan

Freddie Mac, an unmarried man, has listed his home at 2365 Veterans Boulevard for sale with Friendly Agent Company.

The buyers anticipate that they will be required to pay a 1 point origination fee. The sellers will pay an amount not to exceed $1,100 toward the buyer's non-allowable costs.

The buyers are willing to pay $78,000 for the property. The buyers have full entitlement. The buyers have decided to borrow only $62,400 in order to keep the payments at a comfortable level. The buyers will apply for the loan within four days of the effective date of the agreement and anticipate that they can get financing approval within 30 days. They can obtain a 30-year fixed-rate loan at 7.25 percent annual interest rate.

Scenario 6

Figure 5.19 TREC 20-6 Paragraph 3

3. SALES PRICE:

A. Cash portion of Sales Price payable by Buyer at closing................. $____________________

B. Sum of all financing described below (excluding any loan funding fee or mortgage insurance premium) .... $____________________

C. Sales Price (Sum of A and B) .... $____________________

Figure 5.20 TREC 20-6 Paragraph 4

4. FINANCING: The portion of Sales Price not payable in cash will be paid as follows: (Check applicable boxes below)

❑ A. THIRD PARTY FINANCING: One or more third party mortgage loans in the total amount of $__________________. If the Property does not satisfy the lenders' underwriting requirements for the loan(s), this contract will terminate and the earnest money will be refunded to Buyer. (Check one box only)

❑(1) This contract is subject to Buyer being approved for the financing described in the attached Third Party Financing Condition Addendum.

❑(2) This contract is not subject to Buyer being approved for financing and does not involve FHA or VA financing.

❑ B. ASSUMPTION: The assumption of the unpaid principal balance of one or more promissory notes described in the attached TREC Loan Assumption Addendum.

❑ C. SELLER FINANCING: A promissory note from Buyer to Seller of $______________ bearing ______ % interest per annum, secured by vendor's and deed of trust liens, and containing the terms and conditions described in the attached TREC Seller Financing Addendum. If an owner policy of title insurance is furnished, Buyer shall furnish Seller with a mortgagee policy of title insurance.

Figure 5.21 TREC 20-6 Paragraph 12

12. SETTLEMENT AND OTHER EXPENSES:

A. The following expenses must be paid at or prior to closing:

(1) Expenses payable by Seller (Seller's Expenses):

(a) Releases of existing liens, including prepayment penalties and recording fees; release of Seller's loan liability; tax statements or certificates; preparation of deed; one-half of escrow fee; and other expenses payable by Seller under this contract.

(b) Seller shall also pay an amount not to exceed $ ____________ to be applied in the following order: Buyer's Expenses which Buyer is prohibited from paying by FHA, VA, Texas Veteran's Housing Assistance Program or other governmental loan programs; Buyer's prepaid items; other Buyer's expenses.

(2) Expenses payable by Buyer (Buyer's Expenses):

(a) Loan origination, discount, buy-down, and commitment fees (Loan Fees).

(b) Appraisal fees; loan application fees; credit reports; preparation of loan documents; interest on the notes from date of disbursement to one month prior to dates of first monthly payments; recording fees; copies of easements and restrictions; mortgagee title policy with endorsements required by lender; loan-related inspection fees; photos, amortization schedules, one-half of escrow fee; all prepaid items, including required premiums for flood and hazard insurance, reserve deposits for insurance, ad valorem taxes and special governmental assessments; final compliance inspection; courier fee, repair inspection, underwriting fee and wire transfer, expenses incident to any loan, and other expenses payable by Buyer under this contract.

B. Buyer shall pay Private Mortgage Insurance Premium (PMI), VA Loan Funding Fee, or FHA Mortgage Insurance Premium (MIP) as required by the lender.

C. If any expense exceeds an amount expressly stated in this contract for such expense to be paid by a party, that party may terminate this contract unless the other party agrees to pay such excess. Buyer may not pay charges and fees expressly prohibited by FHA, VA, Texas Veteran's Housing Assistance Program or other governmental loan program regulations.

Figure 5.22 TREC 40-1

02-09-2004

EQUAL HOUSING OPPORTUNITY

PROMULGATED BY THE TEXAS REAL ESTATE COMMISSION (TREC)

THIRD PARTY FINANCING CONDITION ADDENDUM

TO CONTRACT CONCERNING THE PROPERTY AT

____

(Street Address and City)

Buyer shall apply promptly for all financing described below and make every reasonable effort to obtain financing approval including but not limited to furnishing all information and documents required by lender for approval. Financing approval will be deemed to have been obtained when the lender determines that Buyer has satisfied all of lender's financial requirements (those items relating to Buyer's assets, income and credit history). If Buyer cannot obtain financing approval, Buyer must give written notice to Seller within ____ days after the effective date of this contract and this contract will terminate and the earnest money will be refunded to Buyer. **If Buyer does not give such notice within the time allowed, this contract will no longer be subject to Buyer being approved for the financing described below. For purposes of this paragraph, time is of the essence; strict compliance with the times for performance herein stated is required.**

Each note must be secured by vendor's and deed of trust liens.

❑ A. CONVENTIONAL FINANCING:

❑ (1) A first mortgage loan in the principal amount of $ ________________ (excluding any financed PMI premium), due in full in ________ year(s), with interest not to exceed ______% per annum for the first _______year(s) of the loan with Loan Fees (loan origination, discount, buy-down, and commitment fees) not to exceed ________% of the loan.

❑ (2) A second mortgage loan in the principal amount of $________________(excluding any financed PMI premium), due in full in __________year(s), with interest not to exceed ______% per annum for the first ___________year(s) of the loan with Loan Fees (loan origination, discount, buy-down, and commitment fees) not to exceed ________ % of the loan.

❑ B. TEXAS VETERANS' HOUSING ASSISTANCE PROGRAM LOAN: A Texas Veteran's Housing Assistance Program Loan of $______________ for a period of at least ______years at the interest rate established by the Texas Veteran's Land Board at the time of closing.

❑ C. FHA INSURED FINANCING: A Section ______________ FHA insured loan of not less than $________________ (excluding any financed MIP), amortizable monthly for not less than _______years, with interest not to exceed _______% per annum for the first ______year(s) of the loan with Loan Fees (loan origination, discount, buy-down, and commitment fees) not to exceed _________ % of the loan. As required by HUD-FHA, if FHA valuation is unknown, *"It is expressly agreed that, notwithstanding any other provision of this contract, the purchaser (Buyer) shall not be obligated to complete the purchase of the Property described herein or to incur any penalty by forfeiture of earnest money deposits or otherwise unless the purchaser (Buyer) has been given in accordance with HUD/FHA or VA requirements a written statement issued by the Federal Housing Commissioner, Department of Veterans Affairs, or a Direct Endorsement Lender setting forth the appraised value of the Property of not less than $________________. The purchaser (Buyer) shall have the privilege and option of proceeding with consummation of the contract without regard to the amount of the appraised valuation. The appraised valuation is arrived at to determine the maximum mortgage the Department of Housing and Urban Development will insure. HUD does not warrant the value or the condition of the Property. The purchaser (Buyer) should satisfy himself/herself that the price and the condition of the Property are acceptable."*

Initialed for identification by Buyer_______ _______ and Seller________ ________

Figure 5.22 TREC 40-1 (continued)

Third Party Financing Condition Addendum Concerning Page Two 02-09-2004

____
(Address of Property)

☐ D. VA GUARANTEED FINANCING: A VA guaranteed loan of not less than $__________ (excluding any financed Funding Fee), amortizable monthly for not less than_______years, with interest not to exceed________% per annum for the first _______year(s) of the loan with Loan Fees (loan origination, discount, buy-down, and commitment fees) not to exceed _______% of the loan.

VA NOTICE TO BUYER: "*It is expressly agreed that, notwithstanding any other provisions of this contract, the Buyer shall not incur any penalty by forfeiture of earnest money or otherwise or be obligated to complete the purchase of the Property described herein, if the contract purchase price or cost exceeds the reasonable value of the Property established by the Department of Veterans Affairs. The Buyer shall, however, have the privilege and option of proceeding with the consummation of this contract without regard to the amount of the reasonable value established by the Department of Veterans Affairs.*"

If Buyer elects to complete the purchase at an amount in excess of the reasonable value established by VA, Buyer shall pay such excess amount in cash from a source which Buyer agrees to disclose to the VA and which Buyer represents will not be from borrowed funds except as approved by VA. If VA reasonable value of the Property is less than the Sales Price, Seller may reduce the Sales Price to an amount equal to the VA reasonable value and the sale will be closed at the lower Sales Price with proportionate adjustments to the down payment and the loan amount.

Buyer hereby authorizes any lender to furnish to the Seller or Buyer or their representatives information relating only to the status of financing approval of Buyer.

______________________	______________________
Buyer	Seller
______________________	______________________
Buyer	Seller

This form has been approved by the Texas Real Estate Commission for use with similarly approved or promulgated contract forms. Such approval relates to this form only. TREC forms are intended for use only by trained real estate licensees. No representation is made as to the legal validity or adequacy of any provision in any specific transactions. It is not suitable for complex transactions. Texas Real Estate Commission, P.O. Box 12188, Austin, TX 78711-2188, 1-800-250-8732 or (512) 459-6544 (http://www.trec.state.tx.us) TREC No. 40-1. This form replaces TREC No. 40-0.

Scenario 7 Assumption with Seller 2nd

The sellers are offering their duplex for sale and asking $158,000. It is currently financed with a VA guaranteed loan with an outstanding balance of $100,000. The loan is at 5.75 percent annual interest. The sellers are willing to carry back a second for $30,000 at 7 percent annual interest with payments due and payable on the first day of each month during the period of indebtedness. They want a buyer to pay principal payments of $500 per month plus interest to liquidate the loan in 60 months. An escrow account is required unless paid to a first lienholder.

They have no desire to purchase another property using VA guaranteed financing and will not seek a restoration of entitlement.

The buyer finds this a very attractive opportunity and offers the seller the asking price. He will assume the existing note, ask the seller to carry back a second on the terms specified, and pay the difference in cash. Although he believes that the transfer fee will be one-half of a point, he writes the offer for a 1 point transfer fee just to be safe. The seller does want to reserve the right to approve any assumptor for the lien being carried by the seller.

The buyer will provide a credit report, verification of employment, verification of the cash funds on deposit, at the bank and a personal financial statement within three days after the effective date of the contract.

The loan being assumed is owned by Ginnie Mae with current monthly payments of $786 being paid to Chase Manhattan Mortgage Company. Any difference in the unpaid principal balance at closing will cause an adjustment to be made to the cash payable at closing.

Scenario 7

Figure 5.23 TREC 20-6 Paragraph 3

3. SALES PRICE:
A. Cash portion of Sales Price payable by Buyer at closing.................. $__________
B. Sum of all financing described below (excluding any loan funding fee or mortgage insurance premium) .... $__________
C. Sales Price (Sum of A and B) .... $__________

Figure 5.24 TREC 20-6 Paragraph 4

4. FINANCING: The portion of Sales Price not payable in cash will be paid as follows: (Check applicable boxes below)

❑ A. THIRD PARTY FINANCING: One or more third party mortgage loans in the total amount of $__________________. If the Property does not satisfy the lenders' underwriting requirements for the loan(s), this contract will terminate and the earnest money will be refunded to Buyer. (Check one box only)

❑(1) This contract is subject to Buyer being approved for the financing described in the attached Third Party Financing Condition Addendum.

❑(2) This contract is not subject to Buyer being approved for financing and does not involve FHA or VA financing.

❑ B. ASSUMPTION: The assumption of the unpaid principal balance of one or more promissory notes described in the attached TREC Loan Assumption Addendum.

❑ C. SELLER FINANCING: A promissory note from Buyer to Seller of $_______________ bearing ______ % interest per annum, secured by vendor's and deed of trust liens, and containing the terms and conditions described in the attached TREC Seller Financing Addendum. If an owner policy of title insurance is furnished, Buyer shall furnish Seller with a mortgagee policy of title insurance.

Figure 5.25 TREC 20-6 Paragraph 12

12. SETTLEMENT AND OTHER EXPENSES:

A. The following expenses must be paid at or prior to closing:

(1) Expenses payable by Seller (Seller's Expenses):

(a) Releases of existing liens, including prepayment penalties and recording fees; release of Seller's loan liability; tax statements or certificates; preparation of deed; one-half of escrow fee; and other expenses payable by Seller under this contract.

(b) Seller shall also pay an amount not to exceed $ ____________ to be applied in the following order: Buyer's Expenses which Buyer is prohibited from paying by FHA, VA, Texas Veteran's Housing Assistance Program or other governmental loan programs; Buyer's prepaid items; other Buyer's expenses.

(2) Expenses payable by Buyer (Buyer's Expenses):

(a) Loan origination, discount, buy-down, and commitment fees (Loan Fees).

(b) Appraisal fees; loan application fees; credit reports; preparation of loan documents; interest on the notes from date of disbursement to one month prior to dates of first monthly payments; recording fees; copies of easements and restrictions; mortgagee title policy with endorsements required by lender; loan-related inspection fees; photos, amortization schedules, one-half of escrow fee; all prepaid items, including required premiums for flood and hazard insurance, reserve deposits for insurance, ad valorem taxes and special governmental assessments; final compliance inspection; courier fee, repair inspection, underwriting fee and wire transfer, expenses incident to any loan, and other expenses payable by Buyer under this contract.

B. Buyer shall pay Private Mortgage Insurance Premium (PMI), VA Loan Funding Fee, or FHA Mortgage Insurance Premium (MIP) as required by the lender.

C. If any expense exceeds an amount expressly stated in this contract for such expense to be paid by a party, that party may terminate this contract unless the other party agrees to pay such excess. Buyer may not pay charges and fees expressly prohibited by FHA, VA, Texas Veteran's Housing Assistance Program or other governmental loan program regulations.

Figure 5.26 TREC 26-4

PROMULGATED BY THE TEXAS REAL ESTATE COMMISSION (TREC) 10-29-01

EQUAL HOUSING OPPORTUNITY

SELLER FINANCING ADDENDUM

TO CONTRACT CONCERNING THE PROPERTY AT

____

(Street Address and City)

A. **CREDIT DOCUMENTATION.** Within__________days after the effective date of this contract, Buyer shall deliver to Seller ☐ credit report ☐ verification of employment, including salary ☐ verification of funds on deposit in financial institutions ☐ current financial statement to establish Buyer's creditworthiness and ☐ ____
____.
Buyer hereby authorizes any credit reporting agency to furnish to Seller at Buyer's sole expense copies of Buyer's credit reports.

B. **CREDIT APPROVAL.** If Buyer's documentation is not delivered within the specified time, Seller may terminate this contract by notice to Buyer within 7 days after expiration of the time for delivery, and the earnest money will be paid to Seller. If the documentation is timely delivered, and Seller determines in Seller's sole discretion that Buyer's credit is unacceptable, Seller may terminate this contract by notice to Buyer within 7 days after expiration of the time for delivery and the earnest money will be refunded to Buyer. If Seller does not terminate this contract, Seller will be deemed to have accepted Buyer's credit.

C. **PROMISSORY NOTE.** The promissory note (Note) described in Paragraph 4 of this contract payable by Buyer to the order of Seller will be payable at the place designated by Seller. Buyer may prepay the Note in whole or in part at any time without penalty. Any prepayments are to be applied to the payment of the installments of principal last maturing and interest will immediately cease on the prepaid principal. The Note will contain a provision for payment of a late fee of 5% of any installment not paid within 10 days of the due date. The Note will be payable as follows:

☐ (1) In one payment due ______________________________ after the date of the Note with interest payable____.

☐ (2) In ________________ installments of $ ____________________ ☐ including interest ☐ plus interest beginning ______________________________ after the date of the Note and continuing at _____________ intervals thereafter for ________________when the balance of the Note will be due and payable.

☐ (3) Interest only in _____ installments for the first ________________________ month(s) and thereafter in installments of $________________ ☐ including interest ☐ plus interest beginning ______________________________ after the date of the Note and continuing at ______________ intervals thereafter for __________________ when the balance of the Note will be due and payable.

D. **DEED OF TRUST.** The deed of trust securing the Note will provide for the following:

(1) PROPERTY TRANSFERS: (check only one)

☐ (a) Consent Not Required: The Property may be sold, conveyed or leased without the consent of Seller, provided any subsequent buyer assumes the Note.

☐ (b) Consent Required: If all or any part of the Property is sold, conveyed, leased for a period longer than 3 years, leased with an option to purchase, or otherwise sold (including any contract for deed), without the prior written consent of Seller, Seller may declare the

Initialed for identification by Buyer_______ _______ and Seller________ ________ 01A

Figure 5.26 TREC 26-4 (continued)

Seller Financing Addendum Concerning Page Two 10-29-01

(Address of Property)

balance of the Note, to be immediately due and payable. The creation of a subordinate lien, any conveyance under threat or order of condemnation, any deed solely between buyers, the passage of title by reason of the death of a buyer or by operation of law will not entitle Seller to exercise the remedies provided in this paragraph.

(2) TAX AND INSURANCE ESCROW: (check only one)

❑ (a) Escrow Not Required: Buyer shall furnish Seller annually, before the taxes become delinquent, evidence that all taxes on the Property have been paid. Buyer shall furnish Seller annually evidence of paid-up casualty insurance naming Seller as an additional loss payee.

❑ (b) Escrow Required: With each installment Buyer shall deposit with Seller in escrow a pro rata part of the estimated annual ad valorem taxes and casualty insurance premiums for the Property. Buyer shall pay any deficiency within 30 days after notice from Seller. Buyer's failure to pay the deficiency constitutes a default under the deed of trust. Buyer is not required to deposit any escrow payments for taxes and insurance that are deposited with a superior lienholder. The casualty insurance must name Seller as an additional loss payee.

(3) PRIOR LIENS: Any default under any lien superior to the lien securing the Note constitutes default under the deed of trust securing the Note.

Buyer Seller

Buyer Seller

This form has been approved by the Texas Real Estate Commission for use with similarly approved or promulgated contract forms. Such approval relates to this form only. TREC forms are intended for use only by trained real estate licensees. No representation is made as to the legal validity or adequacy of any provision in any specific transactions. It is not suitable for complex transactions. Texas Real Estate Commission, P.O. Box 12188, Austin, TX 78711-2188, 1-800-250-8732 or (512) 459-6544 (http://www.trec.state.tx.us) TREC No. 26-4. This form replaces TREC No. 26-3.

01A

Figure 5.27 TREC 41-0

PROMULGATED BY THE TEXAS REAL ESTATE COMMISSION (TREC) 10-29-01

EQUAL HOUSING OPPORTUNITY

LOAN ASSUMPTION ADDENDUM

TO CONTRACT CONCERNING THE PROPERTY AT

____

(Street Address and City)

A. CREDIT DOCUMENTATION. Within______days after the effective date of this contract, Buyer shall deliver to Seller ❑ credit report ❑ verification of employment, including salary ❑ verification of funds on deposit in financial institutions ❑ current financial statement to establish Buyer's creditworthiness and ❑ ________ ________.

Buyer hereby authorizes any credit reporting agency to furnish to Seller at Buyer's sole expense copies of Buyer's credit reports.

B.CREDIT APPROVAL. If Buyer's documentation is not delivered within the specified time, Seller may terminate this contract by notice to Buyer within 7 days after expiration of the time for delivery, and the earnest money will be paid to Seller. If the documentation is timely delivered, and Seller determines in Seller's sole discretion that Buyer's credit is unacceptable, Seller may terminate this contract by notice to Buyer within 7 days after expiration of the time for delivery and the earnest money will be refunded to Buyer. If Seller does not terminate this contract, Seller will be deemed to have accepted Buyer's credit.

C. ASSUMPTION.

❑ (1) The unpaid principal balance of a first lien promissory note payable to ____________________ ____________________ which unpaid balance at closing will be $ ______________. The total current monthly payment including principal, interest and any reserve deposits is $ ______________. Buyer's initial payment will be the first payment due after closing.

❑ (2) The unpaid principal balance of a second lien promissory note payable to ____________________ ____________________ which unpaid balance at closing will be $ ______________. The total current monthly payment including principal, interest and any reserve deposits is $ ______________. Buyer's initial payment will be the first payment due after closing.

Buyer's assumption of an existing note includes all obligations imposed by the deed of trust securing the note.

If the unpaid principal balance(s) of any assumed loan(s) as of the Closing Date varies from the loan balance(s) stated above, the ❑ cash payable at closing ❑ Sales Price will be adjusted by the amount of any variance; provided, if the total principal balance of all assumed loans varies in an amount greater than $350.00 at closing, either party may terminate this contract and the earnest money will be refunded to Buyer unless the other party elects to eliminate the excess in the variance by an appropriate adjustment at closing. Buyer may terminate this contract and the earnest money will be refunded to Buyer if the noteholder requires (a) payment of an assumption fee in excess of $ ______________in (1) above or $ ______________in (2) above and Seller declines to pay such excess, (b) an increase in the interest rate to more than ______% in (1) above, or ______% in (2) above, (c) any other modification of the loan documents, or (d) consent to the assumption of the loan and fails to consent. A vendor's lien and deed of trust to secure assumption will be required which will automatically be released on execution and delivery of a release by noteholder. If Seller is released from liability on any assumed note, the vendor's lien and deed of trust to secure assumption will not be required.

If noteholder maintains an escrow account, the escrow account must be transferred to Buyer without any deficiency. Buyer shall reimburse Seller for the amount in the transferred accounts.

NOTICE TO BUYER: The monthly payments, interest rates or other terms of some loans may be adjusted by the noteholder at or after closing. If you are concerned about the possibility of future adjustments, do not sign the contract without examining the notes and deeds of trust.

NOTICE TO SELLER: Your liability to pay the note assumed by Buyer will continue unless you obtain a release of liability from the noteholder. If you are concerned about future liability, you should use the TREC Release of Liability Addendum.

____________________	____________________
Buyer	Seller
____________________	____________________
Buyer	Seller

This form has been approved by the Texas Real Estate Commission for use with similarly approved or promulgated contract forms. Such approval relates to this form only. TREC forms are intended for use only by trained real estate licensees. No representation is made as to the legal validity or adequacy of any provision in any specific transactions. It is not suitable for complex transactions. Texas Real Estate Commission, P.O. Box 12188, Austin, TX 78711-2188, 1-800-250-8732 or (512) 459-6544 (http://www.trec.state.tx.us) TREC No. 41-0.

01A

Chapter 6

The Property

Key Terms

abstract
annexation
commitment
earnest money
encumbrance
exception documents
extraterritorial jurisdiction
mortgagee's title policy
notice
objections
restrictive covenants
residential service contract
survey
title policy

The property is defined and identified by its legal description in the second paragraph of the contract. In this chapter, we continue our examination of the building blocks of purchase agreements by examining three key paragraphs: 5. Earnest Money, 6. Title Policy and Survey, and 7. Property Condition. Read and study the content of these paragraphs deliberately and carefully. They account for more than 25 percent of the verbiage of the agreement and address issues that are the basis of the vast majority of the litigation that is brought by one of the parties against the other or against the agents. Proceed carefully!

Earnest Money

Figure 6.1 TREC 20-6 Paragraph 5

> **5. EARNEST MONEY:** Upon execution of this contract by both parties, Buyer shall deposit $__________ as earnest money with ______________________________________, as escrow agent, at ______________________________________ (address). Buyer shall deposit additional earnest money of $______________ with escrow agent within ________days after the effective date of this contract. If Buyer fails to deposit the earnest money as required by this contract, Buyer will be in default.

The **earnest money** serves two purposes. The first is to show good faith and serious intent on the part of the purchaser. Note that earnest money is not necessary to bind the contract. The promise of the purchaser to buy and the promise of the seller to deliver title are adequate consideration to create a legally binding executory contract. A listing agent might want to suggest that the seller ask the buyer to show serious intent by requesting a significant earnest money deposit. Around 3 to 5 percent of the purchase price is ideal; however, the parties may determine that a smaller or larger amount is appropriate for their particular transaction. Please remember that the final decision is in the hands of the buyer and the seller. The second purpose of the deposited money is to serve as liquidated damages in the event of default as addressed in the identified remedies listed in paragraph 15.

The blanks calling for additional earnest money can be used when the buyer is unable to make the full desired deposit at the time of signing the agreement. This might occur when the buyer is waiting for a certificate of deposit to mature and does not want to delay signing the agreement or to cash in early and lose the interest on the instrument. It should be noted that failure to deposit the additional money constitutes a default and gives the seller the right to exercise the default remedies established by agreement of the parties in paragraph 15.

The Texas real estate license holder should note that TREC rule 535.15 requires that earnest money be deposited with the escrow agent selected by the parties by the close of the second business day of the escrow officer following the signing of the agreement. When the buyer has tendered the offer in writing, the seller has accepted the offer by signing the contract, and the buyer has been notified of the seller's acceptance, an executory contract exists, and the agent or the buyer needs to deliver the earnest money to the escrow officer named in paragraph 5 of the contract.

Title Policy

The contract is an agreement between the buyer and the seller and should reflect their wishes. Usually the company selected in paragraph 6 to issue the owner's **title policy** is the same chosen in paragraph 5 to serve as escrow officer; however, it is not mandatory. One may list a title agency, in paragraph 5 and a title company, in paragraph 6. Who should choose the company?

Many would argue that because the seller usually pays for the title policy, the seller should choose. Who pays does not and should not automatically dictate who chooses something in a real estate transaction. For example, the buyer is usually required to pay for an appraisal when the buyer is seeking a new loan, but it is the lender who selects the appraiser and is the client of the appraiser. When utilizing a loan guaranteed by the Department of Veterans Affairs, the government regulations require that the seller pay the legal fees for the preparation of the note and mortgage instrument for the borrower's loan. Before a seller or listing agent attempts to dictate the title company, it should be noted that the owner's title policy is a contract between the buyer and the title company. Also, a review of the Real Estate Settlement Procedures Act (RESPA), covering one-family to four-family residential transactions that have financing related to the federal government, reveals that federal regulation prohibits the seller from requiring the buyer to use the services of a particular title provider. Visit *www.HUD.gov* to locate the RESPA legislation or refer to page 17 of the HUD guide, "Settlement Costs," which is given to buyers at the time of loan application. Why should the seller really care? Providing the title policy is an economical way for the seller to show evidence of clear title and indemnify the buyer from financial loss in the event of title failure. The premium cost is the same at all title companies in the state to insure the title of the property with the same sales price.

The majority of transactions closed in Texas involve the issuance of a title policy to the buyer of the property. Local custom often calls for the owner's policy of title insurance to be furnished at the seller's expense. This is a point to be negotiated by the parties. When the parties have come to an agreement on this matter, check the appropriate box.

License holders should let the parties choose the title company that will issue the title policy. On RESPA-covered transactions involving purchases of a one-family to four-family residential property with a federally related loan, the following regulation applies.

RESPA 2608

(a) No seller of property that will be purchased with the assistance of a federally related mortgage loan shall require, directly or indirectly, as a condition to selling the property, that title insurance covering the property be purchased by the buyer from any particular title company.

(b) Any seller who violates the provisions of subsection (a) shall be liable to the buyer in an amount equal to three times all charges made for such title insurance.

The reader should further consider that it is the buyer who must live with the coverage and deal with the insurance company when a title problem rears its ugly head. A buyer who is asking the seller to pay for the policy may be willing to permit the seller to choose. License holders should not dictate in this area; they should always ask. The same rule should be followed in the selection of a residential service contract provider, when you get to paragraph 7H.

In addition to identifying who issues and who pays for the title policy, paragraph 6A establishes that the policy is subject to the exclusions promulgated by the state insurance board in Austin. The eight exclusions are listed in the contract.

The standard printed exception relates to discrepancies, conflicts, and shortages in area or boundary lines. It may be amended to include only "shortages in area" by the payment of an additional 15 percent to the title insurance premium and by providing a survey acceptable to the title company. Check with the title company about the amount and identify who will pay it as an additional business detail in paragraph 11 of the contract. At the beginning of 2004, the additional cost is 5 percent of the title insurance for single family residential properties and 15 percent for others.

The agreement calls for the seller to furnish the buyer a **commitment** for title insurance and, at the buyer's expense, legible copies of deed restrictions and documentation of any exceptions in the commitment within 20 days. The seller requests that the title company mail or hand deliver the commitment to the buyer's address shown in paragraph 21 of the contract form. The parties agree that if the title company is unable to deliver within 20 days, the time for delivery is automatically extended up to 15 days. After the buyer receives the commitment, the buyer has some days to object in writing to any matters disclosed in the commitment. The number of days will be defined by agreement of the parties.

In 6D there is a space in which the buyer can list anything the buyer may want to do on the property that may be prohibited by deed restrictions, building codes, and zoning ordinances. Examples of what may be listed here include conducting a home-based business from the premises, parking a motor home or boat in the driveway, erecting a basketball net, installing a satellite dish, or erecting a ten-foot privacy fence.

Survey

The contract calls for surveys to be performed by a registered professional land surveyor acceptable to the title company or any lender. The parties will select one of three choices and determine the number of days to furnish the survey or survey and seller's affidavit. The three choices address the issues of who will provide and pay for the survey and when it will be delivered.

Figure 6.2 TREC 20-6 Paragraph 6

Contract Concerning ____ Page Two 01-06-03
(Address of Property)

6. TITLE POLICY AND SURVEY:

A. TITLE POLICY: Seller shall furnish to Buyer at ❑Seller's ❑Buyer's expense an owner policy of title insurance (Title Policy) issued by ______________________________ (Title Company) in the amount of the Sales Price, dated at or after closing, insuring Buyer against loss under the provisions of the Title Policy, subject to the promulgated exclusions (including existing building and zoning ordinances) and the following exceptions:

(1) Restrictive covenants common to the platted subdivision in which the Property is located.
(2) The standard printed exception for standby fees, taxes and assessments.
(3) Liens created as part of the financing described in Paragraph 4.
(4) Utility easements created by the dedication deed or plat of the subdivision in which the Property is located.
(5) Reservations or exceptions otherwise permitted by this contract or as may be approved by Buyer in writing.
(6) The standard printed exception as to marital rights.
(7) The standard printed exception as to waters, tidelands, beaches, streams, and related matters.
(8) The standard printed exception as to discrepancies, conflicts, shortages in area or boundary lines, encroachments or protrusions, or overlapping improvements. Buyer, at Buyer's expense, may have the exception amended to read, "shortages in area".

B. COMMITMENT: Within 20 days after the Title Company receives a copy of this contract, Seller shall furnish to Buyer a commitment for title insurance (Commitment) and, at Buyer's expense, legible copies of restrictive covenants and documents evidencing exceptions in the Commitment (Exception Documents) other than the standard printed exceptions. Seller authorizes the Title Company to mail or hand deliver the Commitment and Exception Documents to Buyer at Buyer's address shown in Paragraph 21. If the Commitment and Exception Documents are not delivered to Buyer within the specified time, the time for delivery will be automatically extended up to 15 days or the Closing Date, whichever is earlier.

C. SURVEY: The survey must be made by a registered professional land surveyor acceptable to the Title Company and any lender. (Check one box only)

❑ (1) Within ______ days after the effective date of this contract, Seller, at Seller's expense, shall furnish a new survey to Buyer.
❑ (2) Within ______ days after the effective date of this contract, Buyer, at Buyer's expense, shall obtain a new survey.
❑ (3) Within ______ days after the effective date of this contract, Seller shall furnish Seller's existing survey of the Property to Buyer and the Title Company, along with Seller's affidavit acceptable to the Title Company for approval of the survey. If the survey is not approved by the Title Company or Buyer's lender, a new survey will be obtained at ❑ Seller's ❑ Buyer's expense no later than 3 days prior to the Closing Date.

D. OBJECTIONS: Within ____ days after Buyer receives the Commitment, Exception Documents and the survey, Buyer may object in writing to defects, exceptions, or encumbrances to title: disclosed on the survey other than items 6A(1) through (7) above; disclosed in the Commitment other than items 6A(1) through (8) above; or which prohibit the following use or activity: ____.
Buyer's failure to object within the time allowed will constitute a waiver of Buyer's right to object; except that the requirements in Schedule C of the Commitment are not waived. Seller shall cure the timely objections of Buyer or any third party lender within 15 days after Seller receives the objections and the Closing Date will be extended as necessary. If objections are not cured within such 15 day period, this contract will terminate and the earnest money will be refunded to Buyer unless Buyer waives the objections.

E. TITLE NOTICES:

(1) ABSTRACT OR TITLE POLICY: Broker advises Buyer to have an abstract of title covering the Property examined by an attorney of Buyer's selection, or Buyer should be furnished with or obtain a Title Policy. If a Title Policy is furnished, the Commitment should be promptly reviewed by an attorney of Buyer's choice due to the time limitations on Buyer's right to object.
(2) MANDATORY OWNERS' ASSOCIATION MEMBERSHIP: The Property ❑ is ❑ is not subject to mandatory membership in an owners' association. If the Property is subject to mandatory membership in an owners' association, Seller notifies Buyer under §5.012, Texas Property Code, that, as a purchaser of property in the residential community in

Initialed for identification by Buyer_____ _____ and Seller ______ _____ **01A** TREC NO. 20-6

Figure 6.2 TREC 20-6 (continued)

Contract Concerning ______________________________ Page Three 01-06-03
(Address of Property)

which the Property is located, you are obligated to be a member of the owners' association. Restrictive covenants governing the use and occupancy of the Property and a dedicatory instrument governing the establishment, maintenance, and operation of this residential community have been or will be recorded in the Real Property Records of the county in which the Property is located. Copies of the restrictive covenants and dedicatory instrument may be obtained from the county clerk. You are obligated to pay assessments to the owners' association. The amount of the assessments is subject to change. Your failure to pay the assessments could result in a lien on and the foreclosure of the Property.

(3) STATUTORY TAX DISTRICTS: If the Property is situated in a utility or other statutorily created district providing water, sewer, drainage, or flood control facilities and services, Chapter 49, Texas Water Code requires Seller to deliver and Buyer to sign the statutory notice relating to the tax rate, bonded indebtedness, or standby fee of the district prior to final execution of this contract.

(4) TIDE WATERS: If the Property abuts the tidally influenced waters of the state, §33.135, Texas Natural Resources Code, requires a notice regarding coastal area property to be included in the contract. An addendum containing the notice promulgated by TREC or required by the parties must be used.

(5) ANNEXATION: If the Property is located outside the limits of a municipality, Seller notifies Buyer under §5.011, Texas Property Code, that the Property may now or later be included in the extraterritorial jurisdiction of a municipality and may now or later be subject to annexation by the municipality. Each municipality maintains a map that depicts its boundaries and extraterritorial jurisdiction. To determine if the Property is located within a municipality's extraterritorial jurisdiction or is likely to be located within a municipality's extraterritorial jurisdiction, contact all municipalities located in the general proximity of the Property for further information.

Required Statutory Notices

In 6E, five required statutory notices are provided for the buyer.

1. The buyer is advised to have the abstract examined by an attorney of the buyer's choosing or to get title insurance. The license holder has responsibility under the provisions of the TRELA to provide this notice in writing prior to having the parties sign the purchase agreement. TREC has made it very easy for the license holder when a promulgated form is being used.
2. The buyer is well advised to learn as much as possible about the restrictions, rules, assessments, and operations of any homeowners association that may exercise control over the property; have the power to collect mandatory assessments; or even bring a foreclosure action against the homeowner and the property. The provisions of the Texas Property Code may be accessed at *www.capitol.state.tx.us* under "Legislative Resources." Click on Texas Statutes and scroll down to and click on Property Code. An addendum addressing Mandatory Membership in an Owner's Association is reproduced on page 92.
3. Statutorily created utility districts have the power to assess and collect significant taxes. A buyer needs to understand what is being faced.

4. Owners of property located near or abutting the tidally influenced waters of Texas take on special risks that need to be thoroughly understood before taking title.
5. Often people choose to live in unincorporated areas for a variety of reasons. When one acquires land outside of a municipality, one needs to be aware of the possibility of **annexation** at a future time. The buyer is advised to research the issue before making a final decision to move forward with the acquisition of the property. A license holder should never attempt to predict what may happen in the future with regard to annexation, zoning, ad valorem taxation, school districts, and related issues. Provide customers and clients with information about where they can find the answers to their questions but do not provide the information. As an attorney friend advises, **be the source of the source but don't become the source.**

Review the notices with the customer or your client and introduce them to the TREC promulgated addenda that may be applicable to their transaction.

Figure 6.3 TREC 36-3

PROMULGATED BY THE TEXAS REAL ESTATE COMMISSION (TREC) 02-09-2004

EQUAL HOUSING OPPORTUNITY

ADDENDUM FOR PROPERTY SUBJECT TO MANDATORY MEMBERSHIP IN AN OWNERS' ASSOCIATION

(NOT FOR USE WITH CONDOMINIUMS)

ADDENDUM TO CONTRACT CONCERNING THE PROPERTY AT

____

(Street Address and City)

____

(Name of Owners' Association)

A. SUBDIVISON INFORMATION: "Subdivision Information" means: (i) the restrictions applying to the subdivision, (ii) the bylaws and rules of the Owners' Association, and (iii) a resale certificate, all of which were provided by the Owners' Association in compliance with Section 207.003 of the Texas Property Code no more than three months before the date of their delivery to Buyer.

(Check only one box):

- ☐ 1. Within _____ days after the effective date of the contract, Seller shall at Seller's expense deliver the Subdivision Information to Buyer. If Buyer does not receive the Subdivision Information, Buyer may terminate the contract at any time prior to closing and the earnest money will be refunded to Buyer. If Seller delivers the Subdivision Information, Buyer may terminate the contract for any reason within 7 days after Buyer receives the Subdivision Information or prior to closing, whichever first occurs, and the earnest money will be refunded to Buyer.
- ☐ 2. Buyer has received and approved the Subdivision Information before signing the contract.
- ☐ 3. Buyer does not require delivery of the Subdivision Information.

If Seller becomes aware of any material changes in the Subdivision Information, Seller shall immediately give notice to Buyer. Buyer may terminate the contract prior to closing by giving written notice to Seller if: (i) any of the Subdivision Information provided was not true; or (ii) any material adverse change in the Subdivision Information occurs prior to closing, and the earnest money will be refunded to Buyer.

B. TRANSFER FEES: Buyer shall pay any Owners' Association transfer fee not to exceed $ ___________ and Seller agrees to pay any excess.

NOTICE TO BUYER REGARDING REPAIRS BY THE OWNERS' ASSOCIATION: The Owners' Association may have the sole responsibility to make certain repairs to the Property. If you are concerned about the condition of any part of the Property which the Owners' Association is required to repair, you should not sign the contract unless you are satisfied that the Owners' Association will make the desired repairs.

____________________	____________________
Buyer	Seller
____________________	____________________
Buyer	Seller

The form of this addendum has been approved by the Texas Real Estate Commission for use only with similarly approved or promulgated forms of contracts. Such approval relates to this contract form only. TREC forms are intended for use only by trained real estate licensees. No representation is made as to the legal validity or adequacy of any provision in any specific transactions. It is not suitable for complex transactions. Texas Real Estate Commission, P.O. Box 12188, Austin, TX 78711-2188, 1-800-250-8732 or (512) 459-6544 (http://www.trec.state.tx.us) TREC No. 36-3. This form replaces TREC No. 36-2.

Figure 6.4 TREC 33-0

12-05-94

PROMULGATED BY THE TEXAS REAL ESTATE COMMISSION (TREC)
P.O. BOX 12188, AUSTIN, TX 78711-2188

ADDENDUM FOR
COASTAL AREA PROPERTY

ADDENDUM TO EARNEST MONEY CONTRACT BETWEEN THE UNDERSIGNED PARTIES CONCERNING THE PROPERTY AT

____

____

(Location of Property)

IN ACCORDANCE WITH SECTION 33.135, TEXAS NATURAL RESOURCES CODE, THE FOLLOWING NOTICE IS INCLUDED AS PART OF THE CONTRACT:

NOTICE REGARDING COASTAL AREA PROPERTY

1. The real property described in and subject to this contract adjoins and shares a common boundary with the tidally influenced submerged lands of the state. The boundary is subject to change and can be determined accurately only by a survey on the ground made by a licensed state land surveyor in accordance with the original grant from the sovereign. The owner of the property described in this contract may gain or lose portions of the tract because of changes in the boundary.

2. The seller, transferor, or grantor has no knowledge of any prior fill as it relates to the property described in and subject to this contract except: ____________________

   ____

   ____.

3. State law prohibits the use, encumbrance, construction, or placing of any structure in, on, or over state-owned submerged lands below the applicable tide line, without proper permission.

4. The purchaser or grantee is hereby advised to seek the advice of an attorney or other qualified person as to the legal nature and effect of the facts set forth in this notice on the property described in and subject to this contract. Information regarding the location of the applicable tide line as to the property described in and subject to this contract may be obtained from the surveying division of the General Land Office in Austin.

____________________	____________________
Buyer	Seller
____________________	____________________
Buyer	Seller

This form has been approved by the Texas Real Estate Commission for use with similarly approved or promulgated contract forms. Such approval relates to this form only. No representation is made as to the legal validity or adequacy of any provision in any specific transactions. It is not suitable for complex transactions. (12-94) TREC No. 33-0.

01A TREC No. 33-0

Figure 6.5 TREC 34-1

PROMULGATED BY THE TEXAS REAL ESTATE COMMISSION (TREC) 10-29-01

EQUAL HOUSING OPPORTUNITY

ADDENDUM FOR PROPERTY LOCATED SEAWARD OF THE GULF INTRACOASTAL WATERWAY

TO CONTRACT CONCERNING THE PROPERTY AT

____

____

(Location of Property)

IN ACCORDANCE WITH SECTION 61.025, TEXAS NATURAL RESOURCES CODE, THE FOLLOWING STATEMENT IS INCLUDED AS PART OF THE CONTRACT:

The real property described in this contract is located seaward of the Gulf Intracoastal Waterway to its southernmost point and then seaward of the longitudinal line also known as 97 degrees, 12', 19" which runs southerly to the international boundary from the intersection of the centerline of the Gulf Intracoastal Waterway and the Brownsville Ship Channel. If the property is in close proximity to a beach fronting the Gulf of Mexico, the purchaser is hereby advised that the public has acquired a right of use or easement to or over the area of any public beach by prescription, dedication, or presumption, or has retained a right by virtue of continuous right in the public since time immemorial, as recognized in law and custom.

The extreme seaward boundary of natural vegetation that spreads continuously inland customarily marks the landward boundary of the public easement. If there is no clearly marked natural vegetation line, the landward boundary of the easement is as provided by Sections 61.016 and 61.017, Natural Resources Code.

State law prohibits any obstruction, barrier, restraint, or interference with the use of the public easement, including the placement of structures seaward of the landward boundary of the easement. STRUCTURES ERECTED SEAWARD OF THE VEGETATION LINE (OR OTHER APPLICABLE EASEMENT BOUNDARY) OR THAT BECOME SEAWARD OF THE VEGETATION LINE AS A RESULT OF NATURAL PROCESSES ARE SUBJECT TO A LAWSUIT BY THE STATE OF TEXAS TO REMOVE THE STRUCTURES.

The purchaser is hereby notified that the purchaser should: (1) determine the rate of shoreline erosion in the vicinity of the real property; and (2) seek the advice of an attorney or other qualified person before executing this contract or instrument of conveyance as to the relevance of these statutes and facts to the value of the property the purchaser is hereby purchasing or contracting to purchase.

____________________	____________________
Buyer	Seller
____________________	____________________
Buyer	Seller

This form has been approved by the Texas Real Estate Commission for use with similarly approved or promulgated contract forms. Such approval relates to this form only. TREC forms are intended for use only by trained real estate licensees. No representation is made as to the legal validity or adequacy of any provision in any specific transactions. It is not suitable for complex transactions. Texas Real Estate Commission, P.O. Box 12188, Austin, TX 78711-2188, 1-800-250-8732 or (512) 459-6544 (http://www.trec.state.tx.us) TREC No. 34-1. This form replaces TREC No. 34-0.

01A

Inspection of the Property

At times license holders, in their enthusiasm and desire to earn a commission, create false expectations on the part of the buyer with regard to the condition of the property. You and the buyer would be better served if you advised them that the physical aspects of the property may be something less than perfect and that they should have it thoroughly inspected and evaluated by professionals. The list of possibilities is long and may involve the use of a wide variety of professionals.

The contract establishes the right of the buyer to have access to bring professional, licensed inspectors to examine the property. The buyer may or may not have the right to terminate as a result of the findings of various inspectors. If a buyer wants the ability to cancel the agreement if something is revealed in the inspection process or for any other reason, the buyer needs to purchase the unrestricted right to do so as provided in paragraph 23 of the promulgated contract.

Figure 6.6 TREC 20-6 Paragraph 23

23. TERMINATION OPTION: This paragraph will be a part of this contract ONLY if both blanks are filled in and Buyer has paid the Option Fee. Buyer has paid Seller $_______________ (Option Fee) for the unrestricted right to terminate this contract by giving notice of termination to Seller within ________ days after the effective date of this contract. If Buyer gives notice of termination within the time specified, the Option Fee will not be refunded, however, any earnest money will be refunded to Buyer. The Option Fee ❑will ❑will not be credited to the Sales Price at closing. For the purposes of this paragraph, time is of the essence; strict compliance with the time for performance stated herein is required.

Please note three things that apply when the option is purchased.

1. Valuable consideration (money) must be tendered to the owner
2. Time is of the essence with regard to the option to terminate
3. The right is unrestricted, it is not limited to the results of inspections

Buyers may elect to use any of a significant number of professionals to help them evaluate a particular property.

- Texas Real Estate Commission licensed real estate inspectors
- Structural engineers
- Electricians
- Plumbers
- Pest control specialists
- Heating and air conditioning contractors
- Lead inspectors
- Governmental agencies
- Environmental specialists

Figure 6.7 TREC 20-6 Paragraph 7

7. PROPERTY CONDITION:

A. INSPECTIONS, ACCESS AND UTILITIES: Buyer may have the Property inspected by inspectors selected by Buyer and licensed by TREC or otherwise permitted by law to make inspections. Seller shall permit Buyer and Buyer's agents access to the Property at reasonable times. Seller shall pay for turning on existing utilities for inspections.

B. SELLER'S DISCLOSURE NOTICE PURSUANT TO §5.008, TEXAS PROPERTY CODE (Notice): (Check one box only)

❑ (1) Buyer has received the Notice.

❑ (2) Buyer has not received the Notice. Within ______ days after the effective date of this contract, Seller shall deliver the Notice to Buyer. If Buyer does not receive the Notice, Buyer may terminate this contract at any time prior to the closing and the earnest money will be refunded to Buyer. If Seller delivers the Notice, Buyer may terminate this contract for any reason within 7 days after Buyer receives the Notice or prior to the closing, whichever first occurs, and the earnest money will be refunded to Buyer.

❑ (3) The Texas Property Code does not require this Seller to furnish the Notice.

C. SELLER'S DISCLOSURE OF LEAD-BASED PAINT AND LEAD-BASED PAINT HAZARDS is required by Federal law for a residential dwelling constructed prior to 1978.

D. ACCEPTANCE OF PROPERTY CONDITION: Buyer accepts the Property in its present condition; provided Seller, at Seller's expense, shall complete the following specific repairs and treatments:____
____.

E. LENDER REQUIRED REPAIRS AND TREATMENTS: Unless otherwise agreed in writing, neither party is obligated to pay for lender required repairs, which includes treatment for wood destroying insects. If the parties do not agree to pay for the lender required repairs or treatments, this contract will terminate and the earnest money will be refunded to Buyer. If the cost of lender required repairs and treatments exceeds 5% of the Sales Price, Buyer may terminate this contract and the earnest money will be refunded to Buyer.

F. COMPLETION OF REPAIRS AND TREATMENTS: Unless otherwise agreed in writing, Seller shall complete all agreed repairs and treatments prior to the Closing Date. All required permits must be obtained, and repairs and treatments must be performed by persons who are licensed or otherwise authorized by law to provide such repairs or treatments. At Buyer's election, any transferable warranties received by Seller with respect to the repairs and treatments will be transferred to Buyer at Buyer's expense. If Seller fails to complete any agreed repairs and treatments prior to the Closing Date, Buyer may do so and receive reimbursement from Seller at closing. The Closing Date will be extended up to 15 days, if necessary, to complete repairs and treatments.

G. ENVIRONMENTAL MATTERS: Buyer is advised that the presence of wetlands, toxic substances, including asbestos and wastes or other environmental hazards, or the presence of a threatened or endangered species or its habitat may affect Buyer's intended use of the Property. If Buyer is concerned about these matters, an addendum promulgated by TREC or required by the parties should be used.

H. RESIDENTIAL SERVICE CONTRACTS: Buyer may purchase a residential service contract from a residential service company licensed by TREC. If Buyer purchases a residential service contract, Seller shall reimburse Buyer at closing for the cost of the residential service contract in an amount not exceeding $______________ . Buyer should review any residential service contract for the scope of coverage, exclusions and limitations. **The purchase of a residential service contract is optional. Similar coverage may be purchased from various companies authorized to do business in Texas.**

Paragraph 7A grants access at reasonable times for the appropriate inspections to be done. It further agrees that the seller, at seller's expense, shall have utilities turned on for inspections.

Effective January 1, 1994, section 5.008 of the Texas Property Code requires sellers of previously occupied residential dwelling units to furnish buyers with a seller's disclosure notice with content and information required by statute. Failure to provide the notice prior to signing an executory contract to purchase creates a voidable contract that may be terminated at the sole discretion of the buyer. If it is furnished after an executory contract of purchase is signed, the buyer has a period of seven days to terminate the contract without penalty or forfeiture of earnest money.

There are 11 exceptions stated in subsection (e) of section 5.008 of the Texas Property Code.

(e) This section does not apply to a transfer:

(1) pursuant to a court order or foreclosure sale;

(2) by a trustee in bankruptcy;

(3) to a mortgagee by a mortgagor or successor in interest, or to a beneficiary of a deed of trust by a trustor or successor in interest;

(4) by a mortgagee or a beneficiary under a deed of trust who has acquired the real property at a sale conducted pursuant to a power of sale under a deed of trust or a sale pursuant to a court ordered foreclosure or has acquired the real property by a deed in lieu of foreclosure;

(5) by a fiduciary in the course of the administration of a decedent's estate, guardianship, conservatorship, or trust;

(6) from one co-owner to one or more other co-owners;

(7) made to a spouse or to a person or persons in the lineal line of consanguinity of one or more of the transferors;

(8) between spouses resulting from a decree of dissolution of marriage or a decree of legal separation or from a property settlement agreement incidental to such a decree;

(9) to or from any governmental entity;

(10) transfers of new residences of not more than one dwelling unit which have not previously been occupied for residential purposes; or

(11) transfers of real property where the value of any dwelling does not exceed five percent (5%) of the value of the property. (Note: This provision typically excludes a ranch or farm sale.)

By checking the appropriate box in 7B, the parties define whether

- the buyer has received the notice,
- the seller has a defined number of days to furnish it, or
- the property is exempt from the requirement pursuant to the Texas Property Code.

Remember also that according to this section of the code and section 1101.556 of the TRELA, there is no duty to disclose specific information. Subsection (c) of 5.008 states:

> Sec. 1101.556. DISCLOSURE OF CERTAIN INFORMATION RELATING TO OCCUPANTS. Notwithstanding other law, a license holder is not required to inquire about, disclose, or release information relating to whether:
>
> (1) a previous or current occupant of real property had, may have had, has, or may have AIDS, an HIV-related illness, or an HIV infection as defined by the Centers for Disease Control and Prevention of the United States Public Health Service; or
>
> (2) a death occurred on a property by natural causes, suicide, or accident unrelated to the condition of the property.

The form that follows is the TREC version of the Seller's Disclosure Notice, which is made available for voluntary use by the customers and clients of license holders. Some license holders prefer to use a format developed by the Texas Association of REALTORS® and some use a form developed by an in-house attorney. As long as the disclosure includes the minimum content established by 5.008, it is acceptable. The widely used Texas Association of REALTORS® form is not included in this book because it may be used only by REALTORS®. The version approved by TREC for voluntary use meets the requirements of Section 5.008 of the Texas Property Code and may be used by all real estate license holders and their clients and customers.

Figure 6.8 TREC OP-H

APPROVED BY THE TEXAS REAL ESTATE COMMISSION (TREC) 10-25-93

EQUAL HOUSING OPPORTUNITY

SELLER'S DISCLOSURE OF PROPERTY CONDITION

(SECTION 5.008, TEXAS PROPERTY CODE)

CONCERNING THE PROPERTY AT ____
(Street Address and City)

THIS NOTICE IS A DISCLOSURE OF SELLER'S KNOWLEDGE OF THE CONDITION OF THE PROPERTY AS OF THE DATE SIGNED BY SELLER AND IS NOT A SUBSTITUTE FOR ANY INSPECTIONS OR WARRANTIES THE PURCHASER MAY WISH TO OBTAIN. IT IS NOT A WARRANTY OF ANY KIND BY SELLER OR SELLER'S AGENTS.

Seller ☐ is ☐ is not occupying the Property. If unoccupied, how long since Seller has occupied the Property? __________

1. The Property has the items checked below [Write Yes (Y), No (N), or Unknown (U)]:

___ Range	___ Oven	___ Microwave
___ Dishwasher	___ Trash Compactor	___ Disposal
___ Washer/Dryer Hookups	___ Window Screens	___ Rain Gutters
___ Security System	___ Fire Detection Equipment	___ Intercom System
___ TV Antenna	___ Cable TV Wiring	___ Satellite Dish
___ Ceiling Fan(s)	___ Attic Fan(s)	___ Exhaust Fan(s)
___ Central A/C	___ Central Heating	___ Wall/Window Air Conditioning
___ Plumbing System	___ Septic System	___ Public Sewer System
___ Patio/Deck	___ Outdoor Grill	___ Fences
___ Pool	___ Sauna	___ Spa ___ Hot Tub
___ Pool Equipment	___ Pool Heater	___ Automatic Lawn Sprinkler System
___ Fireplace(s) & Chimney (Woodburning)	___ Fireplace(s) & Chimney (Mock)	___ Gas Lines (Nat./LP)
___ Gas Fixtures	Garage: ___ Attached ___ Not Attached	___ Carport
Garage Door Opener(s):	___ Electronic	___ Control(s)
Water Heater:	___ Gas	___ Electric
Water Supply: ___City	___ Well ___MUD	___ Co-op

Roof Type: ______________________ Age: ______________________ (approx)

Are you (Seller) aware of any of the above items that are not in working condition, that have known defects, or that are in need of repair? ☐ Yes ☐ No ☐ Unknown. If yes, then describe. (Attach additional sheets if necessary): __________

____

____

2. Are you (Seller) aware of any known defects/malfunctions in any of the following? Write Yes (Y) if you are aware, write No (N) if you are not aware.

___ Interior Walls	___ Ceilings	___ Floors
___ Exterior Walls	___ Doors	___ Windows
___ Roof	___ Foundation/Slab(s)	___ Basement
___ Walls/Fences	___ Driveways	___ Sidewalks
___ Plumbing/Sewers/Septics	___ Electrical Systems	___ Lighting Fixtures

___ Other Structural Components (Describe): ____

____

____

01A TREC No. OP-H

Figure 6.8 TREC OP-H (continued)

Seller's Disclosure Notice Concerning the Property at ______________________ Page 2 10-25-93
(Street Address and City)

If the answer to any of the above is yes, explain. (Attach additional sheets if ______________________

3. Are you (Seller) aware of any of the following conditions? Write Yes (Y) if you are aware, write No (N) if you are not aware.

___ Active Termites (includes wood-destroying insects)
___ Termite or Wood Rot Damage Needing Repair
___ Previous Termite Damage
___ Previous Termite Treatment
___ Previous Flooding
___ Improper Drainage
___ Water Penetration
___ Located in 100-Year Floodplain
___ Present Flood Insurance Coverage
___ Previous Structrural or Roof Repair
___ Hazardous or Toxic Waste
___ Asbestos Components
___ Urea-formaldehyde Insulation
___ Radon Gas
___ Lead Based Paint
___ Aluminum Wiring
___ Previous Fires
___ Unplatted Easements
___ Landfill, Settling, Soil Movement, Fault Lines
___ Subsurface Structure or Pits

If the answer to any of the above is yes, explain. (Attach additional sheets if necessary): ______________________

4. Are you (Seller) aware of any item, equipment, or system in or on the Property that is in need of repair? ☐ Yes (if you are aware) ☐ No (if you are not aware). If yes, explain (attach additional sheets as necessary). ______________________

5. Are you (Seller) aware of any of the following? Write Yes (Y) if you are aware, write No (N) if you are not aware.

__ Room additions, structural modifications, or other alterations or repairs made without necessary permits or not in compliance with building codes in effect at that time.

__ Homeowners' Association or maintenance fees or assessments.

__ Any "common area" (facilities such as pools, tennis courts, walkways, or other areas) co-owned in undivided interest with others.

__ Any notices of violations of deed restrictions or governmental ordinances affecting the condition or use of the Property.

__ Any lawsuits directly or indirectly affecting the Property.

__ Any condition on the Property which materially affects the physical health or safety of an individual.

If the answer to any of the above is yes, explain. (Attach additional sheets if necessary): ______________________

Date	Signature of Seller	Date	Signature of Seller

The undersigned purchaser hereby acknowledges receipt of the foregoing notice.

Date	Signature of Purchaser	Date	Signature of Purchaser

01A TREC No. OP-H

Some license holders have the mistaken idea that the form must be signed by the seller, acknowledged by the buyer, and attached as an addendum to the purchase contract. The statute only requires that the seller complete the written disclosure and give it to the buyer. Do not list it as an addendum in paragraph 21. It is a disclosure of what the seller knows; it is not a representation or warranty and therefore not a promise or covenant exchanged between the parties. Some lawyers we have questioned on this matter feel that to reference it as an addendum in some way converts it from being simply a disclosure to a representation and warranty of the property condition. Courts in both San Antonio and Houston have ruled that the attached seller's disclosure was a representation by the sellers and ruled in favor of the buyers. We suggest that you follow the lead of TREC and simply check the appropriate box in paragraph 7B that provides adequate documentation as to what the parties have done with regard to this matter.

Paragraph 7C addresses the possibility of the presence of lead-based paint or lead-based paint hazards. License holders and sellers must be certain that they follow the HUD guidelines with regard to the seller's disclosure of the presence of lead-based paint and/or lead hazards. If the building permits for the construction of the home were issued prior to January 1, 1978, the addendum must be used to comply with the federal regulation to furnish a lead warning statement. You may use the TREC version that follows or the HUD version.

Figure 6.9 TREC OP-L

APPROVED BY THE TEXAS REAL ESTATE COMMISSION 02-09-2004

EQUAL HOUSING OPPORTUNITY

ADDENDUM FOR SELLER'S DISCLOSURE OF INFORMATION ON LEAD-BASED PAINT AND LEAD-BASED PAINT HAZARDS AS REQUIRED BY FEDERAL LAW

CONCERNING THE PROPERTY AT ______________________________
(Street Address and City)

A. **LEAD WARNING STATEMENT:** "Every purchaser of any interest in residential real property on which a residential dwelling was built prior to 1978 is notified that such property may present exposure to lead from lead-based paint that may place young children at risk of developing lead poisoning. Lead poisoning in young children may produce permanent neurological damage, including learning disabilities, reduced intelligence quotient, behavioral problems, and impaired memory. Lead poisoning also poses a particular risk to pregnant women. The seller of any interest in residential real property is required to provide the buyer with any information on lead-based paint hazards from risk assessments or inspections in the seller's possession and notify the buyer of any known lead-based paint hazards. A risk assessment or inspection for possible lead-paint hazards is recommended prior to purchase."
NOTICE: Inspector must be properly certified as required by federal law.

B. **SELLER'S DISCLOSURE:**
1. PRESENCE OF LEAD-BASED PAINT AND/OR LEAD-BASED PAINT HAZARDS (check on box only):
❑(a) Known lead-based paint and/or lead-based paint hazards are present in the Property (explain): ________
______________________________.
❑(b) Seller has no actual knowledge of lead-based paint and/or lead-based paint hazards in the Property.
2. RECORDS AND REPORTS AVAILABLE TO SELLER (check one box only):
❑(a) Seller has provided the purchaser with all available records and reports pertaining to lead-based paint and/or lead-based paint hazards in the Property (list documents):______________________________
______________________________.
❑(b) Seller has no reports or records pertaining to lead-based paint and/or lead-based paint hazards in the Property.

C. **BUYER'S RIGHTS** (check one box only)**:**
❑1. Buyer waives the opportunity to conduct a risk assessment or inspection of the Property for the presence of lead-based paint or lead-based paint hazards.
❑2. Within ten days after the effective date of this contract, Buyer may have the Property inspected by inspectors selected by Buyer. If lead-based paint or lead-based paint hazards are present, Buyer may terminate this contract by giving Seller written notice within 14 days after the effective date of this contract, and the earnest money will be refunded to Buyer.

D. **BUYER'S ACKNOWLEDGMENT** (check applicable boxes)**:**
❑1. Buyer has received copies of all information listed above.
❑2. Buyer has received the pamphlet *Protect Your Family from Lead in Your Home*.

E. **BROKERS' ACKNOWLEDGMENT:** Brokers have informed Seller of Seller's obligations under 42 U.S.C. 4852d to: (a) provide Buyer with the federally approved pamphlet on lead poisoning prevention; (b) complete this addendum; (c) disclose any known lead-based paint and/or lead-based paint hazards in the Property; (d) deliver all records and reports to Buyer pertaining to lead-based paint and/or lead-based paint hazards in the Property; (e) provide Buyer a period of up to 10 days to have the Property inspected; and (f) retain a completed copy of this addendum for at least 3 years following the sale. Brokers are aware of their responsibility to ensure compliance.

F. **CERTIFICATION OF ACCURACY:** The following persons have reviewed the information above and certify, to the best of their knowledge, that the information they have provided is true and accurate.

Buyer	Date	Seller	Date
Buyer	Date	Seller	Date
Other Broker	Date	Listing Broker	Date

The form of this addendum has been approved by the Texas Real Estate Commission for use only with similarly approved or promulgated forms of contracts. Such approval relates to this contract form only. TREC forms are intended for use only by trained real estate licensees. No representation is made as to the legal validity or adequacy of any provision in any specific transactions. It is not suitable for complex transactions. Texas Real Estate Commission, P.O. Box 12188, Austin, TX 78711-2188, 1-800-250-8732 or (512) 459-6544 (http://www.trec.state.tx.us)

Form OP-L 01A

In 7D the buyer agrees that the property is accepted in its present condition but gives the parties the ability to list some specific repairs that are to be completed by the seller and at the seller's expense prior to closing. An example of something that the buyer might request is that the missing gutter on the back of the home be replaced prior to closing or that the damaged kitchen floor covering be replaced with a specific material prior to closing. Listing agents should take special note of the fact that there is no cap on the seller's financial liability. No seller should agree to complete the repairs listed in this paragraph until they have obtained bids or at least some idea of what the requested repair will cost.

When a lender requires a repair, it is usually something that involves significant dollars. It is not prudent to commit to pay potentially large sums of money until one knows the amount. The agreement of the parties is that neither is committed to pay for any lender-required repair. This can be negotiated by using the TREC promulgated amendment form that follows.

Figure 6.10 TREC 39-4

PROMULGATED BY THE TEXAS REAL ESTATE COMMISSION (TREC) 01-06-03

EQUAL HOUSING OPPORTUNITY

AMENDMENT

TO CONTRACT CONCERNING THE PROPERTY AT

____

(Street Address and City)

Seller and Buyer amend the contract as follows: (check each applicable box)

❑(1) The Sales Price in Paragraph 3 of the contract is:

A. Cash portion of Sales Price payable by Buyer at closing .... $____________

B. Sum of financing described in the contract .... $____________

C. Sales Price (Sum of A and B) .... $____________

❑(2) In addition to any repairs and treatments otherwise required by the contract, Seller, at Seller's expense, shall complete the following repairs and treatments:

❑(3) The Option Fee ❑ will ❑ will not be credited to the Sales Price.

❑(4) The date in Paragraph 9 of the contract is changed to ______________________, 20______.

❑(5) The amount in Paragraph 12A(1)(b) of the contract is changed to $ __________________.

❑(6) The cost of lender required repairs and treatment, as itemized on the attached list, will be paid as follows: $ ____________________ by Seller; $ _____________________ by Buyer.

❑(7) Buyer has paid Seller an additional non-refundable Option Fee of $ ________________ for an extension of the unrestricted right to terminate the contract on or before ______________________, 20_______. This additional Option Fee ❑ will ❑ will not be credited to the Sales Price.

❑(8) Upon final acceptance of this Amendment, Buyer waives the unrestricted right to terminate the contract for which the Option Fee was paid.

❑(9) **Other Modifications**: (Insert only factual statements and business details applicable to this sale.)

EXECUTED the___________day of ____________________, 20 ____ (BROKER: FILL IN THE DATE OF FINAL ACCEPTANCE).

Buyer	Seller
Buyer	Seller

This form has been approved by the Texas Real Estate Commission for use with similarly approved or promulgated contract forms. Such approval relates to this form only. TREC forms are intended for use only by trained real estate licensees. No representation is made as to the legal validity or adequacy of any provision in any specific transactions. It is not suitable for complex transactions. Texas Real Estate Commission, P.O. Box 12188, Austin, TX 78711-2188, 1-800-250-8732 or (512) 459-6544 (http://www.trec.state.tx.us) TREC No. 39-4. This form replaces TREC No. 39-3.

01A

Identify 5 or 6 other uses for the form.

1. ______________________________

2. ______________________________

3. ______________________________

4. ______________________________

5. ______________________________

6. ______________________________

7F provides for an extension of 15 days, if necessary, for the seller to complete repairs and treatments. It also provides, although not at all a practical solution, that the buyer may do the repairs prior to closing and receive reimbursement from the seller for them at closing.

Buyers should always be given the opportunity to have the property inspected for environmental hazards. Whether their concern is about radon, asbestos, mold, or the latest concern, the buyer should be satisfied that the property does not pose a health hazard to the buyer or the buyer's family. Always offer the opportunity to use TREC form 28-0 and be certain to structure the transaction with an adequate time frame to accomplish the desired evaluation and to get the report from the inspector to the buyer prior to the agreed period in the form for the termination of the contract by the buyer.

Figure 6.11 TREC 28-0

EQUAL HOUSING OPPORTUNITY

10-25-93

ENVIRONMENTAL ASSESSMENT, THREATENED OR ENDANGERED SPECIES, AND WETLANDS ADDENDUM

PROMULGATED BY THE TEXAS REAL ESTATE COMMISSION (TREC)

ADDENDUM TO EARNEST MONEY CONTRACT BETWEEN THE UNDERSIGNED PARTIES CONCERNING THE PROPERTY AT ____
(Address)

☐ A. ENVIRONMENTAL ASSESSMENT: Buyer, at Buyer's expense, may obtain an Environmental Assessment Report prepared by an environmental specialist.

☐ B. THREATENED OR ENDANGERED SPECIES: Buyer, at Buyer's expense, may obtain a report from a natural resources professional to determine if there are any threatened or endangered species or their habitats as defined by the Texas Parks and Wildlife Department or the U.S. Fish and Wildlife Service.

☐ C. WETLANDS: Buyer, at Buyer's expense, may obtain a report from an environmental specialist to determine if there are wetlands, as defined by federal or state law or regulation.

Within _________ days after the Effective Date of the contract, Buyer may terminate the contract by furnishing Seller a copy of any report noted above that adversely affects the use of the Property and the Earnest Money shall be refunded to Buyer. If Buyer does not furnish Seller a copy of the unacceptable report within the prescribed time and give Seller notice that Buyer has terminated the contract, Buyer shall be deemed to have accepted the Property.

Buyer	Seller
Buyer	Seller

The form of this addendum has been approved by the Texas Real Estate Commission for use only with similarly approved or promulgated forms of contracts. No representation is made as to the legal validity or adequacy of any provision in any specific transactions. It is not suitable for complex transactions. (10-93) TREC No. 28-0.

01A TREC No. 28-0

Residential service contracts 7H are optional and can be purchased by either the seller or the buyer. The cost is minimal, $300 and up for one year; the risk reduction factor for the seller and the agent is enormous. Some license holders have found it to be such a good thing for consumers that they buy it for them. It is best, regardless of who is paying, that the buyers have the opportunity to review available coverage and to select the desired coverage. The sellers' financial liability for the cost of coverage can be capped by agreement in the contract.

Summary

Make certain that paragraphs 6 and 7 are carefully read by each of the parties. As an agent of either or both parties, you must remember that your role is to identify alternatives, alert them to potential danger areas, and encourage them to read and understand the agreement. Your role is not to make decisions, dictate, or define. Remember that it is their transaction, it is not your transaction unless you are listed as seller or buyer in the first paragraph of the contract.

You are not expected to have all knowledge; however, you are expected and required to advise parties to thoroughly investigate title, survey, and physical condition issues.

CHAPTER 6

REVIEW QUESTIONS

1. If the dollar amount of lender-required repairs exceeds 5 percent of the purchase price, who may terminate the contract?

   A. Seller
   B. Listing broker
   C. Lender
   D. Buyer

2. According to the provisions of the contract, who will purchase a residential service contract if so desired?

   A. Lender
   B. Seller
   C. Listing agent
   D. Buyer

3. How many days does the selected title company have after the title company receives a copy of the contract for the seller to furnish to the buyer a copy of the title commitment?

   A. 7 days
   B. 10 days
   C. 20 days
   D. 30 days

4. The seller always has the right to select the company that will provide escrow services and issue a title policy.

   A. True
   B. False

5. Which of the following is included in the contract's definition of exception documents?

   A. Survey
   B. Restrictive covenants
   C. Commitment
   D. Abstract

6. All residential lots in a platted subdivision are subject to mandatory membership in an owner's association.

   A. True
   B. False

7. How many days after receipt of the commitment does the buyer have to object to defects, exceptions, or encumbrances to title?

   A. A number of days determined by the parties
   B. The statutorily mandated 15 days
   C. 10 days
   D. 7 days

8. If a title policy is furnished as evidence of good title, who should promptly review the commitment upon buyer's receipt of it?

   A. Lender
   B. Buyer's attorney
   C. Seller's attorney
   D. Buyer's agent

9. The Federal law requires the attachment of a lead-based paint and lead-based paint hazards addendum to the purchase agreement for housing units built prior to what year?

   A. 1978
   B. 1977
   C. 1988
   D. 1866

10. Should the seller's disclosure notice pursuant to chapter 5.008 of the Texas Property Code be listed as an addendum to the contract?

    A. Yes
    B. No
    C. Only if required by the lender
    D. Only when required by the seller

Chapter 7

The Remaining Provisions

Key Terms

- assignment
- back-up offer
- business detail
- closing
- default
- escrow
- funding
- general warranty deed
- legal remedy
- liquidated damages
- loan fee
- mediation
- MIP
- PMI
- prevailing party
- temporary lease
- VA loan funding fee
- wetland

Brokers' Fees

License holders are particularly fond of the paragraph that instructs the escrow officer to pay them.

Figure 7.1 TREC 20-6 Paragraph 8

> **8. BROKERS' FEES:** All obligations of the parties for payment of brokers' fees are contained in separate written agreements.

Fees are not a part of the agreement between the seller and the buyer but rather are an issue between the seller and the listing broker and the buyer and the buyer's broker. With regard to a subagent, it is a matter between the listing broker and the selling broker. Commission splits between salespersons and the brokers who sponsor them are to be defined by their employment or independent contractor agreement.

Figure 7.2 TREC 20-6, Broker Information and Ratification of Fee

BROKER INFORMATION AND RATIFICATION OF FEE

Listing Broker has agreed to pay Other Broker ______________________________ of the total sales price when Listing Broker's fee is received. Escrow Agent is authorized and directed to pay Other Broker from Listing Broker's fee at closing.

Other Broker	Listing Broker
License No. Telephone	License No. Telephone
represents ☐ Buyer only as Buyer's agent ☐ Seller as Listing Broker's subagent	represents ☐ Seller and Buyer as an intermediary ☐ Seller only as Seller's agent
Associate Telephone	Listing Associate Telephone
Broker's Address	Listing Associate's Office Address Facsimile
Facsimile	Selling Associate Telephone
	Selling Associate's Office Address Facsimile

Having a clear understanding of who is being represented by whom is required by the TRELA. A box addressing this important issue is found on page 8 of the contract form and is identified as "Broker Information and Ratification of Fee." This box is not a part of the contract between the seller and the buyer. It is set apart from the contract by being printed on a separate page and placed in a separate border. Brokers who represent sellers and buyers in the same transaction are reminded that section 1101.559 of the TRELA requires that the broker have written permission from each of the parties to function as an intermediary. Without a listing signed by the seller(s) and a buyer representation agreement signed by the buyer(s), or by other written authorization, the license holder may face disciplinary action by TREC.

Closing and Possession

Figure 7.3 TREC 20-6 Paragraphs 9 and 10

9. CLOSING:

A. The closing of the sale will be on or before ____________________, 20___, or within 7 days after objections to matters disclosed in the Commitment or by the survey have been cured, whichever date is later (Closing Date). If either party fails to close the sale by the Closing Date, the non-defaulting party may exercise the remedies contained in Paragraph 15.

B. At closing:

(1) Seller shall execute and deliver a general warranty deed conveying title to the Property to Buyer and showing no additional exceptions to those permitted in Paragraph 6 and furnish tax statements or certificates showing no delinquent taxes on the Property.

(2) Buyer shall pay the Sales Price in good funds acceptable to the escrow agent.

(3) Seller and Buyer shall execute and deliver any notices, statements, certificates, affidavits, releases, loan documents and other documents required of them by this contract, the Commitment or law necessary for the closing of the sale and the issuance of the Title Policy.

C. Unless expressly prohibited by written agreement, Seller may continue to show the Property and receive, negotiate and accept back up offers.

D. All covenants, representations and warranties in this contract survive closing.

10. POSSESSION: Seller shall deliver to Buyer possession of the Property in its present or required condition, ordinary wear and tear excepted: ❑ upon closing and funding ❑ according to a temporary residential lease form promulgated by TREC or other written lease required by the parties. Any possession by Buyer prior to closing or by Seller after closing which is not authorized by a written lease will establish a tenancy at sufferance relationship between the parties. *Consult your insurance agent prior to change of ownership or possession because insurance coverage may be limited or terminated. The absence of a written lease or appropriate insurance coverage may expose the parties to economic loss.*

Closing and the buyer's possession of the property are important issues addressed in paragraphs 9 and 10. Closing needs to occur on or before a specific date, while possession should be granted at the happening of a defined event, such as closing or funding.

If a buyer moves in before closing and funding or a seller remains after closing and funding, a landlord/tenant relationship exists. The relationship must be clearly defined by a seller's or buyer's **temporary lease.** Please examine the promulgated TREC forms that follow. Failure to use the appropriate temporary lease will create a tenancy at sufferance. Pay particular attention to the provisions relating to insurance coverage on the property during the tenancy period. A temporary lease may not be used to address any tenancy that exceeds 90 days. If the tenancy exceeds 90 days, the owner will need to bring the property into compliance with Chapter 92 of the Texas Property Code, the chapter that defines security devices, smoke detectors, and other features that must be provided in a residential rental unit.

Figure 7.4 TREC 15-3

12-07-98

(NOTICE: For use only when SELLER occupies the property for no more than 90 days AFTER the closing)

EQUAL HOUSING OPPORTUNITY

SELLER'S TEMPORARY RESIDENTIAL LEASE

PROMULGATED BY THE TEXAS REAL ESTATE COMMISSION (TREC)

1. **PARTIES:** The parties to this Lease are ______________________________ (Landlord) and ______________________________(Tenant).
2. **LEASE:** Landlord leases to Tenant the Property described in the Contract between Landlord as Buyer and Tenant as Seller dated ______________, ______,and known as ______________________________(address).
3. **TERM:** The term of this Lease commences on the date the sale covered by the Contract is closed and terminates ______________________, unless terminated earlier by reason of other provisions.
4. **RENTAL:** Tenant shall pay to Landlord as rental $____________per day with the full amount of rental for the term of the Lease to be paid at the time of funding of the sale. Tenant will not be entitled to a refund of rental if this Lease terminates early due to Tenant's default or voluntary surrender of the Property.
5. **SECURITY DEPOSIT:** Tenant shall pay to Landlord at the time of funding of the sale $ __________ as a deposit to secure performance of this Lease by Tenant. Landlord may use the deposit to satisfy Tenant's obligations under this Lease. Landlord shall refund any unused portion of the deposit to Tenant with an itemized list of all deductions from the deposit within 30 days after Tenant (a) surrenders possession of the Property and (b) provides Landlord written notice of Tenant's forwarding address.
6. **UTILITIES:** Tenant shall pay all utility charges except______________________________, which Landlord shall pay.
7. **USE OF PROPERTY:** Tenant may use the Property only for single family dwelling purposes. Tenant may not assign this Lease or sublet any part of the Property.
8. **PETS:** Tenant may not keep pets on the Property except______________________________.
9. **CONDITION OF PROPERTY:** Tenant accepts the Property in its present condition and state of repair at the commencement of the Lease. Upon termination, Tenant shall surrender the Property to Landlord in the condition required under the Contract at the time of closing, except normal wear and tear and any casualty loss.
10. **ALTERATIONS:** Tenant may not alter the Property or install improvements or fixtures without the prior written consent of Landlord. Any improvements or fixtures placed on the Property during the Lease become the property of Landlord.
11. **SPECIAL PROVISIONS:**

12. **INSPECTIONS:** Landlord may enter at reasonable times to inspect the Property.
13. **LAWS:** Tenant shall comply with all applicable laws, restrictions, ordinances, rules and regulations with respect to the Property.
14. **REPAIRS AND MAINTENANCE:** <u>Tenant shall bear all expense of repairing and maintaining the Property, including but not limited to yard, trees and shrubs, unless otherwise required by the Texas Property Code. Tenant shall promptly repair at Tenant's expense any damage to the Property caused directly or indirectly by any act or omission of the Tenant or any person other than Landlord, Landlord's agents or invitees.</u>

01A TREC NO. 15-3

Initialed for identification by Buyer_______ _______ and Seller_________ _______

Figure 7.4 TREC 15-3 (continued)

Seller's Temporary Residential Lease____Page Two 12-07-98
(Address of Property)

15. **INDEMNITY:** Tenant indemnifies Landlord from the claims of all third parties for injury or damage to the person or property of such third party arising from the use or occupancy of the Property by Tenant. This indemnification includes attorney's fees, costs and expenses incurred by Landlord.
16. **INSURANCE:** Landlord and Tenant shall each maintain such insurance on the contents and Property as each party may deem appropriate during the term of this Lease. NOTE: CONSULT YOUR INSURANCE AGENT PRIOR TO CLOSING. Possession of the Property by Seller as Tenant may change insurance policy coverage.
17. **DEFAULT:** If Tenant fails to perform or observe any provision of this Lease and fails, within 24 hours after notice by Landlord, to commence and diligently pursue to remedy such failure, Tenant will be in default.
18. **TERMINATION:** This Lease terminates upon expiration of the term specified in Paragraph 3 or upon Tenant's default under this Lease.
19. **HOLDING OVER:** Tenant shall surrender possession of the Property upon termination of this Lease. Any possession by Tenant after termination creates a tenancy at sufferance and will not operate to renew or extend this Lease. Tenant shall pay $ ______________ per day during the period of any possession after termination as damages, in addition to any other remedies to which Landlord is entitled.
20. **ATTORNEY'S FEES:** The prevailing party in any legal proceeding brought under or with respect to the transaction described in this Lease is entitled to recover from the non-prevailing party all costs of such proceeding and reasonable attorney's fees.
21. **SMOKE DETECTORS:** The Texas Property Code requires Landlord to install smoke detectors in certain locations within the Property at Landlord's expense. Tenant expressly waives Landlord's duty to inspect and repair smoke detectors.
22. **SECURITY DEVICES:** The requirements of the Texas Property Code relating to security devices do not apply to a residential lease for a term of 90 days or less.
23. **CONSULT YOUR ATTORNEY:** Real estate licensees cannot give legal advice. This Lease is intended to be legally binding. READ IT CAREFULLY. If you do not understand the effect of this Lease, consult your attorney BEFORE signing.
24. **NOTICES:** All notices under this Lease from one party to the other must be in writing and are effective when delivered or transmitted by facsimile machine as follows:

To Landlord:	**To Tenant:**
______________________________	______________________________
______________________________	______________________________
______________________________	______________________________
Facsimile:(____)________________	Facsimile:(____)________________

EXECUTED the ______ day of ____________________________.

______________________________	______________________________
Landlord	Tenant
______________________________	______________________________
Landlord	Tenant

The form of this contract has been approved by the Texas Real Estate Commission. Such approval relates to this contract form only. TREC forms are intended for use only by trained real estate licensees. No representation is made as to the legal validity or adequacy of any provision in any specific transaction. It is not suitable for complex transactions. Extensive riders or additions are not to be used. (12-98) Texas Real Estate Commission, P.O. Box 12188, Austin, TX 78711-2188, 1-800-250-8732 or (512)459-6544 (http://www.trec.state.tx.us) TREC NO. 15-3. This form replaces TREC NO. 15-2.

O1A TREC NO. 15-3

Figure 7.5 TREC 16-3

12-07-98

EQUAL HOUSING OPPORTUNITY

(NOTICE: For use only when BUYER occupies the property for no more than 90 days PRIOR to closing)

BUYER'S TEMPORARY RESIDENTIAL LEASE

PROMULGATED BY THE TEXAS REAL ESTATE COMMISSION (TREC)

1. **PARTIES:** The parties to this Lease are ______________________________ (Landlord) and ______________________________(Tenant).
2. **LEASE:** Landlord leases to Tenant the Property described in the Contract between Landlord as Seller and Tenant as Buyer dated ______________, ______,and known as ______________________________(address).
3. **TERM:** The term of this Lease commences on ______________________ and terminates as specified in Paragraph 18.
4. **RENTAL:** Rental will be $ ______________ per day. Upon commencement of this Lease, Tenant shall pay to Landlord the full amount of rental of $ ______________ for the anticipated term of the Lease (commencement date to the closing date specified in Paragraph 9 of the Contract). If the actual term of this Lease differs from the anticipated term, rent will be prorated and paid at closing through the actual closing date. No portion of the rental will be applied to payment of any items covered by the Contract.
5. **SECURITY DEPOSIT:** Tenant has paid to Landlord $ ______________ as a deposit to secure performance of this Lease by Tenant. If this Lease is terminated before the closing, Landlord may use the deposit to satisfy Tenant's obligations under this Lease. Landlord shall refund to Tenant any unused portion of the deposit together with an itemized list of all deductions from the deposit within 30 days after Tenant (a) surrenders possession of the Property and (b) provides Landlord written notice of Tenant's forwarding address. If this Lease is terminated by the closing of the sale of the Property, the unused portion of the deposit will be refunded to Tenant at closing, together with an itemized list of all deductions from the deposit. NOTICE: The security deposit must be in addition to the earnest money under the Contract.
6. **UTILITIES:** Tenant shall pay all utility connections, deposits and charges except ______________________________, which Landlord shall pay.
7. **USE OF PROPERTY:** Tenant may use the Property only for single family dwelling purposes. Tenant may not assign this Lease or sublet any part of the Property.
8. **PETS:** Tenant may not keep pets on the Property except ______________________________
9. **CONDITION OF PROPERTY**: Tenant accepts the Property in its present condition and state of repair, but Landlord shall make all repairs and improvements required by the Contract. If this Lease is terminated prior to closing, Tenant shall surrender possession of the Property to Landlord in its present condition, as improved by Landlord, except normal wear and tear and any casualty loss.
10. **ALTERATIONS:** Tenant may not: (a) make any holes or drive nails into the woodwork, floors, walls or ceilings (b) alter, paint or decorate the Property or (c) install improvements or fixtures without the prior written consent of Landlord. Any improvements or fixtures placed on the Property during the Lease become a part of the Property.
11. **SPECIAL PROVISIONS:**

12. **INSPECTIONS:** Landlord may enter at reasonable times to inspect, replace, repair or complete the improvements.
13. **LAWS:** Tenant shall comply with all applicable laws, restrictions, ordinances, rules and regulations with respect to the Property.
14. **REPAIRS AND MAINTENANCE:** Tenant shall bear all expense of repairing and maintaining the Property, including but not limited to yard, trees and shrubs, unless otherwise required by the Texas Property Code. Tenant shall promptly repair at Tenant's expense any damage to the Property caused directly or indirectly by any act or omission of the Tenant or any person other than Landlord, Landlord's agents or invitees.

01A TREC NO. 16-3

Initialed for identification by Buyer________ ________ and Seller________ ________

Figure 7.5 TREC 16-3 (continued)

Buyer's Temporary Residential Lease_______________________________________Page Two 12-07-98
(Address of Property)

15. **INDEMNITY:** Tenant indemnifies Landlord from the claims of all third parties for injury or damage to the person or property of such third party arising from the use or occupancy of the Property by Tenant. This indemnification includes attorney's fees, costs and expenses incurred by Landlord.
16. **INSURANCE:** Landlord and Tenant shall each maintain such insurance on the contents and Property as each party may deem appropriate during the term of this Lease. NOTE: CONSULT YOUR INSURANCE AGENT PRIOR TO CLOSING. Possession of the Property by Buyer as Tenant may change insurance policy coverage.
17. **DEFAULT:** If Tenant fails to perform or observe any provision of this Lease and fails, within 24 hours after notice by Landlord, to commence and diligently pursue to remedy such failure, Tenant will be in default.
18. **TERMINATION:** This Lease terminates upon (a) closing of the sale under the Contract, (b) termination of the Contract prior to closing, (c) Tenant's default under this Lease, or (d) Tenant's default under the Contract, whichever occurs first. Upon termination other than by closing of the sale, Tenant shall surrender possession of the Property.
19. **HOLDING OVER:** Any possession by Tenant after termination creates a tenancy at sufferance and will not operate to renew or extend this Lease. Tenant shall pay $ ________________ per day during the period of any possession after termination as damages, in addition to any other remedies to which Landlord is entitled.
20. **ATTORNEY'S FEES:** The prevailing party in any legal proceeding brought under or with respect to the transaction described in this Lease is entitled to recover from the non-prevailing party all costs of such proceeding and reasonable attorney's fees.
21. **SMOKE DETECTORS:** The Texas Property Code requires Landlord to install smoke detectors in certain locations within the Property at Landlord's expense. Tenant expressly waives Landlord's duty to inspect and repair smoke detectors.
22. **SECURITY DEVICES:** The requirements of the Texas Property Code relating to security devices do not apply to a residential lease for a term of 90 days or less.
23. **CONSULT YOUR ATTORNEY:** Real estate licensees cannot give legal advice. This Lease is intended to be legally binding. READ IT CAREFULLY. If you do not understand the effect of this Lease, consult your attorney BEFORE signing.
24. **NOTICES:** All notices under this Lease from one party to the other must be in writing and are effective when delivered or transmitted by facsimile machine as follows:

To Landlord:	**To Tenant:**
____________________	____________________
____________________	____________________
____________________	____________________
Facsimile:(_____)________________	Facsimile:(_____)________________

EXECUTED the _____ day of ____________________________ .

____________________	____________________
Landlord	Tenant
____________________	____________________
Landlord	Tenant

The form of this contract has been approved by the Texas Real Estate Commission. TREC forms are intended for use only by trained real estate licensees. Such approval relates to this contract form only. No representation is made as to the legal validity or adequacy of any provision in any specific transaction. It is not suitable for complex transactions. Extensive riders or additions are not to be used. (12-98) Texas Real Estate Commission, P.O. Box 12188, Austin, TX 78711-2188, 1-800-250-8732 or (512)459-6544 (http://www.trec.state.tx.us) TREC NO. 16-3 This form replaces TREC NO. 16-2.

01A TREC NO. 16-3

Special Provisions

When the parties need to add factual statements or business details to their agreement, they may use paragraph 11. When the parties want to define legal rights and remedies, they should seek competent legal advice.

Figure 7.6 TREC 20-6 Paragraph 11

11. SPECIAL PROVISIONS: (Insert only factual statements and business details applicable to the sale. TREC rules prohibit licensees from adding factual statements or business details for which a contract addendum, lease or other form has been promulgated by TREC for mandatory use.)

Things that can be added in the paragraph include

- inventory list,
- preclosing walk-through inspection,
- documents available for review prior to closing, and
- who will pay for specific costs that may be incurred.

When the provisions are extensive and more than will fit in the space provided, the parties may need to seek the assistance of a competent attorney. TREC has kept the space small for good reason.

The following are examples of things that ***MAY NOT*** be addressed in "special provisions" paragraph 11:

- The transaction is contingent upon the sale of another property (see TREC addendum 10-4).
- The contract is in a second or back-up position (see TREC addendum 11-4).
- The assumption transaction is contingent upon the seller's release of liability or, in the case of a VA guaranteed loan, restoration of VA entitlement (see TREC addendum 12-1).
- Arrangements for the buyer to possess before closing or the seller to stay after closing (see TREC addenda 16-3 and 15-3).
- The contract is contingent upon satisfactory inspections to the buyer.
- The parties agree that in the event of a dispute they will try **mediation** before bringing a lawsuit.
- Any wording that defines legal rights and remedies such as "contingent upon, terminate, refund earnest money on demand, cancel, etc."
- "*Time is of the essence*" (parties should contact an attorney).

Settlement and Other Expenses

Paragraph 12 defines who will pay for what and reflects current custom in Texas at the time of adoption of the form. The paragraph is uncomplicated and can easily be understood with a reasonably careful reading.

Figure 7.7 TREC 20-6 Paragraph 12

12. SETTLEMENT AND OTHER EXPENSES:

A. The following expenses must be paid at or prior to closing:

(1) Expenses payable by Seller (Seller's Expenses):

(a) Releases of existing liens, including prepayment penalties and recording fees; release of Seller's loan liability; tax statements or certificates; preparation of deed; one-half of escrow fee; and other expenses payable by Seller under this contract.

(b) Seller shall also pay an amount not to exceed $ ____________ to be applied in the following order: Buyer's Expenses which Buyer is prohibited from paying by FHA, VA, Texas Veteran's Housing Assistance Program or other governmental loan programs; Buyer's prepaid items; other Buyer's expenses.

(2) Expenses payable by Buyer (Buyer's Expenses):

(a) Loan origination, discount, buy-down, and commitment fees (Loan Fees).

(b) Appraisal fees; loan application fees; credit reports; preparation of loan documents; interest on the notes from date of disbursement to one month prior to dates of first monthly payments; recording fees; copies of easements and restrictions; mortgagee title policy with endorsements required by lender; loan-related inspection fees; photos, amortization schedules, one-half of escrow fee; all prepaid items, including required premiums for flood and hazard insurance, reserve deposits for insurance, ad valorem taxes and special governmental assessments; final compliance inspection; courier fee, repair inspection, underwriting fee and wire transfer, expenses incident to any loan, and other expenses payable by Buyer under this contract.

B. Buyer shall pay Private Mortgage Insurance Premium (PMI), VA Loan Funding Fee, or FHA Mortgage Insurance Premium (MIP) as required by the lender.

C. If any expense exceeds an amount expressly stated in this contract for such expense to be paid by a party, that party may terminate this contract unless the other party agrees to pay such excess. Buyer may not pay charges and fees expressly prohibited by FHA, VA, Texas Veteran's Housing Assistance Program or other governmental loan program regulations.

The seller's typical expenses are listed in 12A(1) and the buyer's in 12A(2). The parties can agree to shift any of these expenses by going to paragraph 11 and setting down their agreement.

The following paragraphs are self-explanatory. Please read them carefully. If the parties want to alter any of the wording, competent legal advice should be sought.

Figure 7.8 TREC 20-6 Paragraphs 13, 14, and 15

13. PRORATIONS: Taxes for the current year, interest, maintenance fees, assessments, dues and rents will be prorated through the Closing Date. If taxes for the current year vary from the amount prorated at closing, the parties shall adjust the prorations when tax statements for the current year are available. If taxes are not paid at or prior to closing, Buyer shall pay taxes for the current year.

14. CASUALTY LOSS: If any part of the Property is damaged or destroyed by fire or other casualty after the effective date of this contract, Seller shall restore the Property to its previous condition as soon as reasonably possible, but in any event by the Closing Date. If Seller fails to do so due to factors beyond Seller's control, Buyer may (a) terminate this contract and the earnest money will be refunded to Buyer (b) extend the time for performance up to 15 days and the Closing Date will be extended as necessary or (c) accept the Property in its damaged condition with an assignment of insurance proceeds and receive credit from Seller at closing in the amount of the deductible under the insurance policy. Seller's obligations under this paragraph are independent of any obligations of Seller under Paragraph 7.

15. DEFAULT: If Buyer fails to comply with this contract, Buyer will be in default, and Seller may (a) enforce specific performance, seek such other relief as may be provided by law, or both, or (b) terminate this contract and receive the earnest money as liquidated damages, thereby releasing both parties from this contract. If, due to factors beyond Seller's control, Seller fails within the time allowed to make any non-casualty repairs or deliver the Commitment, or survey, if required of Seller, Buyer may (a) extend the time for performance up to 15 days and the Closing Date will be extended as necessary or (b) terminate this contract as the sole remedy and receive the earnest money. If Seller fails to comply with this contract for any other reason, Seller will be in default and Buyer may (a) enforce specific performance, seek such other relief as may be provided by law, or both, or (b) terminate this contract and receive the earnest money, thereby releasing both parties from this contract.

Mediation

Please carefully read the paragraph that follows relating to dispute resolution.

Figure 7.9 TREC 20-6 Paragraph 16

16. MEDIATION: It is the policy of the State of Texas to encourage resolution of disputes through alternative dispute resolution procedures such as mediation. Any dispute between Seller and Buyer related to this contract which is not resolved through informal discussion ❏ will ❏ will not be submitted to a mutually acceptable mediation service or provider. The parties to the mediation shall bear the mediation costs equally. This paragraph does not preclude a party from seeking equitable relief from a court of competent jurisdiction.

The parties are advised and encouraged to submit to mediation disputes that cannot be resolved through informal discussion.

Under the provisions of the Texas statute relating to alternative dispute resolution, only a judge has been given authority to compel parties to mediation. License holders can encourage parties to submit disputes to mediation by pointing out the benefits, but they cannot compel. License holders should be familiar with the process, and should be able to explain what it is, and is not, to buyer and seller customers and clients.

In 1987, by the passage of Senate Bill 1436, the Texas Legislature enacted the Dispute Resolution Act.

THE STATUTORY PROVISIONS
SUBCHAPTER B.
ALTERNATIVE DISPUTE RESOLUTION PROCEDURES

Sec. 154.021. REFERRAL OF PENDING DISPUTES FOR ALTERNATIVE DISPUTE RESOLUTION PROCEDURE. (a) A court may, on its own motion or the motion of a party, refer a pending dispute for resolution by an alternative dispute resolution procedure including:

(1) an alternative dispute resolution system established under Chapter 26, Acts of the 68th Legislature, Regular Session, 1983 (Article 2372aa, Vernon's Texas Civil Statutes);

(2) a dispute resolution organization; or

(3) a nonjudicial and informally conducted forum for the voluntary settlement of citizens' disputes through the intervention of an impartial third party, including those alternative dispute resolution procedures described under this subchapter.

(b) The court shall confer with the parties in the determination of the most appropriate alternative dispute resolution procedure.

Sec. 154.022. NOTIFICATION AND OBJECTION. (a) If a court determines that a pending dispute is appropriate for referral under Section 154.021, the court shall notify the parties of its determination.

(b) Any party may, within 10 days after receiving the notice under Subsection (a), file a written objection to the referral.

(c) If the court finds that there is a reasonable basis for an objection filed under Subsection (b), the court may not refer the dispute under Section §154.021.

Sec. 154.023. MEDIATION

(a) Mediation is a forum in which an impartial person, the mediator, facilitates communication between parties to promote reconciliation, settlement, or understanding among them.

(b) A mediator may not impose his own judgment on the issues for that of the parties.

The Mediation Process

Mediation might be defined as a process through which two or more parties to a dispute voluntarily meet and attempt to find a mutually agreeable settlement with the assistance of a neutral third party, a mediator. The mediator *does not:*

- render decisions,
- offer advice,
- pass judgment, or
- resolve the dispute.

The mediator *does:*

- facilitate communication between the parties,
- remain impartial, and
- establish the ground rules for the mediation.

On the day of mediation the parties may bring any information that will help explain their respective positions. However, it is important to remember that mediation is an informal process with no formal rules of evidence, disposition, or witnesses. The mediation meeting is privileged and confidential. Under Texas statute the mediator or any party to the mediation is prohibited from telling the court anything said during the mediation. The most a mediator may report to the court is that the case did or did not settle.

The four most frequently cited advantages of mediation are

1. Low cost
2. Much quicker than litigation
3. Privacy (everything that happens or is said in court is public)
4. Offers opportunity for a *WIN-WIN*

The cost of mediation is shared equally by the parties and can range from a few hundred dollars to $1,500 or more. The fee will be determined by the mediator and will vary, depending on the complexity of the issues, the experience of the mediator, the complexity of the case, and the time involved.

In real estate what type of disputes can be mediated? Almost any dispute between buyers and sellers, landlords and tenants, and brokers and clients can and, in the interest of all parties concerned, should be mediated. The only disputes that cannot and should not be mediated are those that include a possible charge or allegation of criminal misconduct.

When the parties reach a point of agreement, the mediation moves to the final stage of the process, in which the parties set down, or memorialize, the essential terms of their agreement. When signed by each party, the parties are bound to fulfill the terms of their agreement just as they would be bound by any other contract into which they might enter.

Other Provisions

Figure 7.10 TREC 20-6 Paragraph 17

17. ATTORNEY'S FEES: The prevailing party in any legal proceeding related to this contract is entitled to recover reasonable attorney's fees and all costs of such proceeding incurred by the prevailing party.

The attorney's fee wording is straightforward and common to most real estate related agreements. It appears that the committee and TREC intended for the wording to include license holders who might become a party in a legal proceeding brought under or with respect to the subject transaction.

Figure 7.11 TREC 20-6 Paragraph 18

18. ESCROW: The escrow agent is not (a) a party to this contract and does not have liability for the performance or nonperformance of any party to this contract, (b) liable for interest on the earnest money and (c) liable for the loss of any earnest money caused by the failure of any financial institution in which the earnest money has been deposited unless the financial institution is acting as escrow agent. At closing, the earnest money must be applied first to any cash down payment, then to Buyer's Expenses and any excess refunded to Buyer. If both parties make written demand for the earnest money, escrow agent may require payment of unpaid expenses incurred on behalf of the parties and a written release of liability of escrow agent from all parties. If one party makes written demand for the earnest money, escrow agent shall give notice of the demand by providing to the other party a copy of the demand. If escrow agent does not receive written objection to the demand from the other party within 30 days after notice to the other party, escrow agent may disburse the earnest money to the party making demand reduced by the amount of unpaid expenses incurred on behalf of the party receiving the earnest money and escrow agent may pay the same to the creditors. If escrow agent complies with the provisions of this paragraph, each party hereby releases escrow agent from all adverse claims related to the disbursal of the earnest money. Escrow agent's notice to the other party will be effective when deposited in the U. S. Mail, postage prepaid, certified mail, return receipt requested, addressed to the other party at such party's address shown below. Notice of objection to the demand will be deemed effective upon receipt by escrow agent.

The TREC-promulgated contracts have an interesting provision beginning with the fifth word of line 9 in paragraph 18. The parties give the escrow agent the ability to, after due notice, release the earnest money to a party making a written demand for it. The parties agree to release the escrow agent from all adverse claims related to the disbursal of the earnest money when the detailed procedure is followed.

Figure 7.12 TREC 20-6 Paragraph 19

19. REPRESENTATIONS: Seller represents that as of the Closing Date (a) there will be no liens, assessments, or security interests against the Property which will not be satisfied out of the sales proceeds unless securing payment of any loans assumed by Buyer and (b) assumed loans will not be in default. If any representation of Seller in this contract is untrue on the Closing Date, Buyer may terminate this contract and the earnest money will be refunded to Buyer.

Sellers should note that all representations made in the agreement transfer to the warranty deed and survive closing. This is a good reason to keep the seller's disclosure notice addressed by section 5.008 of the property code separate from the contract.

Figure 7.13 TREC 20-6 Paragraph 20

20. FEDERAL TAX REQUIREMENTS: If Seller is a foreign "person," as defined by applicable law, or if Seller fails to deliver an affidavit to Buyer that Seller is not a "foreign person," then Buyer shall withhold from the sales proceeds an amount sufficient to comply with applicable tax law and deliver the same to the Internal Revenue Service together with appropriate tax forms. Internal Revenue Service regulations require filing written reports if currency in excess of specified amounts is received in the transaction.

When closing takes place at a title company, the escrow agent makes certain that IRS regulations are followed. The parties should read the paragraph and seek answers to their questions from qualified sources.

Notices

Figure 7.14 TREC 20-6 Paragraph 21

21. NOTICES: All notices from one party to the other must be in writing and are effective when mailed to, hand-delivered at, or transmitted by facsimile as follows:

To Buyer at:	**To Seller at:**
______________________	______________________
______________________	______________________
______________________	______________________
Telephone:(____) ______________	Telephone:(____) ______________
Facsimile:(____) ______________	Facsimile:(____) ______________

Ask the buyer and seller where notices are to be mailed, delivered, or transmitted by facsimile machine. Texas courts will require validation of a contract evidenced by facsimile signatures. It is best to obtain the original signature of each of the parties at the signature lines.

Please be aware that the contract specifies that notices are effective when delivered to the buyer or the seller. A notice given to a principal's agent may constitute an effective delivery to the buyer or seller. This is known as **imputed notice.** It is presumed that tendering money or notifying one's agent is the same as notifying the person directly. **Be careful here!**

If the buyer is a customer rather than a client, the buyer has no agent. Delivery of the notice to a co-op agent, acting as a subagent, does not constitute delivery of the notice to the buyer. Remember that the subagent works for and represents the seller. When a transaction involves both a seller's agent and a buyer's agent, notifying a client's agent will generally be construed as giving constructive or imputed notice to the client.

The list that follows identifies some of the notices and documents identified in the contract that may need to be delivered.

- Notice of termination during the option period
- Homeowner's association resale certificate
- Financial documentation of buyer as identified in paragraph 4E
- Title commitment
- Survey
- Lender required repairs
- Demand for release of earnest money deposit

Agreement of Parties

Figure 7.15 TREC 20-6 Paragraph 22

22. AGREEMENT OF PARTIES: This contract contains the entire agreement of the parties and cannot be changed except by their written agreement. Addenda which are a part of this contract are (check all applicable boxes):

- ❑ Third Party Financing Condition Addendum
- ❑ Seller Financing Addendum
- ❑ Buyer's Temporary Residential Lease
- ❑ Seller's Temporary Residential Lease
- ❑ Addendum for Sale of Other Property by Buyer
- ❑ Addendum for "Back-Up" Contract
- ❑ Addendum for Seller's Disclosure of Information on Lead-based Paint and Lead-based Paint Hazards as Required by Federal Law
- ❑ Loan Assumption Addendum
- ❑ Addendum for Property Subject to Mandatory Membership in an Owners' Association
- ❑ Environmental Assessment, Threatened or Endangered Species and Wetlands Addendum
- ❑ Addendum for Coastal Area Property
- ❑ Addendum for Property Located Seaward of the Gulf Intracoastal Waterway
- ❑ Addendum for Release of Liability on Assumption of FHA, VA, or Conventional Loan/Restoration of Seller's Entitlement for VA Guaranteed Loan

❑ Other (list): ______________________________

____

Any addenda that are to be a part of the agreement must be identified in the agreement. TREC has made it very easy for the parties and the agents to make certain that all addenda are listed. Failure to list or reference an addendum in the agreement can cause serious problems. If it is not referenced in the contract, a court is not likely to accept the addendum in question as a part of the agreement.

Do not list:

- Seller's disclosure notice
- Information about brokerage services
- TAR Form-027: "Notification of Intermediary Relationship"

Termination Option

Figure 7.16 TREC 20-6 Paragraph 23

23. TERMINATION OPTION: This paragraph will be a part of this contract ONLY if both blanks are filled in and Buyer has paid the Option Fee. Buyer has paid Seller $_______________ (Option Fee) for the unrestricted right to terminate this contract by giving notice of termination to Seller within _________ days after the effective date of this contract. If Buyer gives notice of termination within the time specified, the Option Fee will not be refunded, however, any earnest money will be refunded to Buyer. The Option Fee ❑will ❑will not be credited to the Sales Price at closing. For the purposes of this paragraph, time is of the essence; strict compliance with the time for performance stated herein is required.

This is perhaps the most misunderstood paragraph of the contract. Please note:

1. There is no option until the buyer has paid money to the seller. The word "has" is past tense not future tense. When the seller accepts the terms and the option fee, the seller should execute the agreement and the receipt for the option fee at the top of the last page of the form.

Figure 7.17 TREC 20-6 Receipt

SELLER'S RECEIPT

Receipt of $_______________ (Option Fee) in the form of ____________________ is acknowledged.

______________________________ ______________________________
Seller Date

2. Time is of the essence; therefore, a specific number of days must be defined and the right will end at midnight on the last day of the option period. The first day of the option is the day **after** the effective date of the contract.

3. The right to terminate is an unrestricted right. The buyer may terminate for any reason and has no obligation to give a reason.
4. At the agreement of the parties, the option fee may be credited against the sales price if so indicated by the parties. Failure to make an election by checking one of the boxes creates confusion.
5. To exercise the unrestricted right to terminate, the buyer must deliver the promulgated notice that follows to the seller prior to expiration of the option period. Failure to deliver the notice means that the buyer is obligated to close the transaction according to the terms of the contract.

Figure 7.18 TREC 38.1

10-29-01

EQUAL HOUSING OPPORTUNITY

PROMULGATED BY THE TEXAS REAL ESTATE COMMISSION (TREC)

NOTICE OF TERMINATION OF CONTRACT

To: Seller(s)

In accordance with the unrestricted right of Buyer to terminate the contract between

____

as Seller and ____

as Buyer dated __________________, 20____ for the Property located at ___________

____,

Buyer notifies Seller that the contract is terminated.

Buyer	Date	Buyer	Date

This form has been approved by the Texas Real Estate Commission for use with similarly approved or promulgated contract forms. Such approval relates to this form only. TREC forms are intended for use only by trained real estate licensees. No representation is made as to the legal validity or adequacy of any provision in any specific transactions. It is not suitable for complex transactions. Texas Real Estate Commission, P.O. Box 12188, Austin, TX 78711-2188, 1-800-250-8732 or (512) 459-6544 (http://www.trec.state.tx.us) TREC No. 38-1. This form replaces TREC No. 38-0.

01A

Finalizing the Agreement

When in doubt, consult an expert before signing.

Figure 7.19 TREC 20-6 Paragraph 24

24. CONSULT AN ATTORNEY: Real estate licensees cannot give legal advice. READ THIS CONTRACT CAREFULLY. If you do not understand the effect of this contract, consult an attorney BEFORE signing.

Buyer's Attorney is:______________________	Seller's Attorney is:______________________
______________________	______________________
Telephone: (____)______________	Telephone: (____)______________
Facsimile: (____)______________	Facsimile: (____)______________

EXECUTED the _______day of ________________________, 20____ (EFFECTIVE DATE). (BROKER: FILL IN THE DATE OF FINAL ACCEPTANCE.)

______________________ Buyer	______________________ Seller
______________________ Buyer	______________________ Seller

The form of this contract has been approved by the Texas Real Estate Commission. TREC forms are intended for use only by trained real estate licensees. No representation is made as to the legal validity or adequacy of any provision in any specific transacti ons. It is not suitable for complex transactions.Texas Real Estate Commission, P.O. Box 12188, Austin, TX 78711-2188, 1-800-250-8732 or (512) 459-6544 (http://www.trec.state.tx.us) TREC NO. 20-5. This form replaces TREC NO. 20-4.

Please note that it is the broker's duty to fill in the effective date when the last party has signed **and** the other party has been notified of the acceptance. When the contract form states "Executed the _____ day of ______ 20___," it is identifying the date there has been an offer, acceptance, and notification of the acceptance of the offer. In legal terminology, a fully executed contract is one that has been completed and gone to closing.

The agent should deposit the contract and earnest money, if any, to the escrow agent immediately and obtain a receipted copy of the contract for all affected parties.

Figure 7.20 TREC 20-6 Receipt

RECEIPT

Receipt of ❑ Contract and ❑ $__________ Earnest Money in the form of ______________
is acknowledged.
Escrow Agent: ______________________________ Date: ______________________

By: ______________________________

______________________________ Telephone (_____) ______________
Address

______________________________ Facsimile: (_____) ______________
City State Zip

Note that the receipt is issued by the escrow agent, not the listing or selling license holder. Some escrow agents may choose to use their own receipt form for the contract and the earnest money instead of the form at the end of the contract form. Brokers and salespersons are reminded that TREC rules require that the license holder deposit the earnest money with the escrow agent by the close of business on the second business day after the execution of the contract by the principals. The only exception occurs when the principals agree that a deposit may be delayed and a different time is expressly defined in paragraph 11 of the contract [Rule 535.159 (I)].

Once the contract has been finalized, it can only be altered by the written agreement of all parties. To accomplish a desired change, the parties may use the TREC-promulgated form that follows or consult their attorney.

Figure 7.21 TREC 39-4

PROMULGATED BY THE TEXAS REAL ESTATE COMMISSION (TREC) 01-06-03

EQUAL HOUSING OPPORTUNITY

AMENDMENT

TO CONTRACT CONCERNING THE PROPERTY AT

____

(Street Address and City)

Seller and Buyer amend the contract as follows: (check each applicable box)

☐(1) The Sales Price in Paragraph 3 of the contract is:
A. Cash portion of Sales Price payable by Buyer at closing ....$__________
B. Sum of financing described in the contract..$__________
C. Sales Price (Sum of A and B) ....$__________

☐(2) In addition to any repairs and treatments otherwise required by the contract, Seller, at Seller's expense, shall complete the following repairs and treatments:

☐(3) The Option Fee ☐ will ☐ will not be credited to the Sales Price.

☐(4) The date in Paragraph 9 of the contract is changed to ______________________, 20______.

☐(5) The amount in Paragraph 12A(1)(b) of the contract is changed to $ ______________________.

☐(6) The cost of lender required repairs and treatment, as itemized on the attached list, will be paid as follows: $ ____________________ by Seller; $ ____________________ by Buyer.

☐(7) Buyer has paid Seller an additional non-refundable Option Fee of $ ________________ for an extension of the unrestricted right to terminate the contract on or before ______________________ , 20_______. This additional Option Fee ☐ will ☐ will not be credited to the Sales Price.

☐(8) Upon final acceptance of this Amendment, Buyer waives the unrestricted right to terminate the contract for which the Option Fee was paid.

☐(9) **Other Modifications**: (Insert only factual statements and business details applicable to this sale.)

EXECUTED the__________day of ____________________, 20 ____ (BROKER: FILL IN THE DATE OF FINAL ACCEPTANCE).

______________________	______________________
Buyer	Seller
______________________	______________________
Buyer	Seller

This form has been approved by the Texas Real Estate Commission for use with similarly approved or promulgated contract forms. Such approval relates to this form only. TREC forms are intended for use only by trained real estate licensees. No representation is made as to the legal validity or adequacy of any provision in any specific transactions. It is not suitable for complex transactions. Texas Real Estate Commission, P.O. Box 12188, Austin, TX 78711-2188, 1-800-250-8732 or (512) 459-6544 (http://www.trec.state.tx.us) TREC No. 39-4. This form replaces TREC No. 39-3.

Over the period of time between the execution of the contract, as identified by the effective date entered by the broker, and the closing of the transaction, the contract may be amended any number of times by the mutual agreement of the parties. Please note that, once the agreement has been created, neither party is under any obligation to renegotiate any provision of it. One can always ask, but that does not obligate the other party to say yes.

The following two addenda do not really fit with the discussion of any particular paragraph or provision of the basic contract. Although recently revised, both were created at the time when the Texas real estate markets were very different. In a "seller's market," when demand for available properties exceeded available supply, the first addendum, Addendum for Sale of Other Property by Buyer (TREC 10-4), was created to enter into a contract of purchase but to give the buyer an out if the buyer's current property did not sell. From the seller's perspective, it is not a particularly good idea to take the property off the market while waiting for the buyer's property to sell. While the addendum permits the seller to continue to offer the property and to consider other offers, the reality of the marketplace is that license holders working with buyers show available properties first and only show pending properties with contingencies as a last resort. If you do use the addendum, be sure to give careful attention to the time frames. The wording in the addendum states that "time is of the essence" and demands strict compliance with the times set down. Do not confuse this addendum with the statement in paragraph 9 that addresses the seller's right to continue to show the property for possible consideration of back-up offers.

Figure 7.22 TREC 10-4

10-29-01

PROMULGATED BY THE TEXAS REAL ESTATE COMMISSION (TREC)

EQUAL HOUSING OPPORTUNITY

ADDENDUM FOR
SALE OF OTHER PROPERTY BY BUYER

TO CONTRACT CONCERNING THE PROPERTY AT

____

(Street Address and City)

A. The contract is contingent upon Buyer's receipt of the proceeds from the sale of Buyer's property at ____ (Address) by 5:00 p.m. on ______________________________, 20______ (the Contingency). If the Contingency is not satisfied or waived by Buyer by the above time and date, the contract will terminate automatically and the earnest money will be refunded to Buyer.
NOTICE: The date inserted in this Paragraph should be no later than the date inserted in Paragraph 9 of the contract.

B. If Seller accepts a written offer to sell the Property, Seller shall notify Buyer (1) of such acceptance **AND** (2) that Seller requires Buyer to waive the Contingency. Buyer must waive the Contingency by 5:00 p.m. on the _________________day after delivery of Seller's notice to Buyer; otherwise the contract will terminate automatically and the earnest money will be refunded to Buyer.

C. Buyer may waive the Contingency only by notifying Seller of the waiver and depositing $___________ with escrow agent as additional earnest money. All notices must be in writing and are effective when delivered in accordance with the contract.

D. If Buyer waives the Contingency and Buyer's loan or assumption approval is conditioned upon the sale of Buyer's property described in Paragraph A above, Buyer will be in default if such condition is not satisfied by the date provided for in the contract. If such default occurs, Seller may exercise the remedies specified in Paragraph 15 of the contract. If Buyer fails to obtain loan or assumption approval for any other reason, the provisions of the contract remain in effect.

E. For purposes of this Addendum time is of the essence; strict compliance with the times for performance stated herein is required.

______________________ Buyer	______________________ Seller
______________________ Buyer	______________________ Seller

This form has been approved by the Texas Real Estate Commission for use with similarly approved or promulgated contract forms. Such approval relates to this form only. TREC forms are intended for use only by trained real estate licensees. No representation is made as to the legal validity or adequacy of any provision in any specific transactions. It is not suitable for complex transactions. Texas Real Estate Commission, P.O. Box 12188, Austin, TX 78711-2188, 1-800-250-8732 or (512) 459-6544 (http://www.trec.state.tx.us) TREC No. 10-4. This form replaces TREC No. 10-3.

01A

The second addendum, Addendum for "Back-Up" Contract, is designed to be used when a desired property is under contract with another buyer. The second buyer can create an agreement of purchase in which the buyer is entitled to purchase the property only if the existing contract does not close. It creates a contingency for the seller in which it is agreed that "I'll sell you my property, if the existing contract does not close." Again one must give careful attention to the time frames established by the addendum. For the purpose of the addendum, "time is of the essence." Upon execution of a back-up contract, earnest money is deposited with the named title company and the option fee is paid to the seller.

The form is designed to create only one back-up contract. For multiple back-up contracts, the parties will need to consult legal counsel.

Figure 7.23 TREC 11-5

PROMULGATED BY THE TEXAS REAL ESTATE COMMISSION (TREC) 02-09-2004

EQUAL HOUSING OPPORTUNITY

ADDENDUM FOR "BACK-UP" CONTRACT

TO CONTRACT CONCERNING THE PROPERTY AT

____
(Street Address and City)

A. The Contract to which this Addendum is attached (the Back-Up Contract) is binding upon execution by the parties, and the earnest money and any Option Fee must be paid as provided in the Back-Up Contract. The Back-Up Contract is contingent upon the termination of a previous contract (the First Contract) between Seller and ______________________________________, dated __________________________, 20______, for the sale of Property. Except as provided by this Addendum, neither party is required to perform under the Back-Up Contract while it is contingent upon the First Contract.

B. If the First Contract terminates on or before 5:00 p.m. on __________________________, ________ (the Contingency Date), the Back-Up Contract will no longer be contingent upon the termination of the First Contract. Seller must notify Buyer immediately of the termination of the First Contract. For purposes of performance, the effective date of the Back-Up Contract automatically changes to the date Buyer receives notice of termination of the First Contract or the Contingency Date, whichever is earlier (Amended Effective Date).

C. If the First Contract does not terminate by the Contingency Date, the Back-Up Contract terminates and the earnest money will be refunded to Buyer.

D. An amendment or modification of the First Contract will not terminate the First Contract.

E. If Buyer has the unrestricted right to terminate the Back-Up Contract, the time for giving notice of termination begins on the effective date of the Back-Up Contract, continues after the Amended Effective Date and ends upon the expiration of Buyer's unrestricted right to terminate the Back-Up Contract.

F. For purposes of this Addendum, time is of the essence. Strict compliance with the times for performance stated herein is required.

______________________ Buyer	______________________ Seller
______________________ Buyer	______________________ Seller

This form has been approved by the Texas Real Estate Commission for use with similarly approved or promulgated contract forms. Such approval relates to this form only. TREC forms are intended for use only by trained real estate licensees. No representation is made as to the legal validity or adequacy of any provision in any specific transactions. It is not suitable for complex transactions. Texas Real Estate Commission, P.O. Box 12188, Austin, TX 78711-2188, 1-800-250-8732 or (512) 459-6544 (http://www.trec.state.tx.us) TREC No. 11-5. This form replaces TREC No. 11-4.

Summary

When completing contract forms, make certain to correctly complete all required blanks. In a blank in the main body of the contract form that is not applicable, insert N/A. Remember, some blanks need the word "none." There is a different meaning interpreted between "none" and "not applicable." For blanks that follow a box you have not checked, do nothing.

If the agreement went through a countering process, have all changes been properly initialed by each of the parties? Did you date the contract when the buyer was notified of the seller's written acceptance of the buyer's written offer or, if a counteroffer occurred, when the seller was notified of the buyer's written (initialed the changes) acceptance of the seller's written counteroffer? Remember that it is not a counteroffer if the seller has not responded with a signature and initials to any changes or modifications to the buyer's original offer.

CHAPTER 7

REVIEW QUESTIONS

1. Who determines the amount of liquidated damages?

   A. A court
   B. The parties
   C. The title company
   D. The agent

2. Who is responsible for deciding when and to whom earnest money is released?

   A. The escrow officer
   B. The seller
   C. The buyer
   D. The parties

3. What type of deed is to be delivered by the seller to the buyer at closing?

   A. Quitclaim
   B. Special warranty
   C. Deed of trust
   D. General warranty

4. Loan fees include all of the following except

   A. commitment.
   B. buy-down.
   C. funding fee.
   D. discount.

5. If the parties agree to mediation, they are precluded from seeking equitable relief from the court.

   A. True
   B. False

6. Which of the following is not a proper way to deliver a Notice from one party to another according to the provisions of the promulgated contract form?

   A. U.S. mail
   B. Facsimile
   C. Hand-delivered
   D. E-mail

7. The agent should always write in the "Seller's Disclosure of Property Condition" as a listed addendum after checking the boxes for the various TREC-promulgated addenda that have been used to create the agreement.

   A. True
   B. False

8. How will the taxes for the current year be prorated at closing?

   A. To the day of closing
   B. Through the day of closing
   C. Up to the day of closing
   D. Through the day after closing

9. The seller's obligations in the casualty loss paragraph (14) are included in the obligations of the seller in the property condition paragraph (7).

   A. True
   B. False

10. According to the printed TREC-promulgated form, who is to pay for the copies of easements and restrictions?

    A. The buyer
    B. The seller
    C. The agent
    D. The lender

Chapter 8

The Other Promulgated Contracts and Other Forms

Key Terms

C C & R
completed construction
condominium documents
construction document
incomplete construction
mineral interest
R-factor
rollback tax
royalty
surface lease
timber interest
water rights

Now that we are thoroughly familiar with the provisions of the most frequently used promulgated form (20-6) and the promulgated addenda that may be attached to it, we focus our attention on the other promulgated forms.

New Home Contracts

In Chapter 1, we learned that property owners can instruct the license holders to use a form preferred by the owner rather than a TREC-promulgated form. Most builders will dictate that you use a contract form provided by them. New homes may be sold using one of two TREC forms when the builder does not specify. The two TREC new home forms address two types of new homes:

1. **completed construction** (usually spec homes) (24-5) and
2. **incomplete construction** (23-5).

Each will have different considerations and issues to be addressed, particularly in paragraphs 2 and 7: Property and Property Condition.

The reader is advised to check the TREC Web site at *www.trec.state.tx.us* for current versions before using a new home contract form to structure a transaction.

Federal law requires that builders reveal to the buyer the **R-factors** of the insulation installed in the new home. They may be included in the contract or in an addendum attached to the contract. The TREC-promulgated contracts address them in the property condition paragraph. Other topics that should be addressed include:

- construction documents,
- cost adjustments,
- buyer selections,
- completion dates,
- possible delays, and
- warranties.

It is always prudent for a buyer to seek legal counsel before signing a builders contract or before agreeing to the provisions of a contract that addresses incomplete construction. An already completed home in the builder's inventory should be treated in the same manner as a previously occupied resale home with regard to inspections and evaluations by competent professionals. A buyer should never assume that everything in a new home is properly installed and working properly. A license holder who fails to advise the client to seek the counsel of other professionals is not demonstrating minimum standards of care required by the TREC rules and the fiduciary duties owed to clients.

Farm and Ranch

The farm and ranch form 25-4 calls for a metes-and-bounds legal description rather than reference to a recorded plat. When selling a farm or ranch property, the parties must address issues and items that are not considerations in the other types of properties addressed by TREC-promulgated forms. These elements include:

- crops,
- equipment,
- mineral interests,
- royalties,
- timber interests,
- mineral leases,
- surface leases,
- other restrictions and exceptions already existing or to be created,

- water rights, and
- rights and obligations of applicable government programs and cooperative or association memberships.

A unique feature of the contract is the provision in paragraph 3 that allows for an adjustment to the sales price based on the results of the survey that may be done after the effective date of the contract. The contract caps the adjustment at 10 percent of the sales price and gives either party the ability to terminate the agreement if the needed adjustment exceeds that amount.

Paragraph 13 discusses Rollback Taxes that may be assessed if the sale or the buyer use of the property changes the property's designation as a property entitled to benefit from the Texas agricultural exemption and reduced ad valorem taxes. The obligations imposed by the parties on this matter in the contract will survive closing.

Condominium

The current version of the contract to use for a resale transaction was adopted at the same time as the 1–4 family resale contract. It is parallel to the 20-6 with the exception of the unique provisions relating solely to the condominium transactions and the statutory requirements of the Texas Uniform Condominium Act, chapters 81 and 82 of the Texas Property Code.

A study of paragraph 2 will reveal the primary differences between the condominium form and the one that you have studied so thoroughly. Another significant difference will be found in paragraph 6 where the survey provisions have been deleted. Calling for a survey in a condominium transaction is uncommon.

The Condominium Contract and the Condominium Resale Certificate are available at the TREC Web site for your review and study.

Unimproved Property

Due to the lack of fixtures and accessories, paragraph 2 of the unimproved property form is considerably less involved and complicated than the other five forms. A buyer of an unimproved building lot must carefully research zoning ordinances, restrictive covenants, availability of utilities, access, and other matters that will affect the suitability of the building lot for the buyer's intended use of it. An adequate termination option should be purchased to provide a suitable amount of time to make absolutely certain that the property is suitable.

Noncontract Forms

The forms that follow are published by TREC to address important issues and concerns but are not a part of any contractual agreement between buyer and seller.

The promulgated **"Consumer Information Form,"** TREC 1-1, is to be prominently displayed in the office of every licensed inspector and broker in Texas. Residential brokers must also display the HUD fair housing poster with the equal housing opportunity logo. The license of the designated broker and all license holders working with the firm must also be prominently displayed. All of these might best be displayed in one large locking window case in the lobby of the office.

The optional "Notice Concerning Recognized Hazards," TREC OP-1, warns the consumer that injury or property loss can result from a variety of improperly installed or malfunctioning mechanical equipment. It is not a promulgated for mandatory use form, but rather a convenient tool for the license holder to use to assist the parties in making informed decisions.

Chapter 1101.557, 1101.558, 1101.559, 1101.560, and 1101.561 of the license law addresses agency relationships between license holders and the public. One provision requires that a license holder, at the first face-to-face meeting, provide the prospect with **"Information About Brokerage Services,"** TREC OP-K. A face-to-face meeting is defined as the first meeting at which substantive discussion about a particular property or a prospect's ability to buy or lease occurs. The notice must be no smaller than 10-point type.

The form that follows, **"Notice to Prospective Buyer,"** TREC OP-C, is published by TREC for voluntary use by license holders. It is not a TREC or a statutory requirement that the person receiving it sign it. It is not an addendum to the contract.

The Texas licensing law requires that a license holder notify every buyer, prior to the closing of a sale, that the abstract should be examined by an attorney of the buyer's selection or that the buyer should be furnished with or obtain a policy of title insurance. When the agreement of purchase between the seller and the buyer has been reduced to writing by using one of the TREC-promulgated contract forms, this notice requirement has been fulfilled by the wording of the first in the group of notice in paragraph 6 of the contract.

When the contract is drawn by a party's attorney, the TREC OP-C form may be used to give the notice. The form is not promulgated. It is published for voluntary use by the license holder to make it easier to comply with the law. Failure to deliver this notice when required can lead to loss of the broker's ability to collect a brokerage fee under the provisions of Section 20 of the TRELA and possible disciplinary action by TREC under Section 15 of the TRELA.

Remember that before you attempt to use any TREC-promulgated contract and addendum or any voluntary-use form, carefully read it and understand its content. Help the parties identify the business details that need to be addressed and then carefully fill in the appropriate blanks, check the appropriate boxes, and enter N/A where necessary.

Encourage each party to carefully read the agreement, and advise that competent legal counsel should be consulted if unusual matters are present. It is a good practice to always read paragraph 24 to a party before the contract is signed. Encouraging people to seek legal advice is an effective way to reduce your risk of being sued. Stick to defining the business details. Let attorneys address the legal rights and remedies.

Although the license holder does not complete the promulgated resale certificates, he/she should be thoroughly familiar with the content of both 32-0 and 37-1 found on pages 146–148.

Figure 8.1 Consumer Information Form 1-1

THIS FIRM IS

LICENSED AND REGULATED

BY THE

TEXAS REAL ESTATE

COMMISSION (TREC)

TREC ADMINISTERS TWO RECOVERY FUNDS

WHICH MAY BE USED TO SATISFY JUDGMENTS

AGAINST INSPECTORS AND REAL ESTATE

LICENSEES INVOLVING A VIOLATION OF THE LAW.

COMPLAINTS OR INQUIRIES SHOULD

BE DIRECTED TO

TEXAS REAL ESTATE COMMISSION
P.O. BOX 12188
AUSTIN, TEXAS 78711-2188

(512) 465-3960

Figure 8.2 TREC OP-C

APPROVED BY THE TEXAS REAL ESTATE COMMISSION

NOTICE TO PROSPECTIVE BUYER

As required by law, I advise you to have the abstract covering the property known as ______________________________ ______________________________ (Address) examined by an attorney of your own selection OR you should be furnished with or obtain a policy of title insurance.

If the property is situated in a Utility District, Chapter 49 of the Texas Water Code requires you to sign and acknowledge the statutory notice from the seller of the property relating to the tax rate, bonded indebtedness or standby fee of the District.

DATED: ______________________ , __________ .

____
Brokerage Company Name

____
Broker or Sales Associate

I have received a copy of this **NOTICE TO PROSPECTIVE BUYER.**

____
Prospective Buyer

____
Prospective Buyer

This form has been approved by the Texas Real Estate Commission (TREC) for use when a contract of sale has not been promulgated by TREC. The form should be presented before an offer to purchase is signed by the prospective buyer. Texas Real Estate Commission, P.O. Box 12188, Austin, Texas 78711-2188, 1-800-250-8732 or (512) 459-6544 (http://www.trec.state.tx.us). TREC Notice to Prospective Buyer.(12/99) OP-C replaces MA-C.

01A TREC NO. OP-C

Figure 8.3 TREC 32-0

CONDOMINIUM RESALE CERTIFICATE

04-18-94

PROMULGATED BY THE TEXAS REAL ESTATE COMMISSION (TREC)

EQUAL HOUSING OPPORTUNITY

Condominium Certificate concerning Condominium Unit ________, in Building ________, of ________ ________, a condominium project, located at ________ ________ (Address), City of ________, ________, County, Texas, on behalf of the condominium owners association (the Association) by the Association's governing body (the Board).

A. The Declaration ☐ does ☐ does not contain a right of first refusal or other restraint that restricts the right to transfer the Unit. If a right of first refusal or other restraint exists, see Section _____ of the Declaration.

B. The periodic common expense assessment for the Unit is $________ per ________.

C. There ☐ is ☐ is not a common expense or special assessment due and unpaid by the Seller to the Association. The total unpaid amount is $________ and is for ________.

D. Other amounts ☐ are ☐ are not payable by Seller to the Association. The total unpaid amount is $________ and is for ________.

E. Capital expenditures approved by the Association for the next 12 months are $________.

F. Reserves for capital expenditures are $________; of this amount $________ has been designated for ________.

G. The current operating budget of the Association is attached.

H. The amount of unsatisfied judgments against the Association is $________.

I. There ☐ are ☐ are not any suits pending against the Association. The nature of the suits is ________ ________.

J. The Association ☐ does ☐ does not provide insurance coverage for the benefit of unit owners as per the attached summary from the Association's insurance agent.

K. The Board ☐ has ☐ has no knowledge of alterations or improvements to the Unit or to the limited common elements assigned to the Unit or any portion of the project that violate any provision of the Declaration, by-laws or rules of the Association. Known violations are: ________ ________.

L. The Board ☐ has ☐ has not received notice from a governmental authority concerning violations of health or building codes with respect to the Unit, the limited common elements assigned to the Unit, or any other portion of the condominium project. Notices received are: ________ ________.

M. The remaining term of any leasehold estate that affects the condominium is ________ and the provisions governing an extension or renewal of the lease are: ________ ________ ________.

N. The name, mailing address and telephone number of the Association's managing agent are:

____
(Name) (Telephone Number)

____
(Mailing Address)

REQUIRED ATTACHMENTS:
1. Operating Budget
2. Insurance Summary

____
(Name of Condominium Owners Association)

NOTICE: The Certificate must be prepared no more than three months before the date it is delivered to Buyer.

By: ________

____
Title

Received: ________ 19___

____
Buyer

____
Mailing Address

____
Buyer

____
Date Phone No.

The form of this certificate has been approved by the Texas Real Estate Commission for use only with similarly approved or promulgated forms of contracts. No representation is made as to the legal validity or adequacy of any provision in any specific transactions. (04-94) TREC No. 32-0.

Figure 8.4 TREC 37-1

PROMULGATED BY THE TEXAS REAL ESTATE COMMISSION (TREC) 09-01-99

EQUAL HOUSING OPPORTUNITY

SUBDIVISION INFORMATION, INCLUDING RESALE CERTIFICATE FOR PROPERTY SUBJECT TO MANDATORY MEMBERSHIP IN AN OWNERS' ASSOCIATION
(Section 207.003, Texas Property Code)

(NOT FOR USE WITH CONDOMINIUMS)

Resale Certificate concerning the Property (including any common areas assigned to the Property) located at ______________________ (Street Address), City of ______________, ______________, County, Texas, prepared by the property owners' association (the Owners' Association).

A. The Property ❑ is ❑ is not subject to a right of first refusal or other restraint contained in the restrictions or restrictive covenants that restricts the owner's right to transfer the owner's property.

B. The current regular assessment for the Property is $______________ per ______________.

C. A special assessment for the Property due after the date the resale certificate was prepared is $______________ payable as follows ______________________.

D. The total of all amounts due and unpaid to the Owners' Association that are attributable to the Property is $ ______________ .

E. The capital expenditures approved by the Owners' Association for its current fiscal year are $ ______________.

F. The amount of reserves for capital expenditures is $______________.

G. Unsatisfied judgments against the Owners' Association total $______________.

H. There ❑ are ❑ are not any suits pending against the Owners' Association. The style and cause number of each pending suit is: ______________________
____
______________________.

I. The Owners' Association's board ❑ has actual knowledge ❑ has no actual knowledge of conditions on the Property in violation of the restrictions applying to the subdivision or the bylaws or rules of the Owners' Association. Known violations are: ______________________
____
____

J. The Owners' Association ❑ has ❑ has not received notice from any governmental authority regarding health or building code violations with respect to the Property or any common areas or common facilities owned or leased by the Owners' Association. A summary or copy of each notice is attached.

Figure 8.4 TREC 37-1 (continued)

Subdivision Information Concerning ______________________________ Page Two 09-01-99
(Address)

K. The Owners' Association's administrative transfer fee is $ ____________, payable to ______________________________.

L. The Owners' Association's managing agent is ____________________, ____________________
(Name of Agent) (Mailing Address)

____________________, ____________________, ____________________.
(Telephone Number) (Fax Number)

M. The restrictions ☐ do ☐ do not allow foreclosure of the Owners' Association's lien on the Property for failure to pay assessments.

REQUIRED ATTACHMENTS:

1. Restrictions
2. Rules
3. Bylaws
4. Current Balance Sheet
5. Current Operating Budget
6. Certificate of Insurance concerning Property and Liability Insurance for Common Areas and Facilities
7. Any Governmental Notices of Health or Housing Code Violations

NOTICE: This Subdivision Information may change at any time.

____
Name of Owners' Association

By: ______________________________

Title: ______________________________

Mailing Address: ______________________________

Date: ____________________

This form has been approved by the Texas Real Estate Commission for use only with similarly approved or promulgated contract forms. No representation is made as to the legal validity or adequacy of any provision in any specific transaction. (9-99) Texas Real Estate Commission, P.O. Box 12188, Austin, TX 78711-2188, 1-800-250-8732 or (512) 459-6544 (http://www.trec.state.tx.us) TREC No. 37-1. This form replaces TREC No. 37-0.

01A TREC No. 37-1

CHAPTER 8

REVIEW QUESTIONS

1. Rollback taxes are an issue addressed in the condominium contract promulgated by TREC.

   A. True
   B. False

2. Who will complete the promulgated resale certificate?

   A. Seller
   B. Buyer
   C. Homeowners association
   D. Listing agent

3. The "Notice to Prospective Buyer," TREC OP-C, must be used with every transaction and be included with every contract as an addendum.

   A. True
   B. False

4. Who or what need not prominently display the TREC Consumer Information Form 1-1?

   A. Real estate brokers
   B. Real estate inspectors
   C. Residential service contract companies
   D. Residential real estate brokerage firms

5. How many recovery funds are administered by TREC according to Consumer Information Form 1-1?

   A. 2
   B. 3
   C. 1
   D. 5

Chapter 9

Practice Makes Perfect

Now that we have reviewed some of the basic legal concepts, the contract and addenda forms, the provisions of the license act, and the rules of TREC, let us continue our learning experience by completing eight (8) case studies.

Every transaction is unique. It may have special considerations that may be addressed by promulgated addenda or that may require the services of a real estate attorney to structure language to address certain issues. In the case studies that follow, you have the opportunity to complete promulgated contracts and addenda for some of the more commonly encountered situations. Your instructor may provide additional information for some of the cases or have you experience the countering process. Few addresses are furnished other than the property address. You will need to provide missing addresses. Be creative. No answers for these cases are provided in Appendix B. Your instructor will have suggested answers in the Instructor's Manual prepared for use with this book. It is recommended that these case studies be completed and discussed during class.

1. Read the case information carefully.
2. Complete the forms using a pencil. When your instructor walks through the transaction with you, you can make corrections easily.
3. Be sure to put **N/A** in blanks that are not needed for the particular transaction.
4. Be sure to check all attached addenda in paragraph 22.
5. **Have fun!**

Transaction 1: 80% Conventional Fixed Rate Loan
(Using: TREC 20-6, 40-1, 36-3, 28-0, and 39-4)

John Paul Gordon and his wife, Mary Anne Gordon, want to purchase a home owned by Isabelle Gertrude Gerhard, an unmarried resident of Houston, Texas.

The property is identified as Lot 6, Block 10 in Section 1 of the Windswept Addition of Harris County, Texas. It is more commonly known as 2615 Pleasure Point Drive, Houston, Texas 77084. The property is subject to the rules and assessments of a mandatory owners' association.

The buyers have received and approved a copy of the owners' association resale certificate prior to signing the purchase agreement. The buyers are willing to pay $50 of the $100 transfer fee charged by the owners' association.

Ms. Gerhard will remove the draperies from the master bedroom prior to closing. She will leave all other items listed in paragraph 2 of the standard purchase agreement.

Although Ms. Gerhard is asking $106,000 for the property, the buyers have decided to offer $96,000. They have made loan application and expect that they can have financing approval within 25 days after the effective date of the contract. The contract is to be subject to the Gordon's financing approval. They agree to apply for an 80 percent conventional loan at 6 percent with a 15-year amortization and with no private mortgage insurance required.

To show their serious intent, the buyers deposit $10,000 earnest money with No Cloud Title Company at 1700 South Main, Houston, Texas 77001. They feel that it would be unreasonable for the seller to require that any additional earnest money be deposited.

The buyers are willing to pay for a new survey to be delivered within 20 days after the effective date of the contract and ask that the seller pay for the owner's title policy to demonstrate that the title is free of encumbrances as of the date of closing. The buyers want 5 days to review the title commitment and deed restrictions.

Prior to signing the offer to purchase, the buyers receive and review the seller's property disclosure form required by section 5.008 of the Texas Property Code.

The Gordons are willing to pay Ms. Gerhard $300 for a seven-day option to terminate period. The $300 will be credited to the sale price if they complete the transaction. By attaching the appropriate addendum, the parties agree that the buyers will have 20 days to have environmental assessments performed. Because the home was built in 1985, they have not attached the lead-based paint/hazard addendum. They do not feel that lead is an issue.

They want to close on or before the 30th day after the date of the contract and want possession to be granted at closing or the funding of their loan, whichever is later. The buyers will pay for all typical loan costs required by the lender. They will pay a 1 percent loan origination fee and do not anticipate that the lender will charge any discount points. No commitment fee or buydown will be applicable.

The property has been listed by Smooth Sales Realty Company (TREC# 7657321) and is being sold by a company that represents only buyers, Buyer's Broker Realty (TREC# 1234567). The agents obtain the correct addresses and numbers to be entered in paragraph 21 of the purchase contract. The listing broker, through the local MLS, has agreed to pay the selling broker a fee equal to 3 percent of the sale price. Both agents inform their clients of the advantages of mediation but the parties do not want to make the financial commitment to split the cost of mediation.

Five days into the option period the buyer decides to approach the seller and ask the seller to replace the defective flooring in the kitchen. The seller agrees to credit the buyers $1,400 at closing to replace the floor covering rather than become involved in choosing and installing new flooring.

Figure 9.1 TREC 20-6

PROMULGATED BY THE TEXAS REAL ESTATE COMMISSION (TREC) 01-06-03

EQUAL HOUSING OPPORTUNITY

ONE TO FOUR FAMILY RESIDENTIAL CONTRACT (RESALE)

NOTICE: Not For Use For Condominium Transactions

1. **PARTIES:** ______________________________ (Seller) agrees to sell and convey to ______________________________(Buyer) and Buyer agrees to buy from Seller the Property described below.

2. **PROPERTY:**
   A. LAND: Lot ______________,Block_____, ______________ ______________Addition, City of ____________ , ____________ County, Texas, known as ______________________________ ______________(address/zip code), or as described on attached exhibit.
   B. IMPROVEMENTS: The house, garage and all other fixtures and improvements attached to the above-described real property, including without limitation, the following permanently installed and built-in items, if any: all equipment and appliances, valances, screens, shutters, awnings, wall-to-wall carpeting, mirrors, ceiling fans, attic fans, mail boxes, television antennas and satellite dish system and equipment, heating and air-conditioning units, security and fire detection equipment, wiring, plumbing and lighting fixtures, chandeliers, water softener system, kitchen equipment, garage door openers, cleaning equipment, shrubbery, landscaping, outdoor cooking equipment, and all other property owned by Seller and attached to the above described real property.
   C. ACCESSORIES: The following described related accessories, if any: window air conditioning units, stove, fireplace screens, curtains and rods, blinds, window shades, draperies and rods, controls for satellite dish system, controls for garage door openers, entry gate controls, door keys, mailbox keys, above ground pool, swimming pool equipment and maintenance accessories, and artificial fireplace logs.
   D. EXCLUSIONS: The following improvements and accessories will be retained by Seller and excluded: ______________________________ ______________________________.

   The land, improvements and accessories are collectively referred to as the "Property".

3. **SALES PRICE:**
   A. Cash portion of Sales Price payable by Buyer at closing................. $______________
   B. Sum of all financing described below (excluding any loan funding fee or mortgage insurance premium) .... $______________
   C. Sales Price (Sum of A and B) .... $______________

4. **FINANCING:** The portion of Sales Price not payable in cash will be paid as follows: (Check applicable boxes below)
   ☐ A. THIRD PARTY FINANCING: One or more third party mortgage loans in the total amount of $______________. If the Property does not satisfy the lenders' underwriting requirements for the loan(s), this contract will terminate and the earnest money will be refunded to Buyer. (Check one box only)
      ☐ (1) This contract is subject to Buyer being approved for the financing described in the attached Third Party Financing Condition Addendum.
      ☐ (2) This contract is not subject to Buyer being approved for financing and does not involve FHA or VA financing.
   ☐ B. ASSUMPTION: The assumption of the unpaid principal balance of one or more promissory notes described in the attached TREC Loan Assumption Addendum.
   ☐ C. SELLER FINANCING: A promissory note from Buyer to Seller of $______________, bearing _______ % interest per annum, secured by vendor's and deed of trust liens, and containing the terms and conditions described in the attached TREC Seller Financing Addendum. If an owner policy of title insurance is furnished, Buyer shall furnish Seller with a mortgagee policy of title insurance.

5. **EARNEST MONEY:** Upon execution of this contract by both parties, Buyer shall deposit $__________ as earnest money with ______________________________, as escrow agent, at ______________________________ (address). Buyer shall deposit additional earnest money of $______________ with escrow agent within ________days after the effective date of this contract. If Buyer fails to deposit the earnest money as required by this contract, Buyer will be in default.

01A TREC NO. 20-6

Initialed for identification by Buyer_______ _______ and Seller________ ________

Figure 9.1 TREC 20-6 (continued)

Contract Concerning ____ Page Two 01-06-03
(Address of Property)

6. TITLE POLICY AND SURVEY:

A. TITLE POLICY: Seller shall furnish to Buyer at ❑ Seller's ❑ Buyer's expense an owner policy of title insurance (Title Policy) issued by ______________________________ (Title Company) in the amount of the Sales Price, dated at or after closing, insuring Buyer against loss under the provisions of the Title Policy, subject to the promulgated exclusions (including existing building and zoning ordinances) and the following exceptions:

(1) Restrictive covenants common to the platted subdivision in which the Property is located.
(2) The standard printed exception for standby fees, taxes and assessments.
(3) Liens created as part of the financing described in Paragraph 4.
(4) Utility easements created by the dedication deed or plat of the subdivision in which the Property is located.
(5) Reservations or exceptions otherwise permitted by this contract or as may be approved by Buyer in writing.
(6) The standard printed exception as to marital rights.
(7) The standard printed exception as to waters, tidelands, beaches, streams, and related matters.
(8) The standard printed exception as to discrepancies, conflicts, shortages in area or boundary lines, encroachments or protrusions, or overlapping improvements. Buyer, at Buyer's expense, may have the exception amended to read, "shortages in area".

B. COMMITMENT: Within 20 days after the Title Company receives a copy of this contract, Seller shall furnish to Buyer a commitment for title insurance (Commitment) and, at Buyer's expense, legible copies of restrictive covenants and documents evidencing exceptions in the Commitment (Exception Documents) other than the standard printed exceptions. Seller authorizes the Title Company to mail or hand deliver the Commitment and Exception Documents to Buyer at Buyer's address shown in Paragraph 21. If the Commitment and Exception Documents are not delivered to Buyer within the specified time, the time for delivery will be automatically extended up to 15 days or the Closing Date, whichever is earlier.

C. SURVEY: The survey must be made by a registered professional land surveyor acceptable to the Title Company and any lender. (Check one box only)

❑ (1) Within ______ days after the effective date of this contract, Seller, at Seller's expense, shall furnish a new survey to Buyer.

❑ (2) Within ______ days after the effective date of this contract, Buyer, at Buyer's expense, shall obtain a new survey.

❑ (3) Within ______ days after the effective date of this contract, Seller shall furnish Seller's existing survey of the Property to Buyer and the Title Company, along with Seller's affidavit acceptable to the Title Company for approval of the survey. If the survey is not approved by the Title Company or Buyer's lender, a new survey will be obtained at ❑ Seller's ❑ Buyer's expense no later than 3 days prior to the Closing Date.

D. OBJECTIONS: Within ____ days after Buyer receives the Commitment, Exception Documents and the survey, Buyer may object in writing to defects, exceptions, or encumbrances to title: disclosed on the survey other than items 6A(1) through (7) above; disclosed in the Commitment other than items 6A(1) through (8) above; or which prohibit the following use or activity: ____.
Buyer's failure to object within the time allowed will constitute a waiver of Buyer's right to object; except that the requirements in Schedule C of the Commitment are not waived. Seller shall cure the timely objections of Buyer or any third party lender within 15 days after Seller receives the objections and the Closing Date will be extended as necessary. If objections are not cured within such 15 day period, this contract will terminate and the earnest money will be refunded to Buyer unless Buyer waives the objections.

E. TITLE NOTICES:

(1) ABSTRACT OR TITLE POLICY: Broker advises Buyer to have an abstract of title covering the Property examined by an attorney of Buyer's selection, or Buyer should be furnished with or obtain a Title Policy. If a Title Policy is furnished, the Commitment should be promptly reviewed by an attorney of Buyer's choice due to the time limitations on Buyer's right to object.

(2) MANDATORY OWNERS' ASSOCIATION MEMBERSHIP: The Property ❑ is ❑ is not subject to mandatory membership in an owners' association. If the Property is subject to mandatory membership in an owners' association, Seller notifies Buyer under §5.012, Texas Property Code, that, as a purchaser of property in the residential community in

01A TREC NO. 20-6

Initialed for identification by Buyer_______ _______ and Seller________ ________

Figure 9.1 TREC 20-6 (continued)

Contract Concerning ______________________________ Page Three 01-06-03
(Address of Property)

which the Property is located, you are obligated to be a member of the owners' association. Restrictive covenants governing the use and occupancy of the Property and a dedicatory instrument governing the establishment, maintenance, and operation of this residential community have been or will be recorded in the Real Property Records of the county in which the Property is located. Copies of the restrictive covenants and dedicatory instrument may be obtained from the county clerk. You are obligated to pay assessments to the owners' association. The amount of the assessments is subject to change. Your failure to pay the assessments could result in a lien on and the foreclosure of the Property.

(3) STATUTORY TAX DISTRICTS: If the Property is situated in a utility or other statutorily created district providing water, sewer, drainage, or flood control facilities and services, Chapter 49, Texas Water Code requires Seller to deliver and Buyer to sign the statutory notice relating to the tax rate, bonded indebtedness, or standby fee of the district prior to final execution of this contract.

(4) TIDE WATERS: If the Property abuts the tidally influenced waters of the state, §33.135, Texas Natural Resources Code, requires a notice regarding coastal area property to be included in the contract. An addendum containing the notice promulgated by TREC or required by the parties must be used.

(5) ANNEXATION: If the Property is located outside the limits of a municipality, Seller notifies Buyer under §5.011, Texas Property Code, that the Property may now or later be included in the extraterritorial jurisdiction of a municipality and may now or later be subject to annexation by the municipality. Each municipality maintains a map that depicts its boundaries and extraterritorial jurisdiction. To determine if the Property is located within a municipality's extraterritorial jurisdiction or is likely to be located within a municipality's extraterritorial jurisdiction, contact all municipalities located in the general proximity of the Property for further information.

7. PROPERTY CONDITION:

A. INSPECTIONS, ACCESS AND UTILITIES: Buyer may have the Property inspected by inspectors selected by Buyer and licensed by TREC or otherwise permitted by law to make inspections. Seller shall permit Buyer and Buyer's agents access to the Property at reasonable times. Seller shall pay for turning on existing utilities for inspections.

B. SELLER'S DISCLOSURE NOTICE PURSUANT TO §5.008, TEXAS PROPERTY CODE (Notice):
(Check one box only)

❑ (1) Buyer has received the Notice.

❑ (2) Buyer has not received the Notice. Within ______ days after the effective date of this contract, Seller shall deliver the Notice to Buyer. If Buyer does not receive the Notice, Buyer may terminate this contract at any time prior to the closing and the earnest money will be refunded to Buyer. If Seller delivers the Notice, Buyer may terminate this contract for any reason within 7 days after Buyer receives the Notice or prior to the closing, whichever first occurs, and the earnest money will be refunded to Buyer.

❑ (3) The Texas Property Code does not require this Seller to furnish the Notice.

C. SELLER'S DISCLOSURE OF LEAD-BASED PAINT AND LEAD-BASED PAINT HAZARDS is required by Federal law for a residential dwelling constructed prior to 1978.

D. ACCEPTANCE OF PROPERTY CONDITION: Buyer accepts the Property in its present condition; provided Seller, at Seller's expense, shall complete the following specific repairs and treatments:____
____.

E. LENDER REQUIRED REPAIRS AND TREATMENTS: Unless otherwise agreed in writing, neither party is obligated to pay for lender required repairs, which includes treatment for wood destroying insects. If the parties do not agree to pay for the lender required repairs or treatments, this contract will terminate and the earnest money will be refunded to Buyer. If the cost of lender required repairs and treatments exceeds 5% of the Sales Price, Buyer may terminate this contract and the earnest money will be refunded to Buyer.

F. COMPLETION OF REPAIRS AND TREATMENTS: Unless otherwise agreed in writing, Seller shall complete all agreed repairs and treatments prior to the Closing Date. All required permits must be obtained, and repairs and treatments must be performed by persons who are licensed or otherwise authorized by law to provide such repairs or treatments. At Buyer's election, any transferable warranties received by Seller with respect to the repairs and treatments will be transferred to Buyer at Buyer's expense. If Seller fails to complete any agreed repairs and

01A TREC NO. 20-6

Initialed for identification by Buyer_______ _______ and Seller_________ _______

Figure 9.1 TREC 20-6 (continued)

treatments prior to the Closing Date, Buyer may do so and receive reimbursement from Seller at closing. The Closing Date will be extended up to 15 days, if necessary, to complete repairs and treatments.

G. ENVIRONMENTAL MATTERS: Buyer is advised that the presence of wetlands, toxic substances, including asbestos and wastes or other environmental hazards, or the presence of a threatened or endangered species or its habitat may affect Buyer's intended use of the Property. If Buyer is concerned about these matters, an addendum promulgated by TREC or required by the parties should be used.

H. RESIDENTIAL SERVICE CONTRACTS: Buyer may purchase a residential service contract from a residential service company licensed by TREC. If Buyer purchases a residential service contract, Seller shall reimburse Buyer at closing for the cost of the residential service contract in an amount not exceeding $______________ . Buyer should review any residential service contract for the scope of coverage, exclusions and limitations. **The purchase of a residential service contract is optional. Similar coverage may be purchased from various companies authorized to do business in Texas.**

8. BROKERS' FEES: All obligations of the parties for payment of brokers' fees are contained in separate written agreements.

9. CLOSING:

A. The closing of the sale will be on or before ____________________, 20___, or within 7 days after objections to matters disclosed in the Commitment or by the survey have been cured, whichever date is later (Closing Date). If either party fails to close the sale by the Closing Date, the non-defaulting party may exercise the remedies contained in Paragraph 15.

B. At closing:

(1) Seller shall execute and deliver a general warranty deed conveying title to the Property to Buyer and showing no additional exceptions to those permitted in Paragraph 6 and furnish tax statements or certificates showing no delinquent taxes on the Property.

(2) Buyer shall pay the Sales Price in good funds acceptable to the escrow agent.

(3) Seller and Buyer shall execute and deliver any notices, statements, certificates, affidavits, releases, loan documents and other documents required of them by this contract, the Commitment or law necessary for the closing of the sale and the issuance of the Title Policy.

C. Unless expressly prohibited by written agreement, Seller may continue to show the Property and receive, negotiate and accept back up offers.

D. All covenants, representations and warranties in this contract survive closing.

10. POSSESSION: Seller shall deliver to Buyer possession of the Property in its present or required condition, ordinary wear and tear excepted ❑ upon closing and funding ❑ according to a temporary residential lease form promulgated by TREC or other written lease required by the parties. Any possession by Buyer prior to closing or by Seller after closing which is not authorized by a written lease will establish a tenancy at sufferance relationship between the parties. *Consult your insurance agent prior to change of ownership or possession because insurance coverage may be limited or terminated. The absence of a written lease or appropriate insurance coverage may expose the parties to economic loss.*

11. SPECIAL PROVISIONS: (Insert only factual statements and business details applicable to the sale. TREC rules prohibit licensees from adding factual statements or business details for which a contract addendum, lease or other form has been promulgated by TREC for mandatory use.)

Figure 9.1 TREC 20-6 (continued)

Contract Concerning ____ Page Five 01-06-03
(Address of Property)

12. SETTLEMENT AND OTHER EXPENSES:

A. The following expenses must be paid at or prior to closing:

(1) Expenses payable by Seller (Seller's Expenses):

(a) Releases of existing liens, including prepayment penalties and recording fees; release of Seller's loan liability; tax statements or certificates; preparation of deed; one-half of escrow fee; and other expenses payable by Seller under this contract.

(b) Seller shall also pay an amount not to exceed $ ____________ to be applied in the following order: Buyer's Expenses which Buyer is prohibited from paying by FHA, VA, Texas Veteran's Housing Assistance Program or other governmental loan programs; Buyer's prepaid items; other Buyer's expenses.

(2) Expenses payable by Buyer (Buyer's Expenses):

(a) Loan origination, discount, buy-down, and commitment fees (Loan Fees).

(b) Appraisal fees; loan application fees; credit reports; preparation of loan documents; interest on the notes from date of disbursement to one month prior to dates of first monthly payments; recording fees; copies of easements and restrictions; mortgagee title policy with endorsements required by lender; loan-related inspection fees; photos, amortization schedules, one-half of escrow fee; all prepaid items, including required premiums for flood and hazard insurance, reserve deposits for insurance, ad valorem taxes and special governmental assessments; final compliance inspection; courier fee, repair inspection, underwriting fee and wire transfer, expenses incident to any loan, and other expenses payable by Buyer under this contract.

B. Buyer shall pay Private Mortgage Insurance Premium (PMI), VA Loan Funding Fee, or FHA Mortgage Insurance Premium (MIP) as required by the lender.

C. If any expense exceeds an amount expressly stated in this contract for such expense to be paid by a party, that party may terminate this contract unless the other party agrees to pay such excess. Buyer may not pay charges and fees expressly prohibited by FHA, VA, Texas Veteran's Housing Assistance Program or other governmental loan program regulations.

13. PRORATIONS: Taxes for the current year, interest, maintenance fees, assessments, dues and rents will be prorated through the Closing Date. If taxes for the current year vary from the amount prorated at closing, the parties shall adjust the prorations when tax statements for the current year are available. If taxes are not paid at or prior to closing, Buyer shall pay taxes for the current year.

14. CASUALTY LOSS: If any part of the Property is damaged or destroyed by fire or other casualty after the effective date of this contract, Seller shall restore the Property to its previous condition as soon as reasonably possible, but in any event by the Closing Date. If Seller fails to do so due to factors beyond Seller's control, Buyer may (a) terminate this contract and the earnest money will be refunded to Buyer (b) extend the time for performance up to 15 days and the Closing Date will be extended as necessary or (c) accept the Property in its damaged condition with an assignment of insurance proceeds and receive credit from Seller at closing in the amount of the deductible under the insurance policy. Seller's obligations under this paragraph are independent of any obligations of Seller under Paragraph 7.

15. DEFAULT: If Buyer fails to comply with this contract, Buyer will be in default, and Seller may (a) enforce specific performance, seek such other relief as may be provided by law, or both, or (b) terminate this contract and receive the earnest money as liquidated damages, thereby releasing both parties from this contract. If, due to factors beyond Seller's control, Seller fails within the time allowed to make any non-casualty repairs or deliver the Commitment, or survey, if required of Seller, Buyer may (a) extend the time for performance up to 15 days and the Closing Date will be extended as necessary or (b) terminate this contract as the sole remedy and receive the earnest money. If Seller fails to comply with this contract for any other reason, Seller will be in default and Buyer may (a) enforce specific performance, seek such other relief as may be provided by law, or both, or (b) terminate this contract and receive the earnest money, thereby releasing both parties from this contract.

16. MEDIATION: It is the policy of the State of Texas to encourage resolution of disputes through alternative dispute resolution procedures such as mediation. Any dispute between Seller and Buyer related to this contract which is not resolved through informal discussion ☐ will ☐ will not be submitted to a mutually acceptable mediation service or provider. The parties to the mediation shall bear the mediation costs equally. This paragraph does not preclude a party from seeking equitable relief from a court of competent jurisdiction.

01A TREC NO. 20-6

Initialed for identification by Buyer_______ _______ and Seller________ ________

Figure 9.1 TREC 20-6 (continued)

Contract Concerning ______________________________ Page Six 01-06-03
(Address of Property)

17. ATTORNEY'S FEES: The prevailing party in any legal proceeding related to this contract is entitled to recover reasonable attorney's fees and all costs of such proceeding incurred by the prevailing party.

18. ESCROW: The escrow agent is not (a) a party to this contract and does not have liability for the performance or nonperformance of any party to this contract, (b) liable for interest on the earnest money and (c) liable for the loss of any earnest money caused by the failure of any financial institution in which the earnest money has been deposited unless the financial institution is acting as escrow agent. At closing, the earnest money must be applied first to any cash down payment, then to Buyer's Expenses and any excess refunded to Buyer. If both parties make written demand for the earnest money, escrow agent may require payment of unpaid expenses incurred on behalf of the parties and a written release of liability of escrow agent from all parties. If one party makes written demand for the earnest money, escrow agent shall give notice of the demand by providing to the other party a copy of the demand. If escrow agent does not receive written objection to the demand from the other party within 30 days after notice to the other party, escrow agent may disburse the earnest money to the party making demand reduced by the amount of unpaid expenses incurred on behalf of the party receiving the earnest money and escrow agent may pay the same to the creditors. If escrow agent complies with the provisions of this paragraph, each party hereby releases escrow agent from all adverse claims related to the disbursal of the earnest money. Escrow agent's notice to the other party will be effective when deposited in the U. S. Mail, postage prepaid, certified mail, return receipt requested, addressed to the other party at such party's address shown below. Notice of objection to the demand will be deemed effective upon receipt by escrow agent.

19. REPRESENTATIONS: Seller represents that as of the Closing Date (a) there will be no liens, assessments, or security interests against the Property which will not be satisfied out of the sales proceeds unless securing payment of any loans assumed by Buyer and (b) assumed loans will not be in default. If any representation of Seller in this contract is untrue on the Closing Date, Buyer may terminate this contract and the earnest money will be refunded to Buyer.

20. FEDERAL TAX REQUIREMENTS: If Seller is a "foreign person," as defined by applicable law, or if Seller fails to deliver an affidavit to Buyer that Seller is not a "foreign person," then Buyer shall withhold from the sales proceeds an amount sufficient to comply with applicable tax law and deliver the same to the Internal Revenue Service together with appropriate tax forms. Internal Revenue Service regulations require filing written reports if currency in excess of specified amounts is received in the transaction.

21. NOTICES: All notices from one party to the other must be in writing and are effective when mailed to, hand-delivered at, or transmitted by facsimile as follows:

To Buyer at:	**To Seller at:**
______________________	______________________
______________________	______________________
______________________	______________________
Telephone:(____) ______________	Telephone:(____) ______________
Facsimile:(____) ______________	Facsimile:(____) ______________

22. AGREEMENT OF PARTIES: This contract contains the entire agreement of the parties and cannot be changed except by their written agreement. Addenda which are a part of this contract are (check all applicable boxes):

- ❑ Third Party Financing Condition Addendum
- ❑ Addendum for Property Subject to Mandatory Membership in an Owners' Association
- ❑ Seller Financing Addendum
- ❑ Environmental Assessment, Threatened or Endangered Species and Wetlands Addendum

01A TREC NO. 20-6

Initialed for identification by Buyer_______ _______ and Seller________ ________

Figure 9.1 TREC 20-6 (continued)

Contract Concerning ____ Page Seven 01-06-03
(Address of Property)

❑ Loan Assumption Addendum

❑ Buyer's Temporary Residential Lease

❑ Seller's Temporary Residential Lease

❑ Addendum for Sale of Other Property by Buyer

❑ Addendum for Seller's Disclosure of Information on Lead-based Paint and Lead-based Paint Hazards as Required by Federal Law

❑ Addendum for "Back-Up" Contract

❑ Addendum for Coastal Area Property

❑ Addendum for Property Located Seaward of the Gulf Intracoastal Waterway

❑ Addendum for Release of Liability on Assumption of FHA, VA, or Conventional Loan Restoration of Seller's Entitlement for VA Guaranteed Loan

❑ Other (list): ____

____

23. **TERMINATION OPTION: This paragraph will be a part of this contract ONLY if both blanks are filled in and Buyer has paid the Option Fee.** Buyer has paid Seller $__________ (Option Fee) for the unrestricted right to terminate this contract by giving notice of termination to Seller within ________ days after the effective date of this contract. If Buyer gives notice of termination within the time specified, the Option Fee will not be refunded, however, any earnest money will be refunded to Buyer. The Option Fee ❑ will ❑ will not be credited to the Sales Price at closing. For the purposes of this paragraph, time is of the essence; strict compliance with the time for performance stated herein is required.

24. **CONSULT AN ATTORNEY:** Real estate licensees cannot give legal advice. READ THIS CONTRACT CAREFULLY. If you do not understand the effect of this contract, consult an attorney BEFORE signing.

Buyer's Attorney is: ______________________
____
Telephone: (____)______________________
Facsimile: (____)______________________

Seller's Attorney is: ______________________
____
Telephone: (____)______________________
Facsimile: (____)______________________

EXECUTED the ________day of ______________________, 20____ (EFFECTIVE DATE). (BROKER: FILL IN THE DATE OF FINAL ACCEPTANCE.)

____
Buyer

____
Seller

____
Buyer

____
Seller

The form of this contract has been approved by the Texas Real Estate Commission. TREC forms are intended for use only by trained real estate licensees. No representation is made as to the legal validity or adequacy of any provision in any specific transactions. It is not suitable for complex transactions. Texas Real Estate Commission, P.O. Box 12188, Austin, TX 78711-2188, 1-800-250-8732 or (512) 459-6544 (http://www.trec.state.tx.us) TREC NO. 20-6. This form replaces TREC NO. 20-5.

01A TREC NO. 20-6

Initialed for identification by Buyer_______ _______ and Seller_______ _______

Figure 9.1 TREC 20-6 (continued)

Contract Concerning ____ Page Eight 01-06-03
(Address of Property)

SELLER'S RECEIPT

Receipt of $______________ (Option Fee) in the form of ______________________ is acknowledged.

______________________________ Seller

______________________________ Date

BROKER INFORMATION AND RATIFICATION OF FEE

Listing Broker has agreed to pay Other Broker ______________________ of the total sales price when Listing Broker's fee is received. Escrow Agent is authorized and directed to pay Other Broker from Listing Broker's fee at closing.

Other Broker	Listing Broker
License No. Telephone	License No. Telephone
represents ❑ Buyer only as Buyer's agent ❑ Seller as Listing Broker's subagent	represents ❑ Seller and Buyer as an intermediary ❑ Seller only as Seller's agent
Associate Telephone	Listing Associate Telephone
Broker's Address	Listing Associate's Office Address Facsimile
Facsimile	Selling Associate Telephone
	Selling Associate's Office Address Facsimile

RECEIPT

Receipt of ❑ Contract and ❑ $______________ Earnest Money in the form of ______________________
is acknowledged.
Escrow Agent: ______________________________________ Date: ______________________

By: ______________________________________

______________________________________ Address Telephone (_____) ______________

______________________________________ City State Zip Facsimile: (_____) ______________

01A TREC NO. 20-6

Figure 9.2 TREC 40-1

02-09-2004

EQUAL HOUSING OPPORTUNITY

PROMULGATED BY THE TEXAS REAL ESTATE COMMISSION (TREC)

THIRD PARTY FINANCING CONDITION ADDENDUM

TO CONTRACT CONCERNING THE PROPERTY AT

____

(Street Address and City)

Buyer shall apply promptly for all financing described below and make every reasonable effort to obtain financing approval including but not limited to furnishing all information and documents required by lender for approval. Financing approval will be deemed to have been obtained when the lender determines that Buyer has satisfied all of lender's financial requirements (those items relating to Buyer's assets, income and credit history). If Buyer cannot obtain financing approval, Buyer must give written notice to Seller within _____ days after the effective date of this contract and this contract will terminate and the earnest money will be refunded to Buyer. **If Buyer does not give such notice within the time allowed, this contract will no longer be subject to Buyer being approved for the financing described below. For purposes of this paragraph, time is of the essence; strict compliance with the times for performance herein stated is required.**

Each note must be secured by vendor's and deed of trust liens.

☐ A. CONVENTIONAL FINANCING:

☐ (1) A first mortgage loan in the principal amount of $ ____________________ (excluding any financed PMI premium), due in full in __________ year(s), with interest not to exceed ______% per annum for the first ________year(s) of the loan with Loan Fees (loan origination, discount, buy-down, and commitment fees) not to exceed ________% of the loan.

☐ (2) A second mortgage loan in the principal amount of $___________________(excluding any financed PMI premium), due in full in ___________year(s), with interest not to exceed ______% per annum for the first ____________year(s) of the loan with Loan Fees (loan origination, discount, buy-down, and commitment fees) not to exceed _________ % of the loan.

☐ B. TEXAS VETERANS' HOUSING ASSISTANCE PROGRAM LOAN: A Texas Veteran's Housing Assistance Program Loan of $________________ for a period of at least ______years at the interest rate established by the Texas Veteran's Land Board at the time of closing.

☐ C. FHA INSURED FINANCING: A Section _________________ FHA insured loan of not less than $__________________ (excluding any financed MIP), amortizable monthly for not less than _______years, with interest not to exceed _______% per annum for the first ______year(s) of the loan with Loan Fees (loan origination, discount, buy-down, and commitment fees) not to exceed _________ % of the loan. As required by HUD-FHA, if FHA valuation is unknown, *"It is expressly agreed that, notwithstanding any other provision of this contract, the purchaser (Buyer) shall not be obligated to complete the purchase of the Property described herein or to incur any penalty by forfeiture of earnest money deposits or otherwise unless the purchaser (Buyer) has been given in accordance with HUD/FHA or VA requirements a written statement issued by the Federal Housing Commissioner, Department of Veterans Affairs, or a Direct Endorsement Lender setting forth the appraised value of the Property of not less than $__________________. The purchaser (Buyer) shall have the privilege and option of proceeding with consummation of the contract without regard to the amount of the appraised valuation. The appraised valuation is arrived at to determine the maximum mortgage the Department of Housing and Urban Development will insure. HUD does not warrant the value or the condition of the Property. The purchaser (Buyer) should satisfy himself/herself that the price and the condition of the Property are acceptable."*

Initialed for identification by Buyer_______ _______ and Seller________ ________ 01A

Figure 9.2 TREC 40-1 (continued)

Third Party Financing Condition Addendum Concerning Page Two 02-09-2004

____

(Address of Property)

❑ D. VA GUARANTEED FINANCING: A VA guaranteed loan of not less than $_________________ (excluding any financed Funding Fee), amortizable monthly for not less than________years, with interest not to exceed________% per annum for the first ________year(s) of the loan with Loan Fees (loan origination, discount, buy-down, and commitment fees) not to exceed ________% of the loan.

VA NOTICE TO BUYER: "*It is expressly agreed that, notwithstanding any other provisions of this contract, the Buyer shall not incur any penalty by forfeiture of earnest money or otherwise or be obligated to complete the purchase of the Property described herein, if the contract purchase price or cost exceeds the reasonable value of the Property established by the Department of Veterans Affairs. The Buyer shall, however, have the privilege and option of proceeding with the consummation of this contract without regard to the amount of the reasonable value established by the Department of Veterans Affairs.*"

If Buyer elects to complete the purchase at an amount in excess of the reasonable value established by VA, Buyer shall pay such excess amount in cash from a source which Buyer agrees to disclose to the VA and which Buyer represents will not be from borrowed funds except as approved by VA. If VA reasonable value of the Property is less than the Sales Price, Seller may reduce the Sales Price to an amount equal to the VA reasonable value and the sale will be closed at the lower Sales Price with proportionate adjustments to the down payment and the loan amount.

Buyer hereby authorizes any lender to furnish to the Seller or Buyer or their representatives information relating only to the status of financing approval of Buyer.

________________________	________________________
Buyer	Seller
________________________	________________________
Buyer	Seller

This form has been approved by the Texas Real Estate Commission for use with similarly approved or promulgated contract forms. Such approval relates to this form only. TREC forms are intended for use only by trained real estate licensees. No representation is made as to the legal validity or adequacy of any provision in any specific transactions. It is not suitable for complex transactions. Texas Real Estate Commission, P.O. Box 12188, Austin, TX 78711-2188, 1-800-250-8732 or (512) 459-6544 (http://www.trec.state.tx.us) TREC No. 40-1. This form replaces TREC No. 40-0.

Figure 9.3 TREC 36-3

PROMULGATED BY THE TEXAS REAL ESTATE COMMISSION (TREC) 02-09-2004

EQUAL HOUSING OPPORTUNITY

ADDENDUM FOR PROPERTY SUBJECT TO MANDATORY MEMBERSHIP IN AN OWNERS' ASSOCIATION

(NOT FOR USE WITH CONDOMINIUMS)

ADDENDUM TO CONTRACT CONCERNING THE PROPERTY AT

____

(Street Address and City)

____

(Name of Owners' Association)

A. SUBDIVISON INFORMATION: "Subdivision Information" means: (i) the restrictions applying to the subdivision, (ii) the bylaws and rules of the Owners' Association, and (iii) a resale certificate, all of which were provided by the Owners' Association in compliance with Section 207.003 of the Texas Property Code no more than three months before the date of their delivery to Buyer. (Check only one box):

❑ 1. Within _____ days after the effective date of the contract, Seller shall at Seller's expense deliver the Subdivision Information to Buyer. If Buyer does not receive the Subdivision Information, Buyer may terminate the contract at any time prior to closing and the earnest money will be refunded to Buyer. If Seller delivers the Subdivision Information, Buyer may terminate the contract for any reason within 7 days after Buyer receives the Subdivision Information or prior to closing, whichever first occurs, and the earnest money will be refunded to Buyer.

❑ 2. Buyer has received and approved the Subdivision Information before signing the contract.

❑ 3. Buyer does not require delivery of the Subdivision Information.

If Seller becomes aware of any material changes in the Subdivision Information, Seller shall immediately give notice to Buyer. Buyer may terminate the contract prior to closing by giving written notice to Seller if: (i) any of the Subdivision Information provided was not true; or (ii) any material adverse change in the Subdivision Information occurs prior to closing, and the earnest money will be refunded to Buyer.

B. TRANSFER FEES: Buyer shall pay any Owners' Association transfer fee not to exceed $ ____________ and Seller agrees to pay any excess.

NOTICE TO BUYER REGARDING REPAIRS BY THE OWNERS' ASSOCIATION: The Owners' Association may have the sole responsibility to make certain repairs to the Property. If you are concerned about the condition of any part of the Property which the Owners' Association is required to repair, you should not sign the contract unless you are satisfied that the Owners' Association will make the desired repairs.

______________________	______________________
Buyer	Seller
______________________	______________________
Buyer	Seller

The form of this addendum has been approved by the Texas Real Estate Commission for use only with similarly approved or promulgated forms of contracts. Such approval relates to this contract form only. TREC forms are intended for use only by trained real estate licensees. No representation is made as to the legal validity or adequacy of any provision in any specific transactions. It is not suitable for complex transactions. Texas Real Estate Commission, P.O. Box 12188, Austin, TX 78711-2188, 1-800-250-8732 or (512) 459-6544 (http://www.trec.state.tx.us) TREC No. 36-3. This form replaces TREC No. 36-2.

01A

Figure 9.4 TREC 28-0

EQUAL HOUSING OPPORTUNITY

10-25-93

ENVIRONMENTAL ASSESSMENT, THREATENED OR ENDANGERED SPECIES, AND WETLANDS ADDENDUM

PROMULGATED BY THE TEXAS REAL ESTATE COMMISSION (TREC)

ADDENDUM TO EARNEST MONEY CONTRACT BETWEEN THE UNDERSIGNED PARTIES CONCERNING THE PROPERTY AT ______________________________
(Address)

☐ A. ENVIRONMENTAL ASSESSMENT: Buyer, at Buyer's expense, may obtain an Environmental Assessment Report prepared by an environmental specialist.

☐ B. THREATENED OR ENDANGERED SPECIES: Buyer, at Buyer's expense, may obtain a report from a natural resources professional to determine if there are any threatened or endangered species or their habitats as defined by the Texas Parks and Wildlife Department or the U.S. Fish and Wildlife Service.

☐ C. WETLANDS: Buyer, at Buyer's expense, may obtain a report from an environmental specialist to determine if there are wetlands, as defined by federal or state law or regulation.

Within _________ days after the Effective Date of the contract, Buyer may terminate the contract by furnishing Seller a copy of any report noted above that adversely affects the use of the Property and the Earnest Money shall be refunded to Buyer. If Buyer does not furnish Seller a copy of the unacceptable report within the prescribed time and give Seller notice that Buyer has terminated the contract, Buyer shall be deemed to have accepted the Property.

______________________________	______________________________
Buyer	Seller
______________________________	______________________________
Buyer	Seller

The form of this addendum has been approved by the Texas Real Estate Commission for use only with similarly approved or promulgated forms of contracts. No representation is made as to the legal validity or adequacy of any provision in any specific transactions. It is not suitable for complex transactions. (10-93) TREC No. 28-0.

01A TREC No. 28-0

Figure 9.5 TREC 39-4

PROMULGATED BY THE TEXAS REAL ESTATE COMMISSION (TREC) 01-06-03

EQUAL HOUSING OPPORTUNITY

AMENDMENT

TO CONTRACT CONCERNING THE PROPERTY AT

____

(Street Address and City)

Seller and Buyer amend the contract as follows: (check each applicable box)

❑ (1) The Sales Price in Paragraph 3 of the contract is:
A. Cash portion of Sales Price payable by Buyer at closing .... $__________
B. Sum of financing described in the contract.. $__________
C. Sales Price (Sum of A and B) .... $__________

❑ (2) In addition to any repairs and treatments otherwise required by the contract, Seller, at Seller's expense, shall complete the following repairs and treatments:

❑ (3) The Option Fee ❑ will ❑ will not be credited to the Sales Price.

❑ (4) The date in Paragraph 9 of the contract is changed to ______________________, 20______.

❑ (5) The amount in Paragraph 12A(1)(b) of the contract is changed to $ __________________.

❑ (6) The cost of lender required repairs and treatment, as itemized on the attached list, will be paid as follows: $ ____________________ by Seller; $ ______________________ by Buyer.

❑ (7) Buyer has paid Seller an additional non-refundable Option Fee of $ _______________ for an extension of the unrestricted right to terminate the contract on or before ________________________ , 20_______. This additional Option Fee ❑ will ❑ will not be credited to the Sales Price.

❑ (8) Upon final acceptance of this Amendment, Buyer waives the unrestricted right to terminate the contract for which the Option Fee was paid.

❑ (9) **Other Modifications**: (Insert only factual statements and business details applicable to this sale.)

EXECUTED the___________day of ____________________, 20 ____ (BROKER: FILL IN THE DATE OF FINAL ACCEPTANCE).

______________________	______________________
Buyer	Seller
______________________	______________________
Buyer	Seller

This form has been approved by the Texas Real Estate Commission for use with similarly approved or promulgated contract forms. Such approval relates to this form only. TREC forms are intended for use only by trained real estate licensees. No representation is made as to the legal validity or adequacy of any provision in any specific transactions. It is not suitable for complex transactions. Texas Real Estate Commission, P.O. Box 12188, Austin, TX 78711-2188, 1-800-250-8732 or (512) 459-6544 (http://www.trec.state.tx.us) TREC No. 39-4. This form replaces TREC No. 39-3.

01A

Transaction 2:
90% Conventional Fixed Rate Loan with PMI
(Using: TREC 20-6, 40-1, and OP-L Lead-based Paint Addendum)

John Charles Wayne and his spouse, Sharon Sidekick Wayne, want to buy the home owned by Thomas A. Smith and his wife, Molly Bea Smith. Although the property is subject to mandatory membership in an owners' association, the Waynes do not attach the addendum regarding association membership. There are no excluded fixtures at 3510 Mimosa Lane in Bellaire, Harris County, 77404. On the plat of Shadyacres Addition, the property is identified as Lot 7, Block 7.

The Waynes are willing to pay $180,000 for the property and will promptly apply for a 90 percent, 30-year fixed-rate loan at 7.5 percent annual interest. They anticipate that all lender requirements can be met, approval can be received within 30 days of the effective date of the contract, and that they can close within 40 days. They anticipate that they may have to pay up to one discount point to obtain the desired interest rate, and request that the seller be liable for one-half of any discount required by the lender. The lender is charging a 1 percent loan origination fee.

To show good faith, they deposit $4,000 earnest money with Protective Title Company and will deposit another $4,000 thirty days after the effective date of this contract. As previously agreed at the time of listing, the sellers will pay for the owner's title policy. The buyers want 12 days to obtain the survey required by their lender. They are requesting the Smiths to furnish their existing survey and are willing to pay for a new survey if the existing one is not acceptable to the lender. They want seven days to review the survey and title documents.

Prior to making their offer, the buyers received the sellers' disclosure form. Their purchase agreement contains the lead-based paint addendum because the house was built in 1965. They wish to purchase a ten-day option to terminate period and have given the agent a check for $400 to compensate the sellers for giving the option. The option fee will be credited to the sale price at closing. They plan to have a variety of structural and mechanical evaluations done. They are asking the seller to provide a residential service contract from Home Warranty Inc. in an amount not to exceed $325.

The buyers reserve the opportunity to do a walk-through during the four hours prior to closing and want to be granted possession at funding, which they anticipate will be at the closing table. The parties have agreed to mediate any dispute they cannot resolve by informal negotiation.

The buyers are customers who are purchasing the property at an open house being held by the sellers' agent, Sarah Listalot, Broker (TREC# 0234567).

With regard to the lead-based paint addendum, seller has no knowledge of lead-based paint or hazards and the buyers have no current plans to conduct a risk assessment. The buyers have been furnished the HUD lead pamphlet.

Figure 9.6 TREC 20-6

PROMULGATED BY THE TEXAS REAL ESTATE COMMISSION (TREC) 01-06-03

ONE TO FOUR FAMILY RESIDENTIAL CONTRACT (RESALE)

NOTICE: Not For Use For Condominium Transactions

1. **PARTIES:** ____ (Seller) agrees to sell and convey to ____(Buyer) and Buyer agrees to buy from Seller the Property described below.

2. **PROPERTY:**
   A. LAND: Lot ___________________________,Block_____, ___________________________ ___________________________Addition, City of _______________ , _____________ County, Texas, known as ____ ____________________________(address/zip code), or as described on attached exhibit.
   B. IMPROVEMENTS: The house, garage and all other fixtures and improvements attached to the above-described real property, including without limitation, the following permanently installed and built-in items, if any: all equipment and appliances, valances, screens, shutters, awnings, wall-to-wall carpeting, mirrors, ceiling fans, attic fans, mail boxes, television antennas and satellite dish system and equipment, heating and air-conditioning units, security and fire detection equipment, wiring, plumbing and lighting fixtures, chandeliers, water softener system, kitchen equipment, garage door openers, cleaning equipment, shrubbery, landscaping, outdoor cooking equipment, and all other property owned by Seller and attached to the above described real property.
   C. ACCESSORIES: The following described related accessories, if any: window air conditioning units, stove, fireplace screens, curtains and rods, blinds, window shades, draperies and rods, controls for satellite dish system, controls for garage door openers, entry gate controls, door keys, mailbox keys, above ground pool, swimming pool equipment and maintenance accessories, and artificial fireplace logs.
   D. EXCLUSIONS: The following improvements and accessories will be retained by Seller and excluded: ____ ____.

   The land, improvements and accessories are collectively referred to as the "Property".

3. **SALES PRICE:**
   A. Cash portion of Sales Price payable by Buyer at closing................. $________________
   B. Sum of all financing described below (excluding any loan funding fee or mortgage insurance premium) .... $________________
   C. Sales Price (Sum of A and B) .... $________________

4. **FINANCING:** The portion of Sales Price not payable in cash will be paid as follows: (Check applicable boxes below)
   ❑ A. THIRD PARTY FINANCING: One or more third party mortgage loans in the total amount of $__________________. If the Property does not satisfy the lenders' underwriting requirements for the loan(s), this contract will terminate and the earnest money will be refunded to Buyer. (Check one box only)
      ❑ (1) This contract is subject to Buyer being approved for the financing described in the attached Third Party Financing Condition Addendum.
      ❑ (2) This contract is not subject to Buyer being approved for financing and does not involve FHA or VA financing.
   ❑ B. ASSUMPTION: The assumption of the unpaid principal balance of one or more promissory notes described in the attached TREC Loan Assumption Addendum.
   ❑ C. SELLER FINANCING: A promissory note from Buyer to Seller of $________________, bearing _______ % interest per annum, secured by vendor's and deed of trust liens, and containing the terms and conditions described in the attached TREC Seller Financing Addendum. If an owner policy of title insurance is furnished, Buyer shall furnish Seller with a mortgagee policy of title insurance.

5. **EARNEST MONEY:** Upon execution of this contract by both parties, Buyer shall deposit $___________ as earnest money with ______________________________________, as escrow agent, at ____ (address). Buyer shall deposit additional earnest money of $_________________ with escrow agent within ________days after the effective date of this contract. If Buyer fails to deposit the earnest money as required by this contract, Buyer will be in default.

01A TREC NO. 20-6

Initialed for identification by Buyer_______ _______ and Seller________ ________

Figure 9.6 TREC 20-6 (continued)

Contract Concerning ____ Page Two 01-06-03
(Address of Property)

6. TITLE POLICY AND SURVEY:

A. TITLE POLICY: Seller shall furnish to Buyer at ❑ Seller's ❑ Buyer's expense an owner policy of title insurance (Title Policy) issued by ______________________________ ______________________________ (Title Company) in the amount of the Sales Price, dated at or after closing, insuring Buyer against loss under the provisions of the Title Policy, subject to the promulgated exclusions (including existing building and zoning ordinances) and the following exceptions:

(1) Restrictive covenants common to the platted subdivision in which the Property is located.
(2) The standard printed exception for standby fees, taxes and assessments.
(3) Liens created as part of the financing described in Paragraph 4.
(4) Utility easements created by the dedication deed or plat of the subdivision in which the Property is located.
(5) Reservations or exceptions otherwise permitted by this contract or as may be approved by Buyer in writing.
(6) The standard printed exception as to marital rights.
(7) The standard printed exception as to waters, tidelands, beaches, streams, and related matters.
(8) The standard printed exception as to discrepancies, conflicts, shortages in area or boundary lines, encroachments or protrusions, or overlapping improvements. Buyer, at Buyer's expense, may have the exception amended to read, "shortages in area".

B. COMMITMENT: Within 20 days after the Title Company receives a copy of this contract, Seller shall furnish to Buyer a commitment for title insurance (Commitment) and, at Buyer's expense, legible copies of restrictive covenants and documents evidencing exceptions in the Commitment (Exception Documents) other than the standard printed exceptions. Seller authorizes the Title Company to mail or hand deliver the Commitment and Exception Documents to Buyer at Buyer's address shown in Paragraph 21. If the Commitment and Exception Documents are not delivered to Buyer within the specified time, the time for delivery will be automatically extended up to 15 days or the Closing Date, whichever is earlier.

C. SURVEY: The survey must be made by a registered professional land surveyor acceptable to the Title Company and any lender. (Check one box only)

❑ (1) Within ______ days after the effective date of this contract, Seller, at Seller's expense, shall furnish a new survey to Buyer.

❑ (2) Within ______ days after the effective date of this contract, Buyer, at Buyer's expense, shall obtain a new survey.

❑ (3) Within ______ days after the effective date of this contract, Seller shall furnish Seller's existing survey of the Property to Buyer and the Title Company, along with Seller's affidavit acceptable to the Title Company for approval of the survey. If the survey is not approved by the Title Company or Buyer's lender, a new survey will be obtained at ❑ Seller's ❑ Buyer's expense no later than 3 days prior to the Closing Date.

D. OBJECTIONS: Within ____ days after Buyer receives the Commitment, Exception Documents and the survey, Buyer may object in writing to defects, exceptions, or encumbrances to title: disclosed on the survey other than items 6A(1) through (7) above; disclosed in the Commitment other than items 6A(1) through (8) above; or which prohibit the following use or activity: ______________________________.
Buyer's failure to object within the time allowed will constitute a waiver of Buyer's right to object; except that the requirements in Schedule C of the Commitment are not waived. Seller shall cure the timely objections of Buyer or any third party lender within 15 days after Seller receives the objections and the Closing Date will be extended as necessary. If objections are not cured within such 15 day period, this contract will terminate and the earnest money will be refunded to Buyer unless Buyer waives the objections.

E. TITLE NOTICES:

(1) ABSTRACT OR TITLE POLICY: Broker advises Buyer to have an abstract of title covering the Property examined by an attorney of Buyer's selection, or Buyer should be furnished with or obtain a Title Policy. If a Title Policy is furnished, the Commitment should be promptly reviewed by an attorney of Buyer's choice due to the time limitations on Buyer's right to object.

(2) MANDATORY OWNERS' ASSOCIATION MEMBERSHIP: The Property ❑ is ❑ is not subject to mandatory membership in an owners' association. If the Property is subject to mandatory membership in an owners' association, Seller notifies Buyer under §5.012, Texas Property Code, that, as a purchaser of property in the residential community in

01A TREC NO. 20-6

Initialed for identification by Buyer_______ _______ and Seller_______ _______

Figure 9.6 TREC 20-6 (continued)

Contract Concerning ______________________________ Page Three 01-06-03
(Address of Property)

which the Property is located, you are obligated to be a member of the owners' association. Restrictive covenants governing the use and occupancy of the Property and a dedicatory instrument governing the establishment, maintenance, and operation of this residential community have been or will be recorded in the Real Property Records of the county in which the Property is located. Copies of the restrictive covenants and dedicatory instrument may be obtained from the county clerk. You are obligated to pay assessments to the owners' association. The amount of the assessments is subject to change. Your failure to pay the assessments could result in a lien on and the foreclosure of the Property.

(3) STATUTORY TAX DISTRICTS: If the Property is situated in a utility or other statutorily created district providing water, sewer, drainage, or flood control facilities and services, Chapter 49, Texas Water Code requires Seller to deliver and Buyer to sign the statutory notice relating to the tax rate, bonded indebtedness, or standby fee of the district prior to final execution of this contract.

(4) TIDE WATERS: If the Property abuts the tidally influenced waters of the state, §33.135, Texas Natural Resources Code, requires a notice regarding coastal area property to be included in the contract. An addendum containing the notice promulgated by TREC or required by the parties must be used.

(5) ANNEXATION: If the Property is located outside the limits of a municipality, Seller notifies Buyer under §5.011, Texas Property Code, that the Property may now or later be included in the extraterritorial jurisdiction of a municipality and may now or later be subject to annexation by the municipality. Each municipality maintains a map that depicts its boundaries and extraterritorial jurisdiction. To determine if the Property is located within a municipality's extraterritorial jurisdiction or is likely to be located within a municipality's extraterritorial jurisdiction, contact all municipalities located in the general proximity of the Property for further information.

7. PROPERTY CONDITION:

A. INSPECTIONS, ACCESS AND UTILITIES: Buyer may have the Property inspected by inspectors selected by Buyer and licensed by TREC or otherwise permitted by law to make inspections. Seller shall permit Buyer and Buyer's agents access to the Property at reasonable times. Seller shall pay for turning on existing utilities for inspections.

B. SELLER'S DISCLOSURE NOTICE PURSUANT TO §5.008, TEXAS PROPERTY CODE (Notice): (Check one box only)

❑ (1) Buyer has received the Notice.

❑ (2) Buyer has not received the Notice. Within _______ days after the effective date of this contract, Seller shall deliver the Notice to Buyer. If Buyer does not receive the Notice, Buyer may terminate this contract at any time prior to the closing and the earnest money will be refunded to Buyer. If Seller delivers the Notice, Buyer may terminate this contract for any reason within 7 days after Buyer receives the Notice or prior to the closing, whichever first occurs, and the earnest money will be refunded to Buyer.

❑ (3) The Texas Property Code does not require this Seller to furnish the Notice.

C. SELLER'S DISCLOSURE OF LEAD-BASED PAINT AND LEAD-BASED PAINT HAZARDS is required by Federal law for a residential dwelling constructed prior to 1978.

D. ACCEPTANCE OF PROPERTY CONDITION: Buyer accepts the Property in its present condition; provided Seller, at Seller's expense, shall complete the following specific repairs and treatments:____
____.

E. LENDER REQUIRED REPAIRS AND TREATMENTS: Unless otherwise agreed in writing, neither party is obligated to pay for lender required repairs, which includes treatment for wood destroying insects. If the parties do not agree to pay for the lender required repairs or treatments, this contract will terminate and the earnest money will be refunded to Buyer. If the cost of lender required repairs and treatments exceeds 5% of the Sales Price, Buyer may terminate this contract and the earnest money will be refunded to Buyer.

F. COMPLETION OF REPAIRS AND TREATMENTS: Unless otherwise agreed in writing, Seller shall complete all agreed repairs and treatments prior to the Closing Date. All required permits must be obtained, and repairs and treatments must be performed by persons who are licensed or otherwise authorized by law to provide such repairs or treatments. At Buyer's election, any transferable warranties received by Seller with respect to the repairs and treatments will be transferred to Buyer at Buyer's expense. If Seller fails to complete any agreed repairs and

Initialed for identification by Buyer_______ _______ and Seller________ ________

Figure 9.6 TREC 20-6 (continued)

treatments prior to the Closing Date, Buyer may do so and receive reimbursement from Seller at closing. The Closing Date will be extended up to 15 days, if necessary, to complete repairs and treatments.

G. ENVIRONMENTAL MATTERS: Buyer is advised that the presence of wetlands, toxic substances, including asbestos and wastes or other environmental hazards, or the presence of a threatened or endangered species or its habitat may affect Buyer's intended use of the Property. If Buyer is concerned about these matters, an addendum promulgated by TREC or required by the parties should be used.

H. RESIDENTIAL SERVICE CONTRACTS: Buyer may purchase a residential service contract from a residential service company licensed by TREC. If Buyer purchases a residential service contract, Seller shall reimburse Buyer at closing for the cost of the residential service contract in an amount not exceeding $_______________ . Buyer should review any residential service contract for the scope of coverage, exclusions and limitations. **The purchase of a residential service contract is optional. Similar coverage may be purchased from various companies authorized to do business in Texas.**

8. BROKERS' FEES: All obligations of the parties for payment of brokers' fees are contained in separate written agreements.

9. CLOSING:

A. The closing of the sale will be on or before _____________________, 20___, or within 7 days after objections to matters disclosed in the Commitment or by the survey have been cured, whichever date is later (Closing Date). If either party fails to close the sale by the Closing Date, the non-defaulting party may exercise the remedies contained in Paragraph 15.

B. At closing:

(1) Seller shall execute and deliver a general warranty deed conveying title to the Property to Buyer and showing no additional exceptions to those permitted in Paragraph 6 and furnish tax statements or certificates showing no delinquent taxes on the Property.

(2) Buyer shall pay the Sales Price in good funds acceptable to the escrow agent.

(3) Seller and Buyer shall execute and deliver any notices, statements, certificates, affidavits, releases, loan documents and other documents required of them by this contract, the Commitment or law necessary for the closing of the sale and the issuance of the Title Policy.

C. Unless expressly prohibited by written agreement, Seller may continue to show the Property and receive, negotiate and accept back up offers.

D. All covenants, representations and warranties in this contract survive closing.

10. POSSESSION: Seller shall deliver to Buyer possession of the Property in its present or required condition, ordinary wear and tear excepted ❑ upon closing and funding ❑ according to a temporary residential lease form promulgated by TREC or other written lease required by the parties. Any possession by Buyer prior to closing or by Seller after closing which is not authorized by a written lease will establish a tenancy at sufferance relationship between the parties. *Consult your insurance agent prior to change of ownership or possession because insurance coverage may be limited or terminated. The absence of a written lease or appropriate insurance coverage may expose the parties to economic loss.*

11. SPECIAL PROVISIONS: (Insert only factual statements and business details applicable to the sale. TREC rules prohibit licensees from adding factual statements or business details for which a contract addendum, lease or other form has been promulgated by TREC for mandatory use.)

Figure 9.6 TREC 20-6 (continued)

Contract Concerning ____ Page Five 01-06-03
(Address of Property)

12. SETTLEMENT AND OTHER EXPENSES:

A. The following expenses must be paid at or prior to closing:

(1) Expenses payable by Seller (Seller's Expenses):

(a) Releases of existing liens, including prepayment penalties and recording fees; release of Seller's loan liability; tax statements or certificates; preparation of deed; one-half of escrow fee; and other expenses payable by Seller under this contract.

(b) Seller shall also pay an amount not to exceed $ ____________ to be applied in the following order: Buyer's Expenses which Buyer is prohibited from paying by FHA, VA, Texas Veteran's Housing Assistance Program or other governmental loan programs; Buyer's prepaid items; other Buyer's expenses.

(2) Expenses payable by Buyer (Buyer's Expenses):

(a) Loan origination, discount, buy-down, and commitment fees (Loan Fees).

(b) Appraisal fees; loan application fees; credit reports; preparation of loan documents; interest on the notes from date of disbursement to one month prior to dates of first monthly payments; recording fees; copies of easements and restrictions; mortgagee title policy with endorsements required by lender; loan-related inspection fees; photos, amortization schedules, one-half of escrow fee; all prepaid items, including required premiums for flood and hazard insurance, reserve deposits for insurance, ad valorem taxes and special governmental assessments; final compliance inspection; courier fee, repair inspection, underwriting fee and wire transfer, expenses incident to any loan, and other expenses payable by Buyer under this contract.

B. Buyer shall pay Private Mortgage Insurance Premium (PMI), VA Loan Funding Fee, or FHA Mortgage Insurance Premium (MIP) as required by the lender.

C. If any expense exceeds an amount expressly stated in this contract for such expense to be paid by a party, that party may terminate this contract unless the other party agrees to pay such excess. Buyer may not pay charges and fees expressly prohibited by FHA, VA, Texas Veteran's Housing Assistance Program or other governmental loan program regulations.

13. PRORATIONS: Taxes for the current year, interest, maintenance fees, assessments, dues and rents will be prorated through the Closing Date. If taxes for the current year vary from the amount prorated at closing, the parties shall adjust the prorations when tax statements for the current year are available. If taxes are not paid at or prior to closing, Buyer shall pay taxes for the current year.

14. CASUALTY LOSS: If any part of the Property is damaged or destroyed by fire or other casualty after the effective date of this contract, Seller shall restore the Property to its previous condition as soon as reasonably possible, but in any event by the Closing Date. If Seller fails to do so due to factors beyond Seller's control, Buyer may (a) terminate this contract and the earnest money will be refunded to Buyer (b) extend the time for performance up to 15 days and the Closing Date will be extended as necessary or (c) accept the Property in its damaged condition with an assignment of insurance proceeds and receive credit from Seller at closing in the amount of the deductible under the insurance policy. Seller's obligations under this paragraph are independent of any obligations of Seller under Paragraph 7.

15. DEFAULT: If Buyer fails to comply with this contract, Buyer will be in default, and Seller may (a) enforce specific performance, seek such other relief as may be provided by law, or both, or (b) terminate this contract and receive the earnest money as liquidated damages, thereby releasing both parties from this contract. If, due to factors beyond Seller's control, Seller fails within the time allowed to make any non-casualty repairs or deliver the Commitment, or survey, if required of Seller, Buyer may (a) extend the time for performance up to 15 days and the Closing Date will be extended as necessary or (b) terminate this contract as the sole remedy and receive the earnest money. If Seller fails to comply with this contract for any other reason, Seller will be in default and Buyer may (a) enforce specific performance, seek such other relief as may be provided by law, or both, or (b) terminate this contract and receive the earnest money, thereby releasing both parties from this contract.

16. MEDIATION: It is the policy of the State of Texas to encourage resolution of disputes through alternative dispute resolution procedures such as mediation. Any dispute between Seller and Buyer related to this contract which is not resolved through informal discussion ☐ will ☐ will not be submitted to a mutually acceptable mediation service or provider. The parties to the mediation shall bear the mediation costs equally. This paragraph does not preclude a party from seeking equitable relief from a court of competent jurisdiction.

01A TREC NO. 20-6

Initialed for identification by Buyer_______ _______ and Seller________ ________

Figure 9.6 TREC 20-6 (continued)

Contract Concerning ______________________________ Page Six 01-06-03
(Address of Property)

17. ATTORNEY'S FEES: The prevailing party in any legal proceeding related to this contract is entitled to recover reasonable attorney's fees and all costs of such proceeding incurred by the prevailing party.

18. ESCROW: The escrow agent is not (a) a party to this contract and does not have liability for the performance or nonperformance of any party to this contract, (b) liable for interest on the earnest money and (c) liable for the loss of any earnest money caused by the failure of any financial institution in which the earnest money has been deposited unless the financial institution is acting as escrow agent. At closing, the earnest money must be applied first to any cash down payment, then to Buyer's Expenses and any excess refunded to Buyer. If both parties make written demand for the earnest money, escrow agent may require payment of unpaid expenses incurred on behalf of the parties and a written release of liability of escrow agent from all parties. If one party makes written demand for the earnest money, escrow agent shall give notice of the demand by providing to the other party a copy of the demand. If escrow agent does not receive written objection to the demand from the other party within 30 days after notice to the other party, escrow agent may disburse the earnest money to the party making demand reduced by the amount of unpaid expenses incurred on behalf of the party receiving the earnest money and escrow agent may pay the same to the creditors. If escrow agent complies with the provisions of this paragraph, each party hereby releases escrow agent from all adverse claims related to the disbursal of the earnest money. Escrow agent's notice to the other party will be effective when deposited in the U. S. Mail, postage prepaid, certified mail, return receipt requested, addressed to the other party at such party's address shown below. Notice of objection to the demand will be deemed effective upon receipt by escrow agent.

19. REPRESENTATIONS: Seller represents that as of the Closing Date (a) there will be no liens, assessments, or security interests against the Property which will not be satisfied out of the sales proceeds unless securing payment of any loans assumed by Buyer and (b) assumed loans will not be in default. If any representation of Seller in this contract is untrue on the Closing Date, Buyer may terminate this contract and the earnest money will be refunded to Buyer.

20. FEDERAL TAX REQUIREMENTS: If Seller is a "foreign person," as defined by applicable law, or if Seller fails to deliver an affidavit to Buyer that Seller is not a "foreign person," then Buyer shall withhold from the sales proceeds an amount sufficient to comply with applicable tax law and deliver the same to the Internal Revenue Service together with appropriate tax forms. Internal Revenue Service regulations require filing written reports if currency in excess of specified amounts is received in the transaction.

21. NOTICES: All notices from one party to the other must be in writing and are effective when mailed to, hand-delivered at, or transmitted by facsimile as follows:

To Buyer at:	**To Seller at:**
______________________	______________________
______________________	______________________
______________________	______________________
Telephone:(____) ____________	Telephone:(____) ____________
Facsimile:(____) ____________	Facsimile:(____) ____________

22. AGREEMENT OF PARTIES: This contract contains the entire agreement of the parties and cannot be changed except by their written agreement. Addenda which are a part of this contract are (check all applicable boxes):

- ❑ Third Party Financing Condition Addendum
- ❑ Addendum for Property Subject to Mandatory Membership in an Owners' Association
- ❑ Seller Financing Addendum
- ❑ Environmental Assessment, Threatened or Endangered Species and Wetlands Addendum

01A TREC NO. 20-6

Initialed for identification by Buyer_______ _______ and Seller_______ _______

Figure 9.6 TREC 20-6 (continued)

Contract Concerning ______________________________ Page Seven 01-06-03
(Address of Property)

- ❑ Loan Assumption Addendum
- ❑ Buyer's Temporary Residential Lease
- ❑ Seller's Temporary Residential Lease
- ❑ Addendum for Sale of Other Property by Buyer
- ❑ Addendum for Seller's Disclosure of Information on Lead-based Paint and Lead-based Paint Hazards as Required by Federal Law
- ❑ Addendum for "Back-Up" Contract
- ❑ Addendum for Coastal Area Property
- ❑ Addendum for Property Located Seaward of the Gulf Intracoastal Waterway
- ❑ Addendum for Release of Liability on Assumption of FHA, VA, or Conventional Loan Restoration of Seller's Entitlement for VA Guaranteed Loan
- ❑ Other (list): ______________________________

____

23. **TERMINATION OPTION: This paragraph will be a part of this contract ONLY if both blanks are filled in and Buyer has paid the Option Fee.** Buyer has paid Seller $____________ (Option Fee) for the unrestricted right to terminate this contract by giving notice of termination to Seller within ________ days after the effective date of this contract. If Buyer gives notice of termination within the time specified, the Option Fee will not be refunded, however, any earnest money will be refunded to Buyer. The Option Fee ❑ will ❑ will not be credited to the Sales Price at closing. For the purposes of this paragraph, time is of the essence; strict compliance with the time for performance stated herein is required.

24. **CONSULT AN ATTORNEY:** Real estate licensees cannot give legal advice. READ THIS CONTRACT CAREFULLY. If you do not understand the effect of this contract, consult an attorney BEFORE signing.

Buyer's
Attorney is:______________________

____

Telephone: (____)______________________

Facsimile: (____)______________________

Seller's
Attorney is:______________________

____

Telephone: (____)______________________

Facsimile: (____)______________________

EXECUTED the ______day of ______________________, 20____ (EFFECTIVE DATE). (BROKER: FILL IN THE DATE OF FINAL ACCEPTANCE.)

____
Buyer

____
Seller

____
Buyer

____
Seller

The form of this contract has been approved by the Texas Real Estate Commission. TREC forms are intended for use only by trained real estate licensees. No representation is made as to the legal validity or adequacy of any provision in any specific transactions. It is not suitable for complex transactions. Texas Real Estate Commission, P.O. Box 12188, Austin, TX 78711-2188, 1-800-250-8732 or (512) 459-6544 (http://www.trec.state.tx.us) TREC NO. 20-6. This form replaces TREC NO. 20-5.

01A TREC NO. 20-6

Initialed for identification by Buyer_______ _______ and Seller_______ _______

Figure 9.6 TREC 20-6 (continued)

Contract Concerning ______________________________ Page Eight 01-06-03
(Address of Property)

SELLER'S RECEIPT

Receipt of $______________ (Option Fee) in the form of ________________ is acknowledged.

Seller ______________________ Date ______________________

BROKER INFORMATION AND RATIFICATION OF FEE

Listing Broker has agreed to pay Other Broker ____________________ of the total sales price when Listing Broker's fee is received. Escrow Agent is authorized and directed to pay Other Broker from Listing Broker's fee at closing.

Other Broker	Listing Broker
License No. Telephone	License No. Telephone
represents ☐ Buyer only as Buyer's agent ☐ Seller as Listing Broker's subagent	represents ☐ Seller and Buyer as an intermediary ☐ Seller only as Seller's agent
Associate Telephone	Listing Associate Telephone
Broker's Address	Listing Associate's Office Address Facsimile
Facsimile	Selling Associate Telephone
	Selling Associate's Office Address Facsimile

RECEIPT

Receipt of ☐ Contract and ☐ $____________ Earnest Money in the form of ________________ is acknowledged.
Escrow Agent: ______________________ Date: ______________

By: ______________________

Address ______________________ Telephone (____) ______________

City State Zip ______________________ Facsimile: (____) ______________

01A TREC NO. 20-6

Figure 9.7 TREC 40-1

02-09-2004

EQUAL HOUSING OPPORTUNITY

PROMULGATED BY THE TEXAS REAL ESTATE COMMISSION (TREC)

THIRD PARTY FINANCING CONDITION ADDENDUM

TO CONTRACT CONCERNING THE PROPERTY AT

____

(Street Address and City)

Buyer shall apply promptly for all financing described below and make every reasonable effort to obtain financing approval including but not limited to furnishing all information and documents required by lender for approval. Financing approval will be deemed to have been obtained when the lender determines that Buyer has satisfied all of lender's financial requirements (those items relating to Buyer's assets, income and credit history). If Buyer cannot obtain financing approval, Buyer must give written notice to Seller within _____ days after the effective date of this contract and this contract will terminate and the earnest money will be refunded to Buyer. **If Buyer does not give such notice within the time allowed, this contract will no longer be subject to Buyer being approved for the financing described below. For purposes of this paragraph, time is of the essence; strict compliance with the times for performance herein stated is required.**

Each note must be secured by vendor's and deed of trust liens.

❑ A. CONVENTIONAL FINANCING:

❑ (1) A first mortgage loan in the principal amount of $ ___________________ (excluding any financed PMI premium), due in full in _________ year(s), with interest not to exceed ______% per annum for the first ________year(s) of the loan with Loan Fees (loan origination, discount, buy-down, and commitment fees) not to exceed ________% of the loan.

❑ (2) A second mortgage loan in the principal amount of $__________________(excluding any financed PMI premium), due in full in ___________year(s), with interest not to exceed ______% per annum for the first ____________year(s) of the loan with Loan Fees (loan origination, discount, buy-down, and commitment fees) not to exceed _________ % of the loan.

❑ B. TEXAS VETERANS' HOUSING ASSISTANCE PROGRAM LOAN: A Texas Veteran's Housing Assistance Program Loan of $________________ for a period of at least ______years at the interest rate established by the Texas Veteran's Land Board at the time of closing.

❑ C. FHA INSURED FINANCING: A Section ________________ FHA insured loan of not less than $__________________ (excluding any financed MIP), amortizable monthly for not less than _______years, with interest not to exceed _______% per annum for the first ______year(s) of the loan with Loan Fees (loan origination, discount, buy-down, and commitment fees) not to exceed _________ % of the loan. As required by HUD-FHA, if FHA valuation is unknown, *"It is expressly agreed that, notwithstanding any other provision of this contract, the purchaser (Buyer) shall not be obligated to complete the purchase of the Property described herein or to incur any penalty by forfeiture of earnest money deposits or otherwise unless the purchaser (Buyer) has been given in accordance with HUD/FHA or VA requirements a written statement issued by the Federal Housing Commissioner, Department of Veterans Affairs, or a Direct Endorsement Lender setting forth the appraised value of the Property of not less than $__________________. The purchaser (Buyer) shall have the privilege and option of proceeding with consummation of the contract without regard to the amount of the appraised valuation. The appraised valuation is arrived at to determine the maximum mortgage the Department of Housing and Urban Development will insure. HUD does not warrant the value or the condition of the Property. The purchaser (Buyer) should satisfy himself/herself that the price and the condition of the Property are acceptable."*

Initialed for identification by Buyer_______ _______ and Seller________ ________

Figure 9.7 TREC 40-1 (continued)

Third Party Financing Condition Addendum Concerning Page Two 02-09-2004

____

(Address of Property)

☐ D. VA GUARANTEED FINANCING: A VA guaranteed loan of not less than $_________________ (excluding any financed Funding Fee), amortizable monthly for not less than________years, with interest not to exceed________% per annum for the first ________year(s) of the loan with Loan Fees (loan origination, discount, buy-down, and commitment fees) not to exceed ________% of the loan.

VA NOTICE TO BUYER: "*It is expressly agreed that, notwithstanding any other provisions of this contract, the Buyer shall not incur any penalty by forfeiture of earnest money or otherwise or be obligated to complete the purchase of the Property described herein, if the contract purchase price or cost exceeds the reasonable value of the Property established by the Department of Veterans Affairs. The Buyer shall, however, have the privilege and option of proceeding with the consummation of this contract without regard to the amount of the reasonable value established by the Department of Veterans Affairs.*"

If Buyer elects to complete the purchase at an amount in excess of the reasonable value established by VA, Buyer shall pay such excess amount in cash from a source which Buyer agrees to disclose to the VA and which Buyer represents will not be from borrowed funds except as approved by VA. If VA reasonable value of the Property is less than the Sales Price, Seller may reduce the Sales Price to an amount equal to the VA reasonable value and the sale will be closed at the lower Sales Price with proportionate adjustments to the down payment and the loan amount.

Buyer hereby authorizes any lender to furnish to the Seller or Buyer or their representatives information relating only to the status of financing approval of Buyer.

____________________	____________________
Buyer	Seller
____________________	____________________
Buyer	Seller

This form has been approved by the Texas Real Estate Commission for use with similarly approved or promulgated contract forms. Such approval relates to this form only. TREC forms are intended for use only by trained real estate licensees. No representation is made as to the legal validity or adequacy of any provision in any specific transactions. It is not suitable for complex transactions. Texas Real Estate Commission, P.O. Box 12188, Austin, TX 78711-2188, 1-800-250-8732 or (512) 459-6544 (http://www.trec.state.tx.us) TREC No. 40-1. This form replaces TREC No. 40-0.

Figure 9.8 TREC OP-L

APPROVED BY THE TEXAS REAL ESTATE COMMISSION 02-09-2004

EQUAL HOUSING OPPORTUNITY

ADDENDUM FOR SELLER'S DISCLOSURE OF INFORMATION ON LEAD-BASED PAINT AND LEAD-BASED PAINT HAZARDS AS REQUIRED BY FEDERAL LAW

CONCERNING THE PROPERTY AT ______________________________
(Street Address and City)

A. **LEAD WARNING STATEMENT:** "Every purchaser of any interest in residential real property on which a residential dwelling was built prior to 1978 is notified that such property may present exposure to lead from lead-based paint that may place young children at risk of developing lead poisoning. Lead poisoning in young children may produce permanent neurological damage, including learning disabilities, reduced intelligence quotient, behavioral problems, and impaired memory. Lead poisoning also poses a particular risk to pregnant women. The seller of any interest in residential real property is required to provide the buyer with any information on lead-based paint hazards from risk assessments or inspections in the seller's possession and notify the buyer of any known lead-based paint hazards. A risk assessment or inspection for possible lead-paint hazards is recommended prior to purchase."

NOTICE: Inspector must be properly certified as required by federal law.

B. **SELLER'S DISCLOSURE:**

1. PRESENCE OF LEAD-BASED PAINT AND/OR LEAD-BASED PAINT HAZARDS (check on box only):
   ☐(a) Known lead-based paint and/or lead-based paint hazards are present in the Property (explain): ______________________________.
   ☐(b) Seller has no actual knowledge of lead-based paint and/or lead-based paint hazards in the Property.
2. RECORDS AND REPORTS AVAILABLE TO SELLER (check one box only):
   ☐(a) Seller has provided the purchaser with all available records and reports pertaining to lead-based paint and/or lead-based paint hazards in the Property (list documents): ______________________________.
   ☐(b) Seller has no reports or records pertaining to lead-based paint and/or lead-based paint hazards in the Property.

C. **BUYER'S RIGHTS** (check one box only):

☐1. Buyer waives the opportunity to conduct a risk assessment or inspection of the Property for the presence of lead-based paint or lead-based paint hazards.
☐2. Within ten days after the effective date of this contract, Buyer may have the Property inspected by inspectors selected by Buyer. If lead-based paint or lead-based paint hazards are present, Buyer may terminate this contract by giving Seller written notice within 14 days after the effective date of this contract, and the earnest money will be refunded to Buyer.

D. **BUYER'S ACKNOWLEDGMENT** (check applicable boxes):

☐1. Buyer has received copies of all information listed above.
☐2. Buyer has received the pamphlet *Protect Your Family from Lead in Your Home*.

E. **BROKERS' ACKNOWLEDGMENT:** Brokers have informed Seller of Seller's obligations under 42 U.S.C. 4852d to: (a) provide Buyer with the federally approved pamphlet on lead poisoning prevention; (b) complete this addendum; (c) disclose any known lead-based paint and/or lead-based paint hazards in the Property; (d) deliver all records and reports to Buyer pertaining to lead-based paint and/or lead-based paint hazards in the Property; (e) provide Buyer a period of up to 10 days to have the Property inspected; and (f) retain a completed copy of this addendum for at least 3 years following the sale. Brokers are aware of their responsibility to ensure compliance.

F. **CERTIFICATION OF ACCURACY:** The following persons have reviewed the information above and certify, to the best of their knowledge, that the information they have provided is true and accurate.

Buyer	Date	Seller	Date
Buyer	Date	Seller	Date
Other Broker	Date	Listing Broker	Date

The form of this addendum has been approved by the Texas Real Estate Commission for use only with similarly approved or promulgated forms of contracts. Such approval relates to this contract form only. TREC forms are intended for use only by trained real estate licensees. No representation is made as to the legal validity or adequacy of any provision in any specific transactions. It is not suitable for complex transactions. Texas Real Estate Commission, P.O. Box 12188, Austin, TX 78711-2188, 1-800-250-8732 or (512) 459-6544 (http://www.trec.state.tx.us)

Form OP-L 01A

Transaction 3: 80% Conventional ARM
(Using: TREC 20-6 and 40-1)

Susan Helen Seller, an unmarried woman, will sell her lake home to Henry A. Homebuyer and his spouse, Hanna S. Homebuyer. Not being located in a city, town, or village, the property is described by metes and bounds as evidenced in the purchase agreement by attached Exhibit A. The property is not in a plated subdivision. It is located in Harrison County and has a mailing address of 42 Pleasure Lake Drive, Podunk, Texas 77072. Ms. Seller will have the leased security system and the water softener removed prior to closing.

The buyers will pay $126,000 for the property and have already applied for an 80 percent ARM loan. They have not yet been approved for this financing. They feel they can get approval within 20 days and close within 30 days after the effective date of the contract. They have researched the market and know they can get a 15-year ARM loan with an interest rate of 6 percent or less for the first three years of the loan.

The Homebuyers have written a check for $1,500 made payable to Buyer's Choice Title Company. They will pay for the owner's title policy as well as the survey that is to be delivered within 15 days after the date of the contract. They want three days to review the survey that will be furnished to their lender.

The house was built in 1979, so the lead addendum is not attached. The buyers have received the seller's disclosure notice. The buyers accept the property in its present condition, provided the seller will repair the septic system and bring it up to current county code as evidenced by a county inspection certificate.

The buyers want possession at closing and funding and will pay for the appraisal required by the lender. The buyers want all of their notices delivered to their attorney's office at 2225 High Street, Podunk, Texas 77071. Attorney Michael Phelps will review the offer prior to signing by the buyers.

The seller will receive her notices through the listing agent.

The buyers are customers who were shown the property by salesperson Sam Smith, from Happy Buyer Realty. Seller's Choice Realty Services promoted the property through the MLS. Lester Listor is the listing associate. The selling commission is 3.5 percent of the sales price.

The parties feel that it is a good idea to agree to try mediation before resorting to litigation. They agree to split the cost of mediation should it become necessary.

Figure 9.9 TREC 20-6

01-06-03

PROMULGATED BY THE TEXAS REAL ESTATE COMMISSION (TREC)

ONE TO FOUR FAMILY RESIDENTIAL CONTRACT (RESALE)

NOTICE: Not For Use For Condominium Transactions

1. PARTIES: ______________________________ (Seller) agrees to sell and convey to ______________________________(Buyer) and Buyer agrees to buy from Seller the Property described below.

2. PROPERTY:

A. LAND: Lot ______________________,Block_____, ______________________ ______________________Addition, City of ______________ , ____________ County, Texas, known as ______________________________ ______________________(address/zip code), or as described on attached exhibit.

B. IMPROVEMENTS: The house, garage and all other fixtures and improvements attached to the above-described real property, including without limitation, the following permanently installed and built-in items, if any: all equipment and appliances, valances, screens, shutters, awnings, wall-to-wall carpeting, mirrors, ceiling fans, attic fans, mail boxes, television antennas and satellite dish system and equipment, heating and air-conditioning units, security and fire detection equipment, wiring, plumbing and lighting fixtures, chandeliers, water softener system, kitchen equipment, garage door openers, cleaning equipment, shrubbery, landscaping, outdoor cooking equipment, and all other property owned by Seller and attached to the above described real property.

C. ACCESSORIES: The following described related accessories, if any: window air conditioning units, stove, fireplace screens, curtains and rods, blinds, window shades, draperies and rods, controls for satellite dish system, controls for garage door openers, entry gate controls, door keys, mailbox keys, above ground pool, swimming pool equipment and maintenance accessories, and artificial fireplace logs.

D. EXCLUSIONS: The following improvements and accessories will be retained by Seller and excluded: ______________________________ ______________________________.

The land, improvements and accessories are collectively referred to as the "Property".

3. SALES PRICE:

A. Cash portion of Sales Price payable by Buyer at closing................. $______________

B. Sum of all financing described below (excluding any loan funding fee or mortgage insurance premium) .... $______________

C. Sales Price (Sum of A and B) .... $______________

4. FINANCING: The portion of Sales Price not payable in cash will be paid as follows: (Check applicable boxes below)

❑ A. THIRD PARTY FINANCING: One or more third party mortgage loans in the total amount of $____________________. If the Property does not satisfy the lenders' underwriting requirements for the loan(s), this contract will terminate and the earnest money will be refunded to Buyer. (Check one box only)

❑(1) This contract is subject to Buyer being approved for the financing described in the attached Third Party Financing Condition Addendum.

❑(2) This contract is not subject to Buyer being approved for financing and does not involve FHA or VA financing.

❑ B. ASSUMPTION: The assumption of the unpaid principal balance of one or more promissory notes described in the attached TREC Loan Assumption Addendum.

❑ C. SELLER FINANCING: A promissory note from Buyer to Seller of $______________, bearing _______ % interest per annum, secured by vendor's and deed of trust liens, and containing the terms and conditions described in the attached TREC Seller Financing Addendum. If an owner policy of title insurance is furnished, Buyer shall furnish Seller with a mortgagee policy of title insurance.

5. EARNEST MONEY: Upon execution of this contract by both parties, Buyer shall deposit $____________ as earnest money with ______________________________, as escrow agent, at ______________________________ (address). Buyer shall deposit additional earnest money of $____________________ with escrow agent within _________days after the effective date of this contract. If Buyer fails to deposit the earnest money as required by this contract, Buyer will be in default.

Initialed for identification by Buyer______ ______ and Seller _______ ______ **01A** TREC NO. 20-6

Figure 9.9 TREC 20-6 (continued)

Contract Concerning ____ Page Two 01-06-03
(Address of Property)

6. TITLE POLICY AND SURVEY:

A. TITLE POLICY: Seller shall furnish to Buyer at ❑Seller's ❑Buyer's expense an owner policy of title insurance (Title Policy) issued by ______________________________ ______________________________ (Title Company) in the amount of the Sales Price, dated at or after closing, insuring Buyer against loss under the provisions of the Title Policy, subject to the promulgated exclusions (including existing building and zoning ordinances) and the following exceptions:

(1) Restrictive covenants common to the platted subdivision in which the Property is located.
(2) The standard printed exception for standby fees, taxes and assessments.
(3) Liens created as part of the financing described in Paragraph 4.
(4) Utility easements created by the dedication deed or plat of the subdivision in which the Property is located.
(5) Reservations or exceptions otherwise permitted by this contract or as may be approved by Buyer in writing.
(6) The standard printed exception as to marital rights.
(7) The standard printed exception as to waters, tidelands, beaches, streams, and related matters.
(8) The standard printed exception as to discrepancies, conflicts, shortages in area or boundary lines, encroachments or protrusions, or overlapping improvements. Buyer, at Buyer's expense, may have the exception amended to read, "shortages in area".

B. COMMITMENT: Within 20 days after the Title Company receives a copy of this contract, Seller shall furnish to Buyer a commitment for title insurance (Commitment) and, at Buyer's expense, legible copies of restrictive covenants and documents evidencing exceptions in the Commitment (Exception Documents) other than the standard printed exceptions. Seller authorizes the Title Company to mail or hand deliver the Commitment and Exception Documents to Buyer at Buyer's address shown in Paragraph 21. If the Commitment and Exception Documents are not delivered to Buyer within the specified time, the time for delivery will be automatically extended up to 15 days or the Closing Date, whichever is earlier.

C. SURVEY: The survey must be made by a registered professional land surveyor acceptable to the Title Company and any lender. (Check one box only)

❑ (1) Within ______ days after the effective date of this contract, Seller, at Seller's expense, shall furnish a new survey to Buyer.
❑ (2) Within ______ days after the effective date of this contract, Buyer, at Buyer's expense, shall obtain a new survey.
❑ (3) Within ______ days after the effective date of this contract, Seller shall furnish Seller's existing survey of the Property to Buyer and the Title Company, along with Seller's affidavit acceptable to the Title Company for approval of the survey. If the survey is not approved by the Title Company or Buyer's lender, a new survey will be obtained at ❑ Seller's ❑ Buyer's expense no later than 3 days prior to the Closing Date.

D. OBJECTIONS: Within ____ days after Buyer receives the Commitment, Exception Documents and the survey, Buyer may object in writing to defects, exceptions, or encumbrances to title: disclosed on the survey other than items 6A(1) through (7) above; disclosed in the Commitment other than items 6A(1) through (8) above; or which prohibit the following use or activity: ______________________________.
Buyer's failure to object within the time allowed will constitute a waiver of Buyer's right to object; except that the requirements in Schedule C of the Commitment are not waived. Seller shall cure the timely objections of Buyer or any third party lender within 15 days after Seller receives the objections and the Closing Date will be extended as necessary. If objections are not cured within such 15 day period, this contract will terminate and the earnest money will be refunded to Buyer unless Buyer waives the objections.

E. TITLE NOTICES:

(1) ABSTRACT OR TITLE POLICY: Broker advises Buyer to have an abstract of title covering the Property examined by an attorney of Buyer's selection, or Buyer should be furnished with or obtain a Title Policy. If a Title Policy is furnished, the Commitment should be promptly reviewed by an attorney of Buyer's choice due to the time limitations on Buyer's right to object.
(2) MANDATORY OWNERS' ASSOCIATION MEMBERSHIP: The Property ❑ is ❑ is not subject to mandatory membership in an owners' association. If the Property is subject to mandatory membership in an owners' association, Seller notifies Buyer under §5.012, Texas Property Code, that, as a purchaser of property in the residential community in

Initialed for identification by Buyer______ ______ and Seller ______ ______ **01A** TREC NO. 20-6

Figure 9.9 TREC 20-6 (continued)

Contract Concerning ______________________________ Page Three 01-06-03
(Address of Property)

which the Property is located, you are obligated to be a member of the owners' association. Restrictive covenants governing the use and occupancy of the Property and a dedicatory instrument governing the establishment, maintenance, and operation of this residential community have been or will be recorded in the Real Property Records of the county in which the Property is located. Copies of the restrictive covenants and dedicatory instrument may be obtained from the county clerk. You are obligated to pay assessments to the owners' association. The amount of the assessments is subject to change. Your failure to pay the assessments could result in a lien on and the foreclosure of the Property.

(3) STATUTORY TAX DISTRICTS: If the Property is situated in a utility or other statutorily created district providing water, sewer, drainage, or flood control facilities and services, Chapter 49, Texas Water Code requires Seller to deliver and Buyer to sign the statutory notice relating to the tax rate, bonded indebtedness, or standby fee of the district prior to final execution of this contract.

(4) TIDE WATERS: If the Property abuts the tidally influenced waters of the state, §33.135, Texas Natural Resources Code, requires a notice regarding coastal area property to be included in the contract. An addendum containing the notice promulgated by TREC or required by the parties must be used.

(5) ANNEXATION: If the Property is located outside the limits of a municipality, Seller notifies Buyer under §5.011, Texas Property Code, that the Property may now or later be included in the extraterritorial jurisdiction of a municipality and may now or later be subject to annexation by the municipality. Each municipality maintains a map that depicts its boundaries and extraterritorial jurisdiction. To determine if the Property is located within a municipality's extraterritorial jurisdiction or is likely to be located within a municipality's extraterritorial jurisdiction, contact all municipalities located in the general proximity of the Property for further information.

7. PROPERTY CONDITION:

A. INSPECTIONS, ACCESS AND UTILITIES: Buyer may have the Property inspected by inspectors selected by Buyer and licensed by TREC or otherwise permitted by law to make inspections. Seller shall permit Buyer and Buyer's agents access to the Property at reasonable times. Seller shall pay for turning on existing utilities for inspections.

B. SELLER'S DISCLOSURE NOTICE PURSUANT TO §5.008, TEXAS PROPERTY CODE (Notice):
(Check one box only)

❑ (1) Buyer has received the Notice.

❑ (2) Buyer has not received the Notice. Within _______ days after the effective date of this contract, Seller shall deliver the Notice to Buyer. If Buyer does not receive the Notice, Buyer may terminate this contract at any time prior to the closing and the earnest money will be refunded to Buyer. If Seller delivers the Notice, Buyer may terminate this contract for any reason within 7 days after Buyer receives the Notice or prior to the closing, whichever first occurs, and the earnest money will be refunded to Buyer.

❑ (3) The Texas Property Code does not require this Seller to furnish the Notice.

C. SELLER'S DISCLOSURE OF LEAD-BASED PAINT AND LEAD-BASED PAINT HAZARDS is required by Federal law for a residential dwelling constructed prior to 1978.

D. ACCEPTANCE OF PROPERTY CONDITION: Buyer accepts the Property in its present condition; provided Seller, at Seller's expense, shall complete the following specific repairs and treatments:____
____.

E. LENDER REQUIRED REPAIRS AND TREATMENTS: Unless otherwise agreed in writing, neither party is obligated to pay for lender required repairs, which includes treatment for wood destroying insects. If the parties do not agree to pay for the lender required repairs or treatments, this contract will terminate and the earnest money will be refunded to Buyer. If the cost of lender required repairs and treatments exceeds 5% of the Sales Price, Buyer may terminate this contract and the earnest money will be refunded to Buyer.

F. COMPLETION OF REPAIRS AND TREATMENTS: Unless otherwise agreed in writing, Seller shall complete all agreed repairs and treatments prior to the Closing Date. All required permits must be obtained, and repairs and treatments must be performed by persons who are licensed or otherwise authorized by law to provide such repairs or treatments. At Buyer's election, any transferable warranties received by Seller with respect to the repairs and treatments will be transferred to Buyer at Buyer's expense. If Seller fails to complete any agreed repairs and

Figure 9.9 TREC 20-6 (continued)

Contract Concerning ____ Page Four 01-06-03
(Address of Property)

treatments prior to the Closing Date, Buyer may do so and receive reimbursement from Seller at closing. The Closing Date will be extended up to 15 days, if necessary, to complete repairs and treatments.

G. ENVIRONMENTAL MATTERS: Buyer is advised that the presence of wetlands, toxic substances, including asbestos and wastes or other environmental hazards, or the presence of a threatened or endangered species or its habitat may affect Buyer's intended use of the Property. If Buyer is concerned about these matters, an addendum promulgated by TREC or required by the parties should be used.

H. RESIDENTIAL SERVICE CONTRACTS: Buyer may purchase a residential service contract from a residential service company licensed by TREC. If Buyer purchases a residential service contract, Seller shall reimburse Buyer at closing for the cost of the residential service contract in an amount not exceeding $_______________ . Buyer should review any residential service contract for the scope of coverage, exclusions and limitations. **The purchase of a residential service contract is optional. Similar coverage may be purchased from various companies authorized to do business in Texas.**

8. BROKERS' FEES: All obligations of the parties for payment of brokers' fees are contained in separate written agreements.

9. CLOSING:

A. The closing of the sale will be on or before ________________________, 20___, or within 7 days after objections to matters disclosed in the Commitment or by the survey have been cured, whichever date is later (Closing Date). If either party fails to close the sale by the Closing Date, the non-defaulting party may exercise the remedies contained in Paragraph 15.

B. At closing:

(1) Seller shall execute and deliver a general warranty deed conveying title to the Property to Buyer and showing no additional exceptions to those permitted in Paragraph 6 and furnish tax statements or certificates showing no delinquent taxes on the Property.

(2) Buyer shall pay the Sales Price in good funds acceptable to the escrow agent.

(3) Seller and Buyer shall execute and deliver any notices, statements, certificates, affidavits, releases, loan documents and other documents required of them by this contract, the Commitment or law necessary for the closing of the sale and the issuance of the Title Policy.

C. Unless expressly prohibited by written agreement, Seller may continue to show the Property and receive, negotiate and accept back up offers.

D. All covenants, representations and warranties in this contract survive closing.

10. POSSESSION: Seller shall deliver to Buyer possession of the Property in its present or required condition, ordinary wear and tear excepted: ☐ upon closing and funding ☐ according to a temporary residential lease form promulgated by TREC or other written lease required by the parties. Any possession by Buyer prior to closing or by Seller after closing which is not authorized by a written lease will establish a tenancy at sufferance relationship between the parties. *Consult your insurance agent prior to change of ownership or possession because insurance coverage may be limited or terminated. The absence of a written lease or appropriate insurance coverage may expose the parties to economic loss.*

11. SPECIAL PROVISIONS: (Insert only factual statements and business details applicable to the sale. TREC rules prohibit licensees from adding factual statements or business details for which a contract addendum, lease or other form has been promulgated by TREC for mandatory use.)

Initialed for identification by Buyer_____ _____ and Seller _____ _____ **01A** TREC NO. 20-6

Figure 9.9 TREC 20-6 (continued)

Contract Concerning ____ Page Five 01-06-03
(Address of Property)

12. SETTLEMENT AND OTHER EXPENSES:

A. The following expenses must be paid at or prior to closing:

(1) Expenses payable by Seller (Seller's Expenses):

(a) Releases of existing liens, including prepayment penalties and recording fees; release of Seller's loan liability; tax statements or certificates; preparation of deed; one-half of escrow fee; and other expenses payable by Seller under this contract.

(b) Seller shall also pay an amount not to exceed $ ____________ to be applied in the following order: Buyer's Expenses which Buyer is prohibited from paying by FHA, VA, Texas Veteran's Housing Assistance Program or other governmental loan programs; Buyer's prepaid items; other Buyer's expenses.

(2) Expenses payable by Buyer (Buyer's Expenses):

(a) Loan origination, discount, buy-down, and commitment fees (Loan Fees).

(b) Appraisal fees; loan application fees; credit reports; preparation of loan documents; interest on the notes from date of disbursement to one month prior to dates of first monthly payments; recording fees; copies of easements and restrictions; mortgagee title policy with endorsements required by lender; loan-related inspection fees; photos, amortization schedules, one-half of escrow fee; all prepaid items, including required premiums for flood and hazard insurance, reserve deposits for insurance, ad valorem taxes and special governmental assessments; final compliance inspection; courier fee, repair inspection, underwriting fee and wire transfer, expenses incident to any loan, and other expenses payable by Buyer under this contract.

B. Buyer shall pay Private Mortgage Insurance Premium (PMI), VA Loan Funding Fee, or FHA Mortgage Insurance Premium (MIP) as required by the lender.

C. If any expense exceeds an amount expressly stated in this contract for such expense to be paid by a party, that party may terminate this contract unless the other party agrees to pay such excess. Buyer may not pay charges and fees expressly prohibited by FHA, VA, Texas Veteran's Housing Assistance Program or other governmental loan program regulations.

13. PRORATIONS: Taxes for the current year, interest, maintenance fees, assessments, dues and rents will be prorated through the Closing Date. If taxes for the current year vary from the amount prorated at closing, the parties shall adjust the prorations when tax statements for the current year are available. If taxes are not paid at or prior to closing, Buyer shall pay taxes for the current year.

14. CASUALTY LOSS: If any part of the Property is damaged or destroyed by fire or other casualty after the effective date of this contract, Seller shall restore the Property to its previous condition as soon as reasonably possible, but in any event by the Closing Date. If Seller fails to do so due to factors beyond Seller's control, Buyer may (a) terminate this contract and the earnest money will be refunded to Buyer (b) extend the time for performance up to 15 days and the Closing Date will be extended as necessary or (c) accept the Property in its damaged condition with an assignment of insurance proceeds and receive credit from Seller at closing in the amount of the deductible under the insurance policy. Seller's obligations under this paragraph are independent of any obligations of Seller under Paragraph 7.

15. DEFAULT: If Buyer fails to comply with this contract, Buyer will be in default, and Seller may (a) enforce specific performance, seek such other relief as may be provided by law, or both, or (b) terminate this contract and receive the earnest money as liquidated damages, thereby releasing both parties from this contract. If, due to factors beyond Seller's control, Seller fails within the time allowed to make any non-casualty repairs or deliver the Commitment, or survey, if required of Seller, Buyer may (a) extend the time for performance up to 15 days and the Closing Date will be extended as necessary or (b) terminate this contract as the sole remedy and receive the earnest money. If Seller fails to comply with this contract for any other reason, Seller will be in default and Buyer may (a) enforce specific performance, seek such other relief as may be provided by law, or both, or (b) terminate this contract and receive the earnest money, thereby releasing both parties from this contract.

16. MEDIATION: It is the policy of the State of Texas to encourage resolution of disputes through alternative dispute resolution procedures such as mediation. Any dispute between Seller and Buyer related to this contract which is not resolved through informal discussion ☐will ☐will not be submitted to a mutually acceptable mediation service or provider. The parties to the mediation shall bear the mediation costs equally. This paragraph does not preclude a party from seeking equitable relief from a court of competent jurisdiction.

Initialed for identification by Buyer_____ _____ and Seller _____ _____ **01A** TREC NO. 20-6

Figure 9.9 TREC 20-6 (continued)

Contract Concerning ______________________________ Page Six 01-06-03
(Address of Property)

17. ATTORNEY'S FEES: The prevailing party in any legal proceeding related to this contract is entitled to recover reasonable attorney's fees and all costs of such proceeding incurred by the prevailing party.

18. ESCROW: The escrow agent is not (a) a party to this contract and does not have liability for the performance or nonperformance of any party to this contract, (b) liable for interest on the earnest money and (c) liable for the loss of any earnest money caused by the failure of any financial institution in which the earnest money has been deposited unless the financial institution is acting as escrow agent. At closing, the earnest money must be applied first to any cash down payment, then to Buyer's Expenses and any excess refunded to Buyer. If both parties make written demand for the earnest money, escrow agent may require payment of unpaid expenses incurred on behalf of the parties and a written release of liability of escrow agent from all parties. If one party makes written demand for the earnest money, escrow agent shall give notice of the demand by providing to the other party a copy of the demand. If escrow agent does not receive written objection to the demand from the other party within 30 days after notice to the other party, escrow agent may disburse the earnest money to the party making demand reduced by the amount of unpaid expenses incurred on behalf of the party receiving the earnest money and escrow agent may pay the same to the creditors. If escrow agent complies with the provisions of this paragraph, each party hereby releases escrow agent from all adverse claims related to the disbursal of the earnest money. Escrow agent's notice to the other party will be effective when deposited in the U. S. Mail, postage prepaid, certified mail, return receipt requested, addressed to the other party at such party's address shown below. Notice of objection to the demand will be deemed effective upon receipt by escrow agent.

19. REPRESENTATIONS: Seller represents that as of the Closing Date (a) there will be no liens, assessments, or security interests against the Property which will not be satisfied out of the sales proceeds unless securing payment of any loans assumed by Buyer and (b) assumed loans will not be in default. If any representation of Seller in this contract is untrue on the Closing Date, Buyer may terminate this contract and the earnest money will be refunded to Buyer.

20. FEDERAL TAX REQUIREMENTS: If Seller is a "foreign person," as defined by applicable law, or if Seller fails to deliver an affidavit to Buyer that Seller is not a "foreign person," then Buyer shall withhold from the sales proceeds an amount sufficient to comply with applicable tax law and deliver the same to the Internal Revenue Service together with appropriate tax forms. Internal Revenue Service regulations require filing written reports if currency in excess of specified amounts is received in the transaction.

21. NOTICES: All notices from one party to the other must be in writing and are effective when mailed to, hand-delivered at, or transmitted by facsimile as follows:

To Buyer at:	**To Seller at:**
______________________	______________________
______________________	______________________
______________________	______________________
Telephone:(____) ______________	Telephone:(____) ______________
Facsimile:(____)______________	Facsimile:(____) ______________

22. AGREEMENT OF PARTIES: This contract contains the entire agreement of the parties and cannot be changed except by their written agreement. Addenda which are a part of this contract are (check all applicable boxes):

- ☐ Third Party Financing Condition Addendum
- ☐ Addendum for Property Subject to Mandatory Membership in an Owners' Association
- ☐ Seller Financing Addendum
- ☐ Environmental Assessment, Threatened or Endangered Species and Wetlands Addendum

Initialed for identification by Buyer_____ _____ and Seller ______ _____ **01A** TREC NO. 20-6

Figure 9.9 TREC 20-6 (continued)

Contract Concerning ____ Page Seven 01-06-03
(Address of Property)

- ❑ Loan Assumption Addendum
- ❑ Buyer's Temporary Residential Lease
- ❑ Seller's Temporary Residential Lease
- ❑ Addendum for Sale of Other Property by Buyer
- ❑ Addendum for Seller's Disclosure of Information on Lead-based Paint and Lead-based Paint Hazards as Required by Federal Law
- ❑ Addendum for "Back-Up" Contract
- ❑ Addendum for Coastal Area Property
- ❑ Addendum for Property Located Seaward of the Gulf Intracoastal Waterway
- ❑ Addendum for Release of Liability on Assumption of FHA, VA, or Conventional Loan Restoration of Seller's Entitlement for VA Guaranteed Loan

❑ Other (list): ____

____

23. TERMINATION OPTION: This paragraph will be a part of this contract ONLY if both blanks are filled in and Buyer has paid the Option Fee. Buyer has paid Seller $_______________ (Option Fee) for the unrestricted right to terminate this contract by giving notice of termination to Seller within _________ days after the effective date of this contract. If Buyer gives notice of termination within the time specified, the Option Fee will not be refunded, however, any earnest money will be refunded to Buyer. The Option Fee ❑will ❑will not be credited to the Sales Price at closing. For the purposes of this paragraph, time is of the essence; strict compliance with the time for performance stated herein is required.

24. CONSULT AN ATTORNEY: Real estate licensees cannot give legal advice. READ THIS CONTRACT CAREFULLY. If you do not understand the effect of this contract, consult an attorney BEFORE signing.

Buyer's
Attorney is:___________________________

____

Telephone: (____)___________________

Facsimile: (____)___________________

Seller's
Attorney is:___________________________

____

Telephone: (____)___________________

Facsimile: (____)___________________

EXECUTED the _______day of ___________________________, 20____ (EFFECTIVE DATE).
(BROKER: FILL IN THE DATE OF FINAL ACCEPTANCE.)

____
Buyer

____
Seller

____
Buyer

____
Seller

The form of this contract has been approved by the Texas Real Estate Commission. TREC forms are intended for use only by trained real estate licensees. No representation is made as to the legal validity or adequacy of any provision in any specific transactions. It is not suitable for complex transactions. Texas Real Estate Commission, P.O. Box 12188, Austin, TX 78711-2188, 1-800-250-8732 or (512) 459-6544 (http://www.trec.state.tx.us) TREC NO. 20-6. This form replaces TREC NO. 20-5.

Figure 9.9 TREC 20-6 (continued)

Contract Concerning ________________________________ Page Eight 01-06-03
(Address of Property)

SELLER'S RECEIPT

Receipt of $______________ (Option Fee) in the form of ______________ is acknowledged.

______________________ Seller ______________________ Date

BROKER INFORMATION AND RATIFICATION OF FEE

Listing Broker has agreed to pay Other Broker ______________ of the total sales price when Listing Broker's fee is received. Escrow Agent is authorized and directed to pay Other Broker from Listing Broker's fee at closing.

Other Broker	Listing Broker
License No. Telephone	License No. Telephone
represents ❑ Buyer only as Buyer's agent ❑ Seller as Listing Broker's subagent	represents ❑ Seller and Buyer as an intermediary ❑ Seller only as Seller's agent
Associate Telephone	Listing Associate Telephone
Broker's Address	Listing Associate's Office Address Facsimile
Facsimile	Selling Associate Telephone
	Selling Associate's Office Address Facsimile

RECEIPT

Receipt of ❑ Contract and ❑ $______________ Earnest Money in the form of ______________ is acknowledged.

Escrow Agent: ______________________ Date: ______________

By: ______________________

______________________ Telephone (____) ______________
Address

______________________ Facsimile: (____) ______________
City State Zip

Figure 9.10 TREC 40-1

02-09-2004

EQUAL HOUSING OPPORTUNITY

PROMULGATED BY THE TEXAS REAL ESTATE COMMISSION (TREC)

THIRD PARTY FINANCING CONDITION ADDENDUM

TO CONTRACT CONCERNING THE PROPERTY AT

____

(Street Address and City)

Buyer shall apply promptly for all financing described below and make every reasonable effort to obtain financing approval including but not limited to furnishing all information and documents required by lender for approval. Financing approval will be deemed to have been obtained when the lender determines that Buyer has satisfied all of lender's financial requirements (those items relating to Buyer's assets, income and credit history). If Buyer cannot obtain financing approval, Buyer must give written notice to Seller within ____ days after the effective date of this contract and this contract will terminate and the earnest money will be refunded to Buyer. **If Buyer does not give such notice within the time allowed, this contract will no longer be subject to Buyer being approved for the financing described below. For purposes of this paragraph, time is of the essence; strict compliance with the times for performance herein stated is required.**

Each note must be secured by vendor's and deed of trust liens.

❑ A. CONVENTIONAL FINANCING:

❑ (1) A first mortgage loan in the principal amount of $ __________________ (excluding any financed PMI premium), due in full in _________ year(s), with interest not to exceed ______% per annum for the first _______year(s) of the loan with Loan Fees (loan origination, discount, buy-down, and commitment fees) not to exceed ________% of the loan.

❑ (2) A second mortgage loan in the principal amount of $__________________(excluding any financed PMI premium), due in full in ___________year(s), with interest not to exceed ______% per annum for the first ____________year(s) of the loan with Loan Fees (loan origination, discount, buy-down, and commitment fees) not to exceed _________ % of the loan.

❑ B. TEXAS VETERANS' HOUSING ASSISTANCE PROGRAM LOAN: A Texas Veteran's Housing Assistance Program Loan of $________________ for a period of at least ______years at the interest rate established by the Texas Veteran's Land Board at the time of closing.

❑ C. FHA INSURED FINANCING: A Section ________________ FHA insured loan of not less than $__________________ (excluding any financed MIP), amortizable monthly for not less than _______years, with interest not to exceed _______% per annum for the first ______year(s) of the loan with Loan Fees (loan origination, discount, buy-down, and commitment fees) not to exceed _________ % of the loan. As required by HUD-FHA, if FHA valuation is unknown, *"It is expressly agreed that, notwithstanding any other provision of this contract, the purchaser (Buyer) shall not be obligated to complete the purchase of the Property described herein or to incur any penalty by forfeiture of earnest money deposits or otherwise unless the purchaser (Buyer) has been given in accordance with HUD/FHA or VA requirements a written statement issued by the Federal Housing Commissioner, Department of Veterans Affairs, or a Direct Endorsement Lender setting forth the appraised value of the Property of not less than $__________________. The purchaser (Buyer) shall have the privilege and option of proceeding with consummation of the contract without regard to the amount of the appraised valuation. The appraised valuation is arrived at to determine the maximum mortgage the Department of Housing and Urban Development will insure. HUD does not warrant the value or the condition of the Property. The purchaser (Buyer) should satisfy himself/herself that the price and the condition of the Property are acceptable."*

Initialed for identification by Buyer_______ _______ and Seller________ ________

Figure 9.10 TREC 40-1 (continued)

Third Party Financing Condition Addendum Concerning Page Two 02-09-2004

____
(Address of Property)

❑ D. VA GUARANTEED FINANCING: A VA guaranteed loan of not less than $________________ (excluding any financed Funding Fee), amortizable monthly for not less than_______years, with interest not to exceed________% per annum for the first _______year(s) of the loan with Loan Fees (loan origination, discount, buy-down, and commitment fees) not to exceed ________% of the loan.

VA NOTICE TO BUYER: "*It is expressly agreed that, notwithstanding any other provisions of this contract, the Buyer shall not incur any penalty by forfeiture of earnest money or otherwise or be obligated to complete the purchase of the Property described herein, if the contract purchase price or cost exceeds the reasonable value of the Property established by the Department of Veterans Affairs. The Buyer shall, however, have the privilege and option of proceeding with the consummation of this contract without regard to the amount of the reasonable value established by the Department of Veterans Affairs.*"

If Buyer elects to complete the purchase at an amount in excess of the reasonable value established by VA, Buyer shall pay such excess amount in cash from a source which Buyer agrees to disclose to the VA and which Buyer represents will not be from borrowed funds except as approved by VA. If VA reasonable value of the Property is less than the Sales Price, Seller may reduce the Sales Price to an amount equal to the VA reasonable value and the sale will be closed at the lower Sales Price with proportionate adjustments to the down payment and the loan amount.

Buyer hereby authorizes any lender to furnish to the Seller or Buyer or their representatives information relating only to the status of financing approval of Buyer.

______________________	______________________
Buyer	Seller
______________________	______________________
Buyer	Seller

This form has been approved by the Texas Real Estate Commission for use with similarly approved or promulgated contract forms. Such approval relates to this form only. TREC forms are intended for use only by trained real estate licensees. No representation is made as to the legal validity or adequacy of any provision in any specific transactions. It is not suitable for complex transactions. Texas Real Estate Commission, P.O. Box 12188, Austin, TX 78711-2188, 1-800-250-8732 or (512) 459-6544 (http://www.trec.state.tx.us) TREC No. 40-1. This form replaces TREC No. 40-0.

Transaction 4: VA Guaranteed Loan
(Using: TREC 20-6, 40-1, 15-3, 10-4, and OP-L Lead-Based Paint Addendum)

Freddie Mac, an unmarried man, has listed his home at 2365 Veterans Boulevard for sale with Friendly Agent Company. He gives the agent permission to put it in the local multiple listing service and offer other companies the opportunity to function as subagents. Sam Smith, an associate at Peter Finch Realty, shows the property to Victor and Victoria Vet who make an offer of purchase. Although Sam has offered them the opportunity for representation, they choose to be customers and understand that anything they say to Sam may be repeated to the listing agent and the seller. Sam will be paid 2.75 percent of the sales price as the selling commission.

The property is legally identified as Lot 64, Block 83 in Section 2 of the Friendly Hills Addition of Austin, Travis County, Texas. Although it is subject to mandatory membership in the owners' association, the buyers elect not to use the HOA addendum to call for the seller to provide information. They have spoken to an officer of the association and feel that they have learned everything they need to know. The property receives mail at zip code 78711.

The buyers write a check for $1,000 to Buyer's Choice Title Company as earnest money and $200 to the seller as an option fee to have eight days to have the property inspected and back out if they find any significant problems. The option fee will be credited to the sale price at closing.

The seller will pay for the owner's title policy, as well as the survey, which is to be done within 10 days of the effective date of the contract. The Vets have not asked the seller to pay any additional buyer closing costs other than the $1,100 buyer non-allowable fees the seller is required to pay by VA. The buyers will pay for the 1 percent VA funding fee. They want three days to examine the lender-required survey.

The lead-based paint addendum is made a part of the contract. Mr. Smith has provided them with the EPA Lead Paint pamphlet. The seller has no knowledge or records concerning lead-based paint. The buyers will have an inspection for lead paint just to be safe. The buyer has not yet received the seller's disclosure notice, but asks the seller to furnish it within three days after the effective date of the contract.

The buyers are willing to pay $78,000 for the property. Although Mrs. Vet has full entitlement, the Vets have decided to borrow only $62,400 in order to keep their payments at a comfortable level. They can get loan approval within 30 days and close on or before October 20. They can obtain a 30-year fixed-rate loan at 7.25 percent annual interest rate.

They would like possession at closing and table funding. They compromise and agree to permit the seller to remain four days after funding because they are making the transaction contingent upon selling their present home at 1565 Travis Lane. It is under contract and should close on or before October 1. The buyers agree to permit the seller to continue to show the property. If the seller receives and accepts a satisfactory offer from another buyer, the seller shall waive the contingency by 5:00 PM on the third day after the buyers receive the seller's notice. To waive the contingency, the buyers agree that $5,000 additional earnest money will be deposited with the escrow agent.

For the seller's temporary leasehold, Mr. Mac will pay $50 per day and $100 per day for any holdover. The buyers waive any requirement for a security deposit. They all agree to mediate any dispute should it become necessary.

Figure 9.11 TREC 20-6

PROMULGATED BY THE TEXAS REAL ESTATE COMMISSION (TREC) 01-06-03

EQUAL HOUSING OPPORTUNITY

ONE TO FOUR FAMILY RESIDENTIAL CONTRACT (RESALE)

NOTICE: Not For Use For Condominium Transactions

1. PARTIES: ____________________ (Seller) agrees to sell and convey to ____________________ (Buyer) and Buyer agrees to buy from Seller the Property described below.

2. PROPERTY:

A. LAND: Lot ____________, Block_____, ____________ ____________ Addition, City of ____________, ____________ County, Texas, known as ____________ ____________ (address/zip code), or as described on attached exhibit.

B. IMPROVEMENTS: The house, garage and all other fixtures and improvements attached to the above-described real property, including without limitation, the following permanently installed and built-in items, if any: all equipment and appliances, valances, screens, shutters, awnings, wall-to-wall carpeting, mirrors, ceiling fans, attic fans, mail boxes, television antennas and satellite dish system and equipment, heating and air-conditioning units, security and fire detection equipment, wiring, plumbing and lighting fixtures, chandeliers, water softener system, kitchen equipment, garage door openers, cleaning equipment, shrubbery, landscaping, outdoor cooking equipment, and all other property owned by Seller and attached to the above described real property.

C. ACCESSORIES: The following described related accessories, if any: window air conditioning units, stove, fireplace screens, curtains and rods, blinds, window shades, draperies and rods, controls for satellite dish system, controls for garage door openers, entry gate controls, door keys, mailbox keys, above ground pool, swimming pool equipment and maintenance accessories, and artificial fireplace logs.

D. EXCLUSIONS: The following improvements and accessories will be retained by Seller and excluded: ____________________ ____________________.

The land, improvements and accessories are collectively referred to as the "Property".

3. SALES PRICE:

A. Cash portion of Sales Price payable by Buyer at closing.................. $____________

B. Sum of all financing described below (excluding any loan funding fee or mortgage insurance premium) .... $____________

C. Sales Price (Sum of A and B) .... $____________

4. FINANCING: The portion of Sales Price not payable in cash will be paid as follows: (Check applicable boxes below)

❑ A. THIRD PARTY FINANCING: One or more third party mortgage loans in the total amount of $____________. If the Property does not satisfy the lenders' underwriting requirements for the loan(s), this contract will terminate and the earnest money will be refunded to Buyer. (Check one box only)

❑(1) This contract is subject to Buyer being approved for the financing described in the attached Third Party Financing Condition Addendum.

❑(2) This contract is not subject to Buyer being approved for financing and does not involve FHA or VA financing.

❑ B. ASSUMPTION: The assumption of the unpaid principal balance of one or more promissory notes described in the attached TREC Loan Assumption Addendum.

❑ C. SELLER FINANCING: A promissory note from Buyer to Seller of $____________, bearing _______ % interest per annum, secured by vendor's and deed of trust liens, and containing the terms and conditions described in the attached TREC Seller Financing Addendum. If an owner policy of title insurance is furnished, Buyer shall furnish Seller with a mortgagee policy of title insurance.

5. EARNEST MONEY: Upon execution of this contract by both parties, Buyer shall deposit $____________ as earnest money with ____________________, as escrow agent, at ____________________ (address). Buyer shall deposit additional earnest money of $____________ with escrow agent within ________days after the effective date of this contract. If Buyer fails to deposit the earnest money as required by this contract, Buyer will be in default.

Initialed for identification by Buyer______ ______ and Seller ______ ______ **01A** TREC NO. 20-6

Figure 9.11 TREC 20-6 (continued)

Contract Concerning ____ Page Two 01-06-03
(Address of Property)

6. TITLE POLICY AND SURVEY:

A. TITLE POLICY: Seller shall furnish to Buyer at ❑ Seller's ❑ Buyer's expense an owner policy of title insurance (Title Policy) issued by ______________________________ ______________________________ (Title Company) in the amount of the Sales Price, dated at or after closing, insuring Buyer against loss under the provisions of the Title Policy, subject to the promulgated exclusions (including existing building and zoning ordinances) and the following exceptions:

(1) Restrictive covenants common to the platted subdivision in which the Property is located.
(2) The standard printed exception for standby fees, taxes and assessments.
(3) Liens created as part of the financing described in Paragraph 4.
(4) Utility easements created by the dedication deed or plat of the subdivision in which the Property is located.
(5) Reservations or exceptions otherwise permitted by this contract or as may be approved by Buyer in writing.
(6) The standard printed exception as to marital rights.
(7) The standard printed exception as to waters, tidelands, beaches, streams, and related matters.
(8) The standard printed exception as to discrepancies, conflicts, shortages in area or boundary lines, encroachments or protrusions, or overlapping improvements. Buyer, at Buyer's expense, may have the exception amended to read, "shortages in area".

B. COMMITMENT: Within 20 days after the Title Company receives a copy of this contract, Seller shall furnish to Buyer a commitment for title insurance (Commitment) and, at Buyer's expense, legible copies of restrictive covenants and documents evidencing exceptions in the Commitment (Exception Documents) other than the standard printed exceptions. Seller authorizes the Title Company to mail or hand deliver the Commitment and Exception Documents to Buyer at Buyer's address shown in Paragraph 21. If the Commitment and Exception Documents are not delivered to Buyer within the specified time, the time for delivery will be automatically extended up to 15 days or the Closing Date, whichever is earlier.

C. SURVEY: The survey must be made by a registered professional land surveyor acceptable to the Title Company and any lender. (Check one box only)

❑ (1) Within ______ days after the effective date of this contract, Seller, at Seller's expense, shall furnish a new survey to Buyer.
❑ (2) Within ______ days after the effective date of this contract, Buyer, at Buyer's expense, shall obtain a new survey.
❑ (3) Within ______ days after the effective date of this contract, Seller shall furnish Seller's existing survey of the Property to Buyer and the Title Company, along with Seller's affidavit acceptable to the Title Company for approval of the survey. If the survey is not approved by the Title Company or Buyer's lender, a new survey will be obtained at ❑ Seller's ❑ Buyer's expense no later than 3 days prior to the Closing Date.

D. OBJECTIONS: Within ____ days after Buyer receives the Commitment, Exception Documents and the survey, Buyer may object in writing to defects, exceptions, or encumbrances to title: disclosed on the survey other than items 6A(1) through (7) above; disclosed in the Commitment other than items 6A(1) through (8) above; or which prohibit the following use or activity: ____.
Buyer's failure to object within the time allowed will constitute a waiver of Buyer's right to object; except that the requirements in Schedule C of the Commitment are not waived. Seller shall cure the timely objections of Buyer or any third party lender within 15 days after Seller receives the objections and the Closing Date will be extended as necessary. If objections are not cured within such 15 day period, this contract will terminate and the earnest money will be refunded to Buyer unless Buyer waives the objections.

E. TITLE NOTICES:

(1) ABSTRACT OR TITLE POLICY: Broker advises Buyer to have an abstract of title covering the Property examined by an attorney of Buyer's selection, or Buyer should be furnished with or obtain a Title Policy. If a Title Policy is furnished, the Commitment should be promptly reviewed by an attorney of Buyer's choice due to the time limitations on Buyer's right to object.
(2) MANDATORY OWNERS' ASSOCIATION MEMBERSHIP: The Property ❑ is ❑ is not subject to mandatory membership in an owners' association. If the Property is subject to mandatory membership in an owners' association, Seller notifies Buyer under §5.012, Texas Property Code, that, as a purchaser of property in the residential community in

01A TREC NO. 20-6

Initialed for identification by Buyer_______ _______ and Seller________ ________

Figure 9.11 TREC 20-6 (continued)

which the Property is located, you are obligated to be a member of the owners' association. Restrictive covenants governing the use and occupancy of the Property and a dedicatory instrument governing the establishment, maintenance, and operation of this residential community have been or will be recorded in the Real Property Records of the county in which the Property is located. Copies of the restrictive covenants and dedicatory instrument may be obtained from the county clerk. You are obligated to pay assessments to the owners' association. The amount of the assessments is subject to change. Your failure to pay the assessments could result in a lien on and the foreclosure of the Property.

(3) STATUTORY TAX DISTRICTS: If the Property is situated in a utility or other statutorily created district providing water, sewer, drainage, or flood control facilities and services, Chapter 49, Texas Water Code requires Seller to deliver and Buyer to sign the statutory notice relating to the tax rate, bonded indebtedness, or standby fee of the district prior to final execution of this contract.

(4) TIDE WATERS: If the Property abuts the tidally influenced waters of the state, §33.135, Texas Natural Resources Code, requires a notice regarding coastal area property to be included in the contract. An addendum containing the notice promulgated by TREC or required by the parties must be used.

(5) ANNEXATION: If the Property is located outside the limits of a municipality, Seller notifies Buyer under §5.011, Texas Property Code, that the Property may now or later be included in the extraterritorial jurisdiction of a municipality and may now or later be subject to annexation by the municipality. Each municipality maintains a map that depicts its boundaries and extraterritorial jurisdiction. To determine if the Property is located within a municipality's extraterritorial jurisdiction or is likely to be located within a municipality's extraterritorial jurisdiction, contact all municipalities located in the general proximity of the Property for further information.

7. PROPERTY CONDITION:

A. INSPECTIONS, ACCESS AND UTILITIES: Buyer may have the Property inspected by inspectors selected by Buyer and licensed by TREC or otherwise permitted by law to make inspections. Seller shall permit Buyer and Buyer's agents access to the Property at reasonable times. Seller shall pay for turning on existing utilities for inspections.

B. SELLER'S DISCLOSURE NOTICE PURSUANT TO §5.008, TEXAS PROPERTY CODE (Notice): (Check one box only)

☐ (1) Buyer has received the Notice.

☐ (2) Buyer has not received the Notice. Within _______ days after the effective date of this contract, Seller shall deliver the Notice to Buyer. If Buyer does not receive the Notice, Buyer may terminate this contract at any time prior to the closing and the earnest money will be refunded to Buyer. If Seller delivers the Notice, Buyer may terminate this contract for any reason within 7 days after Buyer receives the Notice or prior to the closing, whichever first occurs, and the earnest money will be refunded to Buyer.

☐ (3) The Texas Property Code does not require this Seller to furnish the Notice.

C. SELLER'S DISCLOSURE OF LEAD-BASED PAINT AND LEAD-BASED PAINT HAZARDS is required by Federal law for a residential dwelling constructed prior to 1978.

D. ACCEPTANCE OF PROPERTY CONDITION: Buyer accepts the Property in its present condition; provided Seller, at Seller's expense, shall complete the following specific repairs and treatments:____

____.

E. LENDER REQUIRED REPAIRS AND TREATMENTS: Unless otherwise agreed in writing, neither party is obligated to pay for lender required repairs, which includes treatment for wood destroying insects. If the parties do not agree to pay for the lender required repairs or treatments, this contract will terminate and the earnest money will be refunded to Buyer. If the cost of lender required repairs and treatments exceeds 5% of the Sales Price, Buyer may terminate this contract and the earnest money will be refunded to Buyer.

F. COMPLETION OF REPAIRS AND TREATMENTS: Unless otherwise agreed in writing, Seller shall complete all agreed repairs and treatments prior to the Closing Date. All required permits must be obtained, and repairs and treatments must be performed by persons who are licensed or otherwise authorized by law to provide such repairs or treatments. At Buyer's election, any transferable warranties received by Seller with respect to the repairs and treatments will be transferred to Buyer at Buyer's expense. If Seller fails to complete any agreed repairs and

Figure 9.11 TREC 20-6 (continued)

Contract Concerning ____ Page Four 01-06-03
(Address of Property)

treatments prior to the Closing Date, Buyer may do so and receive reimbursement from Seller at closing. The Closing Date will be extended up to 15 days, if necessary, to complete repairs and treatments.

G. ENVIRONMENTAL MATTERS: Buyer is advised that the presence of wetlands, toxic substances, including asbestos and wastes or other environmental hazards, or the presence of a threatened or endangered species or its habitat may affect Buyer's intended use of the Property. If Buyer is concerned about these matters, an addendum promulgated by TREC or required by the parties should be used.

H. RESIDENTIAL SERVICE CONTRACTS: Buyer may purchase a residential service contract from a residential service company licensed by TREC. If Buyer purchases a residential service contract, Seller shall reimburse Buyer at closing for the cost of the residential service contract in an amount not exceeding $______________ . Buyer should review any residential service contract for the scope of coverage, exclusions and limitations. **The purchase of a residential service contract is optional. Similar coverage may be purchased from various companies authorized to do business in Texas.**

8. **BROKERS' FEES:** All obligations of the parties for payment of brokers' fees are contained in separate written agreements.

9. **CLOSING:**

A. The closing of the sale will be on or before ____________________, 20___, or within 7 days after objections to matters disclosed in the Commitment or by the survey have been cured, whichever date is later (Closing Date). If either party fails to close the sale by the Closing Date, the non-defaulting party may exercise the remedies contained in Paragraph 15.

B. At closing:

(1) Seller shall execute and deliver a general warranty deed conveying title to the Property to Buyer and showing no additional exceptions to those permitted in Paragraph 6 and furnish tax statements or certificates showing no delinquent taxes on the Property.

(2) Buyer shall pay the Sales Price in good funds acceptable to the escrow agent.

(3) Seller and Buyer shall execute and deliver any notices, statements, certificates, affidavits, releases, loan documents and other documents required of them by this contract, the Commitment or law necessary for the closing of the sale and the issuance of the Title Policy.

C. Unless expressly prohibited by written agreement, Seller may continue to show the Property and receive, negotiate and accept back up offers.

D. All covenants, representations and warranties in this contract survive closing.

10. **POSSESSION:** Seller shall deliver to Buyer possession of the Property in its present or required condition, ordinary wear and tear excepted ❑ upon closing and funding ❑ according to a temporary residential lease form promulgated by TREC or other written lease required by the parties. Any possession by Buyer prior to closing or by Seller after closing which is not authorized by a written lease will establish a tenancy at sufferance relationship between the parties. *Consult your insurance agent prior to change of ownership or possession because insurance coverage may be limited or terminated. The absence of a written lease or appropriate insurance coverage may expose the parties to economic loss.*

11. **SPECIAL PROVISIONS:** (Insert only factual statements and business details applicable to the sale. TREC rules prohibit licensees from adding factual statements or business details for which a contract addendum, lease or other form has been promulgated by TREC for mandatory use.)

01A TREC NO. 20-6

Initialed for identification by Buyer_______ _______ and Seller________ ________

Figure 9.11 TREC 20-6 (continued)

Contract Concerning ______________________________ Page Five 01-06-03
(Address of Property)

12. SETTLEMENT AND OTHER EXPENSES:

A. The following expenses must be paid at or prior to closing:

(1) Expenses payable by Seller (Seller's Expenses):

(a) Releases of existing liens, including prepayment penalties and recording fees; release of Seller's loan liability; tax statements or certificates; preparation of deed; one-half of escrow fee; and other expenses payable by Seller under this contract.

(b) Seller shall also pay an amount not to exceed $ ____________ to be applied in the following order: Buyer's Expenses which Buyer is prohibited from paying by FHA, VA, Texas Veteran's Housing Assistance Program or other governmental loan programs; Buyer's prepaid items; other Buyer's expenses.

(2) Expenses payable by Buyer (Buyer's Expenses):

(a) Loan origination, discount, buy-down, and commitment fees (Loan Fees).

(b) Appraisal fees; loan application fees; credit reports; preparation of loan documents; interest on the notes from date of disbursement to one month prior to dates of first monthly payments; recording fees; copies of easements and restrictions; mortgagee title policy with endorsements required by lender; loan-related inspection fees; photos, amortization schedules, one-half of escrow fee; all prepaid items, including required premiums for flood and hazard insurance, reserve deposits for insurance, ad valorem taxes and special governmental assessments; final compliance inspection; courier fee, repair inspection, underwriting fee and wire transfer, expenses incident to any loan, and other expenses payable by Buyer under this contract.

B. Buyer shall pay Private Mortgage Insurance Premium (PMI), VA Loan Funding Fee, or FHA Mortgage Insurance Premium (MIP) as required by the lender.

C. If any expense exceeds an amount expressly stated in this contract for such expense to be paid by a party, that party may terminate this contract unless the other party agrees to pay such excess. Buyer may not pay charges and fees expressly prohibited by FHA, VA, Texas Veteran's Housing Assistance Program or other governmental loan program regulations.

13. PRORATIONS: Taxes for the current year, interest, maintenance fees, assessments, dues and rents will be prorated through the Closing Date. If taxes for the current year vary from the amount prorated at closing, the parties shall adjust the prorations when tax statements for the current year are available. If taxes are not paid at or prior to closing, Buyer shall pay taxes for the current year.

14. CASUALTY LOSS: If any part of the Property is damaged or destroyed by fire or other casualty after the effective date of this contract, Seller shall restore the Property to its previous condition as soon as reasonably possible, but in any event by the Closing Date. If Seller fails to do so due to factors beyond Seller's control, Buyer may (a) terminate this contract and the earnest money will be refunded to Buyer (b) extend the time for performance up to 15 days and the Closing Date will be extended as necessary or (c) accept the Property in its damaged condition with an assignment of insurance proceeds and receive credit from Seller at closing in the amount of the deductible under the insurance policy. Seller's obligations under this paragraph are independent of any obligations of Seller under Paragraph 7.

15. DEFAULT: If Buyer fails to comply with this contract, Buyer will be in default, and Seller may (a) enforce specific performance, seek such other relief as may be provided by law, or both, or (b) terminate this contract and receive the earnest money as liquidated damages, thereby releasing both parties from this contract. If, due to factors beyond Seller's control, Seller fails within the time allowed to make any non-casualty repairs or deliver the Commitment, or survey, if required of Seller, Buyer may (a) extend the time for performance up to 15 days and the Closing Date will be extended as necessary or (b) terminate this contract as the sole remedy and receive the earnest money. If Seller fails to comply with this contract for any other reason, Seller will be in default and Buyer may (a) enforce specific performance, seek such other relief as may be provided by law, or both, or (b) terminate this contract and receive the earnest money, thereby releasing both parties from this contract.

16. MEDIATION: It is the policy of the State of Texas to encourage resolution of disputes through alternative dispute resolution procedures such as mediation. Any dispute between Seller and Buyer related to this contract which is not resolved through informal discussion ☐ will ☐ will not be submitted to a mutually acceptable mediation service or provider. The parties to the mediation shall bear the mediation costs equally. This paragraph does not preclude a party from seeking equitable relief from a court of competent jurisdiction.

01A TREC NO. 20-6

Initialed for identification by Buyer_______ _______ and Seller________ ________

Figure 9.11 TREC 20-6 (continued)

Contract Concerning ______________________________ Page Six 01-06-03
(Address of Property)

17. ATTORNEY'S FEES: The prevailing party in any legal proceeding related to this contract is entitled to recover reasonable attorney's fees and all costs of such proceeding incurred by the prevailing party.

18. ESCROW: The escrow agent is not (a) a party to this contract and does not have liability for the performance or nonperformance of any party to this contract, (b) liable for interest on the earnest money and (c) liable for the loss of any earnest money caused by the failure of any financial institution in which the earnest money has been deposited unless the financial institution is acting as escrow agent. At closing, the earnest money must be applied first to any cash down payment, then to Buyer's Expenses and any excess refunded to Buyer. If both parties make written demand for the earnest money, escrow agent may require payment of unpaid expenses incurred on behalf of the parties and a written release of liability of escrow agent from all parties. If one party makes written demand for the earnest money, escrow agent shall give notice of the demand by providing to the other party a copy of the demand. If escrow agent does not receive written objection to the demand from the other party within 30 days after notice to the other party, escrow agent may disburse the earnest money to the party making demand reduced by the amount of unpaid expenses incurred on behalf of the party receiving the earnest money and escrow agent may pay the same to the creditors. If escrow agent complies with the provisions of this paragraph, each party hereby releases escrow agent from all adverse claims related to the disbursal of the earnest money. Escrow agent's notice to the other party will be effective when deposited in the U. S. Mail, postage prepaid, certified mail, return receipt requested, addressed to the other party at such party's address shown below. Notice of objection to the demand will be deemed effective upon receipt by escrow agent.

19. REPRESENTATIONS: Seller represents that as of the Closing Date (a) there will be no liens, assessments, or security interests against the Property which will not be satisfied out of the sales proceeds unless securing payment of any loans assumed by Buyer and (b) assumed loans will not be in default. If any representation of Seller in this contract is untrue on the Closing Date, Buyer may terminate this contract and the earnest money will be refunded to Buyer.

20. FEDERAL TAX REQUIREMENTS: If Seller is a "foreign person," as defined by applicable law, or if Seller fails to deliver an affidavit to Buyer that Seller is not a "foreign person," then Buyer shall withhold from the sales proceeds an amount sufficient to comply with applicable tax law and deliver the same to the Internal Revenue Service together with appropriate tax forms. Internal Revenue Service regulations require filing written reports if currency in excess of specified amounts is received in the transaction.

21. NOTICES: All notices from one party to the other must be in writing and are effective when mailed to, hand-delivered at, or transmitted by facsimile as follows:

To Buyer at:	**To Seller at:**
______________________	______________________
______________________	______________________
______________________	______________________
Telephone:(____) ______________	Telephone:(____) ______________
Facsimile:(____) ______________	Facsimile:(____) ______________

22. AGREEMENT OF PARTIES: This contract contains the entire agreement of the parties and cannot be changed except by their written agreement. Addenda which are a part of this contract are (check all applicable boxes):

- ☐ Third Party Financing Condition Addendum
- ☐ Addendum for Property Subject to Mandatory Membership in an Owners' Association
- ☐ Seller Financing Addendum
- ☐ Environmental Assessment, Threatened or Endangered Species and Wetlands Addendum

01A TREC NO. 20-6

Initialed for identification by Buyer______ ______ and Seller______ ______

Figure 9.11 TREC 20-6 (continued)

❑ Loan Assumption Addendum

❑ Buyer's Temporary Residential Lease

❑ Seller's Temporary Residential Lease

❑ Addendum for Sale of Other Property by Buyer

❑ Addendum for Seller's Disclosure of Information on Lead-based Paint and Lead-based Paint Hazards as Required by Federal Law

❑ Addendum for "Back-Up" Contract

❑ Addendum for Coastal Area Property

❑ Addendum for Property Located Seaward of the Gulf Intracoastal Waterway

❑ Addendum for Release of Liability on Assumption of FHA, VA, or Conventional Loan Restoration of Seller's Entitlement for VA Guaranteed Loan

❑ Other (list): ____

____

23. **TERMINATION OPTION: This paragraph will be a part of this contract ONLY if both blanks are filled in and Buyer has paid the Option Fee.** Buyer has paid Seller $______________ (Option Fee) for the unrestricted right to terminate this contract by giving notice of termination to Seller within ________ days after the effective date of this contract. If Buyer gives notice of termination within the time specified, the Option Fee will not be refunded, however, any earnest money will be refunded to Buyer. The Option Fee ❑ will ❑ will not be credited to the Sales Price at closing. For the purposes of this paragraph, time is of the essence; strict compliance with the time for performance stated herein is required.

24. **CONSULT AN ATTORNEY:** Real estate licensees cannot give legal advice. READ THIS CONTRACT CAREFULLY. If you do not understand the effect of this contract, consult an attorney BEFORE signing.

Buyer's
Attorney is:______________________

____

Telephone: (____)______________________

Facsimile: (____)______________________

Seller's
Attorney is:______________________

____

Telephone: (____)______________________

Facsimile: (____)______________________

EXECUTED the _______day of ________________________, 20____ (EFFECTIVE DATE).
(BROKER: FILL IN THE DATE OF FINAL ACCEPTANCE.)

______________________ Buyer

______________________ Seller

______________________ Buyer

______________________ Seller

The form of this contract has been approved by the Texas Real Estate Commission. TREC forms are intended for use only by trained real estate licensees. No representation is made as to the legal validity or adequacy of any provision in any specific transactions. It is not suitable for complex transactions. Texas Real Estate Commission, P.O. Box 12188, Austin, TX 78711-2188, 1-800-250-8732 or (512) 459-6544 (http://www.trec.state.tx.us) TREC NO. 20-6. This form replaces TREC NO. 20-5.

Figure 9.11 TREC 20-6 (continued)

Contract Concerning ______________________________ Page Eight 01-06-03
(Address of Property)

SELLER'S RECEIPT

Receipt of $______________ (Option Fee) in the form of ______________ is acknowledged.

______________________ Seller ______________________ Date

BROKER INFORMATION AND RATIFICATION OF FEE

Listing Broker has agreed to pay Other Broker ______________ of the total sales price when Listing Broker's fee is received. Escrow Agent is authorized and directed to pay Other Broker from Listing Broker's fee at closing.

Other Broker	Listing Broker
License No. Telephone	License No. Telephone
represents ☐ Buyer only as Buyer's agent ☐ Seller as Listing Broker's subagent	represents ☐ Seller and Buyer as an intermediary ☐ Seller only as Seller's agent
Associate Telephone	Listing Associate Telephone
Broker's Address	Listing Associate's Office Address Facsimile
Facsimile	Selling Associate Telephone
	Selling Associate's Office Address Facsimile

RECEIPT

Receipt of ☐ Contract and ☐ $______________ Earnest Money in the form of ______________ is acknowledged.

Escrow Agent: ______________________ Date: ______________

By: ______________________

______________________ Address Telephone (_____) ______________

______________________ City State Zip Facsimile: (_____) ______________

Figure 9.12 TREC 40-1

02-09-2004

EQUAL HOUSING OPPORTUNITY

PROMULGATED BY THE TEXAS REAL ESTATE COMMISSION (TREC)

THIRD PARTY FINANCING CONDITION ADDENDUM

TO CONTRACT CONCERNING THE PROPERTY AT

____

(Street Address and City)

Buyer shall apply promptly for all financing described below and make every reasonable effort to obtain financing approval including but not limited to furnishing all information and documents required by lender for approval. Financing approval will be deemed to have been obtained when the lender determines that Buyer has satisfied all of lender's financial requirements (those items relating to Buyer's assets, income and credit history). If Buyer cannot obtain financing approval, Buyer must give written notice to Seller within _____ days after the effective date of this contract and this contract will terminate and the earnest money will be refunded to Buyer. **If Buyer does not give such notice within the time allowed, this contract will no longer be subject to Buyer being approved for the financing described below. For purposes of this paragraph, time is of the essence; strict compliance with the times for performance herein stated is required.**

Each note must be secured by vendor's and deed of trust liens.

❑ A. CONVENTIONAL FINANCING:

❑ (1) A first mortgage loan in the principal amount of $ ____________________ (excluding any financed PMI premium), due in full in _________ year(s), with interest not to exceed ______% per annum for the first ________year(s) of the loan with Loan Fees (loan origination, discount, buy-down, and commitment fees) not to exceed ________% of the loan.

❑ (2) A second mortgage loan in the principal amount of $__________________(excluding any financed PMI premium), due in full in ___________year(s), with interest not to exceed ______% per annum for the first _____________year(s) of the loan with Loan Fees (loan origination, discount, buy-down, and commitment fees) not to exceed _________ % of the loan.

❑ B. TEXAS VETERANS' HOUSING ASSISTANCE PROGRAM LOAN: A Texas Veteran's Housing Assistance Program Loan of $________________ for a period of at least ______years at the interest rate established by the Texas Veteran's Land Board at the time of closing.

❑ C. FHA INSURED FINANCING: A Section _________________ FHA insured loan of not less than $__________________ (excluding any financed MIP), amortizable monthly for not less than _______years, with interest not to exceed _______% per annum for the first ______year(s) of the loan with Loan Fees (loan origination, discount, buy-down, and commitment fees) not to exceed _________ % of the loan. As required by HUD-FHA, if FHA valuation is unknown, *"It is expressly agreed that, notwithstanding any other provision of this contract, the purchaser (Buyer) shall not be obligated to complete the purchase of the Property described herein or to incur any penalty by forfeiture of earnest money deposits or otherwise unless the purchaser (Buyer) has been given in accordance with HUD/FHA or VA requirements a written statement issued by the Federal Housing Commissioner, Department of Veterans Affairs, or a Direct Endorsement Lender setting forth the appraised value of the Property of not less than $__________________. The purchaser (Buyer) shall have the privilege and option of proceeding with consummation of the contract without regard to the amount of the appraised valuation. The appraised valuation is arrived at to determine the maximum mortgage the Department of Housing and Urban Development will insure. HUD does not warrant the value or the condition of the Property. The purchaser (Buyer) should satisfy himself/herself that the price and the condition of the Property are acceptable."*

Initialed for identification by Buyer_______ _______ and Seller________ ________ 01A

Figure 9.12 TREC 40-1 (continued)

Third Party Financing Condition Addendum Concerning Page Two 02-09-2004

____

(Address of Property)

❑ D. VA GUARANTEED FINANCING: A VA guaranteed loan of not less than $_______________ (excluding any financed Funding Fee), amortizable monthly for not less than_______years, with interest not to exceed________% per annum for the first ________year(s) of the loan with Loan Fees (loan origination, discount, buy-down, and commitment fees) not to exceed ________% of the loan.

VA NOTICE TO BUYER: "*It is expressly agreed that, notwithstanding any other provisions of this contract, the Buyer shall not incur any penalty by forfeiture of earnest money or otherwise or be obligated to complete the purchase of the Property described herein, if the contract purchase price or cost exceeds the reasonable value of the Property established by the Department of Veterans Affairs. The Buyer shall, however, have the privilege and option of proceeding with the consummation of this contract without regard to the amount of the reasonable value established by the Department of Veterans Affairs.*"

If Buyer elects to complete the purchase at an amount in excess of the reasonable value established by VA, Buyer shall pay such excess amount in cash from a source which Buyer agrees to disclose to the VA and which Buyer represents will not be from borrowed funds except as approved by VA. If VA reasonable value of the Property is less than the Sales Price, Seller may reduce the Sales Price to an amount equal to the VA reasonable value and the sale will be closed at the lower Sales Price with proportionate adjustments to the down payment and the loan amount.

Buyer hereby authorizes any lender to furnish to the Seller or Buyer or their representatives information relating only to the status of financing approval of Buyer.

______________________	______________________
Buyer	Seller
______________________	______________________
Buyer	Seller

This form has been approved by the Texas Real Estate Commission for use with similarly approved or promulgated contract forms. Such approval relates to this form only. TREC forms are intended for use only by trained real estate licensees. No representation is made as to the legal validity or adequacy of any provision in any specific transactions. It is not suitable for complex transactions. Texas Real Estate Commission, P.O. Box 12188, Austin, TX 78711-2188, 1-800-250-8732 or (512) 459-6544 (http://www.trec.state.tx.us) TREC No. 40-1. This form replaces TREC No. 40-0.

01A

Figure 9.13 TREC 15-3

12-07-98

(NOTICE: For use only when SELLER occupies the property for no more than 90 days AFTER the closing)

EQUAL HOUSING OPPORTUNITY

SELLER'S TEMPORARY RESIDENTIAL LEASE
PROMULGATED BY THE TEXAS REAL ESTATE COMMISSION (TREC)

1. **PARTIES:** The parties to this Lease are ______________________________ (Landlord) and ______________________________(Tenant).
2. **LEASE:** Landlord leases to Tenant the Property described in the Contract between Landlord as Buyer and Tenant as Seller dated _______________, _____,and known as ______________________________(address).
3. **TERM:** The term of this Lease commences on the date the sale covered by the Contract is closed and terminates ______________________________, unless terminated earlier by reason of other provisions.
4. **RENTAL:** Tenant shall pay to Landlord as rental $_______________per day with the full amount of rental for the term of the Lease to be paid at the time of funding of the sale. Tenant will not be entitled to a refund of rental if this Lease terminates early due to Tenant's default or voluntary surrender of the Property.
5. **SECURITY DEPOSIT:** Tenant shall pay to Landlord at the time of funding of the sale $ ____________ as a deposit to secure performance of this Lease by Tenant. Landlord may use the deposit to satisfy Tenant's obligations under this Lease. Landlord shall refund any unused portion of the deposit to Tenant with an itemized list of all deductions from the deposit within 30 days after Tenant (a) surrenders possession of the Property and (b) provides Landlord written notice of Tenant's forwarding address.
6. **UTILITIES:** Tenant shall pay all utility charges except______________________________, which Landlord shall pay.
7. **USE OF PROPERTY:** Tenant may use the Property only for single family dwelling purposes. Tenant may not assign this Lease or sublet any part of the Property.
8. **PETS:** Tenant may not keep pets on the Property except______________________________.
9. **CONDITION OF PROPERTY**: Tenant accepts the Property in its present condition and state of repair at the commencement of the Lease. Upon termination, Tenant shall surrender the Property to Landlord in the condition required under the Contract at the time of closing, except normal wear and tear and any casualty loss.
10. **ALTERATIONS:** Tenant may not alter the Property or install improvements or fixtures without the prior written consent of Landlord. Any improvements or fixtures placed on the Property during the Lease become the property of Landlord.
11. **SPECIAL PROVISIONS:**

12. **INSPECTIONS:** Landlord may enter at reasonable times to inspect the Property.
13. **LAWS:** Tenant shall comply with all applicable laws, restrictions, ordinances, rules and regulations with respect to the Property.
14. **REPAIRS AND MAINTENANCE:** Tenant shall bear all expense of repairing and maintaining the Property, including but not limited to yard, trees and shrubs, unless otherwise required by the Texas Property Code. Tenant shall promptly repair at Tenant's expense any damage to the Property caused directly or indirectly by any act or omission of the Tenant or any person other than Landlord, Landlord's agents or invitees.

01A TREC NO. 15-3

Initialed for identification by Buyer_______ _______ and Seller________ ________

Figure 9.13 TREC 15-3 (continued)

Seller's Temporary Residential Lease____Page Two 12-07-98
(Address of Property)

15. **INDEMNITY:** Tenant indemnifies Landlord from the claims of all third parties for injury or damage to the person or property of such third party arising from the use or occupancy of the Property by Tenant. This indemnification includes attorney's fees, costs and expenses incurred by Landlord.
16. **INSURANCE:** Landlord and Tenant shall each maintain such insurance on the contents and Property as each party may deem appropriate during the term of this Lease. NOTE: CONSULT YOUR INSURANCE AGENT PRIOR TO CLOSING. Possession of the Property by Seller as Tenant may change insurance policy coverage.
17. **DEFAULT:** If Tenant fails to perform or observe any provision of this Lease and fails, within 24 hours after notice by Landlord, to commence and diligently pursue to remedy such failure, Tenant will be in default.
18. **TERMINATION:** This Lease terminates upon expiration of the term specified in Paragraph 3 or upon Tenant's default under this Lease.
19. **HOLDING OVER:** Tenant shall surrender possession of the Property upon termination of this Lease. Any possession by Tenant after termination creates a tenancy at sufferance and will not operate to renew or extend this Lease. Tenant shall pay $ _______________ per day during the period of any possession after termination as damages, in addition to any other remedies to which Landlord is entitled.
20. **ATTORNEY'S FEES:** The prevailing party in any legal proceeding brought under or with respect to the transaction described in this Lease is entitled to recover from the non-prevailing party all costs of such proceeding and reasonable attorney's fees.
21. **SMOKE DETECTORS:** The Texas Property Code requires Landlord to install smoke detectors in certain locations within the Property at Landlord's expense. Tenant expressly waives Landlord's duty to inspect and repair smoke detectors.
22. **SECURITY DEVICES:** The requirements of the Texas Property Code relating to security devices do not apply to a residential lease for a term of 90 days or less.
23. **CONSULT YOUR ATTORNEY:** Real estate licensees cannot give legal advice. This Lease is intended to be legally binding. READ IT CAREFULLY. If you do not understand the effect of this Lease, consult your attorney BEFORE signing.
24. **NOTICES:** All notices under this Lease from one party to the other must be in writing and are effective when delivered or transmitted by facsimile machine as follows:

To Landlord:	**To Tenant:**
______________________________	______________________________
______________________________	______________________________
______________________________	______________________________
Facsimile:(_____)_________________	Facsimile:(_____)_________________

EXECUTED the ______ day of ______________________________ .

______________________________	______________________________
Landlord	Tenant
______________________________	______________________________
Landlord	Tenant

The form of this contract has been approved by the Texas Real Estate Commission. Such approval relates to this contract form only. TREC forms are intended for use only by trained real estate licensees. No representation is made as to the legal validity or adequacy of any provision in any specific transaction. It is not suitable for complex transactions. Extensive riders or additions are not to be used. (12-98) Texas Real Estate Commission, P.O. Box 12188, Austin, TX 78711-2188, 1-800-250-8732 or (512)459-6544 (http://www.trec.state.tx.us) TREC NO. 15-3. This form replaces TREC NO. 15-2.

O1A TREC NO. 15-3

Figure 9.14 TREC 10-4

10-29-01

PROMULGATED BY THE TEXAS REAL ESTATE COMMISSION (TREC)

ADDENDUM FOR SALE OF OTHER PROPERTY BY BUYER

TO CONTRACT CONCERNING THE PROPERTY AT

____

(Street Address and City)

A. The contract is contingent upon Buyer's receipt of the proceeds from the sale of Buyer's property at ______________________________ (Address) by 5:00 p.m. on ____________________, 20______ (the Contingency). If the Contingency is not satisfied or waived by Buyer by the above time and date, the contract will terminate automatically and the earnest money will be refunded to Buyer.
NOTICE: The date inserted in this Paragraph should be no later than the date inserted in Paragraph 9 of the contract.

B. If Seller accepts a written offer to sell the Property, Seller shall notify Buyer (1) of such acceptance **AND** (2) that Seller requires Buyer to waive the Contingency. Buyer must waive the Contingency by 5:00 p.m. on the ______________day after delivery of Seller's notice to Buyer; otherwise the contract will terminate automatically and the earnest money will be refunded to Buyer.

C. Buyer may waive the Contingency only by notifying Seller of the waiver and depositing $__________ with escrow agent as additional earnest money. All notices must be in writing and are effective when delivered in accordance with the contract.

D. If Buyer waives the Contingency and Buyer's loan or assumption approval is conditioned upon the sale of Buyer's property described in Paragraph A above, Buyer will be in default if such condition is not satisfied by the date provided for in the contract. If such default occurs, Seller may exercise the remedies specified in Paragraph 15 of the contract. If Buyer fails to obtain loan or assumption approval for any other reason, the provisions of the contract remain in effect.

E. For purposes of this Addendum time is of the essence; strict compliance with the times for performance stated herein is required.

______________________ Buyer	______________________ Seller
______________________ Buyer	______________________ Seller

This form has been approved by the Texas Real Estate Commission for use with similarly approved or promulgated contract forms. Such approval relates to this form only. TREC forms are intended for use only by trained real estate licensees. No representation is made as to the legal validity or adequacy of any provision in any specific transactions. It is not suitable for complex transactions. Texas Real Estate Commission, P.O. Box 12188, Austin, TX 78711-2188, 1-800-250-8732 or (512) 459-6544 (http://www.trec.state.tx.us) TREC No. 10-4. This form replaces TREC No. 10-3.

01A

Figure 9.15 TREC OP-L

APPROVED BY THE TEXAS REAL ESTATE COMMISSION 02-09-2004

EQUAL HOUSING OPPORTUNITY

ADDENDUM FOR SELLER'S DISCLOSURE OF INFORMATION ON LEAD-BASED PAINT AND LEAD-BASED PAINT HAZARDS AS REQUIRED BY FEDERAL LAW

CONCERNING THE PROPERTY AT ______________________________
(Street Address and City)

A. **LEAD WARNING STATEMENT:** "Every purchaser of any interest in residential real property on which a residential dwelling was built prior to 1978 is notified that such property may present exposure to lead from lead-based paint that may place young children at risk of developing lead poisoning. Lead poisoning in young children may produce permanent neurological damage, including learning disabilities, reduced intelligence quotient, behavioral problems, and impaired memory. Lead poisoning also poses a particular risk to pregnant women. The seller of any interest in residential real property is required to provide the buyer with any information on lead-based paint hazards from risk assessments or inspections in the seller's possession and notify the buyer of any known lead-based paint hazards. A risk assessment or inspection for possible lead-paint hazards is recommended prior to purchase."
NOTICE: Inspector must be properly certified as required by federal law.

B. SELLER'S DISCLOSURE:

1. PRESENCE OF LEAD-BASED PAINT AND/OR LEAD-BASED PAINT HAZARDS (check on box only):
   - ☐ (a) Known lead-based paint and/or lead-based paint hazards are present in the Property (explain): ____________
   - ☐ (b) Seller has no actual knowledge of lead-based paint and/or lead-based paint hazards in the Property.
2. RECORDS AND REPORTS AVAILABLE TO SELLER (check one box only):
   - ☐ (a) Seller has provided the purchaser with all available records and reports pertaining to lead-based paint and/or lead-based paint hazards in the Property (list documents): ____________
   - ☐ (b) Seller has no reports or records pertaining to lead-based paint and/or lead-based paint hazards in the Property.

C. BUYER'S RIGHTS (check one box only)**:**

☐ 1. Buyer waives the opportunity to conduct a risk assessment or inspection of the Property for the presence of lead-based paint or lead-based paint hazards.

☐ 2. Within ten days after the effective date of this contract, Buyer may have the Property inspected by inspectors selected by Buyer. If lead-based paint or lead-based paint hazards are present, Buyer may terminate this contract by giving Seller written notice within 14 days after the effective date of this contract, and the earnest money will be refunded to Buyer.

D. BUYER'S ACKNOWLEDGMENT (check applicable boxes)**:**

☐ 1. Buyer has received copies of all information listed above.

☐ 2. Buyer has received the pamphlet *Protect Your Family from Lead in Your Home*.

E. BROKERS' ACKNOWLEDGMENT: Brokers have informed Seller of Seller's obligations under 42 U.S.C. 4852d to: (a) provide Buyer with the federally approved pamphlet on lead poisoning prevention; (b) complete this addendum; (c) disclose any known lead-based paint and/or lead-based paint hazards in the Property; (d) deliver all records and reports to Buyer pertaining to lead-based paint and/or lead-based paint hazards in the Property; (e) provide Buyer a period of up to 10 days to have the Property inspected; and (f) retain a completed copy of this addendum for at least 3 years following the sale. Brokers are aware of their responsibility to ensure compliance.

F. CERTIFICATION OF ACCURACY: The following persons have reviewed the information above and certify, to the best of their knowledge, that the information they have provided is true and accurate.

Buyer	Date	Seller	Date
Buyer	Date	Seller	Date
Other Broker	Date	Listing Broker	Date

The form of this addendum has been approved by the Texas Real Estate Commission for use only with similarly approved or promulgated forms of contracts. Such approval relates to this contract form only. TREC forms are intended for use only by trained real estate licensees. No representation is made as to the legal validity or adequacy of any provision in any specific transactions. It is not suitable for complex transactions. Texas Real Estate Commission, P.O. Box 12188, Austin, TX 78711-2188, 1-800-250-8732 or (512) 459-6544 (http://www.trec.state.tx.us)

Form OP-L 01A

Transaction 5: Seller Finance
(Using: TREC 20-6, 26-4, and 28-0)

Thomas J. Swanson and his wife, Sarah J. Swanson, will purchase a second home. It is known as Lot 6, Block 8 of the Happily-Ever-After Addition of Waco, McLennan County, Texas. They are willing to pay $73,500 for it if the owner, Samuel Jay Johnson (a bachelor), will owner finance $25,000 for five years at 7 percent annual interest. The buyers will pay monthly interest only until maturity when the principal balance is due. They agree to a due-on-sale clause in the deed of trust and will provide paid tax receipts by February 1 of each year the loan is outstanding.

The Swansons request a title policy issued by Secure Title Company and a new survey showing no encroachments or easements other than the 10-foot utility easement at the rear of the lot. The buyers want 10 days for objections to survey and title commitment. The seller will pay for the title policy. The Swansons want to make certain that cable TV services are available. They have received the Seller's Disclosure Notice and buy a 10-day option to terminate for $150 to have the opportunity to thoroughly evaluate the property. The option fee will not be credited to the sales price at closing. Possession will be granted at closing and funding.

The property is not subject to a mandatory homeowners' association assessment. It is listed with Smooth Sails Realty through whom the buyers purchase it without representation. They will close on or before May 27, which is within 15 days of the effective date of the contract. The seller requests that the buyer furnish a current credit report within five days after the effective date of the contract as evidence of good credit.

The property is located at 15630 Paradise Avenue in Waco, Texas 76710. The buyer wants deletion of the common title policy exclusion relating to discrepancies, conflicts and shortages in area or boundary, and is willing to pay the additional 15 percent policy premium required by the title company. Earnest money in the amount of $2,000 has been tendered. The sellers will provide a new survey within ten days at the seller's expense. The survey will be acceptable to the title company. The purchasers want to have an environmental assessment performed to make certain there are no contamination or toxic materials present. This they will do within ten days after the effective date of the contract. The parties also agree to mediate any disputes that may arise.

Figure 9.16 TREC 20-6

PROMULGATED BY THE TEXAS REAL ESTATE COMMISSION (TREC) 01-06-03

ONE TO FOUR FAMILY RESIDENTIAL CONTRACT (RESALE)

NOTICE: Not For Use For Condominium Transactions

1. PARTIES: ______________________________ (Seller) agrees to sell and convey to ______________________________ (Buyer) and Buyer agrees to buy from Seller the Property described below.

2. PROPERTY:

A. LAND: Lot ____________________, Block_____, ____________________ ____________________ Addition, City of ______________, ______________ County, Texas, known as ________________________________ ____________________ (address/zip code), or as described on attached exhibit.

B. IMPROVEMENTS: The house, garage and all other fixtures and improvements attached to the above-described real property, including without limitation, the following permanently installed and built-in items, if any: all equipment and appliances, valances, screens, shutters, awnings, wall-to-wall carpeting, mirrors, ceiling fans, attic fans, mail boxes, television antennas and satellite dish system and equipment, heating and air-conditioning units, security and fire detection equipment, wiring, plumbing and lighting fixtures, chandeliers, water softener system, kitchen equipment, garage door openers, cleaning equipment, shrubbery, landscaping, outdoor cooking equipment, and all other property owned by Seller and attached to the above described real property.

C. ACCESSORIES: The following described related accessories, if any: window air conditioning units, stove, fireplace screens, curtains and rods, blinds, window shades, draperies and rods, controls for satellite dish system, controls for garage door openers, entry gate controls, door keys, mailbox keys, above ground pool, swimming pool equipment and maintenance accessories, and artificial fireplace logs.

D. EXCLUSIONS: The following improvements and accessories will be retained by Seller and excluded: ____ ____.

The land, improvements and accessories are collectively referred to as the "Property".

3. SALES PRICE:

A. Cash portion of Sales Price payable by Buyer at closing................. $______________

B. Sum of all financing described below (excluding any loan funding fee or mortgage insurance premium) .... $______________

C. Sales Price (Sum of A and B) .... $______________

4. FINANCING: The portion of Sales Price not payable in cash will be paid as follows: (Check applicable boxes below)

☐ A. THIRD PARTY FINANCING: One or more third party mortgage loans in the total amount of $____________________. If the Property does not satisfy the lenders' underwriting requirements for the loan(s), this contract will terminate and the earnest money will be refunded to Buyer. (Check one box only)

☐(1) This contract is subject to Buyer being approved for the financing described in the attached Third Party Financing Condition Addendum.

☐(2) This contract is not subject to Buyer being approved for financing and does not involve FHA or VA financing.

☐ B. ASSUMPTION: The assumption of the unpaid principal balance of one or more promissory notes described in the attached TREC Loan Assumption Addendum.

☐ C. SELLER FINANCING: A promissory note from Buyer to Seller of $________________, bearing _______ % interest per annum, secured by vendor's and deed of trust liens, and containing the terms and conditions described in the attached TREC Seller Financing Addendum. If an owner policy of title insurance is furnished, Buyer shall furnish Seller with a mortgagee policy of title insurance.

5. EARNEST MONEY: Upon execution of this contract by both parties, Buyer shall deposit $____________ as earnest money with ____, as escrow agent, at ____ (address). Buyer shall deposit additional earnest money of $__________________ with escrow agent within _________days after the effective date of this contract. If Buyer fails to deposit the earnest money as required by this contract, Buyer will be in default.

Figure 9.16 TREC 20-6 (continued)

Contract Concerning ____ Page Two 01-06-03
(Address of Property)

6. TITLE POLICY AND SURVEY:

A. TITLE POLICY: Seller shall furnish to Buyer at ❑Seller's ❑Buyer's expense an owner policy of title insurance (Title Policy) issued by ____ (Title Company) in the amount of the Sales Price, dated at or after closing, insuring Buyer against loss under the provisions of the Title Policy, subject to the promulgated exclusions (including existing building and zoning ordinances) and the following exceptions:

(1) Restrictive covenants common to the platted subdivision in which the Property is located.
(2) The standard printed exception for standby fees, taxes and assessments.
(3) Liens created as part of the financing described in Paragraph 4.
(4) Utility easements created by the dedication deed or plat of the subdivision in which the Property is located.
(5) Reservations or exceptions otherwise permitted by this contract or as may be approved by Buyer in writing.
(6) The standard printed exception as to marital rights.
(7) The standard printed exception as to waters, tidelands, beaches, streams, and related matters.
(8) The standard printed exception as to discrepancies, conflicts, shortages in area or boundary lines, encroachments or protrusions, or overlapping improvements. Buyer, at Buyer's expense, may have the exception amended to read, "shortages in area".

B. COMMITMENT: Within 20 days after the Title Company receives a copy of this contract, Seller shall furnish to Buyer a commitment for title insurance (Commitment) and, at Buyer's expense, legible copies of restrictive covenants and documents evidencing exceptions in the Commitment (Exception Documents) other than the standard printed exceptions. Seller authorizes the Title Company to mail or hand deliver the Commitment and Exception Documents to Buyer at Buyer's address shown in Paragraph 21. If the Commitment and Exception Documents are not delivered to Buyer within the specified time, the time for delivery will be automatically extended up to 15 days or the Closing Date, whichever is earlier.

C. SURVEY: The survey must be made by a registered professional land surveyor acceptable to the Title Company and any lender. (Check one box only)

❑ (1) Within ______ days after the effective date of this contract, Seller, at Seller's expense, shall furnish a new survey to Buyer.

❑ (2) Within ______ days after the effective date of this contract, Buyer, at Buyer's expense, shall obtain a new survey.

❑ (3) Within ______ days after the effective date of this contract, Seller shall furnish Seller's existing survey of the Property to Buyer and the Title Company, along with Seller's affidavit acceptable to the Title Company for approval of the survey. If the survey is not approved by the Title Company or Buyer's lender, a new survey will be obtained at ❑ Seller's ❑ Buyer's expense no later than 3 days prior to the Closing Date.

D. OBJECTIONS: Within ____ days after Buyer receives the Commitment, Exception Documents and the survey, Buyer may object in writing to defects, exceptions, or encumbrances to title: disclosed on the survey other than items 6A(1) through (7) above; disclosed in the Commitment other than items 6A(1) through (8) above; or which prohibit the following use or activity: ____.
Buyer's failure to object within the time allowed will constitute a waiver of Buyer's right to object; except that the requirements in Schedule C of the Commitment are not waived. Seller shall cure the timely objections of Buyer or any third party lender within 15 days after Seller receives the objections and the Closing Date will be extended as necessary. If objections are not cured within such 15 day period, this contract will terminate and the earnest money will be refunded to Buyer unless Buyer waives the objections.

E. TITLE NOTICES:

(1) ABSTRACT OR TITLE POLICY: Broker advises Buyer to have an abstract of title covering the Property examined by an attorney of Buyer's selection, or Buyer should be furnished with or obtain a Title Policy. If a Title Policy is furnished, the Commitment should be promptly reviewed by an attorney of Buyer's choice due to the time limitations on Buyer's right to object.

(2) MANDATORY OWNERS' ASSOCIATION MEMBERSHIP: The Property ❑ is ❑ is not subject to mandatory membership in an owners' association. If the Property is subject to mandatory membership in an owners' association, Seller notifies Buyer under §5.012, Texas Property Code, that, as a purchaser of property in the residential community in

Initialed for identification by Buyer______ ______ and Seller ______ ______ **01A** TREC NO. 20-6

Figure 9.16 TREC 20-6 (continued)

Contract Concerning ____ Page Three 01-06-03
(Address of Property)

which the Property is located, you are obligated to be a member of the owners' association. Restrictive covenants governing the use and occupancy of the Property and a dedicatory instrument governing the establishment, maintenance, and operation of this residential community have been or will be recorded in the Real Property Records of the county in which the Property is located. Copies of the restrictive covenants and dedicatory instrument may be obtained from the county clerk. You are obligated to pay assessments to the owners' association. The amount of the assessments is subject to change. Your failure to pay the assessments could result in a lien on and the foreclosure of the Property.

(3) STATUTORY TAX DISTRICTS: If the Property is situated in a utility or other statutorily created district providing water, sewer, drainage, or flood control facilities and services, Chapter 49, Texas Water Code requires Seller to deliver and Buyer to sign the statutory notice relating to the tax rate, bonded indebtedness, or standby fee of the district prior to final execution of this contract.

(4) TIDE WATERS: If the Property abuts the tidally influenced waters of the state, §33.135, Texas Natural Resources Code, requires a notice regarding coastal area property to be included in the contract. An addendum containing the notice promulgated by TREC or required by the parties must be used.

(5) ANNEXATION: If the Property is located outside the limits of a municipality, Seller notifies Buyer under §5.011, Texas Property Code, that the Property may now or later be included in the extraterritorial jurisdiction of a municipality and may now or later be subject to annexation by the municipality. Each municipality maintains a map that depicts its boundaries and extraterritorial jurisdiction. To determine if the Property is located within a municipality's extraterritorial jurisdiction or is likely to be located within a municipality's extraterritorial jurisdiction, contact all municipalities located in the general proximity of the Property for further information.

7. PROPERTY CONDITION:

A. INSPECTIONS, ACCESS AND UTILITIES: Buyer may have the Property inspected by inspectors selected by Buyer and licensed by TREC or otherwise permitted by law to make inspections. Seller shall permit Buyer and Buyer's agents access to the Property at reasonable times. Seller shall pay for turning on existing utilities for inspections.

B. SELLER'S DISCLOSURE NOTICE PURSUANT TO §5.008, TEXAS PROPERTY CODE (Notice): (Check one box only)

☐ (1) Buyer has received the Notice.

☐ (2) Buyer has not received the Notice. Within ______ days after the effective date of this contract, Seller shall deliver the Notice to Buyer. If Buyer does not receive the Notice, Buyer may terminate this contract at any time prior to the closing and the earnest money will be refunded to Buyer. If Seller delivers the Notice, Buyer may terminate this contract for any reason within 7 days after Buyer receives the Notice or prior to the closing, whichever first occurs, and the earnest money will be refunded to Buyer.

☐ (3) The Texas Property Code does not require this Seller to furnish the Notice.

C. SELLER'S DISCLOSURE OF LEAD-BASED PAINT AND LEAD-BASED PAINT HAZARDS is required by Federal law for a residential dwelling constructed prior to 1978.

D. ACCEPTANCE OF PROPERTY CONDITION: Buyer accepts the Property in its present condition; provided Seller, at Seller's expense, shall complete the following specific repairs and treatments:____

____.

E. LENDER REQUIRED REPAIRS AND TREATMENTS: Unless otherwise agreed in writing, neither party is obligated to pay for lender required repairs, which includes treatment for wood destroying insects. If the parties do not agree to pay for the lender required repairs or treatments, this contract will terminate and the earnest money will be refunded to Buyer. If the cost of lender required repairs and treatments exceeds 5% of the Sales Price, Buyer may terminate this contract and the earnest money will be refunded to Buyer.

F. COMPLETION OF REPAIRS AND TREATMENTS: Unless otherwise agreed in writing, Seller shall complete all agreed repairs and treatments prior to the Closing Date. All required permits must be obtained, and repairs and treatments must be performed by persons who are licensed or otherwise authorized by law to provide such repairs or treatments. At Buyer's election, any transferable warranties received by Seller with respect to the repairs and treatments will be transferred to Buyer at Buyer's expense. If Seller fails to complete any agreed repairs and

Initialed for identification by Buyer______ ______ and Seller ______ ______ **01A** TREC NO. 20-6

Figure 9.16 TREC 20-6 (continued)

Contract Concerning ____ Page Four 01-06-03
(Address of Property)

treatments prior to the Closing Date, Buyer may do so and receive reimbursement from Seller at closing. The Closing Date will be extended up to 15 days, if necessary, to complete repairs and treatments.

G. ENVIRONMENTAL MATTERS: Buyer is advised that the presence of wetlands, toxic substances, including asbestos and wastes or other environmental hazards, or the presence of a threatened or endangered species or its habitat may affect Buyer's intended use of the Property. If Buyer is concerned about these matters, an addendum promulgated by TREC or required by the parties should be used.

H. RESIDENTIAL SERVICE CONTRACTS: Buyer may purchase a residential service contract from a residential service company licensed by TREC. If Buyer purchases a residential service contract, Seller shall reimburse Buyer at closing for the cost of the residential service contract in an amount not exceeding $_______________ . Buyer should review any residential service contract for the scope of coverage, exclusions and limitations. **The purchase of a residential service contract is optional. Similar coverage may be purchased from various companies authorized to do business in Texas.**

8. **BROKERS' FEES:** All obligations of the parties for payment of brokers' fees are contained in separate written agreements.

9. **CLOSING:**

A. The closing of the sale will be on or before _____________________, 20___, or within 7 days after objections to matters disclosed in the Commitment or by the survey have been cured, whichever date is later (Closing Date). If either party fails to close the sale by the Closing Date, the non-defaulting party may exercise the remedies contained in Paragraph 15.

B. At closing:

(1) Seller shall execute and deliver a general warranty deed conveying title to the Property to Buyer and showing no additional exceptions to those permitted in Paragraph 6 and furnish tax statements or certificates showing no delinquent taxes on the Property.

(2) Buyer shall pay the Sales Price in good funds acceptable to the escrow agent.

(3) Seller and Buyer shall execute and deliver any notices, statements, certificates, affidavits, releases, loan documents and other documents required of them by this contract, the Commitment or law necessary for the closing of the sale and the issuance of the Title Policy.

C. Unless expressly prohibited by written agreement, Seller may continue to show the Property and receive, negotiate and accept back up offers.

D. All covenants, representations and warranties in this contract survive closing.

10. **POSSESSION:** Seller shall deliver to Buyer possession of the Property in its present or required condition, ordinary wear and tear excepted: ☐ upon closing and funding ☐ according to a temporary residential lease form promulgated by TREC or other written lease required by the parties. Any possession by Buyer prior to closing or by Seller after closing which is not authorized by a written lease will establish a tenancy at sufferance relationship between the parties. *Consult your insurance agent prior to change of ownership or possession because insurance coverage may be limited or terminated. The absence of a written lease or appropriate insurance coverage may expose the parties to economic loss.*

11. **SPECIAL PROVISIONS:** (Insert only factual statements and business details applicable to the sale. TREC rules prohibit licensees from adding factual statements or business details for which a contract addendum, lease or other form has been promulgated by TREC for mandatory use.)

Initialed for identification by Buyer_____ _____ and Seller _____ _____ **01A** TREC NO. 20-6

Figure 9.16 TREC 20-6 (continued)

Contract Concerning ______________________________ Page Five 01-06-03
(Address of Property)

12. SETTLEMENT AND OTHER EXPENSES:

A. The following expenses must be paid at or prior to closing:

(1) Expenses payable by Seller (Seller's Expenses):

(a) Releases of existing liens, including prepayment penalties and recording fees; release of Seller's loan liability; tax statements or certificates; preparation of deed; one-half of escrow fee; and other expenses payable by Seller under this contract.

(b) Seller shall also pay an amount not to exceed $ ____________ to be applied in the following order: Buyer's Expenses which Buyer is prohibited from paying by FHA, VA, Texas Veteran's Housing Assistance Program or other governmental loan programs; Buyer's prepaid items; other Buyer's expenses.

(2) Expenses payable by Buyer (Buyer's Expenses):

(a) Loan origination, discount, buy-down, and commitment fees (Loan Fees).

(b) Appraisal fees; loan application fees; credit reports; preparation of loan documents; interest on the notes from date of disbursement to one month prior to dates of first monthly payments; recording fees; copies of easements and restrictions; mortgagee title policy with endorsements required by lender; loan-related inspection fees; photos, amortization schedules, one-half of escrow fee; all prepaid items, including required premiums for flood and hazard insurance, reserve deposits for insurance, ad valorem taxes and special governmental assessments; final compliance inspection; courier fee, repair inspection, underwriting fee and wire transfer, expenses incident to any loan, and other expenses payable by Buyer under this contract.

B. Buyer shall pay Private Mortgage Insurance Premium (PMI), VA Loan Funding Fee, or FHA Mortgage Insurance Premium (MIP) as required by the lender.

C. If any expense exceeds an amount expressly stated in this contract for such expense to be paid by a party, that party may terminate this contract unless the other party agrees to pay such excess. Buyer may not pay charges and fees expressly prohibited by FHA, VA, Texas Veteran's Housing Assistance Program or other governmental loan program regulations.

13. PRORATIONS: Taxes for the current year, interest, maintenance fees, assessments, dues and rents will be prorated through the Closing Date. If taxes for the current year vary from the amount prorated at closing, the parties shall adjust the prorations when tax statements for the current year are available. If taxes are not paid at or prior to closing, Buyer shall pay taxes for the current year.

14. CASUALTY LOSS: If any part of the Property is damaged or destroyed by fire or other casualty after the effective date of this contract, Seller shall restore the Property to its previous condition as soon as reasonably possible, but in any event by the Closing Date. If Seller fails to do so due to factors beyond Seller's control, Buyer may (a) terminate this contract and the earnest money will be refunded to Buyer (b) extend the time for performance up to 15 days and the Closing Date will be extended as necessary or (c) accept the Property in its damaged condition with an assignment of insurance proceeds and receive credit from Seller at closing in the amount of the deductible under the insurance policy. Seller's obligations under this paragraph are independent of any obligations of Seller under Paragraph 7.

15. DEFAULT: If Buyer fails to comply with this contract, Buyer will be in default, and Seller may (a) enforce specific performance, seek such other relief as may be provided by law, or both, or (b) terminate this contract and receive the earnest money as liquidated damages, thereby releasing both parties from this contract. If, due to factors beyond Seller's control, Seller fails within the time allowed to make any non-casualty repairs or deliver the Commitment, or survey, if required of Seller, Buyer may (a) extend the time for performance up to 15 days and the Closing Date will be extended as necessary or (b) terminate this contract as the sole remedy and receive the earnest money. If Seller fails to comply with this contract for any other reason, Seller will be in default and Buyer may (a) enforce specific performance, seek such other relief as may be provided by law, or both, or (b) terminate this contract and receive the earnest money, thereby releasing both parties from this contract.

16. MEDIATION: It is the policy of the State of Texas to encourage resolution of disputes through alternative dispute resolution procedures such as mediation. Any dispute between Seller and Buyer related to this contract which is not resolved through informal discussion ❑will ❑will not be submitted to a mutually acceptable mediation service or provider. The parties to the mediation shall bear the mediation costs equally. This paragraph does not preclude a party from seeking equitable relief from a court of competent jurisdiction.

01A TREC NO. 20-6

Initialed for identification by Buyer_______ _______ and Seller_______ _______

Figure 9.16 TREC 20-6 (continued)

Contract Concerning ____ Page Six 01-06-03
(Address of Property)

17. ATTORNEY'S FEES: The prevailing party in any legal proceeding related to this contract is entitled to recover reasonable attorney's fees and all costs of such proceeding incurred by the prevailing party.

18. ESCROW: The escrow agent is not (a) a party to this contract and does not have liability for the performance or nonperformance of any party to this contract, (b) liable for interest on the earnest money and (c) liable for the loss of any earnest money caused by the failure of any financial institution in which the earnest money has been deposited unless the financial institution is acting as escrow agent. At closing, the earnest money must be applied first to any cash down payment, then to Buyer's Expenses and any excess refunded to Buyer. If both parties make written demand for the earnest money, escrow agent may require payment of unpaid expenses incurred on behalf of the parties and a written release of liability of escrow agent from all parties. If one party makes written demand for the earnest money, escrow agent shall give notice of the demand by providing to the other party a copy of the demand. If escrow agent does not receive written objection to the demand from the other party within 30 days after notice to the other party, escrow agent may disburse the earnest money to the party making demand reduced by the amount of unpaid expenses incurred on behalf of the party receiving the earnest money and escrow agent may pay the same to the creditors. If escrow agent complies with the provisions of this paragraph, each party hereby releases escrow agent from all adverse claims related to the disbursal of the earnest money. Escrow agent's notice to the other party will be effective when deposited in the U. S. Mail, postage prepaid, certified mail, return receipt requested, addressed to the other party at such party's address shown below. Notice of objection to the demand will be deemed effective upon receipt by escrow agent.

19. REPRESENTATIONS: Seller represents that as of the Closing Date (a) there will be no liens, assessments, or security interests against the Property which will not be satisfied out of the sales proceeds unless securing payment of any loans assumed by Buyer and (b) assumed loans will not be in default. If any representation of Seller in this contract is untrue on the Closing Date, Buyer may terminate this contract and the earnest money will be refunded to Buyer.

20. FEDERAL TAX REQUIREMENTS: If Seller is a "foreign person," as defined by applicable law, or if Seller fails to deliver an affidavit to Buyer that Seller is not a "foreign person," then Buyer shall withhold from the sales proceeds an amount sufficient to comply with applicable tax law and deliver the same to the Internal Revenue Service together with appropriate tax forms. Internal Revenue Service regulations require filing written reports if currency in excess of specified amounts is received in the transaction.

21. NOTICES: All notices from one party to the other must be in writing and are effective when mailed to, hand-delivered at, or transmitted by facsimile as follows:

To Buyer at:	**To Seller at:**
______________________	______________________
______________________	______________________
______________________	______________________
Telephone:(____) ______________	Telephone:(____) ______________
Facsimile:(____)______________	Facsimile:(____) ______________

22. AGREEMENT OF PARTIES: This contract contains the entire agreement of the parties and cannot be changed except by their written agreement. Addenda which are a part of this contract are (check all applicable boxes):

- ☐ Third Party Financing Condition Addendum
- ☐ Addendum for Property Subject to Mandatory Membership in an Owners' Association
- ☐ Seller Financing Addendum
- ☐ Environmental Assessment, Threatened or Endangered Species and Wetlands Addendum

Figure 9.16 TREC 20-6 (continued)

Contract Concerning ______________________________ Page Seven 01-06-03
(Address of Property)

- ❑ Loan Assumption Addendum
- ❑ Buyer's Temporary Residential Lease
- ❑ Seller's Temporary Residential Lease
- ❑ Addendum for Sale of Other Property by Buyer
- ❑ Addendum for Seller's Disclosure of Information on Lead-based Paint and Lead-based Paint Hazards as Required by Federal Law
- ❑ Addendum for "Back-Up" Contract
- ❑ Addendum for Coastal Area Property
- ❑ Addendum for Property Located Seaward of the Gulf Intracoastal Waterway
- ❑ Addendum for Release of Liability on Assumption of FHA, VA, or Conventional Loan Restoration of Seller's Entitlement for VA Guaranteed Loan

❑ Other (list): ______________________________

____

23. **TERMINATION OPTION: This paragraph will be a part of this contract ONLY if both blanks are filled in and Buyer has paid the Option Fee.** Buyer has paid Seller $__________ (Option Fee) for the unrestricted right to terminate this contract by giving notice of termination to Seller within ________ days after the effective date of this contract. If Buyer gives notice of termination within the time specified, the Option Fee will not be refunded, however, any earnest money will be refunded to Buyer. The Option Fee ❑will ❑will not be credited to the Sales Price at closing. For the purposes of this paragraph, time is of the essence; strict compliance with the time for performance stated herein is required.

24. **CONSULT AN ATTORNEY:** Real estate licensees cannot give legal advice. READ THIS CONTRACT CAREFULLY. If you do not understand the effect of this contract, consult an attorney BEFORE signing.

Buyer's Attorney is: ______________________

____

Telephone: (____)______________________

Facsimile: (____)______________________

Seller's Attorney is: ______________________

____

Telephone: (____)______________________

Facsimile: (____)______________________

EXECUTED the ________day of ______________________, 20____ (EFFECTIVE DATE). (BROKER: FILL IN THE DATE OF FINAL ACCEPTANCE.)

____
Buyer

____
Seller

____
Buyer

____
Seller

The form of this contract has been approved by the Texas Real Estate Commission. TREC forms are intended for use only by trained real estate licensees. No representation is made as to the legal validity or adequacy of any provision in any specific transactions. It is not suitable for complex transactions. Texas Real Estate Commission, P.O. Box 12188, Austin, TX 78711-2188, 1-800-250-8732 or (512) 459-6544 (http://www.trec.state.tx.us) TREC NO. 20-6. This form replaces TREC NO. 20-5.

Initialed for identification by Buyer______ ______ and Seller ______ ______ **01A** TREC NO. 20-6

Figure 9.16 TREC 20-6 (continued)

Contract Concerning ______________________________ Page Eight 01-06-03
(Address of Property)

SELLER'S RECEIPT

Receipt of $____________ (Option Fee) in the form of ________________ is acknowledged.

______________________ Seller
______________________ Date

BROKER INFORMATION AND RATIFICATION OF FEE

Listing Broker has agreed to pay Other Broker ________________ of the total sales price when Listing Broker's fee is received. Escrow Agent is authorized and directed to pay Other Broker from Listing Broker's fee at closing.

Other Broker	Listing Broker
License No. Telephone	License No. Telephone
represents ❑ Buyer only as Buyer's agent ❑ Seller as Listing Broker's subagent	represents ❑ Seller and Buyer as an intermediary ❑ Seller only as Seller's agent
Associate Telephone	Listing Associate Telephone
Broker's Address	Listing Associate's Office Address Facsimile
Facsimile	Selling Associate Telephone
	Selling Associate's Office Address Facsimile

RECEIPT

Receipt of ❑ Contract and ❑ $____________ Earnest Money in the form of ________________
is acknowledged.
Escrow Agent: ______________________ Date: ______________

By: ______________________

______________________ Telephone (____) ______________
Address

______________________ Facsimile: (____) ______________
City State Zip

01A TREC NO. 20-6

Figure 9.17 TREC 26-4

PROMULGATED BY THE TEXAS REAL ESTATE COMMISSION (TREC) 10-29-01

EQUAL HOUSING OPPORTUNITY

SELLER FINANCING ADDENDUM

TO CONTRACT CONCERNING THE PROPERTY AT

____

(Street Address and City)

A. CREDIT DOCUMENTATION. Within__________days after the effective date of this contract, Buyer shall deliver to Seller ❑ credit report ❑ verification of employment, including salary ❑ verification of funds on deposit in financial institutions ❑ current financial statement to establish Buyer's creditworthiness and ❑ ____.

Buyer hereby authorizes any credit reporting agency to furnish to Seller at Buyer's sole expense copies of Buyer's credit reports.

B. CREDIT APPROVAL. If Buyer's documentation is not delivered within the specified time, Seller may terminate this contract by notice to Buyer within 7 days after expiration of the time for delivery, and the earnest money will be paid to Seller. If the documentation is timely delivered, and Seller determines in Seller's sole discretion that Buyer's credit is unacceptable, Seller may terminate this contract by notice to Buyer within 7 days after expiration of the time for delivery and the earnest money will be refunded to Buyer. If Seller does not terminate this contract, Seller will be deemed to have accepted Buyer's credit.

C. PROMISSORY NOTE. The promissory note (Note) described in Paragraph 4 of this contract payable by Buyer to the order of Seller will be payable at the place designated by Seller. Buyer may prepay the Note in whole or in part at any time without penalty. Any prepayments are to be applied to the payment of the installments of principal last maturing and interest will immediately cease on the prepaid principal. The Note will contain a provision for payment of a late fee of 5% of any installment not paid within 10 days of the due date. The Note will be payable as follows:

❑ (1) In one payment due ______________________ after the date of the Note with interest payable ______________________________.

❑ (2) In ______________ installments of $ ________________ ❑ including interest ❑ plus interest beginning ________________________ after the date of the Note and continuing at __________ intervals thereafter for ______________when the balance of the Note will be due and payable.

❑ (3) Interest only in ______ installments for the first ____________________ month(s) and thereafter in installments of $______________ ❑ including interest ❑ plus interest beginning ________________________ after the date of the Note and continuing at ____________ intervals thereafter for ______________ when the balance of the Note will be due and payable.

D. DEED OF TRUST. The deed of trust securing the Note will provide for the following:

(1) PROPERTY TRANSFERS: (check only one)

❑ (a) Consent Not Required: The Property may be sold, conveyed or leased without the consent of Seller, provided any subsequent buyer assumes the Note.

❑ (b) Consent Required: If all or any part of the Property is sold, conveyed, leased for a period longer than 3 years, leased with an option to purchase, or otherwise sold (including any contract for deed), without the prior written consent of Seller, Seller may declare the

01A

Initialed for identification by Buyer_______ _______ and Seller________ ________

Figure 9.17 TREC 26-4 (continued)

Seller Financing Addendum Concerning Page Two 10-29-01

(Address of Property)

balance of the Note, to be immediately due and payable. The creation of a subordinate lien, any conveyance under threat or order of condemnation, any deed solely between buyers, the passage of title by reason of the death of a buyer or by operation of law will not entitle Seller to exercise the remedies provided in this paragraph.

(2) TAX AND INSURANCE ESCROW: (check only one)

❑ (a) Escrow Not Required: Buyer shall furnish Seller annually, before the taxes become delinquent, evidence that all taxes on the Property have been paid. Buyer shall furnish Seller annually evidence of paid-up casualty insurance naming Seller as an additional loss payee.

❑ (b) Escrow Required: With each installment Buyer shall deposit with Seller in escrow a pro rata part of the estimated annual ad valorem taxes and casualty insurance premiums for the Property. Buyer shall pay any deficiency within 30 days after notice from Seller. Buyer's failure to pay the deficiency constitutes a default under the deed of trust. Buyer is not required to deposit any escrow payments for taxes and insurance that are deposited with a superior lienholder. The casualty insurance must name Seller as an additional loss payee.

(3) PRIOR LIENS: Any default under any lien superior to the lien securing the Note constitutes default under the deed of trust securing the Note.

Buyer Seller

Buyer Seller

This form has been approved by the Texas Real Estate Commission for use with similarly approved or promulgated contract forms. Such approval relates to this form only. TREC forms are intended for use only by trained real estate licensees. No representation is made as to the legal validity or adequacy of any provision in any specific transactions. It is not suitable for complex transactions. Texas Real Estate Commission, P.O. Box 12188, Austin, TX 78711-2188, 1-800-250-8732 or (512) 459-6544 (http://www.trec.state.tx.us) TREC No. 26-4. This form replaces TREC No. 26-3.

01A

Figure 9.18 TREC 28-0

EQUAL HOUSING OPPORTUNITY

10-25-93

ENVIRONMENTAL ASSESSMENT, THREATENED OR ENDANGERED SPECIES, AND WETLANDS ADDENDUM

PROMULGATED BY THE TEXAS REAL ESTATE COMMISSION (TREC)

ADDENDUM TO EARNEST MONEY CONTRACT BETWEEN THE UNDERSIGNED PARTIES CONCERNING THE PROPERTY AT ______________________________
(Address)

☐ A. ENVIRONMENTAL ASSESSMENT: Buyer, at Buyer's expense, may obtain an Environmental Assessment Report prepared by an environmental specialist.

☐ B. THREATENED OR ENDANGERED SPECIES: Buyer, at Buyer's expense, may obtain a report from a natural resources professional to determine if there are any threatened or endangered species or their habitats as defined by the Texas Parks and Wildlife Department or the U.S. Fish and Wildlife Service.

☐ C. WETLANDS: Buyer, at Buyer's expense, may obtain a report from an environmental specialist to determine if there are wetlands, as defined by federal or state law or regulation.

Within _________ days after the Effective Date of the contract, Buyer may terminate the contract by furnishing Seller a copy of any report noted above that adversely affects the use of the Property and the Earnest Money shall be refunded to Buyer. If Buyer does not furnish Seller a copy of the unacceptable report within the prescribed time and give Seller notice that Buyer has terminated the contract, Buyer shall be deemed to have accepted the Property.

______________________________ ______________________________
Buyer Seller

______________________________ ______________________________
Buyer Seller

The form of this addendum has been approved by the Texas Real Estate Commission for use only with similarly approved or promulgated forms of contracts. No representation is made as to the legal validity or adequacy of any provision in any specific transactions. It is not suitable for complex transactions. (10-93) TREC No. 28-0.

01A TREC No. 28-0

Transaction 6: All Cash
(Using: TREC 25-4, OP-L Lead-Based Paint Addendum, and TREC 28-0)

Fannie Phyllis Farmer, a widow, will sell her Pecos County ranch to William Robert (Billy Bob) Richman and his wife, Mae Bea (Sissy) Richman. The property is described by a rather lengthy metes-and-bounds description, which is attached to the purchase agreement and identified as Exhibit A. It is known as 2520 Farmer Road, Pecos, TX 78789. It is not located in a Texas Agricultural Development District.

There are no crops or equipment included in the sale. There are no outstanding mineral or timber interests; however, Fannie will retain 50 percent of the gas and oil interests at closing. The buyers request that the seller furnishes, at her own expense, a new survey of the property within 20 days after the effective date of the contract and are asking for 7 days to review the survey and title documents. They call for an abstract to be furnished within 30 days after the effective date of the contract, and will have it reviewed by their real estate attorney, Ronald Hawkeye Redundant.

The buyers will pay $895,000 cash for the property. According to the seller, the farm is 350 acres. If, after reviewing the survey, it is found to be more or less than 350 acres, the sale price will be adjusted $2,500 per acre over or under. They tender $100,000 earnest money with Pecos County Abstract Company who will close the transaction in about 30 days on December 23.

The buyers choose not to have any inspections done and accept the property in its present condition. They have received the seller's disclosure of property condition form. They have also waived their right to have the farmhouse inspected for lead-based paint hazards, however they request 20 days to have environmental assessments done. They will have all of the present ramshackle buildings demolished to make way for the new 12,000-square-foot house. Rollback taxes will not be an issue because the buyers plan no change in the use of the property.

The listing broker is Rick Knowles, the owner of Country Properties. Philip Schoewe, an independent broker, represents the buyers. The buyer's broker will be paid a selling fee of $10,000, which will be paid from the listing broker's fee at closing.

Figure 9.19 TREC 25-4

PROMULGATED BY THE TEXAS REAL ESTATE COMMISSION (TREC) 01-06-03

EQUAL HOUSING OPPORTUNITY

FARM AND RANCH CONTRACT

1. **PARTIES:** ______________________________ (Seller) agrees to sell and convey to ______________________________ (Buyer) and Buyer agrees to buy from Seller the Property described below.

2. **PROPERTY:** The land, improvements, accessories and crops are collectively referred to as the "Property".

   A. LAND: The land situated in ______________________ County, Texas, described as follows:

   or as described on attached exhibit, also known as ______________________________
   ______________________________ (address/zip code), together with all rights, privileges, and appurtenances pertaining thereto, including but not limited to: water rights, claims, permits, strips and gores, easements, and cooperative or association memberships.

   B. IMPROVEMENTS:

   (1) FARM and RANCH IMPROVEMENTS: The following permanently installed and built-in items, if any: windmills, tanks, barns, pens, fences, gates, sheds, outbuildings, and corrals.

   (2) RESIDENTIAL IMPROVEMENTS: The house, garage, and all other fixtures and improvements attached to the above-described real property, including without limitation, the following permanently installed and built-in items, if any: all equipment and appliances, valances, screens, shutters, awnings, wall-to-wall carpeting, mirrors, ceiling fans, attic fans, mail boxes, television antennas and satellite dish system and equipment, heating and air-conditioning units, security and fire detection equipment, wiring, plumbing and lighting fixtures, chandeliers, water softener system, kitchen equipment, garage door openers, cleaning equipment, shrubbery, landscaping, outdoor cooking equipment, and all other property owned by Seller and attached to the above described real property.

   C. ACCESSORIES:

   (1) FARM AND RANCH ACCESSORIES: The following described related accessories: (check boxes of conveyed accessories) ☐ portable buildings ☐ hunting blinds ☐ game feeders ☐ livestock feeders and troughs ☐ irrigation equipment ☐ fuel tanks ☐ submersible pumps ☐ pressure tanks ☐ corrals ☐ gates ☐ chutes ☐ other: ______________________________
   ____
   ____

   (2) RESIDENTIAL ACCESSORIES: The following described related accessories, if any: window air conditioning units, stove, fireplace screens, curtains and rods, blinds, window shades, draperies and rods, controls for satellite dish system, controls for garage door openers, entry gate controls, door keys, mailbox keys, above ground pool, swimming pool equipment and maintenance accessories, and artificial fireplace logs.

   D. CROPS: Unless otherwise agreed in writing, Seller has the right to harvest all growing crops until delivery of possession of the Property.

   E. EXCLUSIONS: The following improvements, accessories, and crops will be retained by Seller and excluded: ______________________________
   ____
   ____
   ____

   F. RESERVATIONS: Seller reserves the following mineral, water, royalty, timber, or other interests: ______________________________
   ____
   ____
   ____
   ____

01A TREC NO. 25-4

Initialed for identification by Buyer_______ _______ and Seller_______ _______

Figure 9.19 TREC 25-4 (continued)

Farm and Ranch Contract ______________________________________ Page Two 01-06-03
(Address of Property)

3. SALES PRICE:

A. Cash portion of Sales Price payable by Buyer at closing .... $__________________

B. Sum of all financing described below (excluding any loan funding fee or mortgage insurance premium) .... $__________________

C. Sales Price (Sum of A and B) .... $__________________

D. The Sales Price ☐ will ☐ will not be adjusted based on the survey required by Paragraph 6C. If the Sales Price is adjusted, the Sales Price will be calculated on the basis of $ __________ per acre. If the Sales Price is adjusted by more than 10%, either party may terminate this contract by providing written notice to the other party within _____ days after the terminating party receives the survey. If neither party terminates this contract or if the variance is 10% or less, the adjustment will be made to the amount in ☐ 3A ☐ 3B ☐ proportionately to 3A and 3B.

4. FINANCING: The portion of Sales Price not payable in cash will be paid as follows: (Check applicable boxes below)

☐ A. THIRD PARTY FINANCING: One or more third party mortgage loans in the total amount of $_______________. If the Property does not satisfy the lenders' underwriting requirements for the loan(s), this contract will terminate and the earnest money will be refunded to Buyer. (Check one box only)

☐ (1) This contract is subject to Buyer being approved for the financing described in the attached Third Party Financing Condition Addendum.

☐ (2) This contract is not subject to Buyer being approved for financing.

☐ B. ASSUMPTION: The assumption of the unpaid principal balance of one or more promissory notes described in the attached TREC Loan Assumption Addendum.

☐ C. SELLER FINANCING: A promissory note from Buyer to Seller of $_______________, bearing _______ % interest per annum, secured by vendor's and deed of trust liens, and containing the terms and conditions described in the attached TREC Seller Financing Addendum. If an owner policy of title insurance is furnished, Buyer shall furnish Seller with a mortgagee policy of title insurance.

5. EARNEST MONEY: Upon execution of this contract by both parties, Buyer shall deposit $____________ as earnest money with ____, as escrow agent, at ____ (address). Buyer shall deposit additional earnest money of $__________________ with escrow agent within _________days after the effective date of this contract. If Buyer fails to deposit the earnest money as required by this contract, Buyer will be in default.

6. TITLE POLICY AND SURVEY:

A. TITLE POLICY: Seller shall furnish to Buyer at ☐ Seller's ☐ Buyer's expense an owner policy of title insurance (Title Policy) issued by: ______________________________________ (Title Company) in the amount of the Sales Price, dated at or after closing, insuring Buyer against loss under the provisions of the Title Policy, subject to the promulgated exclusions (including existing building and zoning ordinances) and the following exceptions:

(1) The standard printed exception for standby fees, taxes and assessments.

(2) Liens created as part of the financing described in Paragraph 4.

(3) Reservations or exceptions otherwise permitted by this contract or as may be approved by Buyer in writing.

(4) The standard printed exception as to marital rights.

(5) The standard printed exception as to waters, tidelands, beaches, streams, and related matters.

(6) The standard printed exception as to discrepancies, conflicts, shortages in area or boundary lines, encroachments or protrusions, or overlapping improvements. Buyer, at Buyer's expense, may have the exception amended to read, "shortages in area".

B. COMMITMENT: Within 20 days after the Title Company receives a copy of this contract, Seller shall furnish to Buyer a commitment for title insurance (Commitment) and, at Buyer's expense, legible copies of restrictive covenants and documents evidencing exceptions in the Commitment (Exception Documents) other than the standard printed exceptions. Seller authorizes the Title Company to mail or hand deliver the Commitment and Exception Documents to Buyer at Buyer's address shown in Paragraph 21. If the Commitment and Exception Documents are not delivered to Buyer within the specified time, the time for delivery will be automatically extended up to 15 days or the Closing Date, whichever is earlier.

01A TREC NO. 25-4

Initialed for identification by Buyer_______ _______ and Seller________ ________

Figure 9.19 TREC 25-4 (continued)

Farm and Ranch Contract ____ Page Three 01-06-03
(Address of Property)

C. SURVEY: The survey must be made by a registered professional land surveyor acceptable to the Title Company and any lender. (Check one box only):

❑ (1) Within ________ days after the effective date of this contract, Seller, at Seller's expense, shall furnish a new survey to Buyer.

❑ (2) Within ________ days after the effective date of this contract, Buyer, at Buyer's expense, shall obtain a new survey.

❑ (3) Within ________ days after the effective date of this contract, Seller shall furnish Seller's existing survey of the Property to Buyer and the Title Company, along with Seller's affidavit acceptable to the Title Company for approval of the survey. The existing Survey ☐ will ☐ will not be recertified to a date subsequent to the effective date of this contract at the expense of ☐ Buyer ☐ Seller. If the existing survey is not approved by the Title Company or Buyer's lender, a new survey will be obtained at the expense of ☐ Buyer ☐ Seller no later than 3 days prior to the Closing Date.

❑ (4) No survey is required.

D. OBJECTIONS: Within ____ days after Buyer receives the Commitment, Exception Documents and the survey, Buyer may object in writing to (i) defects, exceptions, or encumbrances to title: disclosed on the survey other than items 6A(1) through (5) above; disclosed in the Commitment other than items 6A(1) through (6) above; (ii) any portion of the Property lying in the 100 year flood plain as shown on the current Federal Emergency Management Agency map; or (iii) any exceptions which prohibit the following use or activity: __________

____

____

____

Buyer's failure to object within the time allowed will constitute a waiver of Buyer's right to object; except that the requirements in Schedule C of the Commitment are not waived. Seller shall cure the timely objections of Buyer or any third party lender within 15 days after Seller receives the objections and the Closing Date will be extended as necessary. If objections are not cured within such 15 day period, this contract will terminate and the earnest money will be refunded to Buyer unless Buyer waives the objections.

E. EXCEPTION DOCUMENTS: Prior to the execution of the contract, Seller has provided Buyer with copies of the Exception Documents listed below or on the attached exhibit. Matters reflected in the Exception Documents listed below or on the attached exhibit will be permitted exceptions in the Title Policy and will not be a basis for objection to title:

Document	Date	Recording Reference
______________	________	________
______________	________	________
______________	________	________
______________	________	________
______________	________	________
______________	________	________

F. SURFACE LEASES: Prior to the execution of the contract, Seller has provided Buyer with copies of written leases and given notice of oral leases (Leases) listed below or on the attached exhibit. The following Leases will be permitted exceptions in the Title Policy and will not be a basis for objection to title: ______________________________

____

____

____

01A TREC NO. 25-4

Initialed for identification by Buyer______ ________ and Seller______ ________

Figure 9.19 TREC 25-4 (continued)

G. TITLE NOTICES:

(1) ABSTRACT OR TITLE POLICY: Broker advises Buyer to have an abstract of title covering the Property examined by an attorney of Buyer's selection, or Buyer should be furnished with or obtain a Title Policy. If a Title Policy is furnished, the Commitment should be promptly reviewed by an attorney of Buyer's choice due to the time limitations on Buyer's right to object.

(2) STATUTORY TAX DISTRICTS: If the Property is situated in a utility or other statutorily created district providing water, sewer, drainage, or flood control facilities and services, Chapter 49, Texas Water, Code requires Seller to deliver and Buyer to sign the statutory notice relating to the tax rate, bonded indebtedness, or standby fee of the district prior to final execution of this contract.

(3) TIDE WATERS: If the Property abuts the tidally influenced waters of the state, §33.135, Texas Natural Resources Code, requires a notice regarding coastal area property to be included in the contract. An addendum containing the notice promulgated by TREC or required by the parties must be used.

(4) ANNEXATION: If the Property is located outside the limits of a municipality, Seller notifies Buyer under §5.011, Texas Property Code, that the Property may now or later be included in the extraterritorial jurisdiction of a municipality and may now or later be subject to annexation by the municipality. Each municipality maintains a map that depicts its boundaries and extraterritorial jurisdiction. To determine if the Property is located within a municipality's extraterritorial jurisdiction or is likely to be located within a municipality's extraterritorial jurisdiction, contact all municipalities located in the general proximity of the Property for further information.

(5) UNIMPROVED PROPERTY LOCATED IN A CERTIFICATED SERVICE AREA OF A UTILITY SERVICE PROVIDER: If the Property is located in a certificated service area of a utility service provider and the Property does not receive water or sewer service from the utility service provider on the date the Property is transferred, §13.257, Texas Water Code, requires a notice regarding the cost of providing water or sewer services to the Property. An addendum containing the notice promulgated by TREC or required by the parties must be used.

(6) TEXAS AGRICULTURAL DEVELOPMENT DISTRICT: The Property ❑ is ❑ is not located in a Texas Agricultural Development District.

7. PROPERTY CONDITION:

A. INSPECTIONS, ACCESS AND UTILITIES: Buyer may have the Property inspected by inspectors selected by Buyer and licensed by TREC or otherwise permitted by law to make inspections. Seller shall permit Buyer and Buyer's agents access to the Property at reasonable times. Seller shall pay for turning on existing utilities for inspections.
NOTICE: Buyer should determine the availability of utilities to the Property suitable to satisfy Buyer's needs.

B. SELLER'S DISCLOSURE NOTICE PURSUANT TO §5.008, TEXAS PROPERTY CODE (Notice):
(Check one box only)
❑ (1) Buyer has received the Notice
❑ (2) Buyer has not received the Notice. Within _______ days after the effective date of this contract, Seller shall deliver the Notice to Buyer. If Buyer does not receive the Notice, Buyer may terminate this contract at any time prior to the closing and the earnest money will be refunded to Buyer. If Seller delivers the Notice, Buyer may terminate this contract for any reason within 7 days after Buyer receives the Notice or prior to the closing, whichever first occurs, and the earnest money will be refunded to Buyer.
❑ (3) The Texas Property Code does not require this Seller to furnish the Notice.

C. SELLER'S DISCLOSURE OF LEAD-BASED PAINT AND LEAD-BASED PAINT HAZARDS is required by Federal law for a residential dwelling constructed prior to 1978.

D. ACCEPTANCE OF PROPERTY CONDITION: Buyer accepts the Property in its present condition; provided Seller, at Seller's expense, shall complete the following specific repairs and treatments:

____

____

E. COMPLETION OF REPAIRS: Unless otherwise agreed in writing, Seller shall complete all agreed repairs prior to the Closing Date. All required permits must be obtained, and repairs must be performed by persons who are licensed or otherwise permitted by law to provide such repairs. At Buyer's election, any transferable warranties received by Seller with respect to the repairs will be transferred to Buyer at Buyer's expense. If Seller fails to complete any agreed repairs prior to the Closing Date, Buyer may do so and receive reimbursement from Seller at closing. The Closing Date will be extended up to 15 days, if necessary, to complete repairs.

Figure 9.19 TREC 25-4 (continued)

F. LENDER REQUIRED REPAIRS AND TREATMENTS: Unless otherwise agreed in writing, neither party is obligated to pay for lender required repairs, which includes treatment for wood destroying insects. If the parties do not agree to pay for the lender required repairs or treatments, this contract will terminate and the earnest money will be refunded to Buyer. If the cost of lender required repairs and treatments exceeds 5% of the Sales Price, Buyer may terminate this contract and the earnest money will be refunded to Buyer.

G. ENVIRONMENTAL MATTERS: Buyer is advised that the presence of wetlands, toxic substances, including asbestos and wastes or other environmental hazards, or the presence of a threatened or endangered species or its habitat may affect Buyer's intended use of the Property. If Buyer is concerned about these matters, an addendum promulgated by TREC or required by the parties should be used.

H. SELLER'S DISCLOSURES: Except as otherwise disclosed in this contract, Seller has no knowledge of the following:
   (1) any flooding of the Property which has had a material adverse effect on the use of the Property;
   (2) any pending or threatened litigation, condemnation, or special assessment affecting the Property;
   (3) any environmental hazards or conditions which materially affect the Property;
   (4) any dumpsite, landfill, or underground tanks or containers now or previously located on the Property;
   (5) any wetlands, as defined by federal or state law or regulation, affecting the Property; or
   (6) any threatened or endangered species or their habitat affecting the Property.

I. RESIDENTIAL SERVICE CONTRACTS: Buyer may purchase a residential service contract from a residential service company licensed by TREC. If Buyer purchases a residential service contract, Seller shall reimburse Buyer at closing for the cost of the residential service contract in an amount not exceeding $______________ . Buyer should review any residential service contract for the scope of coverage, exclusions and limitations. **The purchase of a residential service contract is optional. Similar coverage may be purchased from various companies authorized to do business in Texas.**

J. GOVERNMENT PROGRAMS: The Property is subject to the government programs listed below or on the attached exhibit:____

____

Seller shall provide Buyer with copies of all governmental program agreements. Any allocation or proration of payment under governmental programs is made by separate agreement between the parties which will survive closing.

8. **BROKERS' FEES:** All obligations of the parties for payment of brokers' fees are contained in separate written agreements.

9. **CLOSING:**

A. The closing of the sale will be on or before ______________________, 20___, or within 7 days after objections to matters disclosed in the Commitment or by the survey have been cured, whichever date is later (Closing Date). If either party fails to close the sale by the Closing Date, the non-defaulting party may exercise the remedies contained in Paragraph 15.

B. At closing:
   (1) Seller shall execute and deliver a general warranty deed conveying title to the Property to Buyer and showing no additional exceptions to those permitted in Paragraph 6, an assignment of Leases, and furnish tax statements or certificates showing no delinquent taxes on the Property.
   (2) Buyer shall pay the Sales Price in good funds acceptable to the escrow agent.
   (3) Seller and Buyer shall execute and deliver any notices, statements, certificates, affidavits, releases, loan documents and other documents required of them by this contract, the Commitment or law necessary for the closing of the sale and the issuance of the Title Policy.

C. Unless expressly prohibited by written agreement, Seller may continue to show the Property and receive, negotiate and accept back up offers.

D. All covenants, representations and warranties in this contract survive closing.

10. **POSSESSION:** Seller shall deliver to Buyer possession of the Property in its present or required condition, ordinary wear and tear excepted: ☐ upon closing and funding ☐ according to a temporary residential lease form promulgated by TREC or other written lease required by the parties. Any possession by Buyer prior to closing or by Seller after closing which is not authorized by a written lease will establish a tenancy at sufferance relationship between the parties. *Consult your insurance*

Figure 9.19 TREC 25-4 (continued)

agent prior to change of ownership or possession because insurance coverage may be limited or terminated. The absence of a written lease or appropriate insurance coverage may expose the parties to economic loss.

11. SPECIAL PROVISIONS: (Insert only factual statements and business details applicable to the sale. TREC rules prohibit licensees from adding factual statements or business details for which a contract addendum or other form has been promulgated by TREC for mandatory use.)

12. SETTLEMENT AND OTHER EXPENSES:

A. The following expenses must be paid at or prior to closing:

(1) Expenses payable by Seller (Seller's Expenses):

(a) Releases of existing liens, including prepayment penalties and recording fees; release of Seller's loan liability; tax statements or certificates; preparation of deed; one-half of escrow fee; and other expenses payable by Seller under this contract.

(b) Seller shall also pay an amount not to exceed $ ______________ to be applied in the following order: Buyer's Expenses which Buyer is prohibited from paying by FHA, VA, Texas Veteran's Housing Assistance Program or other governmental loan programs; Buyer's prepaid items; other Buyer's expenses.

(2) Expenses payable by Buyer (Buyer's Expenses):

(a) Loan origination, discount, buy-down, and commitment fees (Loan Fees).

(b) Appraisal fees; loan application fees; credit reports; preparation of loan documents; interest on the notes from date of disbursement to one month prior to dates of first monthly payments; recording fees; copies of easements and restrictions; mortgagee title policy with endorsements required by lender; loan-related inspection fees; photos, amortization schedules, one-half of escrow fee; all prepaid items, including required premiums for flood and hazard insurance, reserve deposits for insurance, ad valorem taxes and special governmental assessments; final compliance inspection; courier fee, repair inspection, underwriting fee and wire transfer, expenses incident to any loan, and other expenses payable by Buyer under this contract.

B. Buyer shall pay Private Mortgage Insurance Premium (PMI), VA Loan Funding Fee, or FHA Mortgage Insurance Premium (MIP) as required by the lender.

C. If any expense exceeds an amount expressly stated in this contract for such expense to be paid by a party, that party may terminate this contract unless the other party agrees to pay such excess. Buyer may not pay charges and fees expressly prohibited by FHA, VA, Texas Veteran's Housing Assistance Program or other governmental loan program regulations.

13. PRORATIONS AND ROLLBACK TAXES:

A. PRORATIONS: Taxes for the current year, interest, maintenance fees, assessments, dues and rents will be prorated through the Closing Date. If taxes for the current year vary from the amount prorated at closing, the parties shall adjust the prorations when tax statements for the current year are available. If taxes are not paid at or prior to closing, Buyer shall pay taxes for the current year. Rentals which are unknown at time of closing will be prorated between Buyer and Seller when they become known.

B. ROLLBACK TAXES: If this sale or Buyer's use of the Property after closing results in the assessment of additional taxes, penalties or interest (Assessments) for periods prior to closing, the Assessments will be the obligation of Buyer. If Seller's change in use of the Property prior to closing or denial of a special use valuation on the Property claimed by Seller results in Assessments for periods prior to closing, the Assessments will be the obligation of Seller. Obligations imposed by this paragraph will survive closing.

14. CASUALTY LOSS: If any part of the Property is damaged or destroyed by fire or other casualty after the effective date of this contract, Seller shall restore the Property to its previous condition as soon as reasonably possible, but in any event by the Closing Date. If Seller fails to do so due to factors beyond Seller's control, Buyer may (a) terminate this

Figure 9.19 TREC 25-4 (continued)

contract and the earnest money will be refunded to Buyer (b) extend the time for performance up to 15 days and the Closing Date will be extended as necessary or (c) accept the Property in its damaged condition with an assignment of insurance proceeds and receive credit from Seller at closing in the amount of the deductible under the insurance policy. Seller's obligations under this paragraph are independent of any obligations of Seller under Paragraph 7.

15. DEFAULT: If Buyer fails to comply with this contract, Buyer will be in default, and Seller may (a) enforce specific performance, seek such other relief as may be provided by law, or both, or (b) terminate this contract and receive the earnest money as liquidated damages, thereby releasing both parties from this contract. If, due to factors beyond Seller's control, Seller fails within the time allowed to make any non-casualty repairs or deliver the Commitment, or survey, if required of Seller, Buyer may (a) extend the time for performance up to 15 days and the Closing Date will be extended as necessary or (b) terminate this contract as the sole remedy and receive the earnest money. If Seller fails to comply with this contract for any other reason, Seller will be in default and Buyer may (a) enforce specific performance, seek such other relief as may be provided by law, or both, or (b) terminate this contract and receive the earnest money, thereby releasing both parties from this contract.

16. MEDIATION: It is the policy of the State of Texas to encourage resolution of disputes through alternative dispute resolution procedures such as mediation. Any dispute between Seller and Buyer related to this contract which is not resolved through informal discussion ☐ will ☐ will not be submitted to a mutually acceptable mediation service or provider. The parties to the mediation shall bear the mediation costs equally. This paragraph does not preclude a party from seeking equitable relief from a court of competent jurisdiction.

17. ATTORNEY'S FEES: The prevailing party in any legal proceeding related to this contract is entitled to recover reasonable attorney's fees and all costs of such proceeding incurred by the prevailing party.

18. ESCROW: The escrow agent is not (a) a party to this contract and does not have liability for the performance or nonperformance of any party to this contract, (b) liable for interest on the earnest money and (c) liable for the loss of any earnest money caused by the failure of any financial institution in which the earnest money has been deposited unless the financial institution is acting as escrow agent. At closing, the earnest money must be applied first to any cash down payment, then to Buyer's Expenses and any excess refunded to Buyer. If both parties make written demand for the earnest money, escrow agent may require payment of unpaid expenses incurred on behalf of the parties and a written release of liability of escrow agent from all parties. If one party makes written demand for the earnest money, escrow agent shall give notice of the demand by providing to the other party a copy of the demand. If escrow agent does not receive written objection to the demand from the other party within 30 days after notice to the other party, escrow agent may disburse the earnest money to the party making demand reduced by the amount of unpaid expenses incurred on behalf of the party receiving the earnest money and escrow agent may pay the same to the creditors. If escrow agent complies with the provisions of this paragraph, each party hereby releases escrow agent from all adverse claims related to the disbursal of the earnest money. Escrow agent's notice to the other party will be effective when deposited in the U. S. Mail, postage prepaid, certified mail, return receipt requested, addressed to the other party at such party's address shown below. Notice of objection to the demand will be deemed effective upon receipt by escrow agent.

19. REPRESENTATIONS: Seller represents that as of the Closing Date (a) there will be no liens, assessments, or security interests against the Property which will not be satisfied out of the sales proceeds unless securing payment of any loans assumed by Buyer and (b) assumed loans will not be in default. If any representation of Seller in this contract is untrue on the Closing Date, Buyer may terminate this contract and the earnest money will be refunded to Buyer.

20. FEDERAL TAX REQUIREMENTS: If Seller is a "foreign person," as defined by applicable law, or if Seller fails to deliver an affidavit to Buyer that Seller is not a "foreign person," then Buyer shall withhold from the sales proceeds an amount sufficient to comply with applicable tax law and deliver the same to the Internal Revenue Service together with appropriate tax forms. Internal Revenue Service regulations require filing written reports if currency in excess of specified amounts is received in the transaction.

Initialed for identification by Buyer_______ _______ and Seller________ ________

Figure 9.19 TREC 25-4 (continued)

21. NOTICES: All notices from one party to the other must be in writing and are effective when mailed to, hand-delivered at, or transmitted by facsimile as follows:

To Buyer at:	**To Seller at:**
______________________	______________________
______________________	______________________
______________________	______________________
Telephone:(____)______________	Telephone:(____)______________
Facsimile:(____)______________	Facsimile:(____) ______________

22. AGREEMENT OF PARTIES: This contract contains the entire agreement of the parties and cannot be changed except by their written agreement. Addenda which are a part of this contract are (check all applicable boxes):

- ☐ Third Party Financing Condition Addendum
- ☐ Seller Financing Addendum
- ☐ Loan Assumption Addendum
- ☐ Buyer's Temporary Residential Lease
- ☐ Seller's Temporary Residential Lease
- ☐ Addendum for Sale of Other Property by Buyer
- ☐ Addendum for Unimproved Property Located in a Certificated Service Area of a Utility Service Provider
- ☐ Addendum for Seller's Disclosure of Information on Lead-based Paint and Lead-based Paint Hazards as Required by Federal Law
- ☐ Environmental Assessment, Threatened or Endangered Species and Wetlands Addendum
- ☐ Addendum for Coastal Area Property
- ☐ Addendum for Property Located Seaward of the Gulf Intracoastal Waterway
- ☐ Addendum for "Back-Up" Contract

☐ Other (list): ____
____
____

Initialed for identification by Buyer______ ________ and Seller________ ________

Figure 9.19 TREC 25-4 (continued)

23. TERMINATION OPTION: This paragraph will be a part of this contract ONLY if both blanks are filled in and Buyer has paid the Option Fee. Buyer has paid Seller $________________ (Option Fee) for the unrestricted right to terminate this contract by giving notice of termination to Seller within __________ days after the effective date of this contract. If Buyer gives notice of termination within the time specified, the Option Fee will not be refunded, however, any earnest money will be refunded to Buyer. The Option Fee ☐will ☐will not be credited to the Sales Price at closing. For the purposes of this paragraph, time is of the essence; strict compliance with the time for performance stated herein is required.

24. CONSULT AN ATTORNEY: Real estate licensees cannot give legal advice. READ THIS CONTRACT CAREFULLY. If you do not understand the effect of this contract, consult an attorney BEFORE signing.

Buyer's Attorney is:________________________

____

Telephone: (____) ________________

Facsimile: (____) ________________

Seller's Attorney is:________________________

____

Telephone: (____) ________________

Facsimile: (____) ________________

EXECUTED the ______day of ________________________, 20___ (EFFECTIVE DATE). (BROKER: FILL IN THE DATE OF FINAL ACCEPTANCE.)

________________________ Buyer

________________________ Seller

________________________ Buyer

________________________ Seller

Figure 9.19 TREC 25-4 (continued)

SELLER'S RECEIPT

Receipt of $________________ (Option Fee) in the form of ______________________ is acknowledged.

______________________________ ______________________________
Seller Date

RATIFICATION OF FEE

Listing Broker has agreed to pay Other Broker_____________ of the total Sales Price when Listing Broker's fee is received. Escrow Agent is authorized and directed to pay Other Broker from Listing Broker's fee at closing.

Other Broker: Listing Broker:

By: ______________________________ By: ______________________________

BROKER INFORMATION AND AGREEMENT FOR PAYMENT OF BROKERS' FEES

Other Broker License No.	Listing or Principal Broker License No.
Associate	Associate
Address	Address
City, State Zip	City, State Zip
Telephone Facsimile	Telephone Facsimile
represents ❑ Buyer only as Buyer's agent ❑ Seller as Listing Broker's subagent	represents ❑ Seller only ❑ Buyer only ❑ Seller and Buyer as an intermediary

Upon closing of the sale by Seller to Buyer of the Property described in the contract to which this fee agreement is attached: (a) ❑Seller ❑ Buyer will pay Listing/Principal Broker ❑a cash fee of $ __________________ or ❑ ______% of the total Sales Price; and (b) ❑Seller ❑ Buyer will pay Other Broker ❑a cash fee of $__________ or ❑ ______% of the total Sales Price. Seller/Buyer authorizes and directs Escrow Agent to pay the brokers from the proceeds at closing.

Brokers' fees are negotiable. Brokers' fees or the sharing of fees between brokers are not fixed, controlled, recommended, suggested or maintained by the Texas Real Estate Commission.

______________________________ ______________________________
Seller Buyer

______________________________ ______________________________
Seller Buyer

Do not sign if there is a separate written agreement for payment of Brokers' fees.

RECEIPT

Receipt of ❑ Contract and ❑ $______________ Earnest Money in the form of __________________ is acknowledged.

Escrow Agent: ______________________________ Date: ______________________

By: ______________________________

______________________________ Telephone (_____) ________________
Address

______________________________ Facsimile: (_____) ________________
City State Zip

Figure 9.20 TREC OP-L

APPROVED BY THE TEXAS REAL ESTATE COMMISSION 02-09-2004

EQUAL HOUSING OPPORTUNITY

ADDENDUM FOR SELLER'S DISCLOSURE OF INFORMATION ON LEAD-BASED PAINT AND LEAD-BASED PAINT HAZARDS AS REQUIRED BY FEDERAL LAW

CONCERNING THE PROPERTY AT ______________________________
(Street Address and City)

A. **LEAD WARNING STATEMENT:** "Every purchaser of any interest in residential real property on which a residential dwelling was built prior to 1978 is notified that such property may present exposure to lead from lead-based paint that may place young children at risk of developing lead poisoning. Lead poisoning in young children may produce permanent neurological damage, including learning disabilities, reduced intelligence quotient, behavioral problems, and impaired memory. Lead poisoning also poses a particular risk to pregnant women. The seller of any interest in residential real property is required to provide the buyer with any information on lead-based paint hazards from risk assessments or inspections in the seller's possession and notify the buyer of any known lead-based paint hazards. A risk assessment or inspection for possible lead-paint hazards is recommended prior to purchase."

NOTICE: Inspector must be properly certified as required by federal law.

B. SELLER'S DISCLOSURE:

1. PRESENCE OF LEAD-BASED PAINT AND/OR LEAD-BASED PAINT HAZARDS (check on box only):
   ❑(a) Known lead-based paint and/or lead-based paint hazards are present in the Property (explain): ____________
   ______________________________.
   ❑(b) Seller has no actual knowledge of lead-based paint and/or lead-based paint hazards in the Property.
2. RECORDS AND REPORTS AVAILABLE TO SELLER (check one box only):
   ❑(a) Seller has provided the purchaser with all available records and reports pertaining to lead-based paint and/or lead-based paint hazards in the Property (list documents):____________
   ______________________________.
   ❑(b) Seller has no reports or records pertaining to lead-based paint and/or lead-based paint hazards in the Property.

C. BUYER'S RIGHTS (check one box only):

❑1. Buyer waives the opportunity to conduct a risk assessment or inspection of the Property for the presence of lead-based paint or lead-based paint hazards.

❑2. Within ten days after the effective date of this contract, Buyer may have the Property inspected by inspectors selected by Buyer. If lead-based paint or lead-based paint hazards are present, Buyer may terminate this contract by giving Seller written notice within 14 days after the effective date of this contract, and the earnest money will be refunded to Buyer.

D. BUYER'S ACKNOWLEDGMENT (check applicable boxes):

❑1. Buyer has received copies of all information listed above.

❑2. Buyer has received the pamphlet *Protect Your Family from Lead in Your Home*.

E. BROKERS' ACKNOWLEDGMENT: Brokers have informed Seller of Seller's obligations under 42 U.S.C. 4852d to: (a) provide Buyer with the federally approved pamphlet on lead poisoning prevention; (b) complete this addendum; (c) disclose any known lead-based paint and/or lead-based paint hazards in the Property; (d) deliver all records and reports to Buyer pertaining to lead-based paint and/or lead-based paint hazards in the Property; (e) provide Buyer a period of up to 10 days to have the Property inspected; and (f) retain a completed copy of this addendum for at least 3 years following the sale. Brokers are aware of their responsibility to ensure compliance.

F. CERTIFICATION OF ACCURACY: The following persons have reviewed the information above and certify, to the best of their knowledge, that the information they have provided is true and accurate.

Buyer	Date	Seller	Date
Buyer	Date	Seller	Date
Other Broker	Date	Listing Broker	Date

The form of this addendum has been approved by the Texas Real Estate Commission for use only with similarly approved or promulgated forms of contracts. Such approval relates to this contract form only. TREC forms are intended for use only by trained real estate licensees. No representation is made as to the legal validity or adequacy of any provision in any specific transactions. It is not suitable for complex transactions. Texas Real Estate Commission, P.O. Box 12188, Austin, TX 78711-2188, 1-800-250-8732 or (512) 459-6544 (http://www.trec.state.tx.us)

Form OP-L 01A

Figure 9.21 TREC 28-0

EQUAL HOUSING OPPORTUNITY

10-25-93

ENVIRONMENTAL ASSESSMENT, THREATENED OR ENDANGERED SPECIES, AND WETLANDS ADDENDUM

PROMULGATED BY THE TEXAS REAL ESTATE COMMISSION (TREC)

ADDENDUM TO EARNEST MONEY CONTRACT BETWEEN THE UNDERSIGNED PARTIES CONCERNING THE PROPERTY AT ______________________________
(Address)

☐ A. ENVIRONMENTAL ASSESSMENT: Buyer, at Buyer's expense, may obtain an Environmental Assessment Report prepared by an environmental specialist.

☐ B. THREATENED OR ENDANGERED SPECIES: Buyer, at Buyer's expense, may obtain a report from a natural resources professional to determine if there are any threatened or endangered species or their habitats as defined by the Texas Parks and Wildlife Department or the U.S. Fish and Wildlife Service.

☐ C. WETLANDS: Buyer, at Buyer's expense, may obtain a report from an environmental specialist to determine if there are wetlands, as defined by federal or state law or regulation.

Within ________ days after the Effective Date of the contract, Buyer may terminate the contract by furnishing Seller a copy of any report noted above that adversely affects the use of the Property and the Earnest Money shall be refunded to Buyer. If Buyer does not furnish Seller a copy of the unacceptable report within the prescribed time and give Seller notice that Buyer has terminated the contract, Buyer shall be deemed to have accepted the Property.

______________________	______________________
Buyer	Seller
______________________	______________________
Buyer	Seller

The form of this addendum has been approved by the Texas Real Estate Commission for use only with similarly approved or promulgated forms of contracts. No representation is made as to the legal validity or adequacy of any provision in any specific transactions. It is not suitable for complex transactions. (10-93) TREC No. 28-0.

01A TREC No. 28-0

Transaction 7: Assumption with Release of Liability
(Using: TREC 30-4, 41-0, 11-5, 33-0, 34-1, and 12-1)

Unit 623 of Building B of the condominium project known as Freedom Flats, Phase II in Corpus Christi, Nueces County, Texas is being sold to Bernie Bryan Buyer and spouse, Beverly Barbara Buyer, by Peter Paul Pastor and his wife, Sarah Sue Pastor. The property is more commonly known as 1215 Market Street, Apartment 623. Ownership of the unit includes two parking spaces identified as numbers 1654 and 1658 in the adjoining parking garage. The zip code is 78411.

Prior to signing the agreement of purchase, the buyers received, reviewed, and accepted all of the condominium documents, as well as the Condominium Resale Certificate (TREC No. 32-0), which was prepared and signed by the secretary of the homeowners' association 20 days ago.

The buyers will pay $368,200 for the unit and assume the seller's existing conventional loan with an outstanding balance of $265,008. The loan is a portfolio loan held by Deep Pocket Mortgage Company, Inc. The buyers will apply for assumption approval within three days after the effective date of the contract. They will close within 30 days of the effective date of this contract, which will allow for closing on June 16. The current loan is at 6.75 percent and may be escalated to 7.25 percent upon assumption. If the loan balance is a few dollars more or less at closing, the cash payable at closing will be adjusted to compensate for any variance. The lender will charge a 1-point transfer fee, which will be paid by the buyer.

The buyers will pay for the owner's title policy. The buyer received the seller's disclosure notice and accepts the property in its present condition provided the seller, at seller's expense, shall replace the nonfunctioning garbage disposal and the broken faucet in the bathroom. Because the project was built in 1979, it is not subject to the HUD lead-based paint disclosure requirement. No repairs to any of the common elements are required.

The seller has informed the buyers that the monthly PITI payment is $2,885 and the monthly maintenance fee is $236. The resale certificate furnished by the secretary of the homeowner's association confirmed the amount of the maintenance fee. The buyer will pay any transfer or processing fee charged by the homeowner's association.

The seller will have the purchase agreement reviewed by attorney Michael Holmes prior to signing the agreement.

The unit has been listed with Skyline Realty. The listing company will pay the subagent, Downhome Realty, a selling fee equal to 3.25 percent of the selling price of the property.

$2,000 earnest money is delivered to Buyer's Choice Title Company, who will issue an owner's policy at closing.

The seller will deliver a copy of the note and deed of trust to the buyer for review within three days after the effective date of the purchase agreement. The buyers also request that copies of every document they will be asked to sign at closing be delivered to them for review a minimum of 48 hours prior to closing.

The sellers will permit the loan to be assumed only if they are released from liability and will not close if the lender refuses to release them. The buyers and the sellers will apply for the release within three days after the effective date of the contract.

There is already an existing contract in place, dated May 5, between the sellers and a bachelor by the name of Gordon Robinson. If the seller notifies the buyers on or before 5 PM on May 20 that the contract with Mr. Robinson is terminated, this agreement is no longer subject to the contingency, and the effective date of this contract will be amended to be the date of termination of the previous contract.

The seller has no knowledge of any prior fill as it relates to the property.

Figure 9.22 TREC 30-4

PROMULGATED BY THE TEXAS REAL ESTATE COMMISSION (TREC) 01-06-03
NOTICE: Not For Use Where Seller Owns Fee Simple Title To Land Beneath Unit

RESIDENTIAL CONDOMINIUM CONTRACT (RESALE)

1. PARTIES: ______________________________ (Seller) agrees to sell and convey to ______________________________(Buyer) and Buyer agrees to buy from Seller the Property described below.

2. PROPERTY AND CONDOMINIUM DOCUMENTS:

A. The Condominium Unit, improvements and accessories described below are collectively referred to as the "Property".

(1) CONDOMINIUM UNIT: Unit __________, in Building __________________, of ______________________________, a condominium project, located at ______________________________(address/zip code), City of ____________________, ____________________County, Texas, described in the Condominium Declaration and Plat and any amendments thereto of record in said County; together with such Unit's undivided interest in the Common Elements designated by the Declaration, including those areas reserved as Limited Common Elements appurtenant to the Unit and such other rights to use the Common Elements which have been specifically assigned to the Unit in any other manner. Parking areas assigned to the Unit are:______________________________.

(2) IMPROVEMENTS: All fixtures and improvements attached to the above described real property including without limitation, the following permanently installed and built-in items, if any: all equipment and appliances, valances, screens, shutters, awnings, wall-to-wall carpeting, mirrors, ceiling fans, attic fans, mail boxes, television antennas and satellite dish system and equipment, heating and air conditioning units, security and fire detection equipment, wiring, plumbing and lighting fixtures, chandeliers, shrubbery, landscaping, outdoor cooking equipment, and all other property owned by Seller and attached to the above described Condominium Unit.

(3) ACCESSORIES: The following described related accessories, if any: window air conditioning units, stove, fireplace screens, curtains and rods, blinds, window shades, draperies and rods, controls for satellite dish system, controls for garage door openers, entry gate controls, door keys, mailbox keys, and artificial fireplace logs.

(4) EXCLUSIONS: The following improvements and accessories will be retained by Seller and excluded: ______________________________
______________________________.

B. The Declaration, Bylaws and any Rules of the Association are called "Documents". (Check one box only):

❑ (1) Buyer has received a copy of the Documents. Buyer is advised to read the Documents before signing the contract.

❑ (2) Buyer has not received a copy of the Documents. Seller shall deliver the Documents to Buyer within __________ days after the effective date of the contract. Buyer may cancel the contract before the sixth day after Buyer receives the Documents by hand-delivering or mailing written notice of cancellation to Seller by certified United States mail, return receipt requested.

C. The Resale Certificate from the condominium owners association (the Association) is called the "Certificate". The Certificate must be in a form promulgated by TREC or required by the parties. The Certificate must have been prepared no more than 3 months before the date it is delivered to Buyer and must contain at a minimum the information required by Section 82.157, Texas Property Code.
(Check one box only):

❑ (1) Buyer has received the Certificate.

❑ (2) Buyer has not received the Certificate. Seller shall deliver the Certificate to Buyer within ________days after the effective date of the contract. Buyer may cancel the contract before the sixth day after the date Buyer receives the Certificate by hand-delivering or mailing written notice of cancellation to Seller by certified United States mail, return receipt requested.

❑ (3) Buyer has received Seller's affidavit that Seller requested information from the Association concerning its financial condition as required by the Texas Property Code, and that the Association did not provide a Certificate or information required in the Certificate. Buyer and Seller agree to waive the requirement to furnish the Certificate.

Initialed for identification by Buyer_____ _____ and Seller _____ _____ **01A** TREC NO. 30-4

Figure 9.22 TREC 30-4 (continued)

Contract Concerning____Page Two 01-06-03
(Address of Property)

3. SALES PRICE:

A. Cash portion of Sales Price payable by Buyer at closing .... $__________________

B Sum of all financing described below (excluding any loan funding fee or mortgage insurance premium)... $__________________

C. Sales Price (Sum of A and B).. $__________________

4. FINANCING: The portion of Sales Price not payable in cash will be paid as follows: (Check applicable boxes below)

❑ A. THIRD PARTY FINANCING: One or more third party mortgage loans in the total amount of $____________________. If the Property does not satisfy the lenders' underwriting requirements for the loan(s), this contract will terminate and the earnest money will be refunded to Buyer. (Check one box only)

❑ (1) This contract is subject to Buyer being approved for the financing described in the attached Third Party Financing Condition Addendum.

❑ (2) This contract is not subject to Buyer being approved for financing and does not involve FHA or VA financing.

❑ B. ASSUMPTION: The assumption of the unpaid principal balance of one or more promissory notes described in the attached TREC Loan Assumption Addendum.

❑ C. SELLER FINANCING: A promissory note from Buyer to Seller of $______________, bearing _______ % interest per annum, secured by vendor's and deed of trust liens, and containing the terms and conditions described in the attached TREC Seller Financing Addendum. If an owner policy of title insurance is furnished, Buyer shall furnish Seller with a mortgagee policy of title insurance.

5. EARNEST MONEY: Upon execution of this contract by both parties, Buyer shall deposit $____________ as earnest money with ______________________________________, as escrow agent, at ____ (address). Buyer shall deposit additional earnest money of $_________________ with escrow agent within _______days after the effective date of this contract. If Buyer fails to deposit the earnest money as required by this contract, Buyer will be in default.

6. TITLE POLICY:

A. TITLE POLICY: Seller shall furnish to Buyer at ❑Seller's ❑Buyer's expense an owner policy of title insurance (Title Policy) issued by ____ ____ (Title Company) in the amount of the Sales Price, dated at or after closing, insuring Buyer against loss under the provisions of the Title Policy, subject to the promulgated exclusions (including existing building and zoning ordinances) and the following exceptions:

(1) Restrictive covenants common to the platted subdivision in which the Property is located.

(2) The standard printed exception for standby fees, taxes and assessments.

(3) Liens created as part of the financing described in Paragraph 4.

(4) Terms and provisions of the Documents including the assessments and platted easements.

(5) Reservations or exceptions otherwise permitted by this contract or as may be approved by Buyer in writing.

(6) The standard printed exception as to marital rights.

(7) The standard printed exception as to waters, tidelands, beaches, streams, and related matters.

(8) The standard printed exception as to discrepancies, conflicts, shortages in area or boundary lines, encroachments or protrusions, or overlapping improvements.

B. COMMITMENT: Within 20 days after the Title Company receives a copy of this contract, Seller shall furnish to Buyer a commitment for title insurance (Commitment) and, at Buyer's expense, legible copies of restrictive covenants and documents evidencing exceptions in the Commitment (Exception Documents) other than the standard printed exceptions. Seller authorizes the Title Company to mail or hand deliver the Commitment and Exception Documents to Buyer at Buyer's address shown in Paragraph 21. If the Commitment and Exception Documents are not delivered to Buyer within the specified time, the time for delivery will be automatically extended up to 15 days or the Closing Date, whichever is earlier.

C. OBJECTIONS: Within _______ days after Buyer receives the Commitment and Exception Documents, Buyer may object in writing to defects, exceptions, or encumbrances to title: disclosed in the Commitment other than items 6A(1) through (8) above; or which prohibit the following use or activity: ____.

Initialed for identification by Buyer______ ______ and Seller _______ _______ **01A** TREC NO. 30-4

Figure 9.22 TREC 30-4 (continued)

Contract Concerning____ Page Three 01-06-03
(Address of Property)

Buyer's failure to object within the time allowed will constitute a waiver of Buyer's right to object; except that the requirements in Schedule C of the Commitment are not waived. Seller shall cure the timely objections of Buyer or any third party lender within 15 days after Seller receives the objections and the Closing Date will be extended as necessary. If objections are not cured within such 15 day period, this contract will terminate and the earnest money will be refunded to Buyer unless Buyer waives the objections.

D. TITLE NOTICES:

(1) ABSTRACT OR TITLE POLICY: Broker advises Buyer to have an abstract of title covering the Property examined by an attorney of Buyer's selection, or Buyer should be furnished with or obtain a Title Policy. If a Title Policy is furnished, the Commitment should be promptly reviewed by an attorney of Buyer's choice due to the time limitations on Buyer's right to object.

(2) STATUTORY TAX DISTRICTS: If the Property is situated in a utility or other statutorily created district providing water, sewer, drainage, or flood control facilities and services, Chapter 49, Texas Water Code requires Seller to deliver and Buyer to sign the statutory notice relating to the tax rate, bonded indebtedness, or standby fee of the district prior to final execution of this contract.

(3) TIDE WATERS: If the Property abuts the tidally influenced waters of the state, §33.135, Texas Natural Resources Code, requires a notice regarding coastal area property to be included in the contract. An addendum containing the notice promulgated by TREC or required by the parties must be used.

(4) ANNEXATION: If the Property is located outside the limits of a municipality, Seller notifies Buyer under §5.011, Texas Property Code, that the Property may now or later be included in the extraterritorial jurisdiction of a municipality and may now or later be subject to annexation by the municipality. Each municipality maintains a map that depicts its boundaries and extraterritorial jurisdiction. To determine if the Property is located within a municipality's extraterritorial jurisdiction or is likely to be located within a municipality's extraterritorial jurisdiction, contact all municipalities located in the general proximity of the Property for further information.

7. PROPERTY CONDITION:

A. INSPECTIONS, ACCESS AND UTILITIES: Buyer may have the Property inspected by inspectors selected by Buyer and licensed by TREC or otherwise permitted by law to make inspections. Seller shall permit Buyer and Buyer's agents access to the Property at reasonable times. Seller shall pay for turning on existing utilities for inspections.

B. SELLER'S DISCLOSURE NOTICE PURSUANT TO §5.008, TEXAS PROPERTY CODE (Notice): (Check one box only)

❑ (1) Buyer has received the Notice.

❑ (2) Buyer has not received the Notice. Within ______ days after the effective date of this contract, Seller shall deliver the Notice to Buyer. If Buyer does not receive the Notice, Buyer may terminate this contract at any time prior to the closing and the earnest money will be refunded to Buyer. If Seller delivers the Notice, Buyer may terminate this contract for any reason within 7 days after Buyer receives the Notice or prior to the closing, whichever first occurs, and the earnest money will be refunded to Buyer.

❑ (3) The Texas Property Code does not require this Seller to furnish the Notice.

C. SELLER'S DISCLOSURE OF LEAD-BASED PAINT AND LEAD-BASED PAINT HAZARDS is required by Federal law for a residential dwelling constructed prior to 1978.

D. ACCEPTANCE OF PROPERTY CONDITION: Buyer accepts the Property in its present condition; provided Seller, at Seller's expense, shall complete the following specific repairs and treatments:____
____.

E. LENDER REQUIRED REPAIRS AND TREATMENTS: Unless otherwise agreed in writing, neither party is obligated to pay for lender required repairs, which includes treatment for wood destroying insects. If the parties do not agree to pay for the lender required repairs or treatments, this contract will terminate and the earnest money will be refunded to Buyer. If the cost of lender required repairs and treatments exceeds 5% of the Sales Price, Buyer may terminate this contract and the earnest money will be refunded to Buyer.

F. COMPLETION OF REPAIRS AND TREATMENTS: Unless otherwise agreed in writing, Seller shall complete all agreed repairs and treatments prior to the Closing Date. All required permits must be obtained, and repairs and treatments must be performed by persons who are licensed or otherwise authorized by law to provide such repairs or treatments. At Buyer's

Initialed for identification by Buyer______ ______ and Seller ______ ______ **01A** TREC NO. 30-4

Figure 9.22 TREC 30-4 (continued)

Contract Concerning____Page Four 01-06-03
(Address of Property)

election, any transferable warranties received by Seller with respect to the repairs and treatments will be transferred to Buyer at Buyer's expense. If Seller fails to complete any agreed repairs and treatments prior to the Closing Date, Buyer may do so and receive reimbursement from Seller at closing. The Closing Date will be extended up to 15 days, if necessary, to complete repairs and treatments.

G. ENVIRONMENTAL MATTERS: Buyer is advised that the presence of wetlands, toxic substances, including asbestos and wastes or other environmental hazards or the presence of a threatened or endangered species or its habitat may affect Buyer's intended use of the Property. If Buyer is concerned about these matters, an addendum promulgated by TREC or required by the parties should be used.

H. RESIDENTIAL SERVICE CONTRACTS: Buyer may purchase a residential service contract from from a residential service company licensed by TREC. If Buyer purchases a residential service contract, Seller shall reimburse Buyer at closing for the cost of the residential service contract in an amount not exceeding $____________________ . Buyer should review any residential service contract for the scope of coverage, exclusions and limitations. **The purchase of a residential service contract is optional. Similar coverage may be purchased from various companies authorized to do business in Texas.**

8. BROKERS' FEES: All obligations of the parties for payment of brokers' fees are contained in separate written agreements.

9. CLOSING:

A. The closing of the sale will be on or before ______________________, 20___, or within 7 days after objections to matters disclosed in the Commitment have been cured, whichever date is later (Closing Date). If either party fails to close the sale by the Closing Date, the non-defaulting party may exercise the remedies contained in Paragraph 15.

B. At closing:

(1) Seller shall execute and deliver a general warranty deed conveying title to the Property to Buyer and showing no additional exceptions to those permitted in Paragraph 6 and furnish tax statements or certificates showing no delinquent taxes on the Property.

(2) Buyer shall pay the Sales Price in good funds acceptable to the escrow agent.

(3) Seller and Buyer shall execute and deliver any notices, statements, certificates, affidavits, releases, loan documents and other documents required of them by this contract, the Commitment or law necessary for the closing of the sale and the issuance of the Title Policy.

C. Unless expressly prohibited by written agreement, Seller may continue to show the Property and receive, negotiate and accept back up offers.

D. All covenants, representations and warranties in this contract survive closing.

10. POSSESSION: Seller shall deliver to Buyer possession of the Property in its present or required condition, ordinary wear and tear excepted: ☐ upon closing and funding ☐ according to a temporary residential lease form promulgated by TREC or other written lease required by the parties. Any possession by Buyer prior to closing or by Seller after closing which is not authorized by a written lease will establish a tenancy at sufferance relationship between the parties. *Consult your insurance agent prior to change of ownership or possession because insurance coverage may be limited or terminated. The absence of a written lease or appropriate insurance coverage may expose the parties to economic loss.*

11. SPECIAL PROVISIONS: (Insert only factual statements and business details applicable to the sale. TREC rules prohibit licensees from adding factual statements or business details for which a contract addendum, lease or other form has been promulgated by TREC for mandatory use.)

Initialed for identification by Buyer______ ______ and Seller ______ ______ **01A** TREC NO. 30-4

Figure 9.22 TREC 30-4 (continued)

Contract Concerning____Page Five 01-06-03
(Address of Property)

12. SETTLEMENT AND OTHER EXPENSES:

A. The following expenses must be paid at or prior to closing:

(1) Expenses payable by Seller (Seller's Expenses):

(a) Releases of existing liens, including prepayment penalties and recording fees; lender, FHA, or VA completion requirements; tax statements or certificates; preparation of deed; one-half of escrow fee; and other expenses payable by Seller under this contract.

(b) Seller shall also pay an amount not to exceed $ ____________ to be applied in the following order: Buyer's Expenses which Buyer is prohibited from paying by FHA, VA, Texas Veteran's Housing Assistance Program or other governmental loan programs; Buyer's prepaid items; other Buyer's expenses.

(2) Expenses payable by Buyer (Buyer's Expenses):

(a) Loan origination, discount, buy-down, and commitment fees (Loan Fees).

(b) Appraisal fees; loan application fees; credit reports; preparation of loan documents; interest on the notes from date of disbursement to one month prior to dates of first monthly payments; recording fees; copies of easements and restrictions; mortgagee title policy with endorsements required by lender; loan-related inspection fees; photos, amortization schedules, one-half of escrow fee; all prepaid items, including required premiums for flood and hazard insurance, reserve deposits for insurance, ad valorem taxes and special governmental assessments; final compliance inspection; courier fee, repair inspection, underwriting fee and wire transfer, expenses incident to any loan, and other expenses payable by Buyer under this contract.

(3) Transfer Expenses: Any Association transfer or processing fee will be paid by ❑ Seller ❑ Buyer.

B. Buyer shall pay Private Mortgage Insurance Premium (PMI), VA Loan Funding Fee, or FHA Mortgage Insurance Premium (MIP) as required by the lender.

C. If any expense exceeds an amount expressly stated in this contract for such expense to be paid by a party, that party may terminate this contract unless the other party agrees to pay such excess. Buyer may not pay charges and fees expressly prohibited by FHA, VA, Texas Veteran's Housing Assistance Program or other governmental loan program regulations.

13. PRORATIONS: Taxes for the current year, interest, maintenance fees, regular condominium assessments, dues and rents will be prorated through the Closing Date. If taxes for the current year vary from the amount prorated at closing, the parties shall adjust the prorations when tax statements for the current year are available. If taxes are not paid at or prior to closing, Buyer shall pay taxes for the current year. Cash reserves from regular condominium assessments for deferred maintenance or capital improvements established by the Association will not be credited to Seller. Any special condominium assessment due and unpaid at closing will be the obligation of Seller.

14. CASUALTY LOSS: If any part of the Unit which Seller is solely obligated to maintain and repair under the terms of the Declaration is damaged or destroyed by fire or other casualty, Seller shall restore the same to its previous condition as soon as reasonably possible, but in any event by the Closing Date. If Seller fails to do so due to factors beyond Seller's control, Buyer may (a) terminate this contract and the earnest money will be refunded to Buyer, (b) extend the time for performance up to 15 days and the Closing Date will be extended as necessary or (c) accept the Property in its damaged condition with an assignment of insurance proceeds and receive credit from Seller at closing in the amount of the deductible under the insurance policy. If any part of the Common Elements or Limited Common Elements appurtenant to the Unit is damaged or destroyed by fire or other casualty loss, Buyer will have 7 days from receipt of notice of such casualty loss within which to notify Seller in writing that the contract will be terminated unless Buyer receives written confirmation from the Association that the damaged condition will be restored to its previous condition within a reasonable time at no cost to Buyer. Unless Buyer gives such notice within such time, Buyer will be deemed to have accepted the Property without confirmation of such restoration. Seller will have 7 days from the date of receipt of Buyer's notice within which to cause to be delivered to Buyer such confirmation. If required by Buyer and written confirmation is not delivered to Buyer as required above, Buyer may terminate this contract and the earnest money will be refunded to Buyer. Seller's obligations under this paragraph are independent of any obligations of Seller under Paragraph 7.

15. DEFAULT: If Buyer fails to comply with this contract, Buyer will be in default, and Seller may (a) enforce specific performance, seek such other relief as may be provided by law, or both, or (b) terminate this contract and receive the earnest money as liquidated damages, thereby releasing both parties from this contract. If, due to factors beyond Seller's control, Seller fails within the time allowed to make any non-casualty repairs or deliver the Commitment, if required of Seller,

Initialed for identification by Buyer_____ _____ and Seller _____ _____ **01A** TREC NO. 30-4

Figure 9.22 TREC 30-4 (continued)

Contract Concerning____Page Six 01-06-03
(Address of Property)

Buyer may (a) extend the time for performance up to 15 days and the Closing Date will be extended as necessary or (b) terminate this contract as the sole remedy and receive the earnest money. If Seller fails to comply with this contract for any other reason, Seller will be in default and Buyer may (a) enforce specific performance, seek such other relief as may be provided by law, or both, or (b) terminate this contract and receive the earnest money, thereby releasing both parties from this contract.

16. **MEDIATION:** It is the policy of the State of Texas to encourage resolution of disputes through alternative dispute resolution procedures such as mediation. Any dispute between Seller and Buyer related to this contract which is not resolved through informal discussion ☐will ☐will not be submitted to a mutually acceptable mediation service or provider. The parties to the mediation shall bear the mediation costs equally. This paragraph does not preclude a party from seeking equitable relief from a court of competent jurisdiction.

17. **ATTORNEY'S FEES:** The prevailing party in any legal proceeding related to this contract is entitled to recover reasonable attorney's fees and all costs of such proceeding incurred by the prevailing party.

18. **ESCROW:** The escrow agent is not (a) a party to this contract and does not have liability for the performance or nonperformance of any party to this contract, (b) liable for interest on the earnest money and (c) liable for the loss of any earnest money caused by the failure of any financial institution in which the earnest money has been deposited unless the financial institution is acting as escrow agent. At closing, the earnest money must be applied first to any cash down payment, then to Buyer's Expenses and any excess refunded to Buyer. If both parties make written demand for the earnest money, escrow agent may require payment of unpaid expenses incurred on behalf of the parties and a written release of liability of escrow agent from all parties. If one party makes written demand for the earnest money, escrow agent shall give notice of the demand by providing to the other party a copy of the demand. If escrow agent does not receive written objection to the demand from the other party within 30 days after notice to the other party, escrow agent may disburse the earnest money to the party making demand reduced by the amount of unpaid expenses incurred on behalf of the party receiving the earnest money and escrow agent may pay the same to the creditors. If escrow agent complies with the provisions of this paragraph, each party hereby releases escrow agent from all adverse claims related to the disbursal of the earnest money. Escrow agent's notice to the other party will be effective when deposited in the U. S. Mail, postage prepaid, certified mail, return receipt requested, addressed to the other party at such party's address shown below. Notice of objection to the demand will be deemed effective upon receipt by escrow agent.

19. **REPRESENTATIONS:** Seller represents that as of the Closing Date (a) there will be no liens, assessments, or security interests against the Property which will not be satisfied out of the sales proceeds unless securing payment of any loans assumed by Buyer, (b) assumed loans will not be in default, and (c) Seller has no knowledge of any misrepresentation or errors in the Certificate or any material changes in the information contained therein. If any representation of Seller in this contract or the Certificate is untrue on the Closing Date, Buyer may terminate this contract and the earnest money will be refunded to Buyer.

20. **FEDERAL TAX REQUIREMENTS:** If Seller is a "foreign person," as defined by applicable law, or if Seller fails to deliver an affidavit to Buyer that Seller is not a "foreign person," then Buyer shall withhold from the sales proceeds an amount sufficient to comply with applicable tax law and deliver the same to the Internal Revenue Service together with appropriate tax forms. Internal Revenue Service regulations require filing written reports if currency in excess of specified amounts is received in the transaction.

21. **NOTICES:** All notices from one party to the other must be in writing and are effective when mailed to, hand-delivered at, or transmitted by facsimile as follows:

To Buyer at:	**To Seller at:**
____________________	____________________
____________________	____________________
____________________	____________________
Telephone:(____)____________	Telephone:(____)____________
Facsimile:(____)____________	Facsimile:(____)____________

Initialed for identification by Buyer______ ______ and Seller ______ ______ **01A** TREC NO. 30-4

Figure 9.22 TREC 30-4 (continued)

Contract Concerning____ Page Seven 01-06-03
(Address of Property)

22. AGREEMENT OF PARTIES: This contract contains the entire agreement of the parties and cannot be changed except by their written agreement. Addenda which are a part of this contract are (check all applicable boxes):

- ❑ Third Party Financing Condition Addendum
- ❑ Loan Assumption Addendum
- ❑ Buyer's Temporary Residential Lease
- ❑ Seller's Temporary Residential Lease
- ❑ Addendum for Sale of Other Property by Buyer
- ❑ Addendum for "Back-Up" Contract
- ❑ Seller Financing Addendum
- ❑ Addendum for Property Located Seaward of the Gulf Intracoastal Waterway
- ❑ Addendum for Seller's Disclosure of Information on Lead-based Paint and Lead-based Paint Hazards as Required by Federal Law
- ❑ Environmental Assessment, Threatened or Endangered Species and Wetlands Addendum
- ❑ Addendum for Coastal Area Property
- ❑ Addendum for Release of Liability on Assumption of FHA, VA, or Conventional Loan Restoration of Seller's Entitlement for VA Guaranteed Loan

❑ Other (list): ____
____

23. TERMINATION OPTION: This paragraph will be a part of this contract ONLY if both blanks are filled in and Buyer has paid the Option Fee. Buyer has paid Seller $ __________ (Option Fee) for the unrestricted right to terminate this contract by giving notice of termination to Seller within __________ days after the effective date of this contract. If Buyer gives notice of termination within the time specified, the Option Fee will not be refunded, however, any earnest money will be refunded to Buyer. The Option Fee ❑will ❑will not be credited to the Sales Price at closing. For the purposes of this paragraph, time is of the essence; strict compliance with the time for performance stated herein is required.

24. CONSULT AN ATTORNEY: Real estate licensees cannot give legal advice. READ THIS CONTRACT CAREFULLY. If you do not understand the effect of this contract, consult an attorney BEFORE signing.

Buyer's
Attorney is:______________________________
____

Telephone: (____)______________________

Facsimile: (____)______________________

Seller's
Attorney is:______________________________
____

Telephone: (____)______________________

Facsimile: (____)______________________

EXECUTED the ______day of ______________________________, 20___ (EFFECTIVE DATE). (BROKER: FILL IN THE DATE OF FINAL ACCEPTANCE.)

____
Buyer

____
Seller

____
Buyer

____
Seller

The form of this contract has been approved by the Texas Real Estate Commission. TREC forms are intended for use only by trained real estate licensees. No representation is made as to the legal validity or adequacy of any provision in any specific transactions. It is not suitable for complex transactions. Texas Real Estate Commission, P.O. Box 12188, Austin, TX 78711-2188, 1-800-250-8732 or (512) 459-6544 (http://www.trec.state.tx.us) TREC NO. 30-4. This form replaces TREC NO. 30-3.

Initialed for identification by Buyer______ ______ and Seller ______ ______ **01A** TREC NO. 30-4

Figure 9.22 TREC 30-4 (continued)

Contract Concerning____ Page Eight 01-06-03
(Address of Property)

SELLER'S RECEIPT

Receipt of $________________ (Option Fee) in the form of ____________________ is acknowledged.

Seller

Date

BROKER INFORMATION AND RATIFICATION OF FEE

Listing Broker has agreed to pay Other Broker __________________________ of the total Sales Price when Listing Broker's fee is received. Escrow agent is authorized and directed to pay Other Broker from Listing Broker's fee at closing.

Other Broker

License No. Telephone

represents ❑ Buyer only as Buyer's agent
❑ Seller as Listing Broker's subagent

Associate Telephone

Broker's Address

Facsimile

Listing Broker

License No. Telephone

represents ❑ Seller and Buyer as an intermediary
❑ Seller only as Seller's agent

Listing Associate Telephone

Listing Associate's office address Facsimile

Selling Associate Telephone

Selling Associate's office address Facsimile

RECEIPT

Receipt of ❑ Contract and ❑ $_____________ Earnest Money in the form of ____________________
is acknowledged.
Escrow Agent: ____________________________________ Date: ________________________

By: ____

Address ____________________________________ Telephone (_____) _______________

City State Zip Facsimile: (_____) _______________

01A TREC NO. 30-4

Figure 9.23 TREC 41-0

PROMULGATED BY THE TEXAS REAL ESTATE COMMISSION (TREC) 10-29-01

EQUAL HOUSING OPPORTUNITY

LOAN ASSUMPTION ADDENDUM

TO CONTRACT CONCERNING THE PROPERTY AT

____

(Street Address and City)

A. CREDIT DOCUMENTATION. Within______days after the effective date of this contract, Buyer shall deliver to Seller ❑ credit report ❑ verification of employment, including salary ❑ verification of funds on deposit in financial institutions ❑ current financial statement to establish Buyer's creditworthiness and ❑ ________ __________.
Buyer hereby authorizes any credit reporting agency to furnish to Seller at Buyer's sole expense copies of Buyer's credit reports.

B. CREDIT APPROVAL. If Buyer's documentation is not delivered within the specified time, Seller may terminate this contract by notice to Buyer within 7 days after expiration of the time for delivery, and the earnest money will be paid to Seller. If the documentation is timely delivered, and Seller determines in Seller's sole discretion that Buyer's credit is unacceptable, Seller may terminate this contract by notice to Buyer within 7 days after expiration of the time for delivery and the earnest money will be refunded to Buyer. If Seller does not terminate this contract, Seller will be deemed to have accepted Buyer's credit.

C. ASSUMPTION.

❑ (1) The unpaid principal balance of a first lien promissory note payable to ____________________ ____________________ which unpaid balance at closing will be $ ____________. The total current monthly payment including principal, interest and any reserve deposits is $ ____________. Buyer's initial payment will be the first payment due after closing.

❑ (2) The unpaid principal balance of a second lien promissory note payable to ____________________ ____________________ which unpaid balance at closing will be $ ______________. The total current monthly payment including principal, interest and any reserve deposits is $ ____________. Buyer's initial payment will be the first payment due after closing.

Buyer's assumption of an existing note includes all obligations imposed by the deed of trust securing the note.
If the unpaid principal balance(s) of any assumed loan(s) as of the Closing Date varies from the loan balance(s) stated above, the ❑ cash payable at closing ❑ Sales Price will be adjusted by the amount of any variance; provided, if the total principal balance of all assumed loans varies in an amount greater than $350.00 at closing, either party may terminate this contract and the earnest money will be refunded to Buyer unless the other party elects to eliminate the excess in the variance by an appropriate adjustment at closing. Buyer may terminate this contract and the earnest money will be refunded to Buyer if the noteholder requires (a) payment of an assumption fee in excess of $ ______________in (1) above or $ ______________in (2) above and Seller declines to pay such excess, (b) an increase in the interest rate to more than ______% in (1) above, or ______% in (2) above, (c) any other modification of the loan documents, or (d) consent to the assumption of the loan and fails to consent. A vendor's lien and deed of trust to secure assumption will be required which will automatically be released on execution and delivery of a release by noteholder. If Seller is released from liability on any assumed note, the vendor's lien and deed of trust to secure assumption will not be required.
If noteholder maintains an escrow account, the escrow account must be transferred to Buyer without any deficiency. Buyer shall reimburse Seller for the amount in the transferred accounts.

NOTICE TO BUYER: The monthly payments, interest rates or other terms of some loans may be adjusted by the noteholder at or after closing. If you are concerned about the possibility of future adjustments, do not sign the contract without examining the notes and deeds of trust.

NOTICE TO SELLER: Your liability to pay the note assumed by Buyer will continue unless you obtain a release of liability from the noteholder. If you are concerned about future liability, you should use the TREC Release of Liability Addendum.

______________________	______________________
Buyer	Seller
______________________	______________________
Buyer	Seller

This form has been approved by the Texas Real Estate Commission for use with similarly approved or promulgated contract forms. Such approval relates to this form only. TREC forms are intended for use only by trained real estate licensees. No representation is made as to the legal validity or adequacy of any provision in any specific transactions. It is not suitable for complex transactions. Texas Real Estate Commission, P.O. Box 12188, Austin, TX 78711-2188, 1-800-250-8732 or (512) 459-6544 (http://www.trec.state.tx.us) TREC No. 41-0.

01A

Figure 9.24 TREC 11-5

PROMULGATED BY THE TEXAS REAL ESTATE COMMISSION (TREC) 02-09-2004

EQUAL HOUSING OPPORTUNITY

ADDENDUM FOR "BACK-UP" CONTRACT

TO CONTRACT CONCERNING THE PROPERTY AT

____

(Street Address and City)

A. The Contract to which this Addendum is attached (the Back-Up Contract) is binding upon execution by the parties, and the earnest money and any Option Fee must be paid as provided in the Back-Up Contract. The Back-Up Contract is contingent upon the termination of a previous contract (the First Contract) between Seller and ______________________________, dated ______________________, 20______, for the sale of Property. Except as provided by this Addendum, neither party is required to perform under the Back-Up Contract while it is contingent upon the First Contract.

B. If the First Contract terminates on or before 5:00 p.m. on ______________________, ________ (the Contingency Date), the Back-Up Contract will no longer be contingent upon the termination of the First Contract. Seller must notify Buyer immediately of the termination of the First Contract. For purposes of performance, the effective date of the Back-Up Contract automatically changes to the date Buyer receives notice of termination of the First Contract or the Contingency Date, whichever is earlier (Amended Effective Date).

C. If the First Contract does not terminate by the Contingency Date, the Back-Up Contract terminates and the earnest money will be refunded to Buyer.

D. An amendment or modification of the First Contract will not terminate the First Contract.

E. If Buyer has the unrestricted right to terminate the Back-Up Contract, the time for giving notice of termination begins on the effective date of the Back-Up Contract, continues after the Amended Effective Date and ends upon the expiration of Buyer's unrestricted right to terminate the Back-Up Contract.

F. For purposes of this Addendum, time is of the essence. Strict compliance with the times for performance stated herein is required.

______________________	______________________
Buyer	Seller
______________________	______________________
Buyer	Seller

This form has been approved by the Texas Real Estate Commission for use with similarly approved or promulgated contract forms. Such approval relates to this form only. TREC forms are intended for use only by trained real estate licensees. No representation is made as to the legal validity or adequacy of any provision in any specific transactions. It is not suitable for complex transactions. Texas Real Estate Commission, P.O. Box 12188, Austin, TX 78711-2188, 1-800-250-8732 or (512) 459-6544 (http://www.trec.state.tx.us) TREC No. 11-5. This form replaces TREC No. 11-4.

Figure 9.25 TREC 33-0

12-05-94

EQUAL HOUSING OPPORTUNITY

PROMULGATED BY THE TEXAS REAL ESTATE COMMISSION (TREC)
P.O. BOX 12188, AUSTIN, TX 78711-2188

ADDENDUM FOR
COASTAL AREA PROPERTY

ADDENDUM TO EARNEST MONEY CONTRACT BETWEEN THE UNDERSIGNED PARTIES
CONCERNING THE PROPERTY AT

____

____

(Location of Property)

IN ACCORDANCE WITH SECTION 33.135, TEXAS NATURAL RESOURCES CODE, THE FOLLOWING NOTICE IS INCLUDED AS PART OF THE CONTRACT:

NOTICE REGARDING COASTAL AREA PROPERTY

1. The real property described in and subject to this contract adjoins and shares a common boundary with the tidally influenced submerged lands of the state. The boundary is subject to change and can be determined accurately only by a survey on the ground made by a licensed state land surveyor in accordance with the original grant from the sovereign. The owner of the property described in this contract may gain or lose portions of the tract because of changes in the boundary.

2. The seller, transferor, or grantor has no knowledge of any prior fill as it relates to the property described in and subject to this contract except: ____
____
____.

3. State law prohibits the use, encumbrance, construction, or placing of any structure in, on, or over state-owned submerged lands below the applicable tide line, without proper permission.

4. The purchaser or grantee is hereby advised to seek the advice of an attorney or other qualified person as to the legal nature and effect of the facts set forth in this notice on the property described in and subject to this contract. Information regarding the location of the applicable tide line as to the property described in and subject to this contract may be obtained from the surveying division of the General Land Office in Austin.

Buyer	Seller
Buyer	Seller

This form has been approved by the Texas Real Estate Commission for use with similarly approved or promulgated contract forms. Such approval relates to this form only. No representation is made as to the legal validity or adequacy of any provision in any specific transactions. It is not suitable for complex transactions. (12-94) TREC No. 33-0.

01A TREC No. 33-0

Figure 9.26 TREC 34-1

PROMULGATED BY THE TEXAS REAL ESTATE COMMISSION (TREC) 10-29-01

EQUAL HOUSING OPPORTUNITY

ADDENDUM FOR
PROPERTY LOCATED SEAWARD OF THE
GULF INTRACOASTAL WATERWAY

TO CONTRACT CONCERNING THE PROPERTY AT

____

____

(Location of Property)

IN ACCORDANCE WITH SECTION 61.025, TEXAS NATURAL RESOURCES CODE, THE FOLLOWING STATEMENT IS INCLUDED AS PART OF THE CONTRACT:

The real property described in this contract is located seaward of the Gulf Intracoastal Waterway to its southernmost point and then seaward of the longitudinal line also known as 97 degrees, 12', 19" which runs southerly to the international boundary from the intersection of the centerline of the Gulf Intracoastal Waterway and the Brownsville Ship Channel. If the property is in close proximity to a beach fronting the Gulf of Mexico, the purchaser is hereby advised that the public has acquired a right of use or easement to or over the area of any public beach by prescription, dedication, or presumption, or has retained a right by virtue of continuous right in the public since time immemorial, as recognized in law and custom.

The extreme seaward boundary of natural vegetation that spreads continuously inland customarily marks the landward boundary of the public easement. If there is no clearly marked natural vegetation line, the landward boundary of the easement is as provided by Sections 61.016 and 61.017, Natural Resources Code.

State law prohibits any obstruction, barrier, restraint, or interference with the use of the public easement, including the placement of structures seaward of the landward boundary of the easement. STRUCTURES ERECTED SEAWARD OF THE VEGETATION LINE (OR OTHER APPLICABLE EASEMENT BOUNDARY) OR THAT BECOME SEAWARD OF THE VEGETATION LINE AS A RESULT OF NATURAL PROCESSES ARE SUBJECT TO A LAWSUIT BY THE STATE OF TEXAS TO REMOVE THE STRUCTURES.

The purchaser is hereby notified that the purchaser should: (1) determine the rate of shoreline erosion in the vicinity of the real property; and (2) seek the advice of an attorney or other qualified person before executing this contract or instrument of conveyance as to the relevance of these statutes and facts to the value of the property the purchaser is hereby purchasing or contracting to purchase.

____________________	____________________
Buyer	Seller
____________________	____________________
Buyer	Seller

This form has been approved by the Texas Real Estate Commission for use with similarly approved or promulgated contract forms. Such approval relates to this form only. TREC forms are intended for use only by trained real estate licensees. No representation is made as to the legal validity or adequacy of any provision in any specific transactions. It is not suitable for complex transactions. Texas Real Estate Commission, P.O. Box 12188, Austin, TX 78711-2188, 1-800-250-8732 or (512) 459-6544 (http://www.trec.state.tx.us) TREC No. 34-1. This form replaces TREC No. 34-0.

01A

Figure 9.27 TREC 12-1

EQUAL HOUSING OPPORTUNITY

03-17-92

ADDENDUM FOR

RELEASE OF LIABILITY ON ASSUMPTION OF FHA, VA OR CONVENTIONAL LOAN

RESTORATION OF SELLER'S ENTITLEMENT FOR VA GUARANTEED LOAN

PROMULGATED BY THE TEXAS REAL ESTATE COMMISSION (TREC)

ADDENDUM TO EARNEST MONEY CONTRACT BETWEEN THE UNDERSIGNED PARTIES CONCERNING THE PROPERTY AT______________________________
(Street Address and City)

☐ **A. RELEASE OF SELLER'S LIABILITY ON LOAN TO BE ASSUMED:**

Within __________ days from the effective date of this contract Seller and Buyer shall apply for release of Seller's liability from (a) any conventional lender, (b) VA and any lender whose loan has been guaranteed by VA, or (c) FHA and any lender whose loan has been insured by FHA. Seller and Buyer shall furnish all required information and documents. If any release of liability has not been approved by the Closing Date: (check 1 or 2 below)

☐ 1. This contract shall terminate and the Earnest Money shall be refunded to Buyer.

☐ 2. Failure to obtain release approval shall not delay closing and Seller and Buyer shall continue to seek release of Seller's liability.

☐ **B. RESTORATION OF SELLERS ENTITLEMENT FOR VA LOAN:**

Within __________ days from the effective date of this contract Seller and Buyer shall apply for restoration of Seller's VA entitlement and shall furnish all information and documents required by VA. If restoration has not been approved by the Closing Date: (check 1 or 2 below)

☐ 1. This contract shall terminate and the Earnest Money shall be refunded to Buyer.

☐ 2. Failure to obtain restoration approval shall not delay closing and Seller and Buyer shall continue to seek restoration of Seller's VA entitlement.

NOTICE: VA will not restore Seller's VA entitlement unless Buyer: (a) is a veteran, (b) has sufficient unused VA entitlement and (c) is otherwise qualified. If Seller desires release of liability from VA and the lender together with restoration of VA entitlement, paragraphs A and B should be used.

Seller shall pay the cost of securing the release and restoration. If Seller's cost will exceed $ ________________, and Buyer declines to pay the excess, Seller may (a) waive release or restoration, (b) pay the excess, or (c) terminate this contract and the Earnest Money shall be refunded to Buyer.

Seller's deed shall contain any loan assumption clause required by FHA, VA or any lender. The provisions of this addendum are enforceable after closing.

____________________ Buyer

____________________ Seller

____________________ Buyer

____________________ Seller

The form of this Addendum has been approved by the Texas Real Estate Commission for use with similarly approved or promulgated contract forms. Such approval relates to this form only. No representation is made as to the legal validity or adequacy of any provision in any specific transactions. It is not suitable for complex transactions. (03-92) TREC No. 12-1. This form replaces TREC No. 12-0.

01A TREC No. 12-1

Transaction 8:
90% Conventional Fixed Rate Loan with PMI
(Using: TREC 20-6, 40-1, 36-3, 28-0, 33-0, and 34-1)

Russell A. Janes and his spouse, Anna M. Janes, have agreed to sell their gulf-front home to Peter Paul Prospect and his spouse, Priscilla B. Prospect, for $387,800. The Prospects will obtain a 90 percent conventional loan. It will require one discount point as well as one point for origination, which will be paid by the buyers. The loan will be a 30-year fixed rate at 7 percent. The contract is subject to financing approval.

The property is located at 12656 Rolling Waves Lane in Galveston County, Texas. It is more fully described as Lot 6, Block 6, Sandy Dunes Addition, Section 2 of Galveston County, Texas. Although it is located outside the city limits, it has a Galveston, Texas, mailing address. The zip code is 77573. The house was built in 1981.

Because the property is subject to membership in and the assessments of a very active homeowners' association, the Prospects want the sellers to furnish the resale certificate from the association. This will be obtained within 15 days after the effective date of the contract. The seller will pay the HOA transfer fee of $100.

The sellers will remove the leased security system from the property prior to closing and have agreed to leave the bedspread that matches the draperies in the master bedroom.

The buyers have selected Buyer's Choice Title Company to hold their $25,000 earnest money deposit and want them to issue the owner's title policy at closing. They request ten days to get the survey and two days to make objections. The buyers will pay for the new survey. They anticipate they can get financing approval in 20 days and close in 30 days. The sellers will pay for owners' title policy. Possession will be granted at funding.

The Prospects do not like the looks of some of the plants on the property and want to have the soil tested for toxic materials. They feel that they can have the tests performed and get the results within 20 days after the effective date of the contract.

In exchange for the payment of $500 to the seller, the buyers want an unrestricted five-day right to inspect the property. If they find anything that they consider unusual, they want to be able to terminate the purchase agreement without forfeiture of their earnest money. If they proceed to closing, the $500 will be credited to the purchase price.

Smooth Sales Realty, Inc., who also has a buyer representation agreement with the Prospects, has listed the property. Both parties have signed a written authorization to permit the broker to function as an intermediary and to allow the broker to appoint Susan Smart, salesperson, to work with the sellers and Sammy Sharp, broker associate, to work with and advise the buyers. The broker has given the parties the proper written notification of who has been appointed to whom to give advice.

The seller furnished the seller's disclosure form prior to the offer being made. The parties are all very reasonable people and will probably get to the closing table without a hitch; however, to be on the safe side, they agree to select a mutually acceptable mediator when and if the need arises and to split the mediator's fee equally.

The buyers will take the prepared offer to their attorney, Rachel Review, prior to signing.

At the advice of the attorney, the buyers require that all documents be prepared and made available to them 48 hours prior to closing for review. They will close on or before April 4.

Figure 9.28 TREC 20-6

PROMULGATED BY THE TEXAS REAL ESTATE COMMISSION (TREC) 01-06-03

EQUAL HOUSING OPPORTUNITY

ONE TO FOUR FAMILY RESIDENTIAL CONTRACT (RESALE)

NOTICE: Not For Use For Condominium Transactions

1. PARTIES: ______________________________ (Seller) agrees to sell and convey to ______________________________(Buyer) and Buyer agrees to buy from Seller the Property described below.

2. PROPERTY:

A. LAND: Lot ____________________,Block_____, ________________ ____________________Addition, City of ______________ , ____________ County, Texas, known as ______________________________ ____________________(address/zip code), or as described on attached exhibit.

B. IMPROVEMENTS: The house, garage and all other fixtures and improvements attached to the above-described real property, including without limitation, the following permanently installed and built-in items, if any: all equipment and appliances, valances, screens, shutters, awnings, wall-to-wall carpeting, mirrors, ceiling fans, attic fans, mail boxes, television antennas and satellite dish system and equipment, heating and air-conditioning units, security and fire detection equipment, wiring, plumbing and lighting fixtures, chandeliers, water softener system, kitchen equipment, garage door openers, cleaning equipment, shrubbery, landscaping, outdoor cooking equipment, and all other property owned by Seller and attached to the above described real property.

C. ACCESSORIES: The following described related accessories, if any: window air conditioning units, stove, fireplace screens, curtains and rods, blinds, window shades, draperies and rods, controls for satellite dish system, controls for garage door openers, entry gate controls, door keys, mailbox keys, above ground pool, swimming pool equipment and maintenance accessories, and artificial fireplace logs.

D. EXCLUSIONS: The following improvements and accessories will be retained by Seller and excluded: ______________________________ ______________________________.

The land, improvements and accessories are collectively referred to as the "Property".

3. SALES PRICE:

A. Cash portion of Sales Price payable by Buyer at closing................. $__________

B. Sum of all financing described below (excluding any loan funding fee or mortgage insurance premium) .... $__________

C. Sales Price (Sum of A and B) .... $__________

4. FINANCING: The portion of Sales Price not payable in cash will be paid as follows: (Check applicable boxes below)

☐ A. THIRD PARTY FINANCING: One or more third party mortgage loans in the total amount of $____________________. If the Property does not satisfy the lenders' underwriting requirements for the loan(s), this contract will terminate and the earnest money will be refunded to Buyer. (Check one box only)

☐(1) This contract is subject to Buyer being approved for the financing described in the attached Third Party Financing Condition Addendum.

☐(2) This contract is not subject to Buyer being approved for financing and does not involve FHA or VA financing.

☐ B. ASSUMPTION: The assumption of the unpaid principal balance of one or more promissory notes described in the attached TREC Loan Assumption Addendum.

☐ C. SELLER FINANCING: A promissory note from Buyer to Seller of $______________, bearing _______ % interest per annum, secured by vendor's and deed of trust liens, and containing the terms and conditions described in the attached TREC Seller Financing Addendum. If an owner policy of title insurance is furnished, Buyer shall furnish Seller with a mortgagee policy of title insurance.

5. EARNEST MONEY: Upon execution of this contract by both parties, Buyer shall deposit $__________ as earnest money with ______________________________, as escrow agent, at ______________________________ (address). Buyer shall deposit additional earnest money of $________________ with escrow agent within ________days after the effective date of this contract. If Buyer fails to deposit the earnest money as required by this contract, Buyer will be in default.

Figure 9.28 TREC 20-6 (continued)

Contract Concerning ____ Page Two 01-06-03
(Address of Property)

6. TITLE POLICY AND SURVEY:

A. TITLE POLICY: Seller shall furnish to Buyer at ❑Seller's ❑Buyer's expense an owner policy of title insurance (Title Policy) issued by ______________________________ ______________________________ (Title Company) in the amount of the Sales Price, dated at or after closing, insuring Buyer against loss under the provisions of the Title Policy, subject to the promulgated exclusions (including existing building and zoning ordinances) and the following exceptions:

(1) Restrictive covenants common to the platted subdivision in which the Property is located.
(2) The standard printed exception for standby fees, taxes and assessments.
(3) Liens created as part of the financing described in Paragraph 4.
(4) Utility easements created by the dedication deed or plat of the subdivision in which the Property is located.
(5) Reservations or exceptions otherwise permitted by this contract or as may be approved by Buyer in writing.
(6) The standard printed exception as to marital rights.
(7) The standard printed exception as to waters, tidelands, beaches, streams, and related matters.
(8) The standard printed exception as to discrepancies, conflicts, shortages in area or boundary lines, encroachments or protrusions, or overlapping improvements. Buyer, at Buyer's expense, may have the exception amended to read, "shortages in area".

B. COMMITMENT: Within 20 days after the Title Company receives a copy of this contract, Seller shall furnish to Buyer a commitment for title insurance (Commitment) and, at Buyer's expense, legible copies of restrictive covenants and documents evidencing exceptions in the Commitment (Exception Documents) other than the standard printed exceptions. Seller authorizes the Title Company to mail or hand deliver the Commitment and Exception Documents to Buyer at Buyer's address shown in Paragraph 21. If the Commitment and Exception Documents are not delivered to Buyer within the specified time, the time for delivery will be automatically extended up to 15 days or the Closing Date, whichever is earlier.

C. SURVEY: The survey must be made by a registered professional land surveyor acceptable to the Title Company and any lender. (Check one box only)

❑ (1) Within ______ days after the effective date of this contract, Seller, at Seller's expense, shall furnish a new survey to Buyer.

❑ (2) Within ______ days after the effective date of this contract, Buyer, at Buyer's expense, shall obtain a new survey.

❑ (3) Within ______ days after the effective date of this contract, Seller shall furnish Seller's existing survey of the Property to Buyer and the Title Company, along with Seller's affidavit acceptable to the Title Company for approval of the survey. If the survey is not approved by the Title Company or Buyer's lender, a new survey will be obtained at ❑ Seller's ❑ Buyer's expense no later than 3 days prior to the Closing Date.

D. OBJECTIONS: Within ____ days after Buyer receives the Commitment, Exception Documents and the survey, Buyer may object in writing to defects, exceptions, or encumbrances to title: disclosed on the survey other than items 6A(1) through (7) above; disclosed in the Commitment other than items 6A(1) through (8) above; or which prohibit the following use or activity: ____.
Buyer's failure to object within the time allowed will constitute a waiver of Buyer's right to object; except that the requirements in Schedule C of the Commitment are not waived. Seller shall cure the timely objections of Buyer or any third party lender within 15 days after Seller receives the objections and the Closing Date will be extended as necessary. If objections are not cured within such 15 day period, this contract will terminate and the earnest money will be refunded to Buyer unless Buyer waives the objections.

E. TITLE NOTICES:

(1) ABSTRACT OR TITLE POLICY: Broker advises Buyer to have an abstract of title covering the Property examined by an attorney of Buyer's selection, or Buyer should be furnished with or obtain a Title Policy. If a Title Policy is furnished, the Commitment should be promptly reviewed by an attorney of Buyer's choice due to the time limitations on Buyer's right to object.

(2) MANDATORY OWNERS' ASSOCIATION MEMBERSHIP: The Property ❑ is ❑ is not subject to mandatory membership in an owners' association. If the Property is subject to mandatory membership in an owners' association, Seller notifies Buyer under §5.012, Texas Property Code, that, as a purchaser of property in the residential community in

Initialed for identification by Buyer______ ______ and Seller ______ ______ **01A** TREC NO. 20-6

Figure 9.28 TREC 20-6 (continued)

Contract Concerning ______________________________ Page Three 01-06-03
(Address of Property)

which the Property is located, you are obligated to be a member of the owners' association. Restrictive covenants governing the use and occupancy of the Property and a dedicatory instrument governing the establishment, maintenance, and operation of this residential community have been or will be recorded in the Real Property Records of the county in which the Property is located. Copies of the restrictive covenants and dedicatory instrument may be obtained from the county clerk. You are obligated to pay assessments to the owners' association. The amount of the assessments is subject to change. Your failure to pay the assessments could result in a lien on and the foreclosure of the Property.

(3) STATUTORY TAX DISTRICTS: If the Property is situated in a utility or other statutorily created district providing water, sewer, drainage, or flood control facilities and services, Chapter 49, Texas Water Code requires Seller to deliver and Buyer to sign the statutory notice relating to the tax rate, bonded indebtedness, or standby fee of the district prior to final execution of this contract.

(4) TIDE WATERS: If the Property abuts the tidally influenced waters of the state, §33.135, Texas Natural Resources Code, requires a notice regarding coastal area property to be included in the contract. An addendum containing the notice promulgated by TREC or required by the parties must be used.

(5) ANNEXATION: If the Property is located outside the limits of a municipality, Seller notifies Buyer under §5.011, Texas Property Code, that the Property may now or later be included in the extraterritorial jurisdiction of a municipality and may now or later be subject to annexation by the municipality. Each municipality maintains a map that depicts its boundaries and extraterritorial jurisdiction. To determine if the Property is located within a municipality's extraterritorial jurisdiction or is likely to be located within a municipality's extraterritorial jurisdiction, contact all municipalities located in the general proximity of the Property for further information.

7. PROPERTY CONDITION:

A. INSPECTIONS, ACCESS AND UTILITIES: Buyer may have the Property inspected by inspectors selected by Buyer and licensed by TREC or otherwise permitted by law to make inspections. Seller shall permit Buyer and Buyer's agents access to the Property at reasonable times. Seller shall pay for turning on existing utilities for inspections.

B. SELLER'S DISCLOSURE NOTICE PURSUANT TO §5.008, TEXAS PROPERTY CODE (Notice): (Check one box only)

❑ (1) Buyer has received the Notice.

❑ (2) Buyer has not received the Notice. Within _______ days after the effective date of this contract, Seller shall deliver the Notice to Buyer. If Buyer does not receive the Notice, Buyer may terminate this contract at any time prior to the closing and the earnest money will be refunded to Buyer. If Seller delivers the Notice, Buyer may terminate this contract for any reason within 7 days after Buyer receives the Notice or prior to the closing, whichever first occurs, and the earnest money will be refunded to Buyer.

❑ (3) The Texas Property Code does not require this Seller to furnish the Notice.

C. SELLER'S DISCLOSURE OF LEAD-BASED PAINT AND LEAD-BASED PAINT HAZARDS is required by Federal law for a residential dwelling constructed prior to 1978.

D. ACCEPTANCE OF PROPERTY CONDITION: Buyer accepts the Property in its present condition; provided Seller, at Seller's expense, shall complete the following specific repairs and treatments:____
____.

E. LENDER REQUIRED REPAIRS AND TREATMENTS: Unless otherwise agreed in writing, neither party is obligated to pay for lender required repairs, which includes treatment for wood destroying insects. If the parties do not agree to pay for the lender required repairs or treatments, this contract will terminate and the earnest money will be refunded to Buyer. If the cost of lender required repairs and treatments exceeds 5% of the Sales Price, Buyer may terminate this contract and the earnest money will be refunded to Buyer.

F. COMPLETION OF REPAIRS AND TREATMENTS: Unless otherwise agreed in writing, Seller shall complete all agreed repairs and treatments prior to the Closing Date. All required permits must be obtained, and repairs and treatments must be performed by persons who are licensed or otherwise authorized by law to provide such repairs or treatments. At Buyer's election, any transferable warranties received by Seller with respect to the repairs and treatments will be transferred to Buyer at Buyer's expense. If Seller fails to complete any agreed repairs and

Initialed for identification by Buyer______ ______ and Seller _______ ______ **01A** TREC NO. 20-6

Figure 9.28 TREC 20-6 (continued)

Contract Concerning ____ Page Four 01-06-03
(Address of Property)

treatments prior to the Closing Date, Buyer may do so and receive reimbursement from Seller at closing. The Closing Date will be extended up to 15 days, if necessary, to complete repairs and treatments.

G. ENVIRONMENTAL MATTERS: Buyer is advised that the presence of wetlands, toxic substances, including asbestos and wastes or other environmental hazards, or the presence of a threatened or endangered species or its habitat may affect Buyer's intended use of the Property. If Buyer is concerned about these matters, an addendum promulgated by TREC or required by the parties should be used.

H. RESIDENTIAL SERVICE CONTRACTS: Buyer may purchase a residential service contract from a residential service company licensed by TREC. If Buyer purchases a residential service contract, Seller shall reimburse Buyer at closing for the cost of the residential service contract in an amount not exceeding $______________ . Buyer should review any residential service contract for the scope of coverage, exclusions and limitations. **The purchase of a residential service contract is optional. Similar coverage may be purchased from various companies authorized to do business in Texas.**

8. BROKERS' FEES: All obligations of the parties for payment of brokers' fees are contained in separate written agreements.

9. CLOSING:

A. The closing of the sale will be on or before ____________________, 20___, or within 7 days after objections to matters disclosed in the Commitment or by the survey have been cured, whichever date is later (Closing Date). If either party fails to close the sale by the Closing Date, the non-defaulting party may exercise the remedies contained in Paragraph 15.

B. At closing:

(1) Seller shall execute and deliver a general warranty deed conveying title to the Property to Buyer and showing no additional exceptions to those permitted in Paragraph 6 and furnish tax statements or certificates showing no delinquent taxes on the Property.

(2) Buyer shall pay the Sales Price in good funds acceptable to the escrow agent.

(3) Seller and Buyer shall execute and deliver any notices, statements, certificates, affidavits, releases, loan documents and other documents required of them by this contract, the Commitment or law necessary for the closing of the sale and the issuance of the Title Policy.

C. Unless expressly prohibited by written agreement, Seller may continue to show the Property and receive, negotiate and accept back up offers.

D. All covenants, representations and warranties in this contract survive closing.

10. POSSESSION: Seller shall deliver to Buyer possession of the Property in its present or required condition, ordinary wear and tear excepted: ☐ upon closing and funding ☐ according to a temporary residential lease form promulgated by TREC or other written lease required by the parties. Any possession by Buyer prior to closing or by Seller after closing which is not authorized by a written lease will establish a tenancy at sufferance relationship between the parties. *Consult your insurance agent prior to change of ownership or possession because insurance coverage may be limited or terminated. The absence of a written lease or appropriate insurance coverage may expose the parties to economic loss.*

11. SPECIAL PROVISIONS: (Insert only factual statements and business details applicable to the sale. TREC rules prohibit licensees from adding factual statements or business details for which a contract addendum, lease or other form has been promulgated by TREC for mandatory use.)

Initialed for identification by Buyer_____ _____ and Seller _____ _____ **01A** TREC NO. 20-6

Figure 9.28 TREC 20-6 (continued)

Contract Concerning ______________________________ Page Five 01-06-03
(Address of Property)

12. SETTLEMENT AND OTHER EXPENSES:

A. The following expenses must be paid at or prior to closing:

(1) Expenses payable by Seller (Seller's Expenses):

(a) Releases of existing liens, including prepayment penalties and recording fees; release of Seller's loan liability; tax statements or certificates; preparation of deed; one-half of escrow fee; and other expenses payable by Seller under this contract.

(b) Seller shall also pay an amount not to exceed $ ____________ to be applied in the following order: Buyer's Expenses which Buyer is prohibited from paying by FHA, VA, Texas Veteran's Housing Assistance Program or other governmental loan programs; Buyer's prepaid items; other Buyer's expenses.

(2) Expenses payable by Buyer (Buyer's Expenses):

(a) Loan origination, discount, buy-down, and commitment fees (Loan Fees).

(b) Appraisal fees; loan application fees; credit reports; preparation of loan documents; interest on the notes from date of disbursement to one month prior to dates of first monthly payments; recording fees; copies of easements and restrictions; mortgagee title policy with endorsements required by lender; loan-related inspection fees; photos, amortization schedules, one-half of escrow fee; all prepaid items, including required premiums for flood and hazard insurance, reserve deposits for insurance, ad valorem taxes and special governmental assessments; final compliance inspection; courier fee, repair inspection, underwriting fee and wire transfer, expenses incident to any loan, and other expenses payable by Buyer under this contract.

B. Buyer shall pay Private Mortgage Insurance Premium (PMI), VA Loan Funding Fee, or FHA Mortgage Insurance Premium (MIP) as required by the lender.

C. If any expense exceeds an amount expressly stated in this contract for such expense to be paid by a party, that party may terminate this contract unless the other party agrees to pay such excess. Buyer may not pay charges and fees expressly prohibited by FHA, VA, Texas Veteran's Housing Assistance Program or other governmental loan program regulations.

13. PRORATIONS: Taxes for the current year, interest, maintenance fees, assessments, dues and rents will be prorated through the Closing Date. If taxes for the current year vary from the amount prorated at closing, the parties shall adjust the prorations when tax statements for the current year are available. If taxes are not paid at or prior to closing, Buyer shall pay taxes for the current year.

14. CASUALTY LOSS: If any part of the Property is damaged or destroyed by fire or other casualty after the effective date of this contract, Seller shall restore the Property to its previous condition as soon as reasonably possible, but in any event by the Closing Date. If Seller fails to do so due to factors beyond Seller's control, Buyer may (a) terminate this contract and the earnest money will be refunded to Buyer (b) extend the time for performance up to 15 days and the Closing Date will be extended as necessary or (c) accept the Property in its damaged condition with an assignment of insurance proceeds and receive credit from Seller at closing in the amount of the deductible under the insurance policy. Seller's obligations under this paragraph are independent of any obligations of Seller under Paragraph 7.

15. DEFAULT: If Buyer fails to comply with this contract, Buyer will be in default, and Seller may (a) enforce specific performance, seek such other relief as may be provided by law, or both, or (b) terminate this contract and receive the earnest money as liquidated damages, thereby releasing both parties from this contract. If, due to factors beyond Seller's control, Seller fails within the time allowed to make any non-casualty repairs or deliver the Commitment, or survey, if required of Seller, Buyer may (a) extend the time for performance up to 15 days and the Closing Date will be extended as necessary or (b) terminate this contract as the sole remedy and receive the earnest money. If Seller fails to comply with this contract for any other reason, Seller will be in default and Buyer may (a) enforce specific performance, seek such other relief as may be provided by law, or both, or (b) terminate this contract and receive the earnest money, thereby releasing both parties from this contract.

16. MEDIATION: It is the policy of the State of Texas to encourage resolution of disputes through alternative dispute resolution procedures such as mediation. Any dispute between Seller and Buyer related to this contract which is not resolved through informal discussion ☐will ☐will not be submitted to a mutually acceptable mediation service or provider. The parties to the mediation shall bear the mediation costs equally. This paragraph does not preclude a party from seeking equitable relief from a court of competent jurisdiction.

Initialed for identification by Buyer_____ _____ and Seller _____ _____ **01A** TREC NO. 20-6

Figure 9.28 TREC 20-6 (continued)

Contract Concerning ____ Page Six 01-06-03
(Address of Property)

17. ATTORNEY'S FEES: The prevailing party in any legal proceeding related to this contract is entitled to recover reasonable attorney's fees and all costs of such proceeding incurred by the prevailing party.

18. ESCROW: The escrow agent is not (a) a party to this contract and does not have liability for the performance or nonperformance of any party to this contract, (b) liable for interest on the earnest money and (c) liable for the loss of any earnest money caused by the failure of any financial institution in which the earnest money has been deposited unless the financial institution is acting as escrow agent. At closing, the earnest money must be applied first to any cash down payment, then to Buyer's Expenses and any excess refunded to Buyer. If both parties make written demand for the earnest money, escrow agent may require payment of unpaid expenses incurred on behalf of the parties and a written release of liability of escrow agent from all parties. If one party makes written demand for the earnest money, escrow agent shall give notice of the demand by providing to the other party a copy of the demand. If escrow agent does not receive written objection to the demand from the other party within 30 days after notice to the other party, escrow agent may disburse the earnest money to the party making demand reduced by the amount of unpaid expenses incurred on behalf of the party receiving the earnest money and escrow agent may pay the same to the creditors. If escrow agent complies with the provisions of this paragraph, each party hereby releases escrow agent from all adverse claims related to the disbursal of the earnest money. Escrow agent's notice to the other party will be effective when deposited in the U. S. Mail, postage prepaid, certified mail, return receipt requested, addressed to the other party at such party's address shown below. Notice of objection to the demand will be deemed effective upon receipt by escrow agent.

19. REPRESENTATIONS: Seller represents that as of the Closing Date (a) there will be no liens, assessments, or security interests against the Property which will not be satisfied out of the sales proceeds unless securing payment of any loans assumed by Buyer and (b) assumed loans will not be in default. If any representation of Seller in this contract is untrue on the Closing Date, Buyer may terminate this contract and the earnest money will be refunded to Buyer.

20. FEDERAL TAX REQUIREMENTS: If Seller is a "foreign person," as defined by applicable law, or if Seller fails to deliver an affidavit to Buyer that Seller is not a "foreign person," then Buyer shall withhold from the sales proceeds an amount sufficient to comply with applicable tax law and deliver the same to the Internal Revenue Service together with appropriate tax forms. Internal Revenue Service regulations require filing written reports if currency in excess of specified amounts is received in the transaction.

21. NOTICES: All notices from one party to the other must be in writing and are effective when mailed to, hand-delivered at, or transmitted by facsimile as follows:

To Buyer at:	**To Seller at:**
______________________	______________________
______________________	______________________
______________________	______________________
Telephone:(____) ______________	Telephone:(____) ______________
Facsimile:(____)______________	Facsimile:(____) ______________

22. AGREEMENT OF PARTIES: This contract contains the entire agreement of the parties and cannot be changed except by their written agreement. Addenda which are a part of this contract are (check all applicable boxes):

- ☐ Third Party Financing Condition Addendum
- ☐ Addendum for Property Subject to Mandatory Membership in an Owners' Association
- ☐ Seller Financing Addendum
- ☐ Environmental Assessment, Threatened or Endangered Species and Wetlands Addendum

Initialed for identification by Buyer______ ______ and Seller _______ ______ **01A** TREC NO. 20-6

Figure 9.28 TREC 20-6 (continued)

Contract Concerning ______________________________ Page Seven 01-06-03
(Address of Property)

- ❑ Loan Assumption Addendum
- ❑ Buyer's Temporary Residential Lease
- ❑ Seller's Temporary Residential Lease
- ❑ Addendum for Sale of Other Property by Buyer
- ❑ Addendum for Seller's Disclosure of Information on Lead-based Paint and Lead-based Paint Hazards as Required by Federal Law
- ❑ Addendum for "Back-Up" Contract
- ❑ Addendum for Coastal Area Property
- ❑ Addendum for Property Located Seaward of the Gulf Intracoastal Waterway
- ❑ Addendum for Release of Liability on Assumption of FHA, VA, or Conventional Loan Restoration of Seller's Entitlement for VA Guaranteed Loan
- ❑ Other (list): ______________________________

____

23. TERMINATION OPTION: This paragraph will be a part of this contract ONLY if both blanks are filled in and Buyer has paid the Option Fee. Buyer has paid Seller $______________ (Option Fee) for the unrestricted right to terminate this contract by giving notice of termination to Seller within ________ days after the effective date of this contract. If Buyer gives notice of termination within the time specified, the Option Fee will not be refunded, however, any earnest money will be refunded to Buyer. The Option Fee ❑will ❑will not be credited to the Sales Price at closing. For the purposes of this paragraph, time is of the essence; strict compliance with the time for performance stated herein is required.

24. CONSULT AN ATTORNEY: Real estate licensees cannot give legal advice. READ THIS CONTRACT CAREFULLY. If you do not understand the effect of this contract, consult an attorney BEFORE signing.

Buyer's
Attorney is:______________________

____

Telephone: (____)______________

Facsimile: (____)______________

Seller's
Attorney is:______________________

____

Telephone: (____)______________

Facsimile: (____)______________

EXECUTED the _______day of ______________________, 20____ (EFFECTIVE DATE).
(BROKER: FILL IN THE DATE OF FINAL ACCEPTANCE.)

______________________ Buyer

______________________ Seller

______________________ Buyer

______________________ Seller

The form of this contract has been approved by the Texas Real Estate Commission. TREC forms are intended for use only by trained real estate licensees. No representation is made as to the legal validity or adequacy of any provision in any specific transactions. It is not suitable for complex transactions. Texas Real Estate Commission, P.O. Box 12188, Austin, TX 78711-2188, 1-800-250-8732 or (512) 459-6544 (http://www.trec.state.tx.us) TREC NO. 20-6. This form replaces TREC NO. 20-5.

Initialed for identification by Buyer_____ _____ and Seller _____ _____ **01A** TREC NO. 20-6

Figure 9.28 TREC 20-6 (continued)

Contract Concerning ____ Page Eight 01-06-03
(Address of Property)

SELLER'S RECEIPT

Receipt of $________________ (Option Fee) in the form of ______________________ is acknowledged.

________________________________ Seller

________________________________ Date

BROKER INFORMATION AND RATIFICATION OF FEE

Listing Broker has agreed to pay Other Broker ____________________ of the total sales price when Listing Broker's fee is received. Escrow Agent is authorized and directed to pay Other Broker from Listing Broker's fee at closing.

Other Broker	Listing Broker
License No. Telephone	License No. Telephone
represents ☐ Buyer only as Buyer's agent ☐ Seller as Listing Broker's subagent	represents ☐ Seller and Buyer as an intermediary ☐ Seller only as Seller's agent
Associate Telephone	Listing Associate Telephone
Broker's Address	Listing Associate's Office Address Facsimile
Facsimile	Selling Associate Telephone
	Selling Associate's Office Address Facsimile

RECEIPT

Receipt of ☐ Contract and ☐ $____________ Earnest Money in the form of ________________ is acknowledged.

Escrow Agent: ______________________________ Date: ________________

By: ______________________________

______________________________ Address

Telephone (_____) ________________

______________________________ City State Zip

Facsimile: (_____) ________________

01A TREC NO. 20-6

Figure 9.29 TREC 40-1

02-09-2004

EQUAL HOUSING OPPORTUNITY

PROMULGATED BY THE TEXAS REAL ESTATE COMMISSION (TREC)

THIRD PARTY FINANCING CONDITION ADDENDUM

TO CONTRACT CONCERNING THE PROPERTY AT

____

(Street Address and City)

Buyer shall apply promptly for all financing described below and make every reasonable effort to obtain financing approval including but not limited to furnishing all information and documents required by lender for approval. Financing approval will be deemed to have been obtained when the lender determines that Buyer has satisfied all of lender's financial requirements (those items relating to Buyer's assets, income and credit history). If Buyer cannot obtain financing approval, Buyer must give written notice to Seller within ____ days after the effective date of this contract and this contract will terminate and the earnest money will be refunded to Buyer. **If Buyer does not give such notice within the time allowed, this contract will no longer be subject to Buyer being approved for the financing described below. For purposes of this paragraph, time is of the essence; strict compliance with the times for performance herein stated is required.**

Each note must be secured by vendor's and deed of trust liens.

❑ A. CONVENTIONAL FINANCING:

❑ (1) A first mortgage loan in the principal amount of $ __________________ (excluding any financed PMI premium), due in full in _________ year(s), with interest not to exceed ______% per annum for the first ________year(s) of the loan with Loan Fees (loan origination, discount, buy-down, and commitment fees) not to exceed ________% of the loan.

❑ (2) A second mortgage loan in the principal amount of $__________________(excluding any financed PMI premium), due in full in ___________year(s), with interest not to exceed ______% per annum for the first ____________year(s) of the loan with Loan Fees (loan origination, discount, buy-down, and commitment fees) not to exceed _________ % of the loan.

❑ B. TEXAS VETERANS' HOUSING ASSISTANCE PROGRAM LOAN: A Texas Veteran's Housing Assistance Program Loan of $________________ for a period of at least ______years at the interest rate established by the Texas Veteran's Land Board at the time of closing.

❑C. FHA INSURED FINANCING: A Section _________________ FHA insured loan of not less than $__________________ (excluding any financed MIP), amortizable monthly for not less than _______years, with interest not to exceed _______% per annum for the first ______year(s) of the loan with Loan Fees (loan origination, discount, buy-down, and commitment fees) not to exceed _________ % of the loan. As required by HUD-FHA, if FHA valuation is unknown, *"It is expressly agreed that, notwithstanding any other provision of this contract, the purchaser (Buyer) shall not be obligated to complete the purchase of the Property described herein or to incur any penalty by forfeiture of earnest money deposits or otherwise unless the purchaser (Buyer) has been given in accordance with HUD/FHA or VA requirements a written statement issued by the Federal Housing Commissioner, Department of Veterans Affairs, or a Direct Endorsement Lender setting forth the appraised value of the Property of not less than $__________________. The purchaser (Buyer) shall have the privilege and option of proceeding with consummation of the contract without regard to the amount of the appraised valuation. The appraised valuation is arrived at to determine the maximum mortgage the Department of Housing and Urban Development will insure. HUD does not warrant the value or the condition of the Property. The purchaser (Buyer) should satisfy himself/herself that the price and the condition of the Property are acceptable."*

Initialed for identification by Buyer_______ _______ and Seller________ ________ 01A

Figure 9.29 TREC 40-1 (continued)

Third Party Financing Condition Addendum Concerning Page Two 02-09-2004

____
(Address of Property)

❑ D. VA GUARANTEED FINANCING: A VA guaranteed loan of not less than $___________________ (excluding any financed Funding Fee), amortizable monthly for not less than________years, with interest not to exceed_________% per annum for the first ________year(s) of the loan with Loan Fees (loan origination, discount, buy-down, and commitment fees) not to exceed ________% of the loan.

VA NOTICE TO BUYER: "*It is expressly agreed that, notwithstanding any other provisions of this contract, the Buyer shall not incur any penalty by forfeiture of earnest money or otherwise or be obligated to complete the purchase of the Property described herein, if the contract purchase price or cost exceeds the reasonable value of the Property established by the Department of Veterans Affairs. The Buyer shall, however, have the privilege and option of proceeding with the consummation of this contract without regard to the amount of the reasonable value established by the Department of Veterans Affairs.*"

If Buyer elects to complete the purchase at an amount in excess of the reasonable value established by VA, Buyer shall pay such excess amount in cash from a source which Buyer agrees to disclose to the VA and which Buyer represents will not be from borrowed funds except as approved by VA. If VA reasonable value of the Property is less than the Sales Price, Seller may reduce the Sales Price to an amount equal to the VA reasonable value and the sale will be closed at the lower Sales Price with proportionate adjustments to the down payment and the loan amount.

Buyer hereby authorizes any lender to furnish to the Seller or Buyer or their representatives information relating only to the status of financing approval of Buyer.

__________________________ __________________________
Buyer Seller

__________________________ __________________________
Buyer Seller

This form has been approved by the Texas Real Estate Commission for use with similarly approved or promulgated contract forms. Such approval relates to this form only. TREC forms are intended for use only by trained real estate licensees. No representation is made as to the legal validity or adequacy of any provision in any specific transactions. It is not suitable for complex transactions. Texas Real Estate Commission, P.O. Box 12188, Austin, TX 78711-2188, 1-800-250-8732 or (512) 459-6544 (http://www.trec.state.tx.us) TREC No. 40-1. This form replaces TREC No. 40-0.

Figure 9.30 TREC 36-3

PROMULGATED BY THE TEXAS REAL ESTATE COMMISSION (TREC) 02-09-2004

EQUAL HOUSING OPPORTUNITY

ADDENDUM FOR PROPERTY SUBJECT TO MANDATORY MEMBERSHIP IN AN OWNERS' ASSOCIATION

(NOT FOR USE WITH CONDOMINIUMS)

ADDENDUM TO CONTRACT CONCERNING THE PROPERTY AT

____

(Street Address and City)

____

(Name of Owners' Association)

A. SUBDIVISON INFORMATION: "Subdivision Information" means: (i) the restrictions applying to the subdivision, (ii) the bylaws and rules of the Owners' Association, and (iii) a resale certificate, all of which were provided by the Owners' Association in compliance with Section 207.003 of the Texas Property Code no more than three months before the date of their delivery to Buyer.
(Check only one box):

❑ 1. Within _____ days after the effective date of the contract, Seller shall at Seller's expense deliver the Subdivision Information to Buyer. If Buyer does not receive the Subdivision Information, Buyer may terminate the contract at any time prior to closing and the earnest money will be refunded to Buyer. If Seller delivers the Subdivision Information, Buyer may terminate the contract for any reason within 7 days after Buyer receives the Subdivision Information or prior to closing, whichever first occurs, and the earnest money will be refunded to Buyer.

❑ 2. Buyer has received and approved the Subdivision Information before signing the contract.

❑ 3. Buyer does not require delivery of the Subdivision Information.

If Seller becomes aware of any material changes in the Subdivision Information, Seller shall immediately give notice to Buyer. Buyer may terminate the contract prior to closing by giving written notice to Seller if: (i) any of the Subdivision Information provided was not true; or (ii) any material adverse change in the Subdivision Information occurs prior to closing, and the earnest money will be refunded to Buyer.

B. TRANSFER FEES: Buyer shall pay any Owners' Association transfer fee not to exceed $ ____________ and Seller agrees to pay any excess.

NOTICE TO BUYER REGARDING REPAIRS BY THE OWNERS' ASSOCIATION: The Owners' Association may have the sole responsibility to make certain repairs to the Property. If you are concerned about the condition of any part of the Property which the Owners' Association is required to repair, you should not sign the contract unless you are satisfied that the Owners' Association will make the desired repairs.

______________________ Buyer	______________________ Seller
______________________ Buyer	______________________ Seller

The form of this addendum has been approved by the Texas Real Estate Commission for use only with similarly approved or promulgated forms of contracts. Such approval relates to this contract form only. TREC forms are intended for use only by trained real estate licensees. No representation is made as to the legal validity or adequacy of any provision in any specific transactions. It is not suitable for complex transactions. Texas Real Estate Commission, P.O. Box 12188, Austin, TX 78711-2188, 1-800-250-8732 or (512) 459-6544 (http://www.trec.state.tx.us) TREC No. 36-3. This form replaces TREC No. 36-2.

Figure 9.31 TREC 28-0

10-25-93

ENVIRONMENTAL ASSESSMENT, THREATENED OR ENDANGERED SPECIES, AND WETLANDS ADDENDUM

PROMULGATED BY THE TEXAS REAL ESTATE COMMISSION (TREC)

ADDENDUM TO EARNEST MONEY CONTRACT BETWEEN THE UNDERSIGNED PARTIES CONCERNING THE PROPERTY AT ____
(Address)

☐ A. ENVIRONMENTAL ASSESSMENT: Buyer, at Buyer's expense, may obtain an Environmental Assessment Report prepared by an environmental specialist.

☐ B. THREATENED OR ENDANGERED SPECIES: Buyer, at Buyer's expense, may obtain a report from a natural resources professional to determine if there are any threatened or endangered species or their habitats as defined by the Texas Parks and Wildlife Department or the U.S. Fish and Wildlife Service.

☐ C. WETLANDS: Buyer, at Buyer's expense, may obtain a report from an environmental specialist to determine if there are wetlands, as defined by federal or state law or regulation.

Within _________ days after the Effective Date of the contract, Buyer may terminate the contract by furnishing Seller a copy of any report noted above that adversely affects the use of the Property and the Earnest Money shall be refunded to Buyer. If Buyer does not furnish Seller a copy of the unacceptable report within the prescribed time and give Seller notice that Buyer has terminated the contract, Buyer shall be deemed to have accepted the Property.

______________________	______________________
Buyer	Seller
______________________	______________________
Buyer	Seller

The form of this addendum has been approved by the Texas Real Estate Commission for use only with similarly approved or promulgated forms of contracts. No representation is made as to the legal validity or adequacy of any provision in any specific transactions. It is not suitable for complex transactions. (10-93) TREC No. 28-0.

01A TREC No. 28-0

Figure 9.32 TREC 33-0

12-05-94

EQUAL HOUSING OPPORTUNITY

PROMULGATED BY THE TEXAS REAL ESTATE COMMISSION (TREC)
P.O. BOX 12188, AUSTIN, TX 78711-2188

ADDENDUM FOR
COASTAL AREA PROPERTY

ADDENDUM TO EARNEST MONEY CONTRACT BETWEEN THE UNDERSIGNED PARTIES CONCERNING THE PROPERTY AT

____

____

(Location of Property)

IN ACCORDANCE WITH SECTION 33.135, TEXAS NATURAL RESOURCES CODE, THE FOLLOWING NOTICE IS INCLUDED AS PART OF THE CONTRACT:

NOTICE REGARDING COASTAL AREA PROPERTY

1. The real property described in and subject to this contract adjoins and shares a common boundary with the tidally influenced submerged lands of the state. The boundary is subject to change and can be determined accurately only by a survey on the ground made by a licensed state land surveyor in accordance with the original grant from the sovereign. The owner of the property described in this contract may gain or lose portions of the tract because of changes in the boundary.

2. The seller, transferor, or grantor has no knowledge of any prior fill as it relates to the property described in and subject to this contract except: ________________________________

____

____.

3. State law prohibits the use, encumbrance, construction, or placing of any structure in, on, or over state-owned submerged lands below the applicable tide line, without proper permission.

4. The purchaser or grantee is hereby advised to seek the advice of an attorney or other qualified person as to the legal nature and effect of the facts set forth in this notice on the property described in and subject to this contract. Information regarding the location of the applicable tide line as to the property described in and subject to this contract may be obtained from the surveying division of the General Land Office in Austin.

____________________ Buyer	____________________ Seller
____________________ Buyer	____________________ Seller

This form has been approved by the Texas Real Estate Commission for use with similarly approved or promulgated contract forms. Such approval relates to this form only. No representation is made as to the legal validity or adequacy of any provision in any specific transactions. It is not suitable for complex transactions. (12-94) TREC No. 33-0.

01A TREC No. 33-0

Figure 9.33 TREC 34-1

PROMULGATED BY THE TEXAS REAL ESTATE COMMISSION (TREC) 10-29-01

EQUAL HOUSING OPPORTUNITY

ADDENDUM FOR
PROPERTY LOCATED SEAWARD OF THE
GULF INTRACOASTAL WATERWAY

TO CONTRACT CONCERNING THE PROPERTY AT

____

____

(Location of Property)

IN ACCORDANCE WITH SECTION 61.025, TEXAS NATURAL RESOURCES CODE, THE FOLLOWING STATEMENT IS INCLUDED AS PART OF THE CONTRACT:

The real property described in this contract is located seaward of the Gulf Intracoastal Waterway to its southernmost point and then seaward of the longitudinal line also known as 97 degrees, 12', 19" which runs southerly to the international boundary from the intersection of the centerline of the Gulf Intracoastal Waterway and the Brownsville Ship Channel. If the property is in close proximity to a beach fronting the Gulf of Mexico, the purchaser is hereby advised that the public has acquired a right of use or easement to or over the area of any public beach by prescription, dedication, or presumption, or has retained a right by virtue of continuous right in the public since time immemorial, as recognized in law and custom.

The extreme seaward boundary of natural vegetation that spreads continuously inland customarily marks the landward boundary of the public easement. If there is no clearly marked natural vegetation line, the landward boundary of the easement is as provided by Sections 61.016 and 61.017, Natural Resources Code.

State law prohibits any obstruction, barrier, restraint, or interference with the use of the public easement, including the placement of structures seaward of the landward boundary of the easement. STRUCTURES ERECTED SEAWARD OF THE VEGETATION LINE (OR OTHER APPLICABLE EASEMENT BOUNDARY) OR THAT BECOME SEAWARD OF THE VEGETATION LINE AS A RESULT OF NATURAL PROCESSES ARE SUBJECT TO A LAWSUIT BY THE STATE OF TEXAS TO REMOVE THE STRUCTURES.

The purchaser is hereby notified that the purchaser should: (1) determine the rate of shoreline erosion in the vicinity of the real property; and (2) seek the advice of an attorney or other qualified person before executing this contract or instrument of conveyance as to the relevance of these statutes and facts to the value of the property the purchaser is hereby purchasing or contracting to purchase.

____________________	____________________
Buyer	Seller
____________________	____________________
Buyer	Seller

This form has been approved by the Texas Real Estate Commission for use with similarly approved or promulgated contract forms. Such approval relates to this form only. TREC forms are intended for use only by trained real estate licensees. No representation is made as to the legal validity or adequacy of any provision in any specific transactions. It is not suitable for complex transactions. Texas Real Estate Commission, P.O. Box 12188, Austin, TX 78711-2188, 1-800-250-8732 or (512) 459-6544 (http://www.trec.state.tx.us) TREC No. 34-1. This form replaces TREC No. 34-0.

01A

Chapter 10

Estimating Seller Net and Buyer Move-In

Buyers and sellers are interested in the bottom line and expect the real estate license holder to give a reasonably accurate estimate of those numbers. To be able to provide this information to the client or customer, the license holder needs to become comfortable with calculating closing costs, prepaids, and lender-required reserve deposits. One must be familiar with HUD's Uniform Settlement Statement, which must be used in all transactions covered by the RESPA rules. These rules cover the vast majority of transactions structured with the promulgated forms we have been studying.

To estimate the costs accurately, carefully examine the purchase agreement, know the typical charges incurred with the particular type of financing involved in the transaction, obtain a title insurance rate card, and obtain accurate numbers for the ad valorem taxes, homeowner's association maintenance fee, and homeowner's insurance policy premium.

Most title insurance companies provide real estate license holders with charts to use in estimating closing costs. For our example, we will use the HUD form. By using this form for estimating purposes, your client or customer will be familiar with it when it is presented in its final form at closing. Familiarity with the form contributes to a smoother closing experience.

One of the most commonly encountered transactions involves a buyer purchasing a single-family, previously occupied home with funds obtained from a 90 percent conventional loan. Transaction 8 in Chapter 9 of this book fits the description of *typical* and is used for this example. In our example, we round all line items to the nearest dollar. Rounding is acceptable for giving estimates. Exact numbers must be used at closing.

The Seller's Side

The listing agent will be concerned with accurately estimating the bottom line for the seller. To do this, begin by itemizing the applicable costs on the back of the statement. In Transaction 8, the seller has charges at the following lines:

703	**Commission** (using a commission rate of 7%) Sales price of \$387,800 × .07 = \$27,146	\$ 27,146
1107	**Attorney's Fee** Preparation of General Warranty Deed and Release	\$ 130
1110	**Owner's Title Insurance Policy Premium** Calculated on sale price using title insurance rate card; using current rate card	\$ 2,885
1111	**Escrow Fee** Determined by title company	\$ 75
1113	**Messenger** Determined by title company	\$ 45
1201	**Recording Fees** Release of lien	\$ 20

Enter these numbers in the column labeled "Paid from Seller's Funds at Settlement" on the back of the Uniform Settlement Statement. Total the column and enter your total on the front of the Uniform Settlement Statement at line 502.

On the front of the Uniform Settlement Statement, enter the contract sale price at line 401. The seller paid the homeowners' association maintenance fee of \$660 on January 1. We use a closing date of April 4 and need to prorate the homeowners' association maintenance fee with the seller paying through the day of closing as stipulated in paragraph 13 of the contract. The seller has had the benefit of January 1 through April 4. The buyer will reimburse the seller for the remaining portion of the year.

To calculate the amount involved, we shall use a "banker's year" of 360 days. For the remaining days in April, we subtract the closing date from 30.

April		May-December		Days Due
30 days – 4 = 26	+	240 (30 × 8)	=	266

The annual fee of \$660 is divided by 360 days and multiplied by the days due to calculate the amount the buyer will be charged and the seller will be credited at lines 409 and 109.

$$\$660 \div 360 \text{ days} \times 266 \text{ days due} = \$488 \text{ (rounded)}$$

The seller has an outstanding loan balance of $86,000 after the April 1 payment has been made. The loan is at 8 percent interest and has no prepayment penalty. To calculate the payoff to enter at line 504, we must calculate four days of interest and add it to the principal balance outstanding.

Loan amount $86,000 × .08 = $6,880 annual interest

$6,880 ÷ 360 days × 4 days due = $76 (rounded)

$86,000 + $76 = $86,076 total payoff

Paragraph 13 also calls for the ad valorem taxes to be prorated through the day of closing, April 4. The annual tax bill for this property is $5,648. To prorate this tax bill, count the days from January 1 through April 4, calculate the dollar amount of tax per day and calculate the total amount of tax that will be charged to the seller at line 510 and credited to the buyer at line 210.

Jan		Feb		Mar		Apr		
30	+	30	+	30	+	4	=	94 days due

Annual tax	÷	360	=	$ per day	×	days due	=	lines 510 and 210
$5,648	÷	360	=	$15.69	×	94	=	$1,475 (rounded)

Now you may total all lines in the 400 series and enter your total at lines 420 and 601. Total all lines in the 500 Series and enter your total at lines 520 and 602. Subtract line 602 from line 601 and enter your answer at line 603. Check the box that indicates cash "To" the seller at line 603 and you are ready to give a solid, accurate estimate to your seller client.

The Buyer's Side

Again, begin on the back of the statement. The purchase agreement and a title company closing cost estimating sheet with typical numbers are invaluable tools.

The 800 series of line items relate to costs associated with the buyer's new loan.

1201	**Recording Fees** Paid to the county clerk's office to record the Deed of Trust ($35) and the General Warranty Deed ($23).	$ 58
1204	**Tax Service Fee**	$ 115
1301	**Survey** Every buyer should require a survey prior to closing. Lenders require a survey as part of the loan package.	$ 325

Enter these numbers in the column labeled "Paid from the Borrower's Funds at Settlement" on the back of the Uniform Settlement Statement. Total the column and enter your total on the front of the Uniform Settlement Statement at line 103.

On the front of the Uniform Settlement Statement, enter the contract sale price at line 101. At line 201, enter the earnest money recited in paragraph 5 on the purchase agreement, and enter the amount from paragraph 3B on line 202. The prorated items should be entered on lines 109 (maintenance fee) and 210 (property tax). You are now ready to total the borrower's side.

Total all lines in the 100 series and enter the number at line 120 and at line 301. Total all lines in the 200 series and enter the number at line 220 and at line 302. To accurately estimate the amount the buyer will need to bring to the closing in the form of a cashier's check, subtract line 302 from line 301 and enter the difference at line 303. Check the box that indicates cash "From" the borrower. Check your completed statement with the answer key in Appendix B.

For a further discussion of finding your way through and completing a closing statement, we recommend Chapter 14 in *Mastering Real Estate Math*, seventh edition, by Tamper and published by Dearborn™ Real Estate Education of Chicago. Chapter 13 of the same book will help you prorate taxes, interest, insurance, homeowners' association maintenance fees, and rents.

Good luck and happy selling!

Figure 10.1 Settlement Statement

A. **Settlement Statement**

U.S. Department of Housing and Urban Development

OMB Approval No. 2502-0265

B. Type of Loan	6. File Number:	7. Loan Number:	8. Mortgage Insurance Case Number:
1. ☐ FHA 2. ☐ FmHA 3. ☐ Conv. Unins. 4. ☐ VA 5. ☐ Conv. Ins.			

C. Note: This form is furnished to give you a statement of actual settlement costs. Amounts paid to and by the settlement agent are shown. Items marked "(p.o.c.)" were paid outside the closing; they are shown here for informational purposes and are not included in the totals.

D. Name & Address of Borrower:	E. Name & Address of Seller:	F. Name & Address of Lender:

G. Property Location:	H. Settlement Agent:	
	Place of Settlement:	I. Settlement Date:

J. Summary of Borrower's Transaction		K. Summary of Seller's Transaction	
100. Gross Amount Due From Borrower		**400. Gross Amount Due To Seller**	
101. Contract sales price		401. Contract sales price	
102. Personal property		402. Personal property	
103. Settlement charges to borrower (line 1400)		403.	
104.		404.	
105.		405.	
Adjustments for items paid by seller in advance		**Adjustments for items paid by seller in advance**	
106. City/town taxes to		406. City/town taxes to	
107. County taxes to		407. County taxes to	
108. Assessments to		408. Assessments to	
109.		409.	
110.		410.	
111.		411.	
112.		412.	
120. Gross Amount Due From Borrower		**420. Gross Amount Due To Seller**	
200. Amounts Paid By Or In Behalf Of Borrower		**500. Reductions In Amount Due To Seller**	
201. Deposit or earnest money		501. Excess deposit (see instructions)	
202. Principal amount of new loan(s)		502. Settlement charges to seller (line 1400)	
203. Existing loan(s) taken subject to		503. Existing loan(s) taken subject to	
204.		504. Payoff of first mortgage loan	
205.		505. Payoff of second mortgage loan	
206.		506.	
207.		507.	
208.		508.	
209.		509.	
Adjustments for items unpaid by seller		**Adjustments for items unpaid by seller**	
210. City/town taxes to		510. City/town taxes to	
211. County taxes to		511. County taxes to	
212. Assessments to		512. Assessments to	
213.		513.	
214.		514.	
215.		515.	
216.		516.	
217.		517.	
218.		518.	
219.		519.	
220. Total Paid By/For Borrower		**520. Total Reduction Amount Due Seller**	
300. Cash At Settlement From/To Borrower		**600. Cash At Settlement To/From Seller**	
301. Gross Amount due from borrower (line 120)		601. Gross amount due to seller (line 420)	
302. Less amounts paid by/for borrower (line 220)	( )	602. Less reductions in amt. due seller (line 520)	( )
303. Cash ☐ **From** ☐ **To Borrower**		**603. Cash** ☐ **To** ☐ **From Seller**	

Section 5 of the Real Estate Settlement Procedures Act (RESPA) requires the following: • HUD must develop a Special Information Booklet to help persons borrowing money to finance the purchase of residential real estate to better understand the nature and costs of real estate settlement services; • Each lender must provide the booklet to all applicants from whom it receives or for whom it prepares a written application to borrow money to finance the purchase of residential real estate; • Lenders must prepare and distribute with the Booklet a Good Faith Estimate of the settlement costs that the borrower is likely to incur in connection with the settlement. These disclosures are manadatory.

Section 4(a) of RESPA mandates that HUD develop and prescribe this standard form to be used at the time of loan settlement to provide full disclosure of all charges imposed upon the borrower and seller. These are third party disclosures that are designed to provide the borrower with pertinent information during the settlement process in order to be a better shopper.

The Public Reporting Burden for this collection of information is estimated to average one hour per response, including the time for reviewing instructions, searching existing data sources, gathering and maintaining the data needed, and completing and reviewing the collection of information.

This agency may not collect this information, and you are not required to complete this form, unless it displays a currently valid OMB control number.

The information requested does not lend itself to confidentiality.

Previous editions are obsolete — Page 1 of 2 — form **HUD-1** (3/86) ref Handbook 4305.2

Figure 10.1 Settlement Statement (continued)

L. Settlement Charges	Paid From Borrowers Funds at Settlement	Paid From Seller's Funds at Settlement
700. Total Sales/Broker's Commission based on price $ @ % =		
Division of Commission (line 700) as follows:		
701. $ to		
702. $ to		
703. Commission paid at Settlement		
704.		
800. Items Payable In Connection With Loan		
801. Loan Origination Fee %		
802. Loan Discount %		
803. Appraisal Fee to		
804. Credit Report to		
805. Lender's Inspection Fee		
806. Mortgage Insurance Application Fee to		
807. Assumption Fee		
808.		
809.		
810.		
811.		
900. Items Required By Lender To Be Paid In Advance		
901. Interest from to @$ /day		
902. Mortgage Insurance Premium for months to		
903. Hazard Insurance Premium for years to		
904. years to		
905.		
1000. Reserves Deposited With Lender		
1001. Hazard insurance months@$ per month		
1002. Mortgage insurance months@$ per month		
1003. City property taxes months@$ per month		
1004. County property taxes months@$ per month		
1005. Annual assessments months@$ per month		
1006. months@$ per month		
1007. months@$ per month		
1008. months@$ per month		
1100. Title Charges		
1101. Settlement or closing fee to		
1102. Abstract or title search to		
1103. Title examination to		
1104. Title insurance binder to		
1105. Document preparation to		
1106. Notary fees to		
1107. Attorney's fees to		
(includes above items numbers:)		
1108. Title insurance to		
(includes above items numbers:)		
1109. Lender's coverage $		
1110. Owner's coverage $		
1111.		
1112.		
1113.		
1200. Government Recording and Transfer Charges		
1201. Recording fees: Deed $; Mortgage $; Releases $		
1202. City/county tax/stamps: Deed $; Mortgage $		
1203. State tax/stamps: Deed $; Mortgage $		
1204.		
1205.		
1300. Additional Settlement Charges		
1301. Survey to		
1302. Pest inspection to		
1303.		
1304.		
1305.		
1400. Total Settlement Charges (enter on lines 103, Section J and 502, Section K)		

Previous editions are obsolete Page 2 of 2 form **HUD-1** (3/86) ref Handbook 4305.2

Glossary

Abstract of Title–a full summary of all recorded documents, recorded at the county courthouse, that may affect title to a given parcel of real estate; addressed in paragraph 6 of TREC-promulgated contracts and TREC form 29-1

Acceptance–an expression of intent to be bound by the terms and conditions of an offer. To bind the agreement, the acceptance must be communicated to the person making the offer. An offer pertaining to real estate must be made in writing and accepted in writing

Accessory–an item identified as part of the sale in paragraph 2 of TREC-promulgated contract forms that does not meet the test of a fixture; defined in paragraph 2 of TREC-promulgated contract forms

Acknowledgment–a formal declaration made by a person signing a document to a duly authorized public official that the document was signed by the signor of his own free will. Documents must be acknowledged to be admissible for public recording

Addendum–an addition or amendment to a contract; the contract must reference the addendum, and the addendum must reference the contract; listed in paragraph 22 of TREC-promulgated contracts

Addition–another name for a platted subdivision; identified in paragraph 2 of TREC promulgated contract forms

After–later than. In TREC-promulgated contract forms, the counting of days is from "the day after" the date of signing or execution and does not include the day the document is signed

Amendment–a revision or change to a contract. TREC contracts may be amended by using TREC form 39-3

Annex–to add or attach to a municipality. The possibility is addressed in paragraph 6 E (5) of TREC promulgated contract forms

Arbitration–an alternative, nonjudicial, dispute resolution approach that submits the dispute to a selected third party who renders a decision that may or may not be binding upon the parties

Assign–to transfer one's legal rights to another party

Assumption–to take on personal liability for a legal obligation made by another person

Attorney-in-Fact–a legally competent and neutral party who is authorized by another to act in his or her place as a fiduciary

Back-up contract–a secondary contract; a contract in which the contracting parties recognize the existence of a superior contract between one of the parties and a third party; created by use of the TREC promulgated addendum identified as 11-5

Baron sole–an unmarried man

Bilateral contract–a contractual agreement in which each party agrees to perform or forbear in exchange for the other party's promise to perform or forebear

Breach of contract–nonperformance of the legal terms of a valid contract

Broker–one who is licensed by the state to serve as a special agent to a buyer or seller in a real estate transaction

Broker/lawyer committee–a statutorily created group of six brokers and six lawyers who draft and recommend forms for promulgation by the real estate commission

Broker's fee–the compensation (commission) charged by a broker for professional services rendered; addressed in paragraph 8 of TREC-promulgated contracts

Business detail–a point of agreement in a contract that does not define legal rights and remedies

Buyer's agent–a broker who represents the interests of the buyer and acts as the buyer's special agent

Casualty loss–a financial loss caused by physical damage to the improvements on a parcel of real estate; remedies for a casualty loss are identified in paragraph 14 of the TREC-promulgated contract forms

Chain of title–a history of the succession of ownership of a parcel of land

Closing–the consummation of a real estate transaction when the seller (grantor) delivers title to the buyer (grantee) and the buyer delivers consideration to the seller

Closing costs–expenses paid at closing in addition to the purchase price of the property; paragraph 12 of the TREC-promulgated contracts identifies who is responsible for paying various closing costs

Competent party–a party who has legal capacity to enter into a binding contract

Condominium documents–the enabling and governing documents that create and guide the operations of a condominium project. Chapter 82 of the Texas Property Code establishes the statutory requirements to create a condominium

Consideration–something of value given by one party in exchange for something from another

Contingency–a contractual provision that requires completion of a defined act before the contract is binding; example, the buyer must be approved for a loan before the buyer is obligated to perform and close the transaction

Contract–a legally enforceable agreement between two parties to do (performance) or not to do (forbearance) a particular act

Contract for deed–a purchase agreement that provides for deferred delivery of the title to the buyer (vendee) after the seller (vendor) has received all of the deferred payments due to be paid as the full consideration tendered for the property; identified as Executory Contract for Conveyance in chapter 5.061 of the Texas Property Code

Conventional–third party financing that is neither insured or guaranteed by an agency of government. Third party lending is addressed in paragraph 4 of the TREC-promulgated contracts with conventional financing terms being defined in TREC addendum 40-1

Cooperating broker–the broker who brings the buyer to the transaction who may be functioning as either a subagent of the listing broker or a buyer's agent

Counteroffer–an offer made in response to an unacceptable offer

Declaration–the recorded document that legally establishes a condominium

Deed restriction–also called *restrictive covenant,* a provision placed in deeds, usually by the developer of a subdivision, that control future use of the property

Default–see breach of contract

Disclosure–a revelation of known facts; section 5.008 of the Texas Property Code requires sellers of previously occupied single-family residences to disclose material facts about the physical condition of the property

Dual agent–a broker who has received the informed consent of both the seller and the buyer to represent both of the parties in a real estate transaction under common law principles rather than functioning as an intermediary as defined by statute

Earnest money–the initial and additional cash deposits tendered by the prospective buyer of real property to show good faith. Earnest money and additional earnest money are addressed in paragraph 5 of the TREC-promulgated contracts and in the TREC 11-5 addendum

Effective date–the date on which the offeree accepts the offer and the offeror is notified of the acceptance. The Statute of Frauds requires that the offer and acceptance be written; the notification may be verbal. The TREC contract forms call for the broker to fill in the effective date

Endangered species–certain fish, animal, and plant life that the federal government has determined to be in danger of extinction

Entitlement–the portion of a VA guaranteed loan that is guaranteed to the lender if the veteran defaults on the loan

Escrow–the act of putting money and documents in the care of a third, disinterested party until certain conditions are met. Paragraph 18 of the TREC-promulgated contracts addresses the responsibilities of the escrow agent

Et ux–and wife

Et vir–and husband

Exclusions–items of real or personal property that are not to be included in the conveyance of the property as defined in paragraph 2 of the TREC-promulgated contract forms

Executed–a contract that has been fully performed. Also used to identify the effective date of the contract when all parties have signed and the offeror has been notified of the acceptance of the offer

Executory–a contract that is in the process of being performed

Exhibit–a document that is attached to a contract to provide documentation supporting something in the principal document; example, a metes-and-bounds legal description attached to a purchase agreement

Extraterritorial jurisdiction (ETJ)–the property located outside of the limits of a municipality that is subject to annexation. Chapter 5.011 of the Texas Property Code requires that purchase agreements must contain a statutory notice that property located outside of the city may be in a city's ETJ and subject to annexation

Femme sole–an unmarried woman

FHA–the federal agency under HUD that insures home loans to make loanable funds available to lower income buyers

Fiduciary–a legal relationship between two persons who agree that one party will act on behalf of the other party, subject to the principal's direction and control

Forbearance–refraining from taking action

Fraud–an act of deceit intended to cause someone to part with money or enter into a contract that he or she would not have entered into if the decision had been based on truth and accurate information

Funding–when the seller receives the proceeds from the sale

Funding fee–the fee charged by the Department of Veterans Affairs to guarantee a veteran's loan

General warranty deed–the most widely used deed in Texas; a deed that warrants the title free of encumbrances back to the sovereign of the soil. Paragraph 9B of the TREC-promulgated contracts calls for the seller to deliver title at closing by executing and delivering a general warranty deed

Hazard insurance–insurance to indemnify a property owner against financial loss in the event of a casualty loss

Incompetent party–one who does not have the legal capacity to enter into a legally binding contract; a minor, or one who is under the influence of alcohol or other mind altering substances, or one who has been declared mentally incompetent by a court

Informal property description–a street address

Improvements–physical additions and fixtures added to land

Intermediary–a broker who has been authorized in writing, by the parties to a purchase agreement, to represent both parties following statutory provisions defined in section 1101.559 of the Texas Real Estate License Act

Lawful objective–a lawful purpose

Lease–a contract that transfers possessory rights from the holder of the fee simple estate to a tenant

Legal description–a property description that is of such certainty and accuracy that one can go to it and identify it; a description that is acceptable to the courts; a reference to a recorded plat or a metes-and-bounds description

Lessee–the tenant identified in a lease

Lessor–the landlord or property owner identified in a lease

License holder–one who holds a valid Texas broker or salesperson license

Liquidated damages–monetary damages to be paid by agreement of the parties in the contract when a default occurs

Listing broker–the broker who represents the interests of the property owner and acts as the seller's special agent

Mediation–a forum in which an impartial person, the mediator, facilitates communication between parties to promote reconciliation, settlement or understanding among the parties

Mineral rights–rights to subsurface land and its profits

Money damages–monetary damages awarded by a court when a party defaults and causes a financial loss to the nondefaulting party

Mortgage insurance premium (MIP)–the cost to purchase the insurance issued by FHA to protect the lender's interest in the event of borrower default

Mortgagee–the lender

Mortgagee's title policy–a policy that protects the lender's interest in the event of a failure of title

Mortgagor–the borrower

Mutual agreement–a meeting of the minds between parties to a contract when no fraud, misrepresentation, or undue influence has been present in the negotiations

Mutual assent–mutual agreement

Notice–information that may be required by the terms of a contract. The effective delivery of notices is defined in paragraph 21 of the TREC-promulgated contract forms

Note–a promise to pay

Novation–the substitution of a new contract for an existing one or the substitution of a new party to an existing obligation

Offer–one of the three components of a valid contract (offer, acceptance, notification of the acceptance). Offers involving real property interests should always be in writing

Offeree–the one to whom the offer is directed

Offeror–the one who makes an offer

Option–a contractual right that obligates the seller to sell but gives the buyer the unrestricted right to proceed or terminate within a defined time frame and at an agreed upon price. To be valid in Texas, the buyer must deliver valuable consideration (money) to the seller and time is of the essence

Owner's title policy–an insurance policy that indemnifies a property owner against financial loss in the event of a title failure

Parole evidence rule–evidence that is outside and separate from the written contractual agreement and that is not admissible into court

Parties–the signatories to a contract

Performance–a contractual agreement or promise to do a particular act

Possession–to take occupancy

Prepaids–expense items related to the ownership of a property that are paid in advance such as loan interest from the date of closing to the first of the next month, the first year's hazard insurance premium plus two additional months to establish the reserve impound account, and the prorated tax amount received from the seller plus an additional two months to be deposited in the reserve impound account

Prevailing party–the one who wins in a law suit; see paragraph 17 of the TREC promulgated contract forms for a list of what said party is entitled to receive

Principles–the parties to a contract; the buyer and the seller, or the tenant and the landlord

Private mortgage insurance (PMI)–the insurance that the borrower must acquire to protect the interest of the lender in the event of borrower default on a greater than 80 percent LTV conventional loan

Promulgated–forms published by the Texas Real Estate Commission for mandatory use by licensees assisting buyers and sellers

Ratification–the confirmation of an act already performed

Reasonable time–a fair length of time, as determined by the court, for the performance of contractual obligations

Recorded–placed in the public records of the county in which the property is located

Release–a document that relieves a person from any further legal obligations

Remedy–something used to correct a wrong

Resale certificate–a document issued by a homeowner's association that certifies the requirements that the restrictive covenants and association rules impose upon the owner of the property

Residential service contract–the statutory name for the contract that limits the owner's financial exposure in the event of a malfunction of the property being purchased; commonly referred to as a home warranty. The companies that issue these contracts are licensed and regulated by the Texas Real Estate Commission

Real Estate Settlement Procedures Act (RESPA)–a federal law that addresses closing procedures for residential transactions that are financed with a federally related loan

Restrictive covenant–see deed restrictions

Rollback tax–a tax that is assessed on Texas property when agriculturally exempted property is converted from agricultural use to another use

Seller financing–a transaction in which the seller receives part of the consideration as a note secured by a mortgage as part of the consideration. The details of the seller financing are addressed in TREC addendum 26-4

Seller's agent–the broker representing the owner's interest as a special agent; the listing broker

Settlement–closing of the transaction

Statute of Frauds–a state law that requires certain documents and agreements be reduced to writing to be enforceable in a court of law

Subagent–a broker who brings a buyer customer to the real estate transaction

Subdivision–land that is divided into two or more parcels to be sold separately

Subject to–a clause setting forth any contingencies or special conditions

Survey–the process of determining and measuring land areas and boundaries to identify easements and encroachments

Temporary lease–a leasehold estate that lasts for no more than 90 days

Tenant at sufferance–a tenancy that exists when a party is in possession of the premises after the legal right to occupy those premises has expired

Termination–to bring to an end. Contract termination may occur by completion of the objective, a change in the law, death or insanity of the parties, expiration, mutual agreement, condemnation or destruction of the property, or bankruptcy of either party

Third party financing–financing that involves someone other than the seller of the property; may be conventional or government backed

Tide waters–waters subject to the changing tides in the Gulf of Mexico

Time is of the essence–the contracting parties agree that strict adherence to the time frames recited in the contract is an essential part of their agreement

Timely presentation–Texas real estate licensees are required to present all offers to the client immediately

Title commitment–a document furnished by a title company that establishes the conditions under which the title company will issue an owner's policy of title insurance

TREC–Texas Real Estate Commission

TRELA–the real estate license act

Unenforceable–a contract that was valid but for a variety of possible reasons may no longer be enforced

Unilateral contract–a contract that requires one party to complete a performance before the other party is obligated to act; example, a seller is not obligated to pay a brokerage fee until the agent produces a ready, willing, and able buyer

Unimproved property–a parcel of land that does not have improvements, fixtures, and accessories

VA–the Department of Veterans Affairs

VA funding fee–the fee charged to a veteran by the Department of Veterans Affairs when a VA guaranteed loan is originated; a fee charged to reduce the cost of administering the VA loan guarantee program to the American taxpayer

Valid–an agreement that meets all of the legal requirements of a contract

Valuable consideration–money

Vernon's Texas Civil Statutes–state laws that do not fall into one of the state's legal codes

Void–the absence of something

Voidable–a contract that may be set aside at the sole option of one of the contracting parties

Waive–to give up or voluntarily surrender a legal right

Warranty–a promise or a covenant

Wetlands–land areas protected by the U.S. government that have groundwater at or near the surface enough of the year to support such as swamps and marshlands

Will–an instrument that conveys the real and personal property of a deceased person to a named beneficiary; a devisor conveys a devise (real property) to a devisee

Appendix A
Contract Content Review

According to the terms of the TREC promulgated contract forms:

1. How many days does the seller have to cure the timely buyer objections to title? ____________________

2. How many days does the title company have to furnish, on behalf of the seller, the title commitment to the buyer? ____________________

3. How many days prior to closing does the buyer or seller have to obtain a new survey if the existing survey is not acceptable and approved by the title company? ____________________

4. The closing paragraph calls for the closing of the transaction to occur on or before a date specified by the parties or within how many days after title objections have been cured? ____________________

5. If the seller's disclosure form is delivered to the buyer after the effective date of the contract, for how many days after it is received does the buyer have the unrestricted right to terminate the purchase agreement? _______

6. What is included in the definition of loan fees?

____

____

____

____

7. How many days may the contract be extended to complete repairs caused by a casualty loss after the effective date of the contract?________________

8. Once a purchase contract has been executed and title has been opened, may a seller continue to show the property to prospective buyers and negotiate back-up offers? ____

9. Who pays the taxes and maintenance fees for the actual day of closing? ____

10. If one party makes written demand of the title company for the earnest money, how many days must the title company wait after giving notice by certified mail to the other party before it can release the money to the demanding party? ____

11. Should the Seller's Disclosure Notice be referenced and added to the purchase agreement as an addendum? ______________________________

12. Who drafts the promulgated contracts? ________________________

13. How many brokers sit on the Committee? ______________________

14. When should a buyer or seller consult an attorney? ________________

15. What two blanks must be completed to have a valid termination option? ____ ____

16. If the effective date of the contract is the 15th of the month, when will the option period end if the agreement calls for a seven-day option period? ____

17. The lead-based paint addendum must be added to contracts for the purchase of homes built prior to what year? ______________________________

18. When must a seller permit access for the buyers to have the property inspected by licensed inspectors? ______________________________

19. Who fills in the date of final acceptance after the offeror has been notified of the acceptance? ____

20. Who pays for the Owner Policy of Title Insurance? ________________

21. The buyer may terminate the contract, even if the seller is willing to pay the cost of repairs, when the cost of lender-required repairs exceeds what amount? ______

22. If repairs are needed in order to complete the transactions, by whom must they be performed? ______

23. If the seller fails to complete any agreed repairs and treatments prior to the closing date, may the buyer do so and receive reimbursement from the seller at closing? ______

24. What is the maximum number of days for which a Sellers' or Buyers' Temporary Lease may be used? ______

25. What kind of a deed will the seller execute and deliver to the buyer at closing? ______

26. If the parties agree to submit any dispute to an alternative dispute resolution procedure such as mediation, who will pay the cost? ______

27. Where is the obligation of the parties for payment of broker's fees defined? ______

28. How shall the buyer pay the sales price? ______

29. Who is responsible for the expense related to releasing existing liens at closing? ______

30. Who will pay a required private mortgage insurance (PMI) premium? ______

31. What three things are collectively referred to as the "Property?" ______

______

______

______

32. For the most commonly used reference to a recorded plat type of legal description, what key element of the description has no blank provided? ______

33. In what paragraph do you find the words "time is of the essence?" ______

34. If the title company is unable to deliver the commitment for title insurance within the time frame defined in the contract, is an extension to that time frame possible? ______

35. If a title policy is to be furnished, who should promptly review the commitment? ______

36. Where in the promulgated contract form would a buyer itemize specific repairs that the buyer wants completed at the seller's expense prior to closing? ______

37. Must municipal building permits be obtained by sellers for repairs to be completed prior to closing? ______

38. Unless otherwise agreed in writing, who is obligated to pay for lender required repairs? ______

39. If a casualty loss occurs after the effective date of the contract and the seller is unable to restore the property prior to closing, the buyer may accept an assignment of the seller's insurance proceeds. What is the buyer to receive in addition to the assignment?

______

______

40. A buyer defaults and releases the earnest money to the seller as liquidated damages; can the seller seek additional money damages from the court?

______

41. Does the fact that the parties agree to submit a dispute to an alternative dispute resolution procedure, such as mediation, preclude a party from seeking equitable relief from a court of competent jurisdiction? ______

42. Does the escrow agent have any liability for the performance or nonperformance of any party to the contract? ______

43. Is the option fee automatically credited to the sales price if the buyer proceeds with the closing of the sale? ______

44. Are there any limitations on the reasons for which a buyer may terminate during the option period? ______

45. What is the status of the termination option when the buyer pays the seller no money? ______

46. What should a buyer or seller do if they do not understand the legal effect of any provision of the contract? ________________________________

47. Does a standard Texas Policy of Title Insurance insure against discrepancies, conflicts or shortages in area or boundary lines? ________________

48. Whose responsibility is it to determine if the property is located within a municipality's extraterritorial jurisdiction and may now or at a later time be subject to annexation? ____

____

____

49. What Texas statute requires the seller to notify the buyer that the property is situated in a utility or other statutorily created district providing water, sewer, drainage or flood control facilities and services? ______________

50. When seller financing is used to purchase the property, who is responsible for furnishing the seller with a mortgagee policy of title insurance? _____

____

Practice Exam

1. When should a party consult legal counsel?

   A. Before signing a contract
   B. Before making loan application
   C. Before tendering any money
   D. Anytime prior to closing

2. Which of the following is not listed as part of the defined real estate in the "property" paragraph of the TREC One to Four Family Residential Contract (Resale) form?

   A. Shrubbery
   B. Refrigerator
   C. Ceiling fans
   D. Satellite dish

3. The dollar amount entered on line 3B of the "sales price" paragraph of the TREC One to Four Family Residential Contract (Resale) form excludes any financed PMI.

   A. False
   B. True

4. What is the first consideration recited in the promulgated purchase contracts?

   A. The earnest money
   B. The sales price
   C. The option fee
   D. The exchange of promises in the "parties" paragraph

5. If a seller fails to provide the buyer with the "Seller's Disclosure of Property Condition" as required by section 5.008 of the Texas Property Code, what is the status of the purchase contract?

   A. Unenforceable
   B. Void
   C. Voidable at the option of the buyer
   D. Valid and enforceable

6. Which of the following is acceptable language for Special Provisions in paragraph 11?

   A. Time is of the essence
   B. Buyer will do a walk through
   C. Seller will pay for the survey
   D. Buyer will pay for the owner's title policy

7. The "property condition" paragraph (paragraph 7A) gives the buyer the right to personally inspect the property during the period between contract and closing at any time of the buyer's choosing.

   A. True
   B. False

8. When must a real estate license holder advise a buyer in writing to get an abstract examined by an attorney of the buyer's choice or obtain an owner's title insurance policy?

   A. At first contact
   B. Prior to signing an agreement to purchase
   C. Prior to closing
   D. At the first face-to-face meeting

9. When does an offer become a binding contract?

   A. When the last party has signed and the other party has been notified.
   B. When the signed contract has been delivered to the title company.
   C. When there is a meeting of the minds and earnest money tendered.
   D. When one party states verbally that the written offer is accepted.

10. The maximum tenancy that may be addressed in a TREC Seller's or Buyer's Temporary Lease (Forms 15-3 and 16-3) is:

    A. 180 days
    B. 90 days
    C. 48 hours
    D. 72 hours

11. Which addendum listed below contains the words "time is of the essence?"

    A. Seller Financing Addendum
    B. Property Condition Addendum
    C. Addendum for "Back-Up" Contract
    D. Addendum for Coastal Area Property

12. The Seller's Disclosure of Property Condition form issued by TREC is promulgated and must be used by all Texas real estate license holders.

    A. True
    B. False

13. According to the standard wording in the "Title Policy and Survey" paragraph of the contract, utility easements created by the dedication deed and plat of the subdivision in which the property is located will not be a basis for objection.

    A. True
    B. False

14. Under what circumstances do TREC rules permit an agent not to present an offer to the seller?

    A. If the seller, after entering into a contract to sell the property, instructs the agent in writing not to present further offers
    B. The agent may never withhold on offer
    C. The seller, after entering into a contract to sell the property, instructs the agent verbally not to present further offers
    D. When common business sense dictates otherwise

15. Which of the following is not an essential element of a contract for the purchase of a one to four family residential resale property?

    A. Competent parties
    B. Consideration
    C. Offer and acceptance
    D. Earnest money

16. In the "parties" paragraph (paragraph 1) of a residential resale contract, which of the following is the appropriate way to identify a buyer who is a widow?

    A. Mary Beth Smith, an unmarried person
    B. Mary Beth Smith, as separate property
    C. Mary Beth Smith, tenant in common
    D. Mary Beth Smith, et al and ux

17. Which of the following is the best example of a bilateral contract?

    A. A residential purchase agreement
    B. A residential lease
    C. An option to purchase
    D. Listing agreement

18. When a closing occurs on June 5th, the buyer will pay the property tax attributable to June 5th according to the provisions of the standard wording in the TREC promulgated contract forms.

    A. True
    B. False

19. Which of the following is not a possible addendum to a promulgated TREC contract form?

 A. Information About Brokerage Services
 B. Release of Liability on Assumption
 C. Buyer's Temporary Residential Lease
 D. Property Located Seaward of the Gulf Intracoastal Waterway

20. When may a potential purchaser's offer to buy real estate be withdrawn?

 A. Only after the seller has turned it down
 B. At any time if no earnest money was tendered
 C. At any time prior to seller acceptance and notification
 D. At any time prior to opening title

21. Which of the following is not addressed by a TREC promulgated contract?

 A. Assumption of a FHA insured loan
 B. A purchase using seller financing
 C. A purchase using a contract for deed
 D. The purchase of a fee simple townhouse

22. Who is responsible for filling in the date of final acceptance on the promulgated purchase contracts?

 A. The broker
 B. The seller
 C. The buyer
 D. The last party to sign

23. What are promulgated forms?

 A. Forms written by TREC and then published by the Broker-Lawyer Committee for mandatory use by license holders
 B. Forms written by the Broker-Lawyer Committee and then published by TREC for mandatory use by license holders
 C. Forms written and issued by the Texas Legislature for mandatory use by license holders
 D. Forms written and issued by TREC for recommended use by license holders

24. What is a legal proceeding brought by a party to a contract against another party to compel action called for in the agreement?

 A. A suit for injunction
 B. A suit for specific performance
 C. A motion for release
 D. A writ of forbearance

25. The buyer will have a maximum of 10 days after receipt of the Commitment to object in writing to matters disclosed in the Commitment.

    A. True
    B. False

26. Which of the following items might meet the test of a fixture but not be a part of the real estate because it is leased rather than owned by the seller?

    A. Permanently installed AC equipment
    B. Built-in cleaning equipment
    C. Certain lighting fixtures
    D. Water treatment system

27. Every TREC contract must have at least one TREC addendum.

    A. True
    B. False

28. Neither buyer nor seller is required to pay for the lender required repairs according to the standard wording in the "Property Condition" paragraph (paragraph 7E) of the TREC One to Four Family Residential Contract (Resale).

    A. True
    B. False

29. A buyer must sign the Seller's Disclosure notice as required by Section 5.008 of the Texas Property Code and incorporate it as an addendum to the purchase agreement.

    A. True
    B. False

30. All representations made by either party in a TREC-promulgated contract form will survive closing.

    A. True
    B. False

31. How much additional title insurance premium will be charged to delete the standard exception in a Texas Owner's Title Policy for a single family residential property relating to the standard exception "as to discrepancies, conflicts, shortages in area or boundary lines, encroachment or protrusions, or overlapping improvements?"

    A. An amount established by the state
    B. 10 percent of the sales price
    C. 5 percent of the loan value
    D. 10 percent of the published premium

32. A seller may continue to show the property to prospects after a purchase agreement has been signed unless agreed otherwise in writing.

    A. True
    B. False

33. According to the preprinted language, what type of deed is to be used at closing to convey the title to real property that is being sold using a TREC-promulgated contract form?

    A. Quitclaim
    B. Bargain and Sale
    C. Special Warranty
    D. General Warranty

34. Financing or assumption approval is deemed to have been obtained when the lender determines that the buyer has satisfied all of the lender's financial requirements such as buyer's net worth, income, and creditworthiness.

    A. True
    B. False

35. Anything that is addressed in one of the TREC addenda can adequately and legally be set down in the "Special Provisions" paragraph (paragraph 11) if so desired by a license holder.

    A. True
    B. False

36. The sum entered on the first line of the "Sales Price" paragraph (3A) of TREC-promulgated contracts excludes the buyer's closing costs and prepaids.

    A. True
    B. False

37. An agent may explain the general content, factual statements, and business details contained in the promulgated forms so long as the agent does not give legal advice.

    A. False
    B. True

38. Who shall be entitled to collect reasonable attorney's fees if a legal proceeding is brought under or with relation to a TREC-promulgated contract?

    A. The buyer
    B. The seller
    C. The listing broker
    D. A prevailing party

39. When the buyer makes a request to the seller to amend a contract during the option period and the seller fails to respond, what is the status of the contract two days after the option period has expired?

    A. The contract is null and void because the request to amend serves as adequate notice that the buyer does not wish to proceed.
    B. The contract is enforceable and the buyer is obligated to complete the transaction under the original terms and conditions.
    C. The option period is automatically extended until the seller responds.
    D. The contract incorporates the buyer's requested changes and moves to closing since the seller did not object to the changes.

40. When may the general public use the promulgated forms?

    A. Only when they have the services of an attorney
    B. Only when they have the services of a real estate broker
    C. The general public may not use the promulgated forms
    D. At any time

41. According to the provisions of the "Notices" paragraph in the TREC promulgated contracts, all notices from one party to the other are only valid when physically delivered to the party who is the recipient of the notice.

    A. True
    B. False

42. How many days does the seller have to cure objections to title after the buyer or third party lender has timely delivered objections to the seller when using the residential resale contract?

    A. 5 days
    B. 7 days
    C. 10 days
    D. 15 days

43. If a buyer decides to terminate a contract within the option period where and how **must** the promulgated Notice of Termination of Contract be delivered?

    A. To the listing agent
    B. As specified in "notices" paragraph
    C. To the title company
    D. All of the above

44. When a buyer is purchasing a home that was built prior to 1978, how many days must be given to the buyer to have the property evaluated for the presence of lead-based paint or lead hazards?

    A. 5
    B. 10
    C. 15
    D. 20

45. The fee that the seller is to pay to the listing broker is always stated in and made a part of the purchase agreement when using TREC-promulgated forms.

    A. True
    B. False

46. The TREC-promulgated contract forms require that the buyer always pay the loan origination fee.

    A. False
    B. True

47. What promulgates forms for mandatory use by license holders?

    A. The legislature
    B. The broker-lawyer committee
    C. The Texas Real Estate Commission
    D. The Texas Association of REALTORS®

48. Federal law dictates that an addendum addressing the possible presence of lead-based paint and lead-based paint hazards be attached to the purchase agreement when the house being sold was built before

    A. 1972.
    B. 1978.
    C. 1977.
    D. 1979.

49. How many contract forms are currently promulgated by TREC?

    A. 7
    B. 6
    C. 9
    D. 10

50. According to the standard verbiage in the "Property Condition" paragraph of TREC One to Four Family Residential Contract (Resale) form, who is responsible for paying the fees involved for turning on utilities for inspections and re-inspections?

    A. Buyer
    B. Seller
    C. Whoever's name is filled in the blank
    D. The one who wants to have inspections done

51. If the effective date on a contract is April 26, 2004, and it grants the buyer an option period of 11 days, on what date at midnight will the option period end?

    A. May 10, 2004
    B. May 6, 2004
    C. May 7, 2004
    D. May 8, 2004

52. If a buyer fails to deposit additional earnest money as called for in the "Earnest Money" paragraph (paragraph 5), the buyer is in default and subject to the provisions in the default paragraph.

    A. True
    B. False

Appendix B
Answer Key

Chapter 1	Chapter 2	Chapter 3	Chapter 4	Chapter 6	Chapter 7	Chapter 8
1. D	1. C	1. C	1. C	1. D	1. B	1. B
2. A	2. D	2. B	2. A	2. D	2. D	2. C
3. B	3. B	3. A	3. D	3. C	3. D	3. B
4. A	4. B	4. B	4. B	4. B	4. C	4. C
5. D	5. D	5. B	5. B	5. B	5. B	5. A
6. B	6. B		6. A	6. B	6. D	
7. B	7. C		7. B	7. A	7. B	
8. C	8. B		8. D	8. B	8. B	
9. B	9. D		9. C	9. A	9. B	
10. D	10. B		10. B	10. B	10. A	

Appendix A Contract Content Review

1. 15 [6D]
2. 20 [6B]
3. 3 [6C(3)]
4. 7 [9]
5. 7 [7B(2)]
6. Origination, discount, buy-down, commitment [12A(2)]
7. 15 [14]
8. Yes [9C]
9. Seller [13]
10. 30 [18]
11. No
12. The Texas Broker/Lawyer Committee [TRELA Sec. 16]
13. 6 [TRELA Sec. 16]
14. Before signing the contract [24]
15. Amount of fee, number of days [23]
16. At midnight on the 22nd [16, 17, 18, 19, 20, 21, 22]
17. 1978 [7C]
18. Reasonable time [7A]
19. Broker [In space provided immediately above signature lines for buyer and seller]
20. As agreed by the parties [6A]
21. 5% [7E]

22. Persons licensed or otherwise authorized by law to provide such repairs or treatments [7F]

23. Yes [7F]

24. 90 days [TREC 15-3 or TREC 16-3]

25. General Warranty Deed [9B(1)]

26. Costs will be shared equally [16]

27. In separate agreements between the parties and their brokers [8]

28. In good funds acceptable to the escrow agent [9B(2)]

29. The seller [12A(1)]

30. The buyer [12B]

31. Land, improvements, accessories [2]

32. Section number [2A]

33. Termination Option [23]

34. Yes–15 days [6B]

35. An attorney of the buyer's choice [6E(1)]

36. 7D

37. Yes [7F]

38. Neither party [7E]

39. A credit at closing for the amount of the deductible under the insurance policy [14]

40. No; acceptance of earnest money releases both parties from the obligations of the contract [15]

41. No [16]

42. No [18]

43. No, the parties must make an election [23]

44. No, it is an unrestricted right to terminate [23]

45. There is no option [23 bold print]

46. Consult an attorney prior to signing [24]

47. No [6A(8)]

48. Section 5.001 of the Texas Property Code requires the seller to tell the buyer to investigate [6E(5)]

49. Chapter 49, Texas Water Code [6E(3)]

50. The buyer [TREC 26-4]

Completed Uniform Settlement Statement, page 1 (Figure 10.1)

A. Settlement Statement

U.S. Department of Housing and Urban Development

OMB Approval No. 2502-0265

B. Type of Loan	6. File Number:	7. Loan Number:	8. Mortgage Insurance Case Number:
1. ☐ FHA 2. ☐ FmHA 3. ☐ Conv. Unins. 4. ☐ VA 5. ☒ Conv. Ins.			

C. Note: This form is furnished to give you a statement of actual settlement costs. Amounts paid to and by the settlement agent are shown. Items marked "(p.o.c.)" were paid outside the closing; they are shown here for informational purposes and are not included in the totals.

D. Name & Address of Borrower:	E. Name & Address of Seller:	F. Name & Address of Lender:
232-36-3775 Peter Paul Prospect, et ux Priscilla Bea Prospect 654 Broadway Galveston	492-56-6667 Russell Alan James, et ux Anna Marie James 12656 Rolling Waves Lane Galveston	Deep Pocket Mortgage Company 6000 Money Lane Galveston, Texas

G. Property Location:	H. Settlement Agent:	
12656 Rolling Waves Lane Galveston, Texas 77573	Buyer's Choice Title Company	
	Place of Settlement: Galveston, Texas	I. Settlement Date: April 4

J. Summary of Borrower's Transaction		K. Summary of Seller's Transaction	
100. Gross Amount Due From Borrower		**400. Gross Amount Due To Seller**	
101. Contract sales price	*	401. Contract sales price	*
102. Personal property		402. Personal property	
103. Settlement charges to borrower (line 1400)	*	403.	*
104. Option fee paid	*<500>	404. Option fee received	*<500>
105.		405.	
Adjustments for items paid by seller in advance		**Adjustments for items paid by seller in advance**	
106. City/town taxes to		406. City/town taxes to	
107. County taxes to		407. County taxes to	
108. Assessments to		408. Assessments to	
109. Maintenance fee 4/4-12/31	*	409. Maintenance fee 4/4-12/31	*
110.		410.	
111.		411.	
112.		412.	
120. Gross Amount Due From Borrower	*	**420. Gross Amount Due To Seller**	*
200. Amounts Paid By Or In Behalf Of Borrower		**500. Reductions In Amount Due To Seller**	
201. Deposit or earnest money	*	501. Excess deposit (see instructions)	
202. Principal amount of new loan(s)	*	502. Settlement charges to seller (line 1400)	*
203. Existing loan(s) taken subject to		503. Existing loan(s) taken subject to	
204.		504. Payoff of first mortgage loan	*
205.		505. Payoff of second mortgage loan	
206.		506.	
207.		507.	
208.		508.	
209.		509.	
Adjustments for items unpaid by seller		**Adjustments for items unpaid by seller**	
210. City/town taxes 1/1 through 4/4	*	510. City/town taxes 1/1 through 4/4	*
211. County taxes to		511. County taxes to	
212. Assessments to		512. Assessments to	
213.		513.	
214.		514.	
215.		515.	
216.		516.	
217.		517.	
218.		518.	
219.		519.	
220. Total Paid By/For Borrower		**520. Total Reduction Amount Due Seller**	
300. Cash At Settlement From/To Borrower		**600. Cash At Settlement To/From Seller**	
301. Gross Amount due from borrower (line 120)		601. Gross amount due to seller (line 420)	
302. Less amounts paid by/for borrower (line 220)	( )	602. Less reductions in amt. due seller (line 520)	( )
303. Cash ☐ From ☐ To Borrower		**603. Cash ☐ To ☐ From Seller**	

Section 5 of the Real Estate Settlement Procedures Act (RESPA) requires the following: • HUD must develop a Special Information Booklet to help persons borrowing money to finance the purchase of residential real estate to better understand the nature and costs of real estate settlement services; • Each lender must provide the booklet to all applicants from whom it receives or for whom it prepares a written application to borrow money to finance the purchase of residential real estate; • Lenders must prepare and distribute with the Booklet a Good Faith Estimate of the settlement costs that the borrower is likely to incur in connection with the settlement. These disclosures are manadatory.

Section 4(a) of RESPA mandates that HUD develop and prescribe this standard form to be used at the time of loan settlement to provide full disclosure of all charges imposed upon the borrower and seller. These are third party disclosures that are designed to provide the borrower with pertinent information during the settlement process in order to be a better shopper.

The Public Reporting Burden for this collection of information is estimated to average one hour per response, including the time for reviewing instructions, searching existing data sources, gathering and maintaining the data needed, and completing and reviewing the collection of information.

This agency may not collect this information, and you are not required to complete this form, unless it displays a currently valid OMB control number.

The information requested does not lend itself to confidentiality.

Previous editions are obsolete — Page 1 of 2 — form HUD-1 (3/86) ref Handbook 4305.2

Completed Uniform Settlement Statement, page 2 (Figure 10.1)

L. Settlement Charges

	Paid From Borrowers Funds at Settlement	Paid From Seller's Funds at Settlement
700. Total Sales/Broker's Commission based on price $ @ % =		
Division of Commission (line 700) as follows:		
701. $ to		
702. $ to		
703. Commission paid at Settlement		*
704.		
800. Items Payable In Connection With Loan		
801. Loan Origination Fee 1 % of new loan (rounded)	*	
802. Loan Discount 1 % of new loan (rounded)	*	
803. Appraisal Fee to	*	
804. Credit Report to	*	
805. Lender's Inspection Fee		
806. Mortgage Insurance Application Fee to 1/2% of new loan	*	
807. Assumption Fee Amortization schedule		
808.	*	
809.		
810.		
811.		
900. Items Required By Lender To Be Paid In Advance		
901. Interest from 4/4 to 5/1 @$ /day	*	
902. Mortgage Insurance Premium for months to		
903. Hazard Insurance Premium for 1 year years to	*	
904. years to		
905.		
1000. Reserves Deposited With Lender		
1001. Hazard insurance 2 months @ $ per month	*	
1002. Mortgage insurance months @ $ per month		
1003. City property taxes 7 months @ $ per month (rounded)	*	
1004. County property taxes months @ $ per month		
1005. Annual assessments months @ $ per month		
1006. months @ $ per month		
1007. months @ $ per month		
1008. months @ $ per month		
1100. Title Charges		
1101. Settlement or closing fee to		
1102. Abstract or title search to		
1103. Title examination to		
1104. Title insurance binder to		
1105. Document preparation to For note and deed of trust	*	
1106. Notary fees to		
1107. Attorney's fees to For deed and release		*
(includes above items numbers:)		
1108. Title insurance to		
(includes above items numbers:)		
1109. Lender's coverage $	*	
1110. Owner's coverage $		*
1111.	*	*
1112.		
1113.	*	*
1200. Government Recording and Transfer Charges		
1201. Recording fees: Deed $ Borrower ; Mortgage $ Borrower ; Releases $ Seller	*	*
1202. City/county tax/stamps: Deed $; Mortgage $		
1203. State tax/stamps: Deed $; Mortgage $		
1204. Tax service fee	*	
1205.		
1300. Additional Settlement Charges		
1301. Survey to ABC Survey Company	*	
1302. Pest inspection to		
1303.		
1304.		
1305.		
1400. Total Settlement Charges (enter on lines 103, Section J and 502, Section K)	*	*

Previous editions are obsolete Page 2 of 2 form **HUD-1** (3/86) ref Handbook 4305.2

Practice Exam

1. A
2. B
3. B
4. D
5. C
6. B
7. B
8. C
9. A
10. B
11. C
12. B
13. A
14. A
15. D
16. A
17. C
18. B
19. A
20. C
21. C
22. A
23. B
24. B
25. B
26. D
27. B
28. A
29. B
30. A
31. A
32. A
33. D
34. A
35. B
36. A
37. B
38. D
39. B
40. D
41. B
42. D
43. B
44. B
45. B
46. A
47. C
48. B
49. B
50. B
51. C
52. A

Appendix C
Inventory of TREC Forms

Forms are available in PDF and can be downloaded from the Texas Real Estate Commission (TREC) Web site at *www.trec.state.tx.us*

Promulgated Contracts:

Number	**Name**	**Adoption Date**
9-5	Unimproved Property Contract	01/03
20-6	One to Four Family Residential Contract (Resale)	01/03
23-5	New Home Contract (Incomplete Construction)	01/03
24-5	New Home Contract (Completed Construction)	01/03
25-4	Farm and Ranch Contract	01/03
30-4	Residential Condominium Contract (Resale)	01/03

Promulgated Addenda:

10-4	Addendum for Sale of Other Property by Buyer	10/01
11-5	Addendum for "Back-Up" Contract	2/04
12-1	Release of Liability on Assumption of FHA, VA or Conventional Loan/Restoration of Seller's Entitlement for VA Guaranteed Loan	3/92
15-3	Seller's Temporary Residential Lease	12/98
16-3	Buyer's Temporary Residential Lease	12/98
26-4	Seller Financing Addendum	10/01
28-0	Environmental Assessment, Threatened or Endangered Species, and Wetlands Addendum	10/93
33-0	Addendum for Coastal Area Property	12/94

Promulgated Addenda (continued):

Number	Name	Date
34-1	Addendum for Property Located Seaward of the Gulf Intracoastal Waterway	10/01
36-3	Addendum for Property Subject to Mandatory Membership in an Owners' Association	2/04
40-1	Third Party Financing Condition Addendum	2/04
41-0	Loan Assumption Addendum	10/01
42-0	Notice Pursuant to Third Party Financing Condition Addendum	2/04

Amendment

39-4	Amendment	01/03

Promulgated Resale Certificates:

32-0	Condominium Resale Certificate	4/94
37-1	Subdivision Information, Including Resale Certificate for Property Subject to Mandatory Membership in an Owners' Association	9/99

Promulgated Notice:

38-1	Notice of Termination of Contract	10/01

Promulgated Consumer Disclosure:

•	Consumer Information Form 1-1	8/91

Optional/Voluntary Use Forms:

OP-C	Notice to Prospective Buyer	12/90
OP-H	Seller's Disclosure of Property Condition	10/93
OP-I	Texas Real Estate Consumer Notice Concerning Recognized Hazards	9/94
OP-K	Information About Brokerage Services	
OP-L	Lead-Based Paint Addendum	2/04
OP-M	Addendum for Unimproved Property Located in a Certified Service Area of a Utility Service Provider	7/01

Appendix D
Useful Web Sites

Rather than cut down more trees and increase the number of pages and the cost of this book, we provide this appendix to assist you in locating and reviewing relevant statutory provisions. All Texas statutes are available on the State of Texas Web site.

Go to:

www.capitol.state.tx.us

Under Legislative resources, click on Texas Statutes. Scroll down to locate the following relevant provisions.

Example: Property Code

Title 2, Chapter 5, Section 5.008
5.011
5.012

Title 7, Chapters 81–82, Condominiums

Title 8, Chapters 91–93, Landlord and Tenant

Others of Interest:

Vernon's Texas Civil Statutes	TRELA Residential Service Contract Act
Water Code	Chapter 40 regarding utility service districts
Texas Natural Resources Code	Chapter 33, 135 regarding tidally influenced land

For assistance with financing questions, the following sites can be very useful.

www.Fanniemae.com

www.Freddiemac.com

www.Ginniemae.gov

www.HUD.gov

www.VA.gov

Index

NOTE: Page references in *italics* refer to figures.

U

V

W

Z